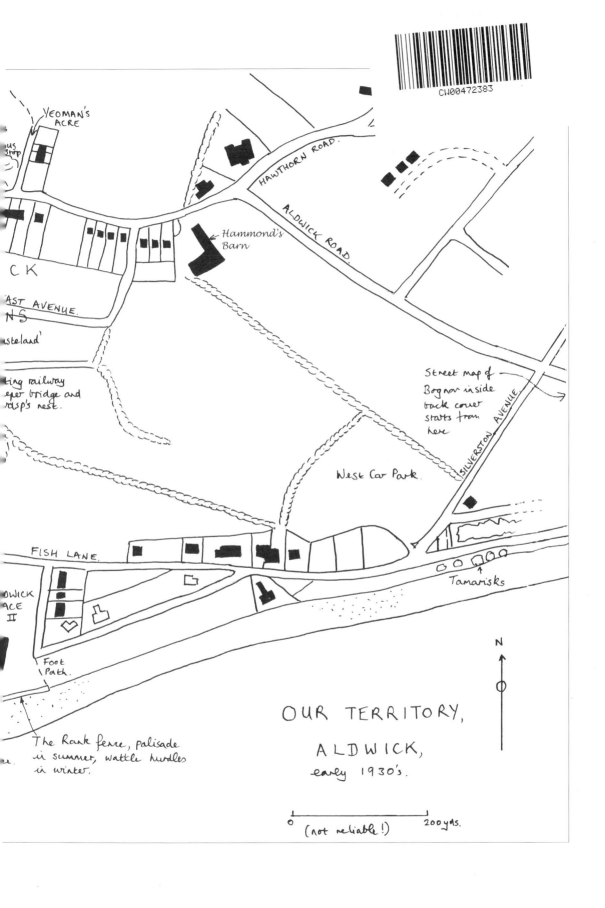

YEOMAN'S
ACRE

us
stop

C K

AST AVENUE.

N S

steland'

ting railway
per bridge and
asp's nest.

HAWTHORN ROAD.

ALDWICK ROAD.

Hammond's
Barn

Street map of
Bognor inside
back cover
starts from
here

SILVERSTON AVENUE.

West Car Park.

FISH LANE.

DWICK
ACE
II

Foot
Path.

Tamarisks

The Rank fence, palisade
in summer, wattle hurdles
in winter.

N

OUR TERRITORY,

ALDWICK,

early 1930's.

0 (not reliable!)   200 yds.

THE PARADISE ROCKS

'Myself and Roger on the Paradise Rocks'. Sketch by Michael Alford.

THE PARADISE ROCKS

A 1930s Childhood in Bognor
and a Little Local History

Michael Alford

edited by Roger Alford

Phillimore

2002

Published by
PHILLIMORE & CO. LTD
Shopwyke Manor Barn, Chichester, West Sussex, England

ISBN 1 86077 234 X

Printed and bound in Great Britain by
THE CROMWELL PRESS
Trowbridge, Wiltshire

Nothing is more fraught with risk than the choice of one's parents. So, to have plumped for a London mother and father who built a bungalow in a field at Aldwick in 1929 for me and my brothers, has to count as a stroke of uncommon good luck.

Michael Alford

Michael Alford died on 29 November 2000 leaving this book virtually completed. It has fallen to me, his brother Roger, who trailed happily along behind him through so many of these pages, to do the final editing and to see it through to publication. This was a labour, but a labour of love.

Roger Alford
March 2002

Contents

List of Illustrations

Preface

I am never quite certain how many people trouble to read prefaces, but in case the current reader is a stickler for this kind of thing, then allow me to explain the curious genesis of *The Paradise Rocks*.

The story begins in the early years of our recently-demised 20th century when, as a little girl, my mother-to-be, with her cousins, spent two holidays on Bognor's golden sands. They must have vividly impressed her, for even in old age she loved to talk of the many little incidents and experiences which had textured those precious childhood days. Better still, she had jotted down some notes. So had I.

For the rest of this narrative, we have to jump to 1929 when the family found itself living at Isleworth, a leafy suburb of west London. It was also the year that my parents – an artist father and a fashion-artist mother – elected to build a bungalow 'in a field' at Aldwick, so that their two sons Michael, the writer of this book, his younger brother Roger and later, a third addition, Julian, could flourish in the south coast's ozone-steeped air during the holidays.

Thus, from a tender age, usually unescorted by any elder, my brother Roger and I spent almost every weekend, school holiday and half-term, tramping and roaming our local lanes, fields, farms, ditches and beaches, and – when so enabled by our fragile finances – trawling the town for such free entertainment as it might have to offer. Soon we could claim a territory measuring much of the known world around Bognor, a world in which we felt more at home than in our west London suburb.

Some time ago, looking through a stack of old photograph albums, my two brothers and I, being in a nostalgic mood, set our ageing minds on a slow trot around the Bognor and Aldwick scene of the 1930s in which we had spent so much of our young lives: '... do you remember when? ... wasn't that the time? ... of course, it's all built over now.'

Afterwards, with so many memories re-kindled, I decided to jot down on a sheet of A4 a short account of some of the adventures, excursions and escapades that we had got up to in those growing-up years when Aldwick was mainly fields and the harvesting was done with horses. You know, just to stick it in a photograph album, just for family eyes.

Then it occurred to me how frequently those expeditions – although we were unaware of it at the time – had brushed against the history of Bognor and Aldwick, a subject in which, meanwhile, I had become keenly interested. And what about those contemporary warp-and-weft events around us of which we were only vaguely aware, but which patterned the times of which we were part? Should I not touch upon those also? And thus I made a noose for my own neck. Research!

It was that fleshing out of the past that took the time: maps, street directories, local newspapers and, when all else failed, Gerard Young's *A History of Bognor Regis*. By now I was sitting on nearly ten pages of A4.

One day, I fell to talking with my good friend Martin Venables (that indefatigable scribe, apple-grower, geologist and custodian of Bognor's history, by then retired to Eastgate House in Chichester) about an idea I had. A 'child's-eye' view of Bognor and our explorations during the 'thirties, which also brushed upon their historic past, was an undertaking which appealed to him enormously. And especially the first chapter – An Edwardian Prelude – which was the account of my mother's holidays at Bognor during the early 1900s, when Martin was born. That was how *A Scene from the Paradise Rocks* came to be written.

What really was the name of those boulders stacked up on the beach at the end of Dark Lane and shown above as they used to be in 1937? 'Barn Rocks', do I hear? Well, that may have been their provenance, but in other respects it is quite wrong as the real Barn Rocks are a reef out at sea which shows up at very low tides. 'Aldwick Rocks' is merely proxy for Barn Rocks. As for 'Grant's Rocks'?* – surely not! In fact, our family knew them simply as 'The Rocks'; the only certainty was that, in 1929, they were piled up at the foot of the sea-wall below Mrs Croxton Johnson's house, Paradise.

So, in this book, for the sake of unambiguity – not to mention euphony – I have christened them 'The Paradise Rocks'. In any case, regardless of their name, 'The Rocks', so evocative of our Aldwick childhood, have all but disappeared in recent years, submerged by the rising sand level. And if that weren't bad enough – while my back was turned – they have had dumped upon them intimidating megaliths chosen by an accountant and climbable only by the most heroic child.

Elsewhere, time has been no kinder. The famous drainpipe has lost its down-turned mouth, and young visitors are no longer encouraged to walk its length in un-sandalled feet. Worse, Dark Lane has been been severed in two by a new road and its sea-end thoughtfully municipalised. It is no longer even particularly 'Dark', the severe gales of some years ago having felled many of the arching elms. The rook calls have fallen to a murmur. Another loss is the cast-iron railings to what was once Aldwick Grange, along which our spades used to rattle with such a satisfying noise, but which have since been replaced by concrete blocks complete with graffiti.

Yet, on a recent summer's evening, as I sat on Aldwick beach, I could still feel a little of its magic so redolent of my childhood days, more than sixty years ago.

MGA
June 2000

---

* Mrs Joan Goodacre told me that her father used to refer to them as 'Grant's Rocks', after the dubious Baron Albert Grant who lived at Aldwick Place during the 1880s; a curious mis-identification.

Acknowledgements

Because without their assistance this book could never have seen the light of day, I have to begin by thanking the staff of the West Sussex Record Office at Chichester – and the county's librarians – not only for assiduously preserving the rich tapestry of our district's past, but also for making it so readily available to amateur historians like myself.

And it is in the same vein that I should like to express my appreciation of the way the Bognor Regis Training College (now the Bognor Regis Campus of the Chichester Institute of Higher Education) have provided such a good – if inevitably cramped – home for the late Gerard Young's incomparable collection of 'Bognoriana', and to their staff who, uncomplainingly, lock and unlock the bulging cabinets each time a researcher calls.

Writing, I soon discovered, can be a lonely occupation. A mentor is needed, one capable of offering encouragement without losing their faculty for fearless – and constructive – criticism. So I am greatly indebted to my dear friend, June Mahon, who not only afforded me both in full measure, but slogged through all the chapters, kindly chuckled at some of the passages, and constantly badgered me to get the thing published!

Another tower of strength has been Ron Iden of the West Sussex Record Office, whose unfailing help in sniffing out the more obscure nuggets of Bognor's history has rescued me from many an historical impasse. And if that weren't enough, he kindly went through the draft with a toothcomb, putting in apostrophes, suggesting *italics* and correcting dates.

Moving to the corpus of the book, it is my dear mother I have to thank for the reminiscences of her holidays spent at Bognor in the early 1900s which fills most of Chapter 1 – the oral tradition. I can still hear her voice.

Next on the list must come John Rank, a friend for many years, without whose insider knowledge of his family's milling business The Miller's Tale must have remained untold. Indeed, much the same can be said of the Tregear family who gave me unstinted help with the chapter bearing their name: Phil and Jack (who, sadly, have since departed the scene), as well as Marion Sleeman, David Tregear and Mary, who are still very much part of it. Jack Tregear's privately published book, *This is the House that Jack Built*, also proved an invaluable – and amusing – source of information.

Mrs Jean Rose – a stalwart ally of long standing – offered me much sound advice on the penultimate chapter, A Postscript from Iraq, which deals *inter alia* with the saving of Hotham Park House from demolition in 1977 when she was (the politically incorrect!) Chairman of the Friends.

Then there was Michael Goodall, the aeronautical historian and author of *The White and Thompson File*, who was noble-spirited enough to read through The Bognor Sky, to which he made some useful amendments, besides letting me have some excellent photographs of early aeroplanes.

I have to thank David Bone for helping me track down much of the information on Martin Venables. I have purposely not dwelt at any length upon Martin's geological work as this has been adequately covered elsewhere, not least by David himself in a series of articles he contributed to geological journal *Tertiary Research.*

I have relied heavily on *H.L.F Guermonprez 1858-1924* by M.D. Crane MSc., PhD, FLS, Assistant Curator (Natural History), Portsmouth City Museum for the paragraphs on Bognor's naturalist.

Finally, I must thank both Mrs Margaret Gowler for checking my notes on her grandfather, Albert Seymour JP, and Mrs Greta Blythe whose memories of her father, Herbert William Seymour, the builder of Bognor's Town Hall, have added life to Chapter 17. Oh yes, and brother Roger, whose memory stretches back to his days at Miss Clear's dame school in Aldwick village, where her grounding in the use of the abacus set him on the path to becoming an Academic Governor of the London School of Economics.

Now I run into difficulties. For this book has been so long in the gestation, that I fear I may have forgotten some of those kind folk like Aubrey Cox, Peter Ide, D.W.K. Jones and Norman Reynolds who, many years ago, helped fill in gaps in my knowledge. To those I have not mentioned I can only apologise profusely.

MGA

Acknowledgements are due to the following publishers and their authors, whose work appears in this book: Putnam Ltd (Harald Penrose on Messrs White and Thompson in his book, *The Great War and Armistice*); Macmillan Ltd (Rudyard Kipling's *Just So Stories*); The Viscount Norwich (*The Rainbow Comes and Goes* and *Trumpets from the Steep* by Lady Diana Cooper).

My thanks also to the *Bognor Regis Observer* and the British Museum Newspaper Library at Colindale, London, for consent to reproduce a number of headlines and advertisements from past copies of the *Observer* and the *Bognor Regis Post*. Past issues of the *West Sussex Gazette* and *Portsmouth Evening News* have also proved invaluable sources of historical information throughout this book. I have also used the minutes of the Bognor Regis UDC and the Bognor Guides and Directories in the West Sussex Record Office.

Illustration Acknowledgements

aerofilms.com, 98; *Aeroplane*/British Museum Newspaper Library, 26, 116; 'After the Battle', 128, 131; Author's Collection, frontispiece, 1, 2, 11-15, 17, 22-4, 28, 33, 41, 56, 61, 65, 67, 74-6, 81, 117, 147; Sonia Beck, 137; Mrs Greta Blythe, 97; *Bognor Guidebook*, 38; Bognor Regis Local History Society, 124; Percy Cartright, 85; Reg Christian, 60; Colin Crudas/Cobham plc, 114; Sylvia Endacott, 36, 122; Allen Eyles, 78; *Flight International*, 66; Donald Francke, 123; Gerard Young Collection, University College Chichester, 3, 4, 7, 8, 19, 25, 30-2, 37, 42, 45, 48, 53, 54, 62, 68, 69, 79, 83, 93, 99, 101, 103, 106, 107, 118, 120, 121, 140, 150; Mike Goodall, 109; Don Hansford, 39; the late Pat Hansford, 40; Phillip Hawes, 63; Jenny Hickman/ the late Frank L'Alhouette, 91, 104, 125, 129, 130, 133-6; Ron Iden, 35; Imperial War Museum, 110, 111; H. Jarvis, 57; P. Jarvis, 132; D.W.K Jones, 65; S. Jordan, 119; Wendy Lines, 49; Middleton Press Collection, 16; Ministry of Defence, 138; David Morris, 50; National Maritime Museum, Greenwich, London, 27; Lee Peck, 18, 20, 21, 44, 46, 55, 58, 70-3, 84, 102, 105, 112, 115; Andrew Perry, ARPS, 139; John Rank, 86-90, 92; Norman Reynolds, 10; RIBA Library, 94, 95; Jean Rose, 141; David Tregear, 47; West Sussex County Council Library Service, 5, 34; West Sussex Record Office, 9 (PH16198/11), 51 (George Garland), 52 (PH486), 80 (PH16198/11), 82 (George Garland), 96, 100 (UD/BR/6511/1), 148, 149; Brian Williams, 142-6; Jon Wynne Tyson, 15.

The endpapers in this book are reproduced from the 1929 Ordnance Survey map. The sketch map 'Our Territory' was specially drawn by R.E.J. Seymour. The street map of Bognor is reproduced from the Ward Lock *Guide to Bognor* (fifth edition) with the consent of Littlehampton Book Services Limited.

Michael Alford approached many friends and contacts for photographs with which to illustrate this book. Following his death, the editor has made every effort to confirm that permission to reproduce them had been given, and whenever providers of photographs have been traced they have agreed that this was so. In only a handful of cases we have been unable to locate the providers, and we apologise in advance for not being able to confirm their permission.

1

An Edwardian Prelude

This story has to begin in London because in 1904 the family were not at all clear where Bognor was. So the first chapter portrays a middle-class Edwardian household at Hampstead only just getting used to the idea of being in the 20th century at a time when the British Empire glowed Imperial pink on page after page of *Philip's World Atlas*, the Royal Navy enjoyed the freehold of the Seven Seas, income tax was 1s. 7d. in the £ and Tom Hayward and the incomparable 'Plum' Warner opened for England.

In the metropolis, depressed-looking cab-horses kept one eye on the noisy new motor carriages and the other on His Majesty's subjects in pursuit of all the wonders of their modern age as, from Tulse Hill to Hammersmith Broadway, Mr Faraday's electricity propelled them prodigious distances in Nestlé's Milk trams for only a penny, the gas-lamps were lit using poles carried by cloth-capped men on bicycles and the Electric Telegraph could send a simple message to an aunt in Sidmouth for only threepence.

Best of all, though, were the railways. Day and night, lovingly polished steam engines rattled and clanked their trains over a mesh of permanent ways which covered the Kingdom. And a glance at Mr Bradshaw's eponymous timetable would have revealed – not before time, many had said* – that the London, Brighton and South Coast Railway had cast one of their lines to fall upon the little Victorian watering-place of Bognor.

Yet, for those prospective travellers to whom change and innovation were anathema, it would have been unwise to stay too long within its ozoned purlieus. For Bognor, too, was awash with the spirit of the age. Nor were instances hard to find. For not only had that indomitable entrepreneur, Mr William Tate, recently built a shopping arcade of startling modernity in the grounds of York House in the High Street, but then, bold fellow, he had gone on to light it with the new 'electric' – not to mention having built the generating station in which the mysterious stuff was made! Indeed there were rumours that this prince amongst constructors was even then toying with yet another scheme, a theatre in Belmont Street and a domed Kursaal of Imperial distinction facing the sea to cater for the roller-skating classes.[†]

At Bognor, then – a name synonymous with culture – Orpheus, too, was wooed. Soon, from opposite the *Royal Norfolk Hotel*, there would fall upon

---

* An allusion to the six thwarted attempts, between 1845 and 1863, to provide Bognor with a direct railway link to the main east-west line running north of the town, thus obviating the maddening 3½-mile trek out to the so-called 'Bognor' station at Woodgate. Success came on 1 June 1864 when the Bognor Railway Company opened their branch line (operated by the LBSCR) from a new station at Barnham.

† There is more historical information on William Tate in the Appendix, p.307.

the public ear the oom-pah-pah of a military band playing from a brand new bandstand, the plans for which had only just been un-pinned from the drawing board of Mr Oswald Bridges, the town's Surveyor and Inspector of Nuisances.*

One could go on and on; Mr Chalmers Kearney was proposing to connect Bognor with Littlehampton by means of a mono-rail[†] and Mr Davies' solid-tyred charabancs were daily probing new frontiers along the dusty Downland tracks. Indeed, to this list could be added the name of a certain Arthur Southerton who, for the sum of six guineas, could furnish the more energetic with a bicycle of Edwardian excellence, handmade in his Sudley Road workshop.

Nor was there any need to look further than this little seaside resort to spot those tell-tale tokens of technological progress, as a glimpse at the

1 Doris Davey as a young girl.

Urban District's Fire Brigade Committee's Minutes will reveal. For, on 5 August 1904, that august body had resolved that the ratepayers be asked to fork up £275 for the purchase of that ultimate quencher of flames, *viz.* an invincible 'Shand Mason Improved Patent Double cylinder Vertical Variable Expansion Fire Engine'.[‡] Around the 20th century's hem, change and innovation were creeping in everywhere. So was the 'electric'. Even at Bognor.

By one of those sublime coincidences of history, it so happened that it was during that same summer that my mother-to-be, Doris Davey – herself a very contemporary young lady of 11 years of age – first made Bognor's acquaintance. By train, she had come down from London with her Doré cousins to stay at the Debt House, the family name for their small Victorian villa in London Road which, had she known it, was to influence all our lives many years later.

In fact, it was to pursue this curious family story, after more than half a century had elapsed, that one afternoon my mother and I were resolved to try to rediscover the exact whereabouts of the house which had – indirectly – brought us to live

---

* The reader interested in the details of Bridges' life can find more in the Appendix, p.307.

† Mr Chalmers Kearney's mono-rail appears to have sunk without trace after being referred to the Roads and Pavings Committee in July 1905.

‡ The late Mr Leslie Walwin, that one-time pillar of Bognor's Fire Brigade, once told me how, just after the First World War, when his father was Leading Fireman at the Fire Station in the High Street, he was employed as 'fuse-boy' at 3d. a week. When the alarm bell sounded, and after the Shand Mason had been pulled out into the road, his job was to put a taper to the oil-soaked cotton-waste in the fire-box. Twelve minutes was all that was needed to raise sufficient steam for the pump to become operational. In those days Albert Florence, the Job Master of Waterloo Square, both provided and drove the horses. The Fire Brigade appears to have had a soft spot for the old Shand Mason. It remained at the fire station doing nothing until 1935 when it was sold for £10. There is a similar 'steamer' at Arundel Castle.

at Bognor. Thus did we set out dutifully to trudge London Road between Spencer Street and the level crossing.* But time had played tricks with her memory and the Improvement Grants had played tricks with the houses. So had the German bombers. Worse, she'd forgotten its name.

Still in her mind was a green-painted entrance door at the front and the sound of the steam-trains at the back; not far from the level crossing yet only a few steps to the corner of Spencer Street, where she remembered the name of Mr Knight, the outfitter, written on the wall above his shop. Our quarry was a 'clerkly' house, white-stuccoed, Victorian. Of course, in that quarter of Bognor there was no shortage of candidates! A dozen fitted the description. Yet few had retained their fanlight-names which might have served to jog an elderly memory.

At all events, that afternoon the Debt House proved an elusive prey. Then it began to rain. Well, we would come back another time – cross our hearts, we would! Meanwhile, she'd ring cousin Sybil. But Sibby's mind proved no longer the address book for which it had once been famous. 'Near the level crossing' was the best she could offer.

But, as the reader may have half-suspected, our stern resolution to return to London Road proved no match for procrastination. For if it wasn't her grandchildren being brought down for the afternoon, then it was panic stations as I tried to catch the next Planning Committee. Or it was the afternoon for Mr Best, her gardener, to spray the apple trees. Or the china cupboard needed turning out. Or the washing machine man cometh on the wrong afternoon with the right part (or was it the gas man who cometh on the right afternoon with the wrong part?). Early closing days were a godsend for inaction. Or it was merely raining again. Anyhow, I expect you know how it is.

Then one day … well, very sadly, one day it was left for me to unravel the mystery of the whereabouts of the Debt House on my own. However, there is no purpose in my keeping hidden from the reader why this small terrace house – (when I can find it!†) – came to have such a curious name. It was disarmingly simple. It had come into Edwin Doré's hands to expiate the wickedness of one of his customers.

Until then, I daresay, there was no reason why the paterfamilias of a family which had hitherto spent most of its holidays on the east coast should have concerned himself with a small seaside town in a part of the country he barely knew. My mother's uncle, Edwin Doré, was – as she was – of Huguenot stock and it was thus predictable that he should have pursued a calling traditionally associated with those enterprising people long before the horrors that befell them in the wake of the Revocation of the Edict of Nantes. Under his father's name of James Doré, Uncle Ted had inherited a substantial cloth importing and tailoring business‡ with showrooms overlooking the Lord Mayor's processional route where it wound its foggy-November way along Cheapside in the City of London.

---

* The level crossing was closed in 1976 when the new road carrying the A29 was built.

† Once I had discovered *Kelly's Street Directories*, the Debt House was swiftly found. In 1904 it was known as Anglesea House. Today, much altered, it is 222 London Road and close to the old level crossing.

‡ Family tradition has it that Oscar Wilde left Reading Jail dressed in a Doré suit.

At half-past three each workday afternoon it was Edwin's habit to make his way down to the 'smoky sewer' of the Metropolitan Railway, settle himself in a first-class compartment and read the *Evening Star* until the train arrived at West Hampstead. From the station a walk of only a few hundred yards brought him to Cleve Road. And it was in this tree-lined thoroughfare of transcendental respectability, behind a tall laurel hedge punctuated with 'In' and 'Out' gates, that Edwin and his wife, Clara, lived with their numerous progeny in a substantial Victorian villa staffed with a complement of servants deemed proper to their circumstances.

Perhaps we can gloss over my mother's imperfect recollection of the exterior of the Doré residence: its monkey-puzzle trees, the central fountain of pampas grass, the box-lined drive and the tennis court marked out 'in woggly white lines'; even the vegetable garden 'full of cabbages and green caterpillars'. Instead – since it is germane to this story – let the reader's imagination dwell for a moment on the stable and carriage house which stood to the east side of this substantial villa. For it was here, above the chestnut mare and the gleaming Victoria, the Beldons lived: Tom the groom and gardener; she the family's 'cooky'. But in the evenings, when so demanded by the social calendar, Mr B. could have been found performing, with becoming gravitas, the exacting role of butler.

Thus, to the *beau monde* of West Hampstead, it was clear beyond any doubt that the Dorés of Cleve Road held credentials enough to qualify for inclusion in that much sought-after social niche reserved for 'carriage folk'. Facilitated by a bottomless pool of cheaply available cooks, gardeners, governesses, housemaids, 'tween maids – not to mention children's nurses – and with the late Dr Spock still a safe way off, middle-class Edwardians were able to absolve themselves of much of the daily grind of raising the offspring they begat with such unbridled vigour.

So when it came to the school holidays, Aunt Clara, defender of the well-honed domestic and social arrangements at Cleve Road and mother of Dorothy, Sybil and Gilbert – from now on referred to collectively as 'the cousins' – drew a firm line at anything which might have been misconstrued as enthusiasm for the forthcoming assault upon her precious citadel by a lot of excited and noisy children. The moment their schools broke up for the holidays, the Doré siblings were handed over lock, sock and satchel to the family's children's nurse – the legendary Wonnie – and under her tutelage remained until the next term hove into view.

Nurse Wansford was the trusted, much loved – yet occasionally feared – family institution who had exerted a benevolently formative influence on a strung-out generation of seven Doré offspring. When taking them out for walks, my mother used to tell me, she wore a nurse's wimple, white starched cuffs, a brown woollen cape and lace-up boots; back in the nursery she smelt delicately of Wright's Coal Tar soap.

Wonnie believed in deep breathing, the benefits to be derived from putting a cold key down the back to stem nose-bleeds, and properly enunciated prayers from the kneeling position – especially on bitterly cold nights. She was also a tireless advocate of the nutritional virtues of spinach, which was another way of saying that it had to be eaten up before going on to the Bakewell Tart. Miss Wansford was, it appears, a safe, uncomplicated supporter of the Edwardian establishment and the British Empire as well as being a firm believer in Our Lord as He might have been revealed in a stained-glass window designed by the late Sir Edward Burne-Jones.

In my mother's affections, though, she had claim to a special place. For there had been that tear-stained winter's afternoon when Wonnie had been asked to draw upon her deep well of compassion to comfort a little girl just bereaved. My mother's father died when she was only seven, just a few years before this story begins. 'So wasn't it ironic', I remember her once saying, 'that the tragic loss of my father marked the beginning of some of the happiest times of my life. For it was in the aftermath of that terrible

2 Wonnie.

experience, with no father, a grief-stricken and partly deaf mother and a much older sister away at a school in Belgium, that Aunt Clara insisted that – at least for the next few years – I should spend all my holidays with her own children, my dear cousins amongst whom, in any case, I had always felt more a sister.'

Behind the slated roof-slopes, finials, bargeboards, lead flashings and dormer windows of this Hampstead mansion lay a large children's nursery overseen by a red-saddled rocking horse with a mane of real hair, the sort that might have fallen from a fairground roundabout. There was also a wooden slide, two doll's houses, a swing and an inventory of toys and books beyond the author's powers to catalogue. And it was over this wax-polished kingdom, with its views of ancient trees and the smoking chimneys of London's suburban sprawl, that Wonnie's writ held sway. It was also where, at the least sign of tears, little Doris had once found comfort enfolded in those well-starched sleeves smelling of Wright's Coal Tar.

So, in that summer of 1904, with school already a hazy memory, excitement mounted in the nursery as the three great moth-ball-scented trunks were brought down from the loft for packing to commence. But not before, upon each, had been slapped a label stating in bold letters its destination: BOGNOR. 'I am sure', declared my mother, 'that was the first time I had heard that funny name! But those trunks I remember well; huge things needing two men to carry them when full. Wherever one went in those days, it was like moving house. Everything was taken: bedding, summer dresses and winter woollies; headwear and footwear, raincoats, umbrellas, parasols and galoshes. No meteorological quirk was overlooked. We packed the picnic things, our Kate Greenaway books, toys, jigsaw puzzles and our dolls – unthinkable that even the scruffiest among them should be denied a few weeks by the sea! Naturally, Gilbert insisted on bringing his cricket gear and his pogo-stick – oh yes, and his revolting-looking pickled conker. I expect I made certain my drawing books and pencils were tucked in somewhere. And I am sure Wonnie wouldn't have travelled any distance without her bottles of Dinneford's Magnesia, Virol and that disgusting castor oil!'

At last, the day of departure arrived. Wonnie, the cousins, young Doris and yet more assorted baggage – the three great trunks had been sent on in advance – were loaded into the Cleve Road carriage under the watchful eyes of Aunt Clara and Doris's mother, Alice. Now it was time for every permutation of good-bye kisses and fervent promises to be good; Wonnie's fingers sought the reassuring feel of the railway tickets. Then Beldon gee'd up the mare, and with that the carriage, accompanied by the whole Doré *menage*, began to move slowly down the gravel drive into Cleve Road where the frantic farewelling continued unabated until it turned into Priory Road and was lost to view.

Quite soon the little holiday party was trotting through the green shadows of a tree-lined and nearly motor carriage-less Maida Vale on their way to Mr Bradshaw's Victoria station and their ultimate destination, the Debt House in London Road at Bognor. Ahead of young Doris Davey and her Doré cousins stretched the prospect of a ripping seven-week holiday at the seaside.

As far back as my memory stretches, I can recall my mother, in her nostalgic moments, telling me of the many little incidents and experiences which had textured those childhood holidays spent at Bognor thirty years earlier; stories I had heard so often that they have become part of me – and of my brothers, too. Then, in later years, curious about family memories – yet devoid of any tangible purpose – I jotted down many of these vignettes on scraps of paper and on backs of envelopes. Fortunately a lot she had noted herself and these I treasure still. Now, at last, they have found a purpose.

Of course, this book does not purport to be a 'history'. Nevertheless, where I felt a little research might add veracity to – or shine a fresh light upon – some ancient local topic, I undertook it at first with resignation, but with increasing zeal as I fell under the spell of Bognor and Aldwick's historical legacy.

Although this chapter began life written in the third person, I soon found the repetitious 'she said' and 'my mother told me' a heavy millstone round my neck – especially as in my head I could hear her voice making what she *had* said sound so much more alive and interesting. So I have taken the liberty of letting her, as it were, write much of the rest of this first chapter herself, using her own phraseology which is as familiar to me as my own.

According to my mother, she came to Bognor with her cousins twice: in the summer of 1904 and again in 1906. In fact, she had to admit that only haziness separated the two visits. But what follows, making due allowance for the inevitable lapses of memory and the distortions of space and time, gives some idea of a child's holiday spent at Bognor nearly a century ago.

* * *

'Well, as you know, dear, it all began with this little house in London Road finding its way – somewhat dubiously by the sound of it! – into Uncle Ted's hands. Of course, for us children, it meant that instead of our holidays

3 Bognor's muddy London Road at the turn of the 19th century, still awaiting its tar-macadam surface and stone pavings. The Debt House is out of sight to the right and near the level crossing.

by the sea being restricted to the usual fortnight, we were able to enjoy it for the whole seven or eight weeks. But even more importantly, as it turned out, it introduced me to a little seaside town which, many years later, your father and I came to love enough to put down part of our roots there.

'As it is, my first memory of Bognor is of us getting off the train at the railway station. Naturally we were all terribly excited. When we got outside – where the horses and carriages used to wait in those days – we looked for the sea. But in vain! What had happened to it? Who'd ever heard of a seaside railway station that didn't command an instant view of the briny with its starfish-studded sands, sailing boats and old tars with wooden legs, all under a cerulean sky dappled with white seagulls? Well, that was what our comics showed and no doubt that was what we were expecting. Bravely, we swallowed our disappointment!

'Meanwhile, Wonnie had hired a carriage and within a few minutes we arrived outside this little house in London Road: a two-storey Victorian terrace house with a dark green front door incorporating a leaded-glass 'tulip' window. Inside, the prevailing colour scheme was various shades of brown to match the linoleum. However, we had not come all this way to discuss interior decoration!

'Clamorously, we demanded to be allowed out to find where this elusive sea had got to! So, as soon as Wonnie had made us spruce ourselves up and we had had our tea, we set off in an animated little crocodile to look for it.

4 Those elusive sands! Glowered over by the *Royal Pier Hotel*, Bognor's 'children's beach' is where my mother and her cousins built their sandcastle and ate their 'hokey pokey'. Between the left-hand breakwaters a beach show is in full swing.

'Well, you can imagine what a great adventure it all was, for everything that met our eyes was new to us; even the most ordinary houses, the street names, the shops, the unfolding views; St John's Church, the Water Tower and the Arcade. But at last we turned into what must have been Clarence Road and there, straight ahead of us, we caught our first glimpse of – the SEA! With squeals of delight, and dragging Wonnie in our wake, we were soon down on the shingle seeing how close we could get to the waves without getting our feet wet. So those are among my earliest recollections of Bognor: Wonnie holding our coats, the crunchy feel of the stones underfoot, the breaking waves and the sight of the bathing-machines and the drawn-up fishing boats receding into the distance towards the Pier.

'Of the house itself I have only the faintest memory. We three girls, I recall, slept in a front bedroom overlooking some large trees on the other side of London Road, which must have been in what is now Hotham Park. Downstairs there was a noisy water closet that seemed attached to a sort of laundry with a clothes boiler and a washbasin. There was no real bathroom, just a big, white-enamelled bath which had to be filled from a tin tub heated up on a primitive gas stove in the kitchen. Also at the back was a small yard in which we did our skipping to that age old jingle, "salt, mustard, vinegar, pepper". We had our meals in the dining-room at the front of the house as Wonnie wouldn't have dreamed of making us use the kitchen, although it would have saved her endless fetching and carrying. But in those days standards were standards.

'In the morning Wonnie's large tin alarm clock used to go off at about half-past six and an hour later she would bring us a jug of hot water for washing and prise us out of bed. At breakfast the prevailing sounds – apart from our incessant chatter! – were the shrill whistles of railway engines and the clinketty-clink of trucks being shunted in the railway yard at the back. I can recall, too, the milkman rat-tatting on the front door with his cry of "milk'o". Then there used to be a rush round for the willow-pattern jugs which he filled from a brass churn carried on his horse-drawn milk float.

'On most days, when the weather was fine, we used to walk down that long footpath behind the Police Station (Church Path) to Clarence Road and then on, past the Roman Catholic church, to the beach. Often we played in the shadows of those bathing machines with their huge wheels; although, as none of us girls could swim, we never actually hired the things. But I do recall climbing up the steps of one of them and being terribly disappointed to find that it had only a rough wooden seat. I think I was expecting it to be furnished with a carpet and chairs like a little room!'

But it was only a matter of time before the cousins discovered that the real 'children's Bognor' lay west of the Pier. Frequently it was Wonnie's habit to walk her young charges along the breezy promenade, past Colebrook Terrace, the *Beach Hotel* and the Olympian Gardens, on their way to the beach below Queen Victoria's drinking fountain opposite the Steyne. And that makes this author wonder whether, during the course of their strolls, they ever caught sight of a stocky little woman on the sands, standing proprietorially amongst the red-and-white striped bathing machines at the end of Lennox Street. Or noticed her weather-beaten face and twinkling eyes under a broad-brimmed hat as she looked out from the little hut on the Esplanade bearing her name above it. Mary Wheatland, Bognor's sea-bathing lady extraordinary! Of course, her renown might not have reached their ears. Sylvia Endacott, in her booklet, *Our Mary*, says that in her lifetime she rescued some thirty people from drowning and held the Bronze Medal and two Certificates of the Royal Humane Society. But she was the commanding sort of figure who might well have attracted their attention. And in 1904 she was a mere 68 years of age and still some way from retirement. Alas, we shall never know. But if I were a betting man ...!

5 Mary Wheatland, Bognor's famous sea-bathing lady.

My mother again: '... so while Wonnie did her crocheting, we slapped and patted our sandcastles into shape with the Union flag fluttering from the topmost sand-pie turret. Meanwhile poor old Gilbert was expected to trot backwards and forwards to the sea in order to fetch pails of water for tipping into the castle's moat – which immediately disappeared into the thirsty sand. But we never had long to wait for the sea to come in and do the job for us, although the trouble was never knowing how to stop it! Oh, the anguish of watching our handiwork gradually dissolve beneath those heedless waves.

'What else did we get up to? Well, the first thing that springs to mind were donkey rides, although I have to admit to never feeling quite secure seated on one. There were trips in goat-carts, too; smellier but safer as far as I was concerned! In those days bicycles could be hired on the sands – which we girls left to Gilbert, he being the only one of us who knew how to remain upright on the things. Splashing around in the rock pools and under the Pier with our shrimping nets – bought from good old Burgess's Bazaar – must have accounted for goodness-knows-how-many hours. Oh yes, then there was our kite which seemed to spend more time tangled up on the beach than in the air.'

One can only commiserate with those Bognor folk and visitors who, now in their mid-fifties or younger, never experienced the joy of paying a visit to Burgess's Bazaar, until 1951 Bognor's Aladdin's Cave of toys. Sited on the corner of Manor Place and Waterloo Square and known as Waterloo House, the little shop was built by William Kimber Wonham just after the Napoleonic Wars. According to Gerard Young, in an article in the *Bognor Regis Post* (30 November 1968), its first occupant was John Kimber's brother, Richard, who was a draper and undertaker. In 1840 Miss Augusta Binstead took over the shop for her library and fancy goods business.

However, it was not until the mid-1870s that the shop found itself in the hands of the first Burgess – James Reeve – a proprietor who dealt in fancy goods as well as in toys. And it was in toys he came to enjoy a near-monopoly in the town until the opening of Toyland in the Arcade in the early 1900s. But it was his successor, Robert Briant Burgess, who erected the famous green glass fascia with gold lettering which became engrained in the psyche of young Bognorians during the first half of the 20th century. He continued in the business until, with his death in the 1930s, the shop was taken over by his brother, William.

In its lifetime, Burgess' Bazaar enjoyed two flurries of excitement. One was when Queen Mary visited the shop while she was staying at Craigweil House in 1929. The other occured when a bullet from a German aircraft was found lodged in a doll during the last war. The end of the line – and the end of a legend – came in 1951 when the business was sold.

Mother continued: 'Somewhere on the beach there was a coconut shy and I remember we all had a few goes at that. A good bit of our time was spent hunting for pretty pebbles, the ones with holes through them being regarded as especially lucky – my dear, you have no idea how superstitious we all were in our younger days! – nor must I forget those splendid whelk shells in which we willingly believed we could hear the roar of the ocean.

'Gilbert – our own Ranji* – couldn't wait for the tide to recede so that he could nag us to play cricket with him. The trouble was he insisted we girls bowled over-arm which clearly nature had never intended. In any case, apart from batting, I found cricket deadly boring and much preferred playing beach-tennis over a breakwater in spite of having to spend half the time retrieving our ball from the little pools.

* R.S. Ranjitsinhji, the Ruling Prince of Nawajar, who batted gloriously for England, Sussex and Cambridge between 1894 and 1912.

6 Built at the cost of £60, the Western Bandstand was opened in 1904. Sometime before the First World War it was enlarged to take the 'Blue Hungarian Band'. But its windswept location proved its undoing. In 1937 it was demolished to make way for the barely less draughty Western Bandstand Enclosure. The size of the telegraph poles indicates the growing popularity of the telephone.

'When the tide was in, or the beach became uncomfortably crowded, as it sometimes did at Bank Holiday weekends, Wonnie had to find something to occupy us. Quite often she took us to listen to the military band playing at the Western Bandstand opposite the *Royal Norfolk Hotel*. Or she might have taken us for a walk through the town or up Linden Road and back along Victoria Drive where cattle used to graze in the field in which St Wilfrid's Church was destined to rise a few years later.

'I can remember seeing leathery-faced old women sitting on chairs on the pavement shelling a sack of peas; perhaps it was in Chapel Street or one of those little ways behind the Southdown bus station.* It was also around there that I can faintly recall seeing a nanny goat being milked in the street. And another thing: in those days Bognor seemed full of pubs which you could smell from a long way off. It was also quite common to see children on errands carrying jugs of beer back to their homes.

'About the furthest east Wonnie ever marched us was to Felpham, which at that time was a quiet, pretty little village with thatched cottages and gravel roads. And, of course, its lovely St Mary's Church which you drew for your exams.† More than once we traipsed down to Felpham's beach so we must have passed Blake's Cottage, although I doubt whether we were aware of the eminence of its one-time occupant.

* The art-deco Southdown bus station, built on the site of the old council offices in 1934, was demolished in 1993. This prime High Street site now languishes as a supermarket car park.

† As part of my post-war studies I was required to measure and draw a building of some architectural note. St Mary's Church at Felpham was nicely convenient. To measure the height of the nave I used a length of twine attached to a dart, a stratagem as irreligious as it was effective. The drawing still hangs in my studio.

'Instead, I still carry a picture in my mind of an amusing little incident which occurred on one of those walks. We were near the bridge over the (Aldingbourne) Rife, where a large traction engine had stopped to take on water. Naturally, Gilbert ran on ahead to have a look. Imagine, then, Wonnie's anguish when the driver – and a pretty oil-stained one at that – picked him up and deposited him in amongst all the coal dust, the hissing valves, levers and other greasy things! Of course Gilbert loved it but as he was wearing his best clothes there was a lot of fretting from Wonnie after that!

'Another of our well-worn walks was past the Pier, the *Rock Garden's Hotel* and Culver Cottage to Nyewood Lane, where we discovered the tamarisk hedge, Gray's huts and the little fishermen's settlement that nestled amongst them; this was another new experience for us and accounted for the hours we spent watching them bringing in their catches and repairing their lobster pots and nets. Then, if we had been very good, Wonnie might have bought us a couple of crabs to take home for our high tea.

'Of course, that part of Bognor was just country then – cornfields. Only on the north side of Aldwick Road were there a few houses, although I recall Tregear's stores was there even then. So, too, was what we called the Bailey Home before it became Watney House. Further along was Arthur's Home and those little Victorian and Edwardian villas amongst which lay Forrabury and your own first taste of Bognor in 1928. But in 1904 Aldwick Road was just a dusty lane.'

The 'Bailey Home' is the substantial Edwardian building of 1898 on the north side of Aldwick Road, east of its junction with Nyewood Lane. When my mother first encountered it in 1904, it would have still been known as the Princess Mary Convalescent Home, run by the East London Hospital for Children. In about 1920 it became the seaside branch of the Princess Elizabeth of York Hospital, Shadwell and was renamed the Bailey Home. And thus it remained until 1947, when it passed into the hands of Watney's the brewers, who re-christened it Watney House and used it as a rest home for their staff and dependants. In more recent times, United Response turned it into a home for the mentally handicapped with the new name of Lantern House, and in 1994 the building underwent extensive alterations to re-emerge as the *Royal Bay Retirement Hotel*.

Mother again: 'When we awoke to rain-flecked windows and gurgling downpipes – which seemed all too often! – we were well prepared. Then out came our games of ludo, dominoes, Happy Families and the jigsaw puzzles – beautiful things in thick plywood, not the miserable cardboard stuff you see today. Gilbert, I remember, had a constructional set not unlike Meccano. For myself, I daresay I was content to do some drawing or write up my little picture-book of our holiday. For years I kept it, but you know how these things just disappear.

'Writing and acting little plays was another thing we had up our sleeves for when it rained. A table, some chairs, a walking stick and a piece of paper rolled up to look like a cigarette were all the props we needed to make us believe that we were treading the Lyceum's boards – with poor old Wonnie the captive audience. But even our most tear-jerking melodramas nearly always ended up with us rolling about in paroxysms of laughter! Anyway, it was impossible to be bored with these cousins of mine around. Just think of it, though, dear, no wireless or gramophone – and television beyond anyone's comprehension. Yet, even from Wonnie's tea-leaf readings we used to get a lot of fun.

'A bad-weather treat was for us to be taken to the little concert party at the Olympian Gardens which Wonnie always made an "occasion" by insisting we were properly togged up in our best dresses and straw boaters. Then, to make it even more special, she used to buy us a bag of sugared almonds.

'In those days Bognor was full of nurses with their little skeins of children in tow – just like ourselves, in fact. They seemed to enjoy a cheerful camaraderie. Often Wonnie used to stop and speak to one or other of them. Perhaps they were known to her in London. Anyway, I am sure they used to swap stories about what little horrors we all were!

'Another everyday sight on the Esplanade was bath-chairs. Of course, you don't see them nowadays as they've been replaced by these marvellous little electric things. But my impression is that their occupants were usually old ladies dressed in black bombazine, net-veiled and wrapped up in a plaid rug. Often they were dragged around by desiccated old men who looked as if they ought to have been in the chair as well!

'But, you know, in Edwardian times – as in Queen Victoria's – women only just the wrong side of 60 were regarded as being quite ancient, objects of sympathy, the elbow to be held. Indeed, they were expected to dress and behave in an "elderly" manner. Many of my aunts were like that, and since most of them were widows they dressed in black for the rest of their lives which made them look even older.

'Yet, today, many of those "poor old things" would be driving around in their Minis or – like me when I was getting on for 80 – off in an aeroplane to the Rhineland on a package tour and dressed in clothes quite suited to a woman of half my years. I think my mother would have been surprised and gratified to see the way "elderliness" is being pushed further and further away from whatever age we happen to have attained, until only a select few in their late nineties will be permitted to qualify as "poor old things!"

'One day Wonnie took us to a big fair somewhere near Argyle Road. I can still recall the swings, helter-skelter, coconut shies – and of course we all had to have a go on the beautiful gas-lit roundabout with its twisted brass poles, prancing horses and piping organ music. Anyway, it was a great contrast to the Esplanade where, in those days, there was very little in the way of entertainment for children. You know, if Butlins had been around in 1904, it would have taken wild horses to have dragged us away! But isn't it amusing to think that Billy Butlin then would have been only about our own age and probably unaware of Bognor's existence.

'Another source of entertainment were the little beach shows which I think Wonnie enjoyed as much as we. There was one, I remember, which had a performing dog and most of them ran to a bit of that hoped-for slapstick. But, to tell you the truth, I was always apprehensive of sitting too near the front as I had a secret fear of being asked to get up on the stage to take part in one of their acts. Dorothy and Sybil revelled in that sort of thing. Then, of course, there was the Punch and Judy show to which we all became addicts. In fact, I think it was in the same groyne – next to that man who used to draw those marvellous pictures in the sand – when you boys used to watch him thirty years later.

'During our time at Bognor there seemed quite a lot of beach vendors selling their wares: things like toffee-apples, pies, beach toys and, of course, that delicious ice-cream, or "hokey pokey" as it was sometimes called in London – and perhaps at Bognor, too – but in London it had the apocryphal cachet of having spent the night under the Italian vendor's bed! But while it was socially quite acceptable to eat ice-cream on the beach, we wouldn't have dreamed of eating it in the street. Supposing one of our mistresses from the Latimer and Godolphin [her school in Hammersmith] happened to be holidaying in Bognor and saw me? Expulsion must have surely followed! Today, of course, it sounds ridiculous. But 1904 wasn't 1977! In those days, I can tell you, our consciences were often sorely tried. However, Wonnie used to take us to little cafés – one of which I am sure was the Bijou in York Road, and there was another in West Bognor – where ice-cream could be consumed free of stigma.

'Visits to the Pier were regarded as highlights of our holiday. Well, for four young suburban landlubbers and their nurse to find themselves hanging on to their hats in a stiff breeze only a few feet above the roaring waves, surrounded by anglers and looking back at a far-off Esplanade where the bathing machines, drawn-up boats and the holiday throng suddenly looked so small, had to count as something of an adventure!

'And now you wring from me a terrible confession about a game we used to play on the Pier. The object was to avoid walking on the joints in

7 The junction of High Street and London Road. But the date? Staley's womenswear shop was in the garden of Mrs W. Cox's Camden House (right) in 1914. The car suggests about 1912. The horticultural nurseries to the north also belonged to Mrs Cox. The trees are in the grounds of the Congregationalist church.

the boards; one wobbly step spelt being gobbled up by a Great Black Bear, played stoically and *ad nauseam* by Wonnie – with added sound effects!

'Of course, in those days there was no Pier Theatre, but Wonnie used sometimes to take us to the little Pavilion at the sea-end where a small orchestra played; Pierrots, too, for I am sure that was where one of them gave me a grease-painty kiss as he handed me a string bag of chocolate coins, although for what, I've forgotten.

'Gilbert's faultless memory for the paddle-steamer's timetable meant that every now and then we were dragged onto the Pier to watch one arrive. But really they were beautiful things with their great paddles thrashing, flags fluttering and their decks lined with "foreigners" from Worthing and East-bourne. Yet, I cannot recall us ever having been for a voyage on one. I think the best that we managed were a couple of trips in sailing boats which we boarded near the Pier.'

I asked my mother about pocket money. 'Well, apart from that which my mother gave me, I think Uncle Ted slipped us all half-a-sovereign apiece before we left – which at that time was pretty generous. Clara, I remember, gave us exercise books; you know, the sort with multiplication tables on the backs, in which we were meant to account for our spending, although I have a guilty feeling that I used mine for drawing in.

'Quite a lot of our money must have been spent at Burgess' Bazaar in Waterloo Square. That was where I bought a doll with two pairs of sweet little shoes. Lead cart-horses were amongst our other purchases: beautiful, shiny things with harness and bridles. Our shrimping nets came from there, too. Dorothy, I remember, bought a wooden hoop. Now, I am sure Wonnie would not have let her buy the iron kind guided by a hook, as these were regarded as being rather 'common' on account of their association with working-class children! Well, they certainly made a great din running on stone pavements or over cobbles – and a very "Londony" sound it was, too.

'Nearly every day I used to send my dear mother a postcard, often purchased from Webster and Webb's in the High Street. So that must have accounted for a little of my outgoings, although the cost of a stamp then was only a ha'penny. The Post Office at that time was in the Arcade, opposite Toyland – which I see is still there.*

'Other shops I remember from those days and which were still in business in the 'thirties were Long and Strickland the chemists, Buckle and Clidero the grocers and Isted's the corn-chandlers in London Road; Lemmon's and Reynolds' existed as well. So, too, did Mant's the pork butchers in West Street where we and Wonnie were frequent customers.

'Often we used to buy our penn'orths of sweets at "Queen Victoria's Little Shop" on the corner of Gloucester Road. They stocked liquorice "bootlaces" and sherbert dabs – both great favourites in their day. Oh yes, and pink and white sugar mice with string tails. Humbugs cost four-a-farthing and toffee came in large slabs which had to be broken into pieces with a small brass hammer before being slid off the scales into a conical bag formed from a piece of newspaper. Really it was quite criminal to have

---

* In fact, Toyland closed in December of that same year (1977). With Goodacres and Burgess's Bazaar already gone, it marked the end of Bognor's indigenous toyshops.

8 Queen Victoria's little shop' on the north-east corner of Gloucester Road. It was sold as hardcore for £22 10s. in 1967, the victim of a road-widening scheme.

pulled down such a unique little building. All that history and all I remembered, snuffed out just like that!'

Insignificant as the shop may have been architecturally, this small cottage at the north-east end of Gloucester Road nevertheless enjoyed a special place in the hearts of Bognor folk. Originally part of a farm owned by the Munday family and known as Brook Cottage, it was used by one of them as a cobbler's shop. In the early 1800s, while the little Princess Victoria and her mother, the Duchess of Kent, were staying at nearby Bognor Lodge – Sir Richard Hotham's first mansion in the town – the young Queen-to-be was taken to Mr Munday to be fitted with a pair of shoes, a tumultuous event from which Bognor has still barely recovered! But by the time my mother knew it it had become a sweet shop, popular with pupils from the nearby schools. In 1967 there was public outcry when it was announced that it was proposed to demolish 'Ye Olde Tucke Shoppe' – as the mid-20th century coyly knew it – to make way for road widening. Had the will been there, no doubt it could have been saved to remain an asset to Bognor's tourist industry. But the authorities in those days were deaf to that sort of entreaty. Instead it was sold as hardcore to Mr Harry Geal, the demolition contractor, for £22 10s. As the Chairman of the Highways Committee explained, 'We are not vandals; we are not destroying Bognor. We are only acting as agents!'

Mother again: 'Most of our shopping was done at Hawke's in the High Street, where presumably Aunt Clara had opened an account. It meant that even the smallest purchases were delivered to the house by a whistling errand boy on a bike; we never seemed to carry anything away. But tell me, dear, where have all those whistling errand boys gone? To universities? In the City? Or making thousands of pounds in pop groups? Anyway, all who call at my back door nowadays are gloomy, monosyllabic young van-drivers in jeans.

'Of course, the Bognor of those days wasn't much more than a large village. I can well remember the cart- and cab-horses queuing up to drink in the horse-trough by the *Bedford Hotel* and I have a faint memory of seeing sheep being driven along, I think, West Street. And where the bus station and those new shops stand in the High Street were front gardens of the premises behind them, filled with trees and shrubs; the Fitzleet House grounds were a veritable forest. In fact, when we first came here, in 1928, there were still some private gardens with quite large trees in London Road,* all of which added to the town's charm.

'So it is sad to see what appears to be a determined effort afoot to make Bognor ugly. It has become the plaything of developers and young planners. Slowly, its Victorian and Edwardian seaside character – which is, after all, one of its few assets – is being inexorably eroded. I mean, how could they have allowed those huge blocks of flats to go up in Queensway? And what about our poor old Pier bereft of its little sea-end Pavilion? Do you honestly think it will ever be replaced? Really, our only consolation is that at least we knew the town when it still retained a vestige of its more elegant past.'

One day Wonnie's name came up in conversation and I learned a little more of her. 'She was the youngest daughter of a Lincolnshire farmhand whose family were driven to becoming "soup-kitchen" folk by the agricultural depression of the 1880s. I remember her telling me that she had gone "into service" in London when she was fourteen. Yet somehow she had picked up a little education and was able to read and write moderately well – well enough for us children, anyway. But Wonnie never lost her Lincolnshire accent. I believe that at heart she was a Wesleyan which explains how she could quote great tracts of the Bible from memory.

'But she could be quite strict. For instance she was absolutely intolerant of us skipping in the street or even playing "touch" or leapfrog. Nor was Dorothy allowed to bowl her hoop. Raised voices or any form of rumbustiousness had immediately to be quelled by that famous Wonnie "hush-hush".

'Of course she was careful to see we were always properly dressed. Self-indulgent scruffiness was quite unheard of in the 1900s. Indeed, our wardrobes contained none of what we now call "casuals"; just our "velvets", house dresses and pinafores. Cleaning our teeth with Odol toothpaste twice a day and saying our prayers – kneeling – before going to bed were other things on which she kept her eye. Oh yes, and then there was our Virol, a spoonful each after lunch – I can still taste the stuff! Another of her foibles

---

* Moreton Swinburne, editor of the *Bognor Regis Post* noticed these changes even earlier. On 28 January 1938 he wrote, 'During the last ten years the transformation of London Road, from a comparatively quiet and still-residential road into a busy road of large shops, illustrates more than anything else the rapid growth of Bognor Regis.' What might he have said to a shopping precinct, I wonder?

was making us breath deeply and count ten before exhaling, although its only effect on me was to make me feel faint!

'Wonnie was completely devoted to the Dorés, having spent the best part of thirty years helping raise their spread-out family. Then, when old age began to take its toll of Clara and Uncle Ted, she became the mainstay of their lives. I think she was with the family for something like forty-five years.'

Yet, notwithstanding her many virtues, I couldn't help thinking that Wonnie on holiday sounded a bit of a drag! Immediately my mother sprang to her defence. 'I daresay she sounds a bit of a martinet to you, dear, because you were born into a world that had been transformed by the Great War. Our circumstances had completely changed. No longer were we in a position to pay for a full-time children's nurse whose wage levels were being set by the proliferation of the so-called "Norland"* nurses. In any case, we hadn't the accommodation for one at Aldwick. Instead, it meant that we had to make do with "dailies". But they had other duties than keeping their eyes on you children all the time. Gradually you began to wander off on your own; down to the beach and out into the countryside, a countryside which began at the bottom of Aldwick Garden when we first came here. My reward was seeing my sons becoming daily more self-reliant as they sought their own little adventures and diversions. I can never remember feeling concerned for your safety.

'But returning to Wonnie. You have to remember that she was charged with bringing us up to fit into the middle-class, Edwardian mould of the early 1900s; to conform to "The Code". And in those days children didn't expect to be pandered to by the grown-ups – unlike today when parents hardly dare refuse their offspring's slightest whim.

'Good behaviour, a grasp of etiquette, a proper respect for our elders and a belief in God – or at least a working knowledge of the New Testament and where to find the Epistle for the fourteenth Sunday after Trinity in the *Book of Common Prayer* – were the keystones of our Edwardian edifice. Of course, there were other things like well-scrubbed hands and eating up every disgusting scrap on our plates. Oh yes, and forever practising our scales on the piano.

'But we never questioned any of this. We were surrounded by examples; Uncle Ted used to address his father as "Sir" when he was a grown man. And old James continued to hold prayers once a week in the panelled room in The Grange at Clapton – to which the staff had to be dragged – until a few weeks before he died. Naturally we all learned to curtsey, and dear old Aunt Louise – the Eastbourne one – used to rate at least a small curtsey at Cleve Road on Christmas morning.

'And yet, when I think how much my sons enjoyed just being allowed to mess around on their own, I have to admit that my cousins and I rather missed out on that sort of thing. I really think it would have done us a lot of good to have escaped sometimes from Wonnie's over-protectiveness. But at the time we never gave it a thought. We simply accepted our Edwardian

---

* My mother would have been surprised to have learned that in 1910 Mrs Mary Ward, foundress of the Norland Institute (training super-nannies), had set up a branch in Gloucester Road while she was staying at Sudley Lodge.

9 'Pile 'em high and sell 'em cheap' might be the caption for this picture of a cane-ware vendor in Waterloo Square. Perhaps he is also a horse-dealer which would explain the three ponies in tow. Around 1890 the Burgess family would have been running the Bognor library, already well-known for its stocks of children's toys. This picture is by the well-known local amateur photographer, A.R. Dressler.

circumstances. Although it was sometimes irksome, Wonnie's tight rein served to set us apart from street urchins and no doubt induced in us a sense of security. But the main thing was that we expected to do as we were told. Democracy or arguing back didn't come into it!'

Well, there it was; no jeans and trainers at the Debt House! But when they were out with Wonnie, my mother used to tell us, they wore their Daniel Neal button-up boots, cotton dresses, a bow for their necks and another two for their pigtails, and, on their heads, school boaters. For his pains, Gilbert was condemned to being dressed in a plum-coloured jacket, baggy knickerbockers and his school cap. But at least he was spared being dolled up like a little Jack Tar which, in my mother's recollection, was the lot of many small boys at Bognor at that time.

On Sundays Gilbert's unruly hair was subdued with brilliantine and the girls pulled on their white kid gloves for the walk to St Mary's Church at South Bersted, where the incumbent never tired of reminding them of how full of sin and empty of goodness they all were; verities to which the cousins responded by forgetting the Collects and playing surreptitious games

10 Reynolds' steam lorry and trailer in use during the early 'twenties.

of noughts-and-crosses behind piously opened hymn books! 'And in those days, dear', exclaimed my mother, 'sermons were sermons; three-quarters of an hour of anaesthetising declamation from the pulpit!'

Here is another of her Bognor reminiscences. During their arboreal strolls around Aldwick Manor (now Hotham Park House) and The Dome, the little party quite often encountered a smartly turned-out man mounted upon a bob-tailed hack who used to give them a smile and lift his top hat in salutation. Evidently he was a gentleman of some substance, although whom they had no idea. I wonder, myself.

Could she remember there being many cars in Bognor when she was there? This was a question I once put to her. 'Well, there were a few, of course – charabancs, too, for that matter. Gilbert, I recall, used to note down their numbers in a little book. But there was certainly no mistaking a motor car when it went past; they made a great racket, raised clouds of dust and people still stopped to look at them.

'Indeed, it must have been at about that time that Uncle Ted bought a huge thing with brass headlamps and a folding hood. But apparently he was so terrified of driving it that eventually Beldon was called upon to do the chauffeuring. It must have been happening all over the country. And another thing I can remember about that car was how, after a trip to Highgate on a bitterly cold day, Aunt Clara went straight to Whiteley's store in Bayswater and ordered a large opossum rug to improve the passenger's prospects of survival.' The author can remember this rug's declining years, draped over the back of a chair at home.

There appear to have been more motor cars in Bognor in 1904 than my mother gave credit for. As an example, there was motor car racing on the sands. It was sanctioned by the council (13 April 1904) 'providing that the AA Club take entire responsibility for all arrangements and relieves the Council from all liability in case of an accident'. By the following year the the BUDC had come to regard cars on the untarred roads as an unmitigated nuisance, *vide* the Council Minutes of 5 July 1905: '... the Council feels it is impossible and unjust to have to maintain the roads between the Urban centres owing to the extra amount of through traffic thrown upon them by the ever-increasing and devastating motors.' On 5 May 1905 Mr Bridges reported the erection of 'five signs warning drivers of dangerous corners'. And as as early as July 1903 a Mrs Bowring had written to the council complaining of the noise made by a car belonging to 'a driver touting for business' in front of Cotswold Terrace. Another sign of the times was to be seen at the *Victoria Hotel* in West Bognor, where visitors were offered lessons in motor car driving as well as horse-riding. Verily, the writing was on the wall!

So it was apposite that my mother should have mentioned charabancs. For it was in just such a conveyance that Wonnie had promised the cousins a trip. 'I think it must have been to somewhere around Slindon – well, lots of narrow lanes with overhanging hedges which threatened to decapitate its human cargo. And I well remember the affront suffered by the teetotal Wonnie when the driver stopped at a rural beer house, filled with cyclists, for his passengers to slake their thirst!' But surely it was an act of compassion, for on those unmade Downland tracks they must have swallowed a lot of dust.

One day, the arrival of a postcard at London Road caused a flurry of excitement. Shamelessly, Uncle Ted and Clara had elected to break their vows of non-participation in their children's holidays! They were coming down by train from Hampstead for the day – and to Doris' delight her mother Alice was coming too.

To mark the occasion Wonnie ordered cream puffs for tea instead of the perennial sand cake; the girls put on their 'velvets' and a display of pebbles, shells and marine bric-à-brac was arranged on the dining room table. Later Wonnie took them to meet the train. 'How lovely it was to see my dear, sad little mother again. I just put my arms round her neck and wept!'

When time hung heavily at the Debt House, there was a diversion close at hand: to stand on the over-bridge by the level crossing and enjoy being blanketed in the steam of the passing London, Brighton and South Coast Railway locomotives. But when Gilbert overstepped the bounds of propriety by trying to spit down their chimneys, Wonnie was wrathful. 'You disgusting little urchin', she exclaimed, 'I shall tell your mother!' But by the time I tried it, in the 1930s, the chimneys had changed hands and by then belonged to the Southern Railway.

Then, one wet and blustery afternoon, Doris and her cousins peered through the parlour window to witness a passing funeral cortège, a little white coffin in a glass-sided hearse pulled by two horses with nodding black plumes. 'But it certainly wasn't the first child-funeral we'd seen. In those days they were all too common in London and everywhere else.'

Surrounding this birth-of-the-20th-century scene, she reminded me, was the all-pervading smell of horse dung, the whiff of cesspits and smell of dustbins awaiting emptying into the council's open, horse-drawn dust-cart. 'As you say, dear, it was all a very far cry from the Beatles, washing machines, nylon underwear and these huge airliners flying all over the world – things beyond our wildest childhood dreams. And come to that, who amongst my generation could have envisaged the National Health Service or State Old Age Pensions? But what about landing those men on the moon! Wasn't that absolutely incredible? And to think that I was able to watch it minute by minute on that other miracle of our time, television!

'Yet, you know, there is something I find quite nostalgic about these young girls in their granny-shawls, for they remind me of the flower-sellers in Piccadilly before the First World War. But at my age [she was 83 in 1977], one has a curious perspective on time. I mean, even the "flappers" of the 'twenties – "the thin and emancipated", as someone called them – strike me as being still quite modern.'

Evidently, Queen Victoria's 'dear little Bognor' struck a chord with young Doris Davey. So at the end of those holidays – which I daresay passed all too quickly – it was, perhaps, predictable that one day she would seek its reacquaintance. And how she did, the reader will learn in the pages which follow.

* * *

In 1985, Doris Alford passed from this world having known and lived at Bognor, off and on, for the best part of her 91 years.

2

Lest We Forget

With the passing years, the green-baize door leading to Wonnie's wax-polished kingdom at Cleve Road came to swing less often as her young charges grew up. Sybil had buckled down to a course in Domestic Science at Regent Street Polytechnic; Dorothy was doing Pitman's shorthand and typing, while Gilbert had been perched on one of the lower rungs of the banking business. Meanwhile, their cousin Doris had put up her hair and was now at Miss Emant's studio, overlooking Kew Green, where she was daily discovering more of her talent for drawing beautiful women dressed in the latest *haut couture*. The future must have looked full of summers.

Then, on 28 June 1914, at Sarajevo in Bosnia, Gavrilo Princip, a politically inflamed Serbian schoolboy, jumped on to the running board of an open motor carriage and fired two shots from his pistol. The first killed the Archduke Franz Ferdinand, the other his wife, Sophie.

'Immediately news of the war broke,' my mother used to tell us, 'a great wave of patriotism swept the country. Union flags appeared on all the important buildings and many were unfurled from the top windows of ordinary houses where they'd been kept rolled up since the end of the Boer War. A great crowd assembled in Trafalgar Square to give vent to its approval of war. Outside the Army Recruiting Office in Acton, pinch-faced young chaps in cloth caps and fine-looking young fellows in boaters queued up to 'sign on' for the Services. At the Music Halls, the ballads and ditties became steeped in nationalistic fervour.

'The Doré boys and most of their friends had been in their school OTCs [Officer Training Corps], so they were among the first to volunteer for Commissions in the Army – and with such enthusiasm! It was almost as if they were looking forward to some great sporting event; they couldn't wait to get to France "to give the Boche a good hiding". Gilbert, I remember, was dreadfully concerned lest he should "miss all the fun" when he learned that Reggie Berisford's regiment was to embark from Dover before his own.

'I think we really did believe that after a few gentlemanly skirmishes, the Hun would run up the white flag, there'd be handshakes all round and our boys would be home for Christmas! I don't suppose it entered our heads that the Germans were probably thinking on the same lines – but with us doing the surrendering! Of course, those poor dears had no inkling of what lay ahead of them; no conception of those damnable trenches, the mud, the barbed wire, the gas clouds and those wicked day-long artillery barrages.

'Eventually, we began to read of the great battles – Mons, the Marne, Ypres and the unspeakable Somme. Day after day the casualty lists in the papers grew longer. And those were mainly officers. I think they played down the losses among the ordinary soldiers. Looking through those columns of names, to see whether they mentioned some young boy we knew, was terrible. And I remember how our hearts used to sink when we saw a telegraph boy pedalling down our road. At which house would he stop? Whose life was about to be shattered by those dread words "We regret to inform you …" scrawled on a scrap of fawn paper? Gradually a shroud of grief was drawn over the whole country as men's lives became cheaper and cheaper until, by 1918, it was as though half the women in our part of London were dressed in black.

'Naturally, the loss of so many of those boys I had been brought up with affected me deeply – mere kids at school when the war started. Pupils at St Paul's, Chigwell and Merchant Taylors, clad in their school caps and blazers one moment, and the next – there they stood, bold-looking one-pippers wearing their regimental badges and shiny Sam Browne belts. But within a short time, many of them lay dead under the poppies of northern France: Harold Williams, Robert Just, and Phyllis Hinde's fiancée, Peter; poor Henry Carter, too, who crashed in an aeroplane; oh, and lots of others, Reggie Berisford among them.

11 My grandmother, Alice Davey (Nana).

'Do you know, dear, for years I couldn't hear that ghastly name "Somme" without my eyes filling with tears – in fact, they do still. I can remember Gilbert coming home on leave looking grey and haggard and quite unable to tell us anything he'd been through. So that war not only finished off half the young men of my generation; it also put paid to a middle-class way of life which – until then – we had no reason to believe was not our birthright! And then to think you had to go through the whole thing again twenty years later!'

The Armistice signed, a war-numbed Britain counted her 760,000 dead, inscribed their names on war memorials scattered throughout the towns and shires and put their trust in them being 'Remembered for Evermore'. Somehow Gilbert had survived the Somme's 'demented guns' with only a scarred mind for his pains. Safe, too, my father-in-waiting thanks to the rear hoof of a compassionate horse which consigned him to hospital and prolonged convalescence with a ruptured spleen just before his Battery was shovelled into the third battle of Ypres.

With their fair share of orders for officer's uniforms, James Doré and Sons also survived the war. But with the peace came new problems. Many of their customers were content to use up their pre-war garments, and by the time they looked for new ones, the cheaper and now better ready-made suits had become much more widely acceptable.

But tribulations seldom travel singly. For now had to be added the anxieties of old age. First Clara became ill and then Edwin's heart began to give trouble. The business was handed over to their eldest son, Graham. Gradually, Wonnie became his parents' lifeline. At last, too expensive to run, the Cleve Road mansion had to go. They moved into a smaller house in Blenheim Road nearby – and of course Wonnie went too. And there, not long afterwards, Clara died.

Widowed, Uncle Ted moved his life to Crewkerne in Somerset, where he survived his wife by only a year or two. But time enough to honour a certain debt which hung heavily upon his conscience. Provision was made for Wonnie to receive a small pension, sufficient for self-esteem in a modest room off Kilburn High Road.

Mercifully, the future had kept its wicked secrets to itself during those carefree, turn-of-the-century holidays my mother and her cousins had spent on Bognor's golden sands.

* * *

In 1919, while Doris was still attending life classes at Lime Grove Art School in Shepherds Bush, she became friendly with a gifted young artist working in the next studio who had insisted on painting her portrait. His name was Frank Alford. She had also learned how he had just realised his most cherished ambition. Long an admirer of the work of Frank Brangwyn,* regarded as one of Britain's greatest living painters, he had persuaded the Master to cast a critical eye over some of his work. Now Doris could share in Frank's hour of triumph. For at the end of that anxious afternoon he had been invited to become Brangwyn's painting assistant and to work on the Master's world-famous murals† at his Temple Lodge studio at Hammersmith.

Ambition, however, lay not only with this brilliant young artist. For its flame burned just as brightly in his sweetheart, Doris Davey. Which explains why, one day, she bade a fond farewell to Miss Emant, picked up her portfolio and set off to peddle her work among the steely-eyed dragonesses who edited the women's pages of some of Fleet Street's best-known papers and periodicals. 'My knees used to knock as I waited to go in', she more than once confessed. 'What if they took one look at my work and pointed to the door?' Well, of course, they didn't. And at least they took down a few of her details. Then one day she met an editress more sympathetic than most. 'Your work deserves a good agent, dear. Now there's a Mrs Alcock who handles your sort of thing. Here's her address.'

Thus, Amelia Alcock entered my mother's life. Soon it became clear that Mrs A. was on pink-gin and De Reske Minor terms with every editorial dragoness in the kingdom! Quite soon a trickle of commissions began dropping through the letterplate of No. 36 Grafton Road at Acton. One thing eventually led to another, and so it came about that at the unfashionable hour of 10.15 on a July morning in 1920, much to the jubilation of the 12-

---

* Later Sir Frank Brangwyn RA.

† Many of Frank Brangwyn's murals were on a massive scale needing to be painted off ladders and trestles. After sketching in the main composition and painting in a few salient details himself, the Master would leave the completion of much of the rest of the work to my father, whose painting style was remarkably similar to Brangwyn's own.

strong wedding party – which, needless to say, included the Doré cousins and a white-haired Wonnie – Frank and Doris emerged from the porch of Acton parish church joined together as man and wife.

Of course, it would have made a prettier story had I been able to relate how the happy couple had been last seen boarding the night train *en route* for their Paris honeymoon. More prosaic the truth, though. For suddenly the trickle of Fleet Street commissions had swollen to a flood. Only by working all God's hours could she cope. For D.D. (as she continued to sign herself) was on the threshold of becoming a top-flight fashion artist. And not even a honeymoon was going to get in the way of that! Acton would have to do.

Eventually, the young Alfords settled down in my grandmother's house at Grafton Road, first as a comfortable threesome and later – after I had been gently introduced into this world – a foursome. Thus, for the next few years, my life revolved round not only my mother and father, but nearly as much around my grandmother, Nana. For it was she who helped hand-raise her grandson: kept him fragrant, tied his laces, combed his hair and read him the more difficult passages from *Chick's Own*. And when she had done with young Michael, she ran the house, did the laundering, helped with the cooking and spent the evenings mending everything that was worn and torn. And all so that my parents could pursue their respective professions as far as possible absolved from domestic distractions. No wonder that my father claimed Nana to be the best mother-in-law in the business!

Some years later my father left Brangwyn's studio at Temple Lodge to pursue a career on his own, first as a painter and muralist before side-stepping into the architectural profession with offices at No. 19 Hanover

12 My father painting in his studio.

13 'Vegetables and Jug', a still life by Frank Alford.

Square, WC1. In due course, success attended his endeavours when, by a set of circumstances he could never have foreseen, he came to enjoy the consistent patronage of the Duke of Newcastle: inheritor of the priceless Hope diamond, a world-renowned art collection, Clumber Castle in the Dukeries, two country houses, Box Hill and 38,000 acres of land, much of it in the better parts of Surrey, all of which may help explain the Duke's antipathy towards the Bolshevik regime!

From her studio-world of drawing boards, lay figures, easels, Indian ink, sketching pens, reams of Bristol board, a dozen exquisite gowns – and a hundred good ideas – my mother continued to meet, week after week, for the next fifteen years, the treadmill discipline of Fleet Street deadlines. By 1930 her drawings were appearing in the *Daily Mail, Daily Express, Westminster Gazette, Glasgow Herald*, the *Evening News* and *Punch*. In addition, she drew the catalogues and illustrations for Dickens and Jones, Peter Robinson, Selfridge's, and Kendall Milne of Manchester. She was also a contributor with fashion sketches to *Weldon's Weekly* and *Home Chat*.

The rest of the time she spent encouraging and supporting my father in his ever-increasing work. And when Nana became too frail, she produced thousands of good wholesome meals containing neither garlic nor yoghurt. She was also a compulsive poet with much of her work appearing in two hardbacks, *The Kindling Light* and *Snow Upon the Hearth*, published in the late 'fifties by the Fortune Press. One of her poems, celebrating the building of the Chichester Festival Theatre, hangs there in a position of honour in the foyer, under the portrait of the founder of the theatre, Leslie Evershed-Martin.

Nor should I fail to mention that somehow she found time to produce, mould, raise and partly educate three sons – each passable in his own way – as well as nurturing a seedling apple which the reader will meet in the last chapter.

By 1923 the family had moved to Isleworth, a privet-hedged suburb of west London and a village still, where the ancient hostelry walls of the *London Apprentice* stood reflected in the lingering waters of the River

14 One of the many hundreds of pen-and-ink sketches my mother produced in the 'twenties and 'thirties.

Thames, with a view similar to that of Sir Joshua Reynolds' house over-looking the nearby Eyot. In the Isleworth hinterland, Van Gogh had stayed at No.160 Twickenham Road and John Adam had refurbished Syon House for the Duke of Northumberland ...

But enough with name dropping! In any case, where we actually lived the Thames had long given up lingering. Instead, our nearest neighbours of any note were Watney's Isleworth Brewery and Pears Soap factory. When the wind blew southerly, it brought to our noses the scent of hops and a delicious soapy compound of rosemary, cedar and thyme; and it brought to our ears the scream of their clocking-on hooters. In a broad avenue lined with imperious chestnuts and without a parked car in sight, the family lived in a comfortable Edwardian house which echoed to the cry of the rag-and-bone man on Wednesday afternoons and the calls of tawny owls and distant river tugs throughout the night.

Then, on a day full of whispers and winks, I was packed off to spend a few days with my cousin, Elizabeth. When I returned, I was invited to peer into a flouncy cot containing a bundle of swaddling clothes out of one end of which protruded a small, wizened head. It purported to be my new brother. I must say, left to me, I'd have chosen something a bit bigger. Anyway, its name was Roger.

3

A Little Piece of Sussex

In twenty years time the whole face of the country will be covered with bungaloid growth in which childless couples will sleep after racing around the roads in their little cars ...

Dean Inge (c.1927)

In the summer of 1927 my parents decided the time had come to introduce their first-born and his small brother to the seaside. From the pages of *The Lady* came forth the felicitously descriptive Red Roof, a 'furn'd bung nr sea' in Seal Road at Selsey. My mother and I travelled down with my father in our first car, a grease-gun-and-nipples two-seater Singer with a rear 'dickey', folding hood and a bulbous rubber horn tuned to the honk of a London taxi.

As the car came to a halt outside the bungalow, I awoke to a disquieting sight: a road consisting of an anarchic compilation of flints, hardcore, sand, tufts of dusty grass and potholes punctuated with little piles of horse dung. Of course, as a child of the London suburbs, I knew only of well-ordered pavements and sleeked-down tarmacadam. I had seen my first unmade road.

Mrs Sayers, the owner, greeted us at the garden gate, showed my mother the shilling-in-the-slot meters and water stopcock's hiding place and handed her the keys. Then she was off and we moved in. Soon I discovered that Mrs Sayers' sort of house had no stairs: my first bungalow. Selsey was to prove full of 'firsts'.

The next day my father drove over to Chichester to pick up my brother and Marjory, our maid, who had travelled down from London by train; this pointed to the inadequacy of three-seater family cars. Now our holiday could properly begin. In the afternoon, accompanied by Marjory, we went for a walk and that was the first time I had ever come across people living in wooden shacks and converted railway carriages.

One glance at its beach pointed to Selsey's heritage consisting largely of pebbles. Miles of them. But before I had a chance to question this dubious excess of nature, I discovered that among the clumps of sea-kale and sorrel that grew out of the stones, there lurked an abundance of little brown sand lizards which used to stare and flick their impertinent tongues at us as we ate our picnics on the East Beach. But they had to be held with care, otherwise they shed their tails and this used to precipitate the womenfolk into hysterics. It was also on Selsey's strand that my first sandcastle rose: to the purblind, a small eruption in the sand, but to its architect and builder, a triumph of constructional and aesthetic judgment.

After a few days, I was promised a treat. We were going to Chichester by train. And thus I was introduced to the 'West Sussex Railway – Selsey Tramway Section',* with its operatic little steam engines which pre-Emetted Rowland Emett by many years. Twice we set out for Chichester. The first time we were hauled by just such an engine, which leaked steam from every joint, and I can vividly recall the bumpy rails, the excitement of crossing the lifting-bridge at Hunston and my mother trying to get a bit of ash out of my eye with the corner of her hanky. So that was another 'first' of a very high order.

The next time we used Selsey's Tramway, we climbed on board an eccentric-looking Ford bus on which the tyres had been replaced with flanged railway wheels.† It was, though, from the beginning, a journey doomed. For at Ferry Halt the train stopped – as if this time it really meant it! There, we waited … and waited until, about an hour later, a wheezy steam engine arrived and pulled us back to the safety of Selsey station. Eventually we found our way up to the top deck of a No. 52 green-and-cream Southdown bus which ran a pneumatic-tyred service to Chichester. This, exclaimed my mother triumphantly, was the travel of the future. And with that we bade farewell to the Manhood's ricketty little railway.

Other images of Selsey remain clearly etched on my mind: its bleach-thatched cottages, the regiments of lobster pots, the fishing boats and nets drying in a wind smelling of tar and seaweed. And in my ears the sibilant monotony of pebbles running through the fingers of the waves.

Selsey was also where I first made the acquaintance of a freshly caught swordfish, learned how to hold a crab so it couldn't nip me, saw my first Clyno motor car and had my first ride on a horse – which surely must have been at Scrimgeour's riding stables. The Owers flashing beam, too, was quite the first lightship to be brought to my notice. And I nearly forgot Medmerry Mill, where we all got drenched in a sudden monsoon which washed out the Boy Scout's tents and turned their fires into heaps of sodden ashes.

If Selsey had a soul, she must have kept it in the recently built (1927) Lifeboat Station. In fact, apart from the *Marine Hotel*, Red Roof and the Coastguard's Station, it is the only other building I can remember. And little wonder. For daily I held it in vigil hoping against hope for a bit of maritime drama. You know the sort of thing: exploding maroons, pouring rain, thunder-and-lightning and bearded sea-dogs launching their boat into crashing seas. It was a scenario dearly held. But for the whole of that fortnight the waves remained resolutely un-crashing until, in the end, my father had to take me to see my first lifeboat, the *Jane Holland*‡ – for such was her name in those days – behind chocks in her new home. As I said, Selsey was just one 'first' after another.

---

* The pre-1924 name of 'Hundred of Manhood and Selsey Tramway Company Limited' had more resonance.
† These Model 'T' Ford traction units were made by Edmunds Ltd of Thetford, Norfolk and worked in pairs separated by an open truck. In 1928 they were superseded by a later version known as 'Shefflex' cars.
‡ The *Jane Holland* was transferred to Eastbourne in 1929 and replaced by the lifeboat *Canadian Pacific*. In June 1940 *Jane Holland* took part in the Dunkirk evacuation. See also Chapter 21.

15 The replacement Selsey Lifeboat Station in about 1927. Because of coastal erosion yet another shed had to be built closer to the land in 1960.

Only our being cut off in Seal Road from the mainstream of Selsey's historic past, can excuse the three score years which elapsed before I discovered, from reading Edward Heron-Allen's *Selsey Bill; Historic and Pre-Historic*, that the town had once hit the big-time in the mouse-trap-making business. Well, at least it makes a change from Bishop Wilfrid castigating the local folk for profitlessly trapping eels instead of netting fish from the sea.

It happened in the 1860s. Yet, of Colin Pullinger, that doyen of entrepreneurs, who started the enterprise and invented the grisly-sounding 'Automaton and Perpetual' trap, the casual visitor enters and leaves Selsey unreminded. Apparently, Pullinger rates no obelisk; the eye seeks in vain an Ionic marble mouse-trap raised high above the city gate; there is no Pullinger Boulevard, Parade or Ave. Only a dismissive silence. And that seems less than his due. For once upon a time, his 'self-setting' design was all the talk in mouse-trap circles and, around 1880, nearly a thousand such

16 A Ford railcar unit of the Selsey Tramway in about 1927.

traps were being made every week at his 'Inventive' Factory in the High Street. At 2s. 6d. they sound quite expensive. But not to Mr P. 'They're cheap at the price and will last a lifetime', he retorts. And if you couldn't afford to buy the 'Perpetual', the mice still weren't safe. 'Mouse Traps Let on Hire', his brochure threatens.

In fact there seems nothing to which this homespun Leonardo da Vinci and Clerk to the Selsey Sparrow club couldn't turn his hand:

COLIN PULLINGER,
Selsey, near Chichester
Contractor, Inventor, Fisherman and Mechanic.
Following the various trades of a
Builder, Carpenter, Joiner, Sawyer, Undertaker, Turner, Cooper
Painter, Glazier, Wooden pump maker.
PAPER HANGER, BELL HANGER, SIGN PAINTER, BOAT BUILDER
Clock cleaner, Repairer of Locks, and Keys fitted.
Repairer of umbrellas and parasols, Mender of china and glass.
Copying Clerk, Letter writer, Accountant, Teacher of Navigation.
GROCER, BAKER, FARMER
Assessor and Collector of Taxes, Surveyor, House Agent, Engineer,
Land Measurer, Assistant Overseer, Clerk of the Parish Vestry Meetings,
Clerk to the Selsey Police, Clerk to the Selsey Sparrow Club.....
Has Served at Sea in the Four Quarters of the World as
Seaman, Cook, Steward, Mate and Navigator.

The Maker and Inventor of the following:
AN IMPROVED HORSE HOE, AN IMPROVED SCARIFIER
A newly-invented Couch Grass Rake, A machine to tar ropes.
A model of of a Vessel to Cut Asunder Chains put across a Harbour Mouth.
A CURIOUS MOUSE TRAP
Made on a scientific Principle, where each one caught resets the trap to catch
its neighbour, requires no fresh baiting, and will catch them by dozens
A Rat Trap on a peculiar construction that will catch them
and put them in a trap.
An improved Mole Trap, an improved Velocipede, a Model of a fast-sailing yacht
on improved construction, 2 feet long and challenged to sail against
any Boat of the same length in the World etc., etc.,
CRABS, LOBSTERS AND PRAWNS SENT TO ANY PART OF
ENGLAND.
MOUSE TRAPS LET ON HIRE.

But in the late 1880s, just along the coast at Bognor, this historical nugget had a significance bordering on the dolorous. For according to Gerard Young, had we been around at the time, we might have observed that *Black's Guide* was so desperate to find something to take the visitors' minds off the paucity of the the town's entertainment facilities that it was reduced to the 'heroic hopelessness' of recommending trips to Selsey for a look round Mr Pullinger's thriving manufactory. Alas, statistics are sparse which might reveal how many visitors availed themselves of the punishing 25-mile-round trip along those dusty roads, via Lagness, Hunston and Sidlesham, to visit this mouse-trap Shangri-la!

In fact, as far as Bognor's entertainment facilities were concerned, things hadn't improved very much by 1904, the year my mother stayed there. On 13 January, in the *West Sussex Gazette*, a correspondent under the pseudonym *Quis Quis* felt compelled to comment: 'Bognor may well pose as a "quiet place" this winter, for never in my experience have its entertainments been at such a low ebb. What with the cessation (one might say 'extinction'), of the Subscription Concerts and the dearth of Theatrical entertainments, we appear to have been asleep.'

But during the succeeding years this little Victorian watering place had pulled up its socks. So much so that, by 1927, it could offer its visitors not only record-breaking hours of sunshine, unusually pure water, excellent drains and hygienic abattoirs, but also safe sea-bathing ('children may perambulate its sands which decline gradually to the native bed of the ocean'), golden beaches washed twice a day by an obliging tide as well as a plethora of excellent family hotels and boarding houses promising every kind of 'civil attention, liberal tables and all home comforts'. It could also boast a theatre, two cinemas, a brace of bandstands, a Victorian Pier and a modest range of child-oriented diversions. And if that wasn't enough, Bognor was also about to get a new Town Hall.

One day my parents ventured over to this paragon of seaside resorts in the Singer, my mother to refresh her childhood memories; my father – well, because he was the one who could drive. They made their way slowly through its main streets, obedient to its 10 m.p.h. speed limit, parked the car on the Esplanade and left their footmarks in the sand on their stroll to Nyewood Lane. And it was while they were sitting in the Marine Café's wicker chairs, toying with their chocolate sundaes, that my father confided in his wife that he was rather taken by the look of Bognor. So, that must explain why, that afternoon, he insisted upon stopping and peering into the windows of every estate agent they passed. The prospects looked good!

The following summer my parents rented the ground floor of Mr Hutchinson's Victorian villa, Forrabury – a few doors east of Arthur's Home and next door to Ozone in Aldwick Road. From the front parlour it enjoyed an uninterrupted view across a cornfield to the far-off tamarisk hedge, Gray's huts and the sea beyond. It is my earliest vignette of Bognor.

Now we had a new maid, Joan Boxall. Sitting on the beach at the end of Nyewood Lane – just below Mrs Cass' wheelbarrow stall on the Promenade – she used to read her Mills and Boones, do her nails in Oyster Pink and keep an eye on where I had buried my brother in the sand. Meanwhile, my parents were off examining further particulars of 'Land for Sale', parleying with estate agents and visiting innumerable building plots to which the term 'unsuitable' came merely to indicate that it was within their budget.

Whilst at Forrabury I quickly made two discoveries: one was the ashy shoe-destroying footpath which wended its way from opposite Richmond Avenue to Fish Lane; the other was the Ide family's little fishing settlement amongst Gray's bathing huts. Accompanied by Joan, I spent a large part of that holiday watching the fishermen wrest their living from the sea just as my mother and her cousins had a quarter of a century earlier. The footpath disappeared long ago under the houses in Silverston Avenue.

17 An early expedition discovered Gray's huts at Aldwick.

In the course of our walks and shopping expeditions, the jigsaw of Bognor's street plan began gradually to imprint itself upon my mind. Landmarks fell into place: the Pier, the Western Bandstand, the Arcade and the Pavilion to which my mother took me to see a clown on stilts. Unmissable, too, the Fire Station and its fine red fire engine, opposite the High Street Post Office. I discovered that, for a penny, a bus would take me from outside Webster and Webb's shop to a stop close to Forrabury.

With Joan, I explored the Esplanade and discovered Sait's sunken tea garden of sticky memory as well as Mr Cheer's tea rooms and Mr Cass' shop full of Bognor rock. Then there was the day, with Roger in his pram, we plodded the backwaters of Chapel Street and Manor Place before unaccountably ending up chatting to the horses at the Swansea Riding School behind the *Royal Norfolk Hotel*. Other expeditions revealed the whereabouts of Albert Seymour's Marble Works in Station Road, the Bognor Steam Laundry in Hawthorn Road and the Picturedrome in Canada Grove. I was able to reassure myself that if I could see the tower of St John's chapel in the Steyne I wasn't lost. So, at the end of that holiday, already I carried in my head a rudimentary map of Bognor. It was all good, pioneering stuff!

In 1928, though, the local geography differed greatly from today. Where Marine Park Gardens now lie there was a large car park. There was no King's Parade. Marine Drive lay unmacadamed and led to the West Car Park opened only the year before. Mr H.W. Seymour, the builder, had not yet commenced his Marine Park Estate development which was one day to give us Princess, Wessex, Selsey and Silverston Avenues. In Nyewood Lane, The

Crescent was still a notion in the head of its builder, Algy Booker. From Richmond Avenue to the Duck Pond there were mainly fields, and most of Aldwick Road remained unpavemented, unlit and much narrower than now. West of the Pier, Mr Jenkins continued to hire out bathing machines.

The purchase of the land for Marine Park Gardens was something of a *coup* for Bognor Council. When W.H.B. Fletcher put part of his great estate up for auction in May 1926, Mr Jubb, the Town Clerk, was instructed to purchase the parcel of land bounded by Aldwick Road, Nyewood Lane, Marine Drive and what is now Silverston Avenue. After carving out of it the area required for the proposed gardens, the remaining land was re-sold and eventually developed by H.W. Seymour, the builder, as the West Marine Park Estate. Marine Park Gardens were declared open by William Fletcher, lord of the manor of Aldwick, on 22 July 1935.

In the town, the Congregational chapel – although under sentence for demolition to make way for Timothy White's new emporium – still stood at the High Street end of London Road, its front garden softened with trees. Shrubs and more trees grew in the London Road gardens of Mr Palmer's Ivy Lodge and The Lawns before they fell to M&S and Burton's made-to-measure suits a few years later. In Station Road, the Southern Railway station remained unobscured by Station Parade – only recently demolished (1994) to reveal once more this fine Edwardian railway building. There was no Odeon cinema, the Southdown bus office remained in a little hutch next to the *Beach Hotel* on the Esplanade, and the Public Library was still in the Lyon Street School. At the Olympian Gardens on the corner of Lennox Street, Leonard Henry, the comedian, was appearing in *The Mountebanks*. And as for Mr Billy Butlin ... Mr Who?

Meawhile, frustration continued to dog my parent's search for the perfect building site at a knock-down price. For heaven's sake, where was that artistic old Marquess, sitting on a fine marine site, who would have regarded it a privilege to have swapped his sea-girt acres for a couple of my father's paintings and a cheque for £100? But 1928 proved a poor year for gullible old Marquesses. So, having stubbed their toes on the reality of land prices, my parents took a second look at a fraction of a meadow in the Hundred of Aldwick, scattered with buttercups and daisies, the home of bubbling skylarks and grazed by friendly riding-school horses. The quest was over.

Access to this self-effacing plot turned out to be via a chalky, unmade track off Aldwick Road, a few yards west of Yeoman's Acre and opposite a sculptural elm tree that might have come from Arthur Rackham's etching press. On a piece of wood was painted the road's name, 'Aldwick Gardens'. But where the Gardens' primitive surface could go no further, it turned west and unaccountably changed its name to 'South Avenue'. And that was us. Over a rustic stile and across a field of ripening corn, the seashore lay a ten-minute stroll from the family's new semi-marine estate at Plot No.2. Upon its clay my parents were invited to build a roof and sink their roots in this unfinished quarter of Aldwick.

Indeed, if the *Bognor Regis Town Guide* of 1930 was anything to go by, we had chosen a rather select area in which to settle: 'Many of the estates

18 A scene soon to become part of our lives: Aldwick village and the *Ship Inn* in 1929. Does the flag flying on Mr Parson's Aldwick Motors indicate that King George V was still at Craigweil House? The sloping roof by the small touring car belonged to Pippins, the village café.

(west of Bognor) are being laid out on well-thought-out lines and are of pleasing design. Amongst such estates are the West Marine Park and, a short distance away, Aldwick Gardens Estate, both being worth a visit.' According to Lindsay Fleming (*History of Pagham in Sussex*, vol. III, page clx, appendix G, Land holdings in Aldwick Manor, 1608, 1768 and 1786), Aldwick Gardens was built on the southern part of a copyhold of some forty acres disposed on either side 'of the road leading from South Bersted to Aldwick Green' (now Aldwick Road). Fleming goes on to point out that the boundaries of this part of the holding have remained unaltered since 1608 – and possibly earlier. In that year John Greenleafe is shown as proprietor. In 1849 the Pagham Tithe Award refers to the Trustees of George Gatehouse, a Chichester brewer, with one William Follett as occupant who 'farmed 25 acres with one man'. In the 1890s it was part of Slated Farm (the Slated Barn alludes) and had as its sometime tenant the Countess of Portarlington.

In about 1926 an unmetalled road was formed roughly on the line of the old footpath in Footpath Field (1849) and became known as Aldwick Gardens. When I was a child the footpath recommenced at Yeomans Acre and wended its way through the fields to Chalcraft Lane. Cambridge Drive in Westmeads appears to follow part of its track. In 1798 the southern end of this same footpath, which today connects Aldwick Gardens with Fish Lane, ran through part of Aldwick Farm, which at that date belonged to Sir

Richard Hotham. According to the Tithe Award, this field was known as 'Hog Brook' (after a large ditch?) and was in the ownership of John Ballett Fletcher, father of William Fletcher who eventually inherited it. Today it lies under Aldwick Felds.

(The cost of our plot in South Avenue was, I believe, three guineas 'per foot frontage', which was the manner in which many building plots were sold before they became like gold in more recent times. Since it was about forty feet wide, our plot would have cost my father all of £126!)

Back in their Isleworth studio, much midnight oil was burned as my parents applied their pencils to sketching out alternative ideas for the last word in bungalow design – only to see them stumble and fall, one after another, tripped up by that old ruffian … cost! But at last most of the *multum* had been squeezed into the available *parvo* – which was another way of saying that any notions of grandeur finally bowed to the barely adequate. Anyway, the plans passed muster with the Westhampnett RDC and permission to build was granted in November 1928.

Meanwhile, Mr C.D. Chuter, a builder of East Avenue, had undertaken to erect our modest residence for the sum of £500. With lofty contempt for those family faint-hearts who raised their eyebrows at such profligacy, my father gave orders for building to begin in the following spring. So, as February 1929 gave way to March, all was bustle on Plot No. 2 as Mr Chuter and his Wellington-booted cohorts first erected a hut-full of builderly smells and then, with string, poles, pegs, a wooden square – and my father's drawings – began the arcane rites of 'setting out' the walls of the new bungalow. And within a few days their shiny grafters were slicing into the damp earth, digging out the foundation trenches.

Soon a procession of horse-drawn carts began bringing in loads of 'beach' from the end of Barrack Lane,* and a lorry filled with stock bricks from Hawes' sulphurous clamps in Westloats Lane was unloaded and stacked by men wearing mittens cut from pink inner-tubes. And, from time to time, Hall & Co.'s muscle-operated Albion tipper delivered its avalanches of Thakeham sand. Next, it was the turn of Peppers of Amberley to begin bringing in the 1 cwt jute bags of Blue Circle cement (at 4s. 11d. each) from their depot in Station Yard, as well as lime for slaking.

With no water piped to the site, Mr Chuter's men had first to dig a six-foot well … and, lo, before their backs were turned it had filled with clean, cool water. So too, the next day, had the foundation trenches. But that was rain. For this sort of emergency the resourceful Mr Chuter had a hand-pump and soon they were dry enough for concreting to commence. A day or two later the steely ring of trowels could be heard across the meadow as the bricklayers bent to their task, and within a short time the new bungalow began to peer shyly above South Avenue's yellow clay.

My first visit to Aldwick was marked by a momentous discovery. For at the end of our plot I found a wide, slow-moving body of water the colour of Mother Earth and barely contained within its banks. Why had my father never revealed that our new bungalow was to be built on the banks of this

* This was the sideline of Mr Holbrook, the Duff Cooper's butler, who made a small fortune selling off his employer's beach at the end of Barrack Lane. See also Chapter 10.

uncharted rife? Immediately my thoughts sprang to hook and line – or, more precisely, bent pin and string – and the sudden tug of something about three feet long with sharp teeth! I couldn't wait to return.

Many weeks dragged by before the ball-and-chain of school was once more grudgingly unlocked. Eventually, my father and I arrived in Bognor where our only call was at Osborne's, the bakers in the High Street: Eccles cakes and doughnuts for our tea. Then it was on to South Avenue, where a dust cloud enveloped anything that dared move and showed how much more primitive our thoroughfare was than anything Selsey had had to offer. For by now I could claim to be something of an authority on unmade roads.

As soon as the car had rocked to a halt, clasping my fishing line I was off down to the end of the garden to inspect our pike-filled tributary. Expectantly I peered over the hedge ... but oh! Did my eyes deceive me? For our 'rife' had disappeared – gone! Instead I found myself looking at a paltry six inches of stagnant water in which floated a whisky bottle, thoughtfully presented by a member of the drinking classes, homeward-bound from *The Ship* inn in the village. Well, of course, the truth was that it hadn't rained for weeks!

Rubbing shoulders with real builders was a new experience for me. Here, I thought, were men of the world whom one might emulate with confidence and to advantage. For instance, I had observed that to hold a spade properly Mr Chuter found it necessary first to spit lustily on the palms of his hands; it seemed a very grown-up thing to do; a pointer to my parents that they had begotten a natural little spitter. But not a bit of it. For as soon as I practised my manly technique with a wooden spade in the course of making sandcastles, my mother swiftly held the habit to be depraved and disgusting and banned it on the spot!

Our carpenter was another of my mentors. It was he who pointed out that when one was not actually using one's short, well-chewed and nearly leadless pencil, it was properly stored behind the right ear – providing the space was not already taken up by a half-smoked Woodbine. But at school the pencil-behind-the-ear idea was greeted by my conservative, Ealing-born teacher with about as much rapture as the spitting-on-hands thing had been by my mother. Oh, luckless boy! Clearly, it was safer just to watch.

Mr Chuter's bricklayer, though, was less contentious. To see this master of the burnished trowel perform his craft made cheap of those sixty miles. Standing in his shadow, I patiently awaited that most dramatic operation in bricklaying – cropping a brick in two with powerful, ringing blows from the edge of a trowel. Then he 'buttered' (I assure the reader that is the correct term) both ends of the 'bat' (less than a full brick's length) with 'compo' (mortar) before deftly tapping into position with the handle. When I grew up, I thought, I wouldn't mind being a bricklayer.

The plasterer, with whom I shared a taste for Glacier Mints, was another of our star performers. With consummate dexterity, and drawing upon an arsenal of nails protruding from his mouth, he first fixed the wooden lathes to the ceiling joists. Then – when I had ceased questioning him about the why-and-how of his trade – he ferociously attacked the lathes with trowels full of sloshy plaster mixed with ox-hair, squeezing it into the slots where, in defiance of what little I knew about gravity, it stayed put. Anyway, it looked a smashing job. So, when the intellectual demands of bricklaying became insupportable, perhaps this young dreamer might try his hand at a spot of dilettante plastering.

But this does illustrate how, compared with the constructional techniques used in building houses today, the lower end of the industry in 1929 functioned at a nearly medieval level. The smaller builders employed no mechanical aids that I can recall: muscle, spit and sinew dug the trenches, mixed the concrete and sawed the timber. So it was the pulley-wheels and the pump with which Mr Chuter emptied our foundations of water. In those days it was all sweat and graft to raise even a bungalow from the soil.

By now the Grim Reaper has likely crossed off all of Mr Chuter's little labour force. But enough of their misty images remain to remind me what a different breed they were compared with their hard-hatted successors of the transistor-touting days of the building boom which followed the Second World War. Most of them spoke with the local Sussex 'burr' and addressed my father as 'sir'. I was 'the young man', occasionally 'the young master'. They wore flat caps over hair cut 'short back and sides'; shirts were of flannel, collarless, with the bone stud left showing or sometimes covered up with a coloured neckchief; braces, rather than belts, kept their trousers up. Footwear was either Dunlop wellingtons patched with pink inner tubes or ex-Army 'ammo' boots with Blakey toe protectors. Lager bellies were conspicuous only by their absence.

19 Aldwick's duckpond.

A lot of men in those days had served in France in the late war, which accounted for the British Legion badges many wore in their jacket lapels. On Empire Day they arrived with medal ribbons: 'Ypres and Mons', whispered my father, late of 'The Gunners'.

The war was also reflected in the Army Surplus greatcoats worn by many workers; the khaki haversacks, too, in which they brought their cheese-and-pickle 'doorsteps' and wedges of wife-made fruit cake stashed in Huntley and Palmer biscuit tins. Over a wood-fire that stung the eyes, they brewed up the definitive 'builder's char', the sort in which – apocryphally – a teaspoon will stand upright! Copious pourings of Ideal Milk, ladles of sugar and the smell of wood smoke were the secrets, but it only tasted right when stirred with a carpenter's pencil and drunk from a chipped enamel mug.

Nearly all the men came to work on bicycles fitted with carbide lamps – the kind into which you peed to make them burn more brightly. But one of the 'brickies' had an old BSA motorcycle which he rode wearing his goggles over a flatcap turned back-to-front. When it rained Mr Chuter's men tied pieces of cord round their calves to keep their trousers out of the mud, draped a jute cement sack over their shoulders and continued working with water dripping off the ends of their noses. It was how they earned their £3 9s. 2d. for a 52-hour week.

Smoking on building sites was endemic: Will's Woodbines, Player's Weights or BDV; tuppence-ha'penny for five; more 'fags' than cigarettes. A few men made their own with Rizla papers and a rubber roller. And all held the lighted end shielded by the palm of the hand – a sign of the good infantryman, trained not to let the enemy see that tell-tale glow. But it was a briar pipe that brought solace to the hod-carrier. Charged with 'plug' 'baccy, it produced an aroma sweet enough for me to ask him for a sniff as he rubbed it in the rough palms of his hands.

Although denied my 25lb pike on this occasion, another event proved nearly as exciting. For, just as we were about to leave for home, there came a distant roar that grew louder and louder as into view, flying low over our new bungalow, swept three silver-coloured biplanes with RAF markings on their wings: Armstrong-Whitworth Siskin fighters from Tangmere. At school it was a story which improved with each telling!

Throughout that spring each visit to the site revealed more of our bungalow's secrets; the position of the front door became clear; the kitchen showed off its lead pipes, and the different rooms dropped hints of shape and purpose. I found the bedroom I was to share with my brother and pro-visionally bagged the best position for my bed. 'Now be careful you don't fall off,' warned my father as his son, intent on helping the carpenter shape the eaves, teetered round the unguarded larch-pole scaffolding.

At this time King George V was convalescing at Craigweil House. 'Where is Craigweil House?' I asked my father. He pointed in its direction. 'Can we go and see the King?' I inquired. 'No, the place is swarming with police and we aren't allowed to park. And in any case we haven't time to walk along the beach.' So I had to be content with a handed-down account from our plumber's wife, who had seen the royal ambulance pass Aldwick

20 The sands below Goodman Drive (now Marine Drive West). Note the bathing huts on stilts which had their admirers and detractors in equal numbers.

crossroads. But how my father had the pleasure of meeting the Queen of England under rather curious circumstances I will reveal later.

At last came the 'topping-out', an age-old custom marking the completion of the highest point of a building. My father bought a small Union Jack from Cummings in West Bognor and tied it to the chimney. Now it was time for Penfolds of Barnham to deliver the roof tiles in their fiery Sentinel steam-lorry. Soon the bungalow was watertight. Inside, work began to gather speed.

Meanwhile, at Isleworth, excitement mounted as the date of our move to Aldwick drew closer. Already my father had begun taking down small pieces of furniture in his new car, a maroon-coloured Floating Power Citroen tourer with celluloid side-screens, an electric horn, a self-starter and Dunlop balloon tyres. Our arrival in South Avenue promised to be in style.

And so it came about that, one Saturday afternoon in the middle of July 1929, the Citroen, laden with blankets, eiderdowns, oil-stoves, cutlery, crates of books and two excited young boys, came to a halt outside the new bungalow. The key found beneath the cement bag on the step, my father opened the back door. And thus, forgetful of any ceremony, the family crossed the threshold of its semi-completed bungalow for the first time. Over the carpetless floors, our London shoes clicketty-clacked alienly as we looked into rooms which held us strangers. Dust lay on every ledge, arris, shelf and moulding. Paint tins huddled in corners; wood shavings littered the floor and the air was heavy with the smell of distemper and creosote. Upon window-boards stood empty milk bottles and tins of nails garnished with cigarette ends and daddy-long-legs, crisply mummified. Awaiting electricity, bulbless flexes dangled from unpainted ceilings. Firmly, I informed my brother of the position of my bed. 'No, no – that's the place I wanted, it's not fair,' he wailed. Then my father barked, and with that we were put to work unloading the car, still smelling of Abdullas and Nuttall's Mintoes. 'And to think, dears, it's all our very own,' murmured my mother as she gazed through the putty-smeared windows at a garden sown with brick-bats and shards of broken tiles.

Soon, hot-water bottles were placed in all the beds, mattresses were leaned against clothes-horses in front of an unseasonal fire, and blankets were draped over the backs of chairs. For our bungalow proved a martyr to condensation. With neither gas nor electricity supplies connected, Aladdin lamps and candles were our only means of illumination. As the last hours of day yielded to our first night at Aldwick, the Valor oil-stoves stencilled their stellar designs on unfamiliar ceilings and the oil-lamps cast the grotesque shadows of flapping beasties on the freshly plastered walls. The day's excitement spent, at last it was time for bed. As we confided our prayers to darkened pillows, my brother and I became aware of a sound strange to our suburban ears: a far-off hiss that rose and fell, rose and fell. It took a little time to puzzle out what it was. At last it dawned on us. It was the sea playing with Aldwick's shingly beach! And thereafter it became a sound ever evocative of our seaside bungalow.

Beyond the leaded window panes not a lamp glimmered; just the purple night and the unfolding stars. The only sounds were the far-off roar of the shingle and Mr Crockett's cows tearing at the dew-laden grass.

With a 'New World' gasless and a 'Belling' voltless, my mother was reduced to preparing our stewy meals on a neurotic primus stove and finishing them off in her hay-box – that fuel-saving dodge of Great War necessity. But if we were too hungry to wait, then lunch became bowls of oxtail soup made from Foster and Clarke's crumbly cubes, followed by Harnett's beef sausages cooked on the end of a telescopic toasting fork stuck over the living-room fire. In the kitchen we ate our for-what-we-are-about-to-receive meals off a table-top covered with yesterday's *Morning Post*. 'Elbows off, dears, and sit up straight,' adjured my mother, unforgetful of Wonnie's precepts.

Each passing day marked some small improvement in our circum-stances; the dust was vanquished by broom, brush and besom and the decoration completed. Soon, superannuated blankets became surrogate cur-tains secured to the window frames with drawing-pins. Next, geriatric carpets, discarded by the more discerning branches of the family, were laid in the principal rooms, their bald patches and stains cunningly camouflaged by such furniture as we could muster. In the bathroom and kitchen we found ourselves treading on new linoleum of a design less beguiling than its price tag. Eventually, a wooden plate-rack appeared above the fire-clay sink.

Then, one afternoon, the Southern Railway's horse-drawn delivery van brought to our door a 'repro' sideboard not quite to the taste of a Hampstead aunt. A few days later it was joined by the battle-worn sofa and armchairs relegated to Bognor from the Isleworth house. A plate-glass mirror, with a clothes-brush above it, was fixed by the front door and my father's red-chalk drawings hung on the living room walls. And, throughout the summer, always fresh-cut flowers in long-necked vases.

21 A view of the High Street east of the Arcade. Behind the 'tourer' lies the Fire Station. Nearer the camera the white-painted building on the left is the *Sussex Hotel* (now the *William Hardwicke*).

With no fence to mark our plot, the riding-school horses quickly learned to thrust expectant heads through the open kitchen window in claim of their daily tithe of apples and crusts, while the rooks and rabbits remained unconvinced that our garden wan't still their field. Then, during a weekend, authentic in its Gothic, the name 'Idlewylde' appeared beside the front door to advise strangers, hawkers, circulars and the postman that this was how, henceforth, the new bungalow at 3 South Avenue was to be addressed. In the meadow beyond our domain, Mr Crockett's cows scratched themselves thoughtfully against the fence-posts and decided that such a disgraceful carry-on was best ignored.

My grandmother, hitherto an occasional spectator of the Aldwick scene, now, on the pretext of 'doing one or two little jobs', began staying at the bungalow on her own. At first for days, then for weeks, and eventually for months at a time. She enjoyed pottering over to the village and loved the beach. She joined the Public Library and spoke glowingly of the weather and Bognor's shops. Eventually she expressed a wish to settle at Idlewylde permanently, a sea-change that proved to be an admirable arrangement for the rest of the family. Now, at weekends, we had waiting for us a well run home, a stocked-up larder, her Abergelly puddings on demand and hot-water bottles in the beds during freeze-ups.

In due course, monthly accounts were opened with the local shops. Each morning our bread was delivered by Osborne's from their High Street bakery. Milk came from Crockett's Dairy at Aldwick Farm – with the treat of a carton of cream on Saturdays. From West Bognor, Targett's the butchers supplied our meat – with the occasional profligate chicken for visitors; for fish we looked either to Joe Ragless at No.2 The Parade or else to the Ide family's little open-air fishery amongst the tamarisk huts.

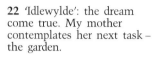

22 'Idlewylde': the dream come true. My mother contemplates her next task – the garden.

Over in the village, our day-to-day grocery needs were under the personal supervision of Mr and Mrs George Gates at their Aldwick Stores, where Mrs G. displayed an uncanny gift for remembering all those things my grandmother had absent-mindedly omitted from her list. Most of the shops brought our orders to the back door – unlocked 24 hours a day – and if there were no one at home, the delivery boy let himself in and placed the goods on the kitchen table. In those days we trusted everyone. Meanwhile, Mrs Duffin at the Slated Barn Stores in Aldwick Road continued to be our source for Standard paraffin at 6d. a gallon, as well as meeting the two young Alford boys' insatiable appetites for Lyon's Buzz chocolate bars and Button's coconut squares – not to mention cashing their postal orders on birthdays and other celebratory occasions.

Adjoining Mrs Duffin's stores were two other shops which were destined to play cardinal roles in our new life at Aldwick. In the first, the smell of heelball and leather announced the business of Mr Burchfell, the cobbler, whom we kept busy for the next ten years, soling and heeling and generally breathing a bit more life into those of our shoes we hadn't grown out of. From next door to the cobbler, Mr Bartholomew, the electrician, provided us with our weekly three-penn'orth of charged-up acid battery for the Detex portable. Finally, if we required postage stamps or to send a telegram, Mrs Charlie Tooze was at our service behind the counter of the Post Office, over in Aldwick village just west of the *Ship* inn. All that remained now was for the GPO to turn up one afternoon and install that wonder of modern communication, a black 'daffodil' telephone. And thus Idlewylde joined the 20th century.

Hitherto children of the western suburbs of the Great Wen, my brother and I prepared for the exciting prospect of exploring our new home on the edge of the Sussex countryside at Aldwick and our territory, deemed to stretch from the Paradise Rocks on Aldwick beach to our outback of uncouth roads, stubbly cornfields and cow-pat footpaths. This did not take into account our licence to pry into the private lives of the buzzers, stingers, belly-crawlers, bubblers, peckers, munchers and all those other living things that awaited our inquiring eyes in the yet-untapped world of ditches, meads, wastes and tulgy slyps that lay between our bungalow and those far-off Sussex Downs.

As our mother never ceased to remind us, we were very lucky boys.

4

Home Sweet Home

With the passing months, the settlers from west London gradually came to consider themselves citizens of this obscure quarter of Aldwick. By courtesy of Reynolds' Auction Rooms in Canada Grove, the vacant spaces between the combings from the Isleworth house gradually began to fill with a variety of pieces of pre-loved furniture suggesting little rivalry in their procurement. That was where our bedroom table came from; also a tallboy with drawers nearly unopenable, once opened as resolutely uncloseable.

Another visit to Canada Grove resulted in the acquisition of a Vono mattress and a metal bed with four detachable legs that drew blood every time it was erected. And there was that nervous nod in the direction of the auctioneer's desk that resulted in my mother's triumphant homecoming, the richer by three stone hot-water bottles and an Acme wringer. Come to think of it, the HMV wind-up gramophone and its box of Harry Roy records also bore that unmistakable Reynolds' stamp. How, a few years later, my 12-year-old brother became the proud owner of a cracked glass case containing half-a-dozen crumbling passerines for a shilling need not detain the reader. Getting it home had been the saga.

Next, it was the turn of the dangling electric light bulbs to be made chaste with lamp-shades. A few came from Lewis's in London Road but most were conjured out of the silk of First World War parachutes, dyed various colours and run up on my grandmother's Willcox and Gibbs' sewing machine. One by one, the surrogate curtains surrendered to oddment lengths of Sanderson's fabrics and the net ones were hung on stretched wires designed to sag. The carpet stains we got used to.

In those days South Avenue was as notorious for its absence of tempering trees as it was for the intemperate abundance of its puddles. Mercilessly, the midsummer sun beat down on the living room and its perspiring occupants. So my father had a striped roller-blind installed above the loggia and, behold! the room was transformed into a cool oasis. In winter our enemy was the tenacious clay, only partly repelled by a boot-scraper placed outside the back door. The fieldmice were a problem, too.

Woolworth's proved a life-line for my parent's overstretched pockets. Our six table settings of bright red cups, saucers, plates and a cheese dish were theirs – and if we had them still, they would no doubt rate a short paragraph in Sotheby's catalogue. 'Nothing over Sixpence' was also the source of a heterogeneous selection of cutlery which was to prove an acute embarrassment to the Doré-monogrammed silver for the next fifty years.

To Pipers in the High Street could be traced the provenance of my mother's tea service – yellow daffodils its theme. Yet, set upon the damasked garden table (after it had been de-woggled with a piece of cardboard), it presented a certain innocent charm, awaiting only the lace doilies, bone-handled cutlery and the silver-plated kettle on its methylated spirit burner. Next to the table stood that other Reynolds orphan, the three-tiered cake-stand bearing its plates of Shippam's bloater-paste sandwiches, 'dainties' and a Victoria sponge. All that was missing was the Hampstead aunt and the hint of *Eau de Cologne*.

In fact, the only jarring note known to have marred these tranquil occasions was the unwelcome appearance of my mother's two ditch-stained sons, socks at half-mast, hair awry and holding a dead water-rat by the tail.

Resembling the aftermath of a Vicarage jumble sale, the remainder of our culinary infrastructure resided in the kitchen china cupboard. On its shelves, in permanent asylum, were to be found a teapot brain-washed into believing itself to be a thatched cottage, a biscuit jar masquerading as a beer-barrel and a honey pot with a bas-relief bee crawling over its lid and placing it firmly in that category of artefacts clearly won rather than purchased. It was an orphanage for cup-less saucers and saucer-less cups; a sanatorium for cracked Victorian water jugs and a rest home for retired blancmange and jelly moulds of many ingenious designs. It was a retreat for numerous small pieces of earthenware and china bearing such messages as 'East or West, Old Friends are Best' and 'Never say Die, Up Man and Try', their stirring eloquence making up for their lack of any obvious purpose.

On the bottom shelf – besides the egg-slicer engineered to reduce to a yellow-and-white crumble any egg that crossed its path – lay a spectacular array of Victorian cruets, although finding a vessel which retained both its stopper at the bottom and allowed the flow of its contents out of the top

23 Aldwick village, looking westwards towards the *Ship*. In 1930 the white house on the right was called Almora. The gates to Aldwick Place are behind the camera.

was the cause of much unsuccessful experiment. It was a museum of unused rolling pins, multifarious strainers and carving sets capable of dealing with buffaloes, as well as being the last known address of a cardboard box containing the enigmatic remains of a glass chandelier. On the top shelf, though, lay our one treasure. Frank Brangwyn had recently given my parents a fine Royal Doulton 'Harvest' tea service, designed by himself. It is in the family, still.

Many of my grandmother's cooking pots were of 19th-century cast-iron, manufactured to the same sturdy specification as the Forth Bridge. Two hands were needed to lift them empty; on the stove the handles became quickly incandescent. In her capacious cast-iron bread bin the smaller kind of missionary might have been simmered to a turn. But the 20th century had its niche: a green Bakelite lemon squeezer.

In 1929 the kitchen's furnishments were sparse: a glazed china-clay sink with a teak draining board, a 'New World' gas stove, a wooden plate-rack and my grandmother's well-thumbed copy of *Mrs Beeton*. The meat we stored in a perforated-zinc box, while the milk spent the summer standing in a bowl of water under a terracotta cooler.

In the centre of the room stood an American-cloth-covered table on which, a year or two earlier, I had been parted from my adenoids in the breakfast room at Isleworth. Still wearing his spats, the peripatetic surgeon had scrubbed his hands in a washing-up bowl of Lysol in the kitchen sink before choosing his knife. In those days it was chloroform.

From May onwards the hordes of flies drove us mad. But sticky fly-papers and spraying with Flit only turned them into 'heroes of the state', to be avenged by the bottomless reinforcements stationed all over Sussex. It was Mr Crockett's cows, vowed my grandmother, as she struck out valiantly with her Timothy White's flyswat.

For a long time the back boiler in the living room had been the cause of much muttering among the womenfolk; filling the bath – at least, with hot water – was clearly beyond it. So my father installed a Pollard Geyser ('A Penny a Bath') in the bathroom. But no one had reckoned on its terrifying virility. Only after the window had been flung open and the family shepherded to safety on the other side of the door, dared anyone show it a lighted match. There followed a thunderous explosion and the roar of the flames could be heard at the bottom of the garden. But at least we had some lovely hot baths on which to float our celluloid ducks and Hornby speedboats.

Readers to whom 1929 must sound almost pre-Devonian may wonder how my mother survived such primitive conditions. But somehow she did, along with millions of other housewives in similarly sparsely equipped and detergentless kitchens – *sans* 'fridge, deep freezer, washing machine or liquidiser. Yet, from it flowed a steady stream of garlic- and yoghurt-free family meals, quite unaffected by the lack of panelled-oak wall-fittings and mother-of-pearl working tops. But, then, of course, she enjoyed the unfair advantage of her ubiquitous hay-box!

Since there is no record of the *Ideal Home*'s photographer ever having risked professional ostracism by being seen in South Avenue, let me describe briefly the living room at Idlewylde. Like most of the bungalows in our road, it had two long and two short sides – although the rear 'short' side was really the french windows leading onto the loggia. The vari-stained carpets, cream-distempered walls and the brass hearth-tidy from Woolworth's – 6d. each part, stand, shovel, poker and brush – can be taken as read. So, too, the two threadbare armchairs and a huge crettoned sofa which, rather than lack springs, had them piled up where no one ever sat. 'Bouncing,' groaned my mother accusingly.

If the living room could have boasted anything which might have been termed 'a feature', it was over the fireplace: a large oak-framed mirror which had seen better times in the Portland Place home of the author, Ian Hay, before my father's plans for refurbishment made it redundant in WC1. Generously, he had given it to my father for 'his little place at Bognor'. On the other hand, my father's red-chalk drawings and his painting of my mother were worth a second look; so too the signed etching of Rudyard Kipling, one of my mother's literary heroes. Mine too, come to that.

Otherwise, the rest of the living room consisted of a general amalgam of the Hampstead Aunt's sideboard, a rupturing oak gate-leg table, six wheelback chairs and an electric radiator. Oh yes, and a wobbly butler's tray just then occupied by my mother's needlework box and my herd of leaden Friesian cows. All the remaining interstices were taken up with bookcases. So, together with the usual scattering of half-completed jigsaw puzzles, comics, silvery gliders, my mother's drawing-boards and assorted copies of *Vogue*, that was our living room in 1929. But homely and better than a beach-hut.

The mention of bookcases brings me to books. And in those we could hold up our head, for Arthur Davey, my maternal grandfather, had been appointed Headmaster of St John's Boys School, Waterloo, when he was only twenty-seven. Books were his life and he died at the tragically premature age of forty-seven. (He was born too early; antibiotics would have made short work of his pneumonia – and it was only small compensation that Lilian Bayliss of the Old Vic was influential in having a stained-glass window erected to his memory in St John's Church, Waterloo). He left behind a sizeable heavy-duty Victorian library. Over the years, my mother – herself well-versed in English literature – added to it with wisdom and lighter touch.

Thus, from an early age, I was inspected daily by the intimidating spines of Plutarch's *Lives*, Milton's *Areopagitica* and *Seven Discourses on Art* by Sir Joshua Reynolds and, for good measure, by Carlyle's *Essays on Goethe*, too. One glance at their contents, though, soon revealed that they were not of the funny-ha-ha genre. So, for the time being, I stuck with things like *The Rainbow* and A.A. Milne's *Pooh* books, mandatory on middle-class bookshelves in the 'thirties. 'Mother, if I go to bed early will you read me about the Heffalump?' was a cherished prospect. *Black Beauty* and Kingsley's *Water Babies* also helped me make sense of strung-together words.

Then, one day, hunting for something that might serve as a railway station platform for my Hornby trains, my eyes fell upon a set of maroon-coloured volumes in one of the bookcases. They turned out to be the original Macmillan series of Rudyard Kipling's works published in the early 1900s. In time I suppose I must have tired of the railway, but prevailed upon my grandmother to read me something from the books. She chose the shallow end: 'The Sing-Song of Old Man Kangaroo' (or how the kangaroo got his legs) from the *Just So Stories*. You know the thing: '… Still ran Dingo ~ Yellow Dog Dingo ~ always hungry, grinning like a rat-trap, never getting nearer, never getting farther,–ran after Kangaroo. He had to!' … etc., etc.

I laughed uproariously … this chap wasn't bad at all. 'Oh, please read me some more, Nana, please,' I implored. Yes, but only if I tried to read some of it myself. Thus I put my first sandal on the road to serious reading, concentration measured by the length of my protruding tongue. From my favourite reading position – on my knees in front of the living room fire – I haltingly worked my way through those rich tapestries of words, only seeking a little grown-up help with some of the more difficult ones like 'Nqa', 'Djinn' and 'Phoenicians'.

Nana and my mother – when she could tear herself away from her drawing-board – kept their part of the bargain by sharing with me *The Jungle Book*, *Kim* and *Puck of Pook's Hill*. It was a great leap forward from the *Rupert* books, *Bubbles Annual* and *Pip, Squeak and Wilfred*. Before long, I could read quite well, with literary tastes as liberal as they were indiscriminate: everything from Lewis Carroll's *Alice* books to *The Autocar*; from Defoe's *A Journal of the Plague Year* to *Exchange and Mart*; from H.G. Wells' *An Outline of History* to the weekly *Passing Show*, via the *Bognor Post* and the backs of Players cigarette cards.

Then came that well-remembered birthday when my mother – in a moment of enlightened self-interest – presented me with Lansborough Thompson's *Britain's Birds*, four solid inches of ornithological wisdom. Immediately I became glued to its contents, although I somehow got the impression that the red-throated diver stood about five feet high at the shoulder due to a certain lack of scale in the illustration. But my life-long fascination with birds commenced the moment I opened that book.

Inevitably the time came for a bit of Dickens; first *A Child's History of England* in the Hall and Chapman series, murderously small print excused only by the Cruikshank illustrations. Over cups of cocoa, my mother and I read its pages, turn-and-turn-about, during the long evenings of a bitterly cold Christmas holiday at Aldwick. For many years it was the main source of what little history I absorbed. Next came *David Copperfield* and a few chapters of *Nicholas Nickleby* before the longer days and the arrival of my new bike brought a temporary halt to my literary studies. Twelve years later I finished off the latter on board His Majesty's Troopship *Athlone Castle* while we waited to dock at Freetown.

Then, from 1935 onwards, our shelves enjoyed a general cheering up with the introduction of the orange-and-white covers of Allen Lane's 6d. Penguin paperbacks starting, I seem to remember, with André Maurois' *Ariel*. Soon we were able to place Dorothy L. Sayers' *The Unpleasantness at the Bellona Club* and *Murder on the Links* by Agatha Christie on either side of Plato's *Phaedo and Crito* – and hoped he might see the funny side of it! But I think my mother might have drawn a line at *No Orchids for Miss Blandish*. Anyway, by then I was a safe distance away in a Transit Camp at Naples. At all events, in books we weren't too badly placed.

Even as the ink dried on the building plot contract, my parents had set their hearts on our new home being flattered by well manicured lawns and graced with the sort of floral and frondescent excesses they had seen illustrated so seductively in *Amateur Gardening* and *Ideal Home*. At Aldwick a restless variety of garden layouts sketched on odd pieces of paper littered the living room. At last, the design was settled. Now it was gardener's dream-time! But first, a five-foot close-boarded fence had to be put up to enclose the garden – much to the chagrin of the riding-school horses who saw the end of their daily apples. But it was they who had the last laugh. For no sooner had the fence been put up than it was blown down by a fierce sou'wester and had to be buttressed with long steel rods before it felt able to face another gale on equal terms.

The new garden's centrepiece was to be a semi-circular ornamental pond girdled by low brick walls culminating in a graceful central brick arch with a lion's head at its crown out of which water would pour. The rest of the garden was to consist of a circular lawn bounded by a brick path with the quadrant corner beds in Horsham stone. But the fountain's brickwork had 'high cost' stamped all over it; the builder's estimates didn't bear looking at. How could the thing be constructed more cheaply? Painfully the solution became abundantly clear ... so my father went off and bought himself a book on 'Practical Bricklaying' and studied it diligently. Then he bought a trowel, a spirit-level and a few assorted tools. Next, he took me with him to visit Mr Harry Humphry, a dealer in *objets d'art* who lived at Bah-singh-to in Gossamer Lane, and came away with a lion's head cast in lead.

A few days later, a load of Dorking handmade facing bricks was delivered to Idlewylde, followed by a lorry load of York stone cappings. In due course, some sand and a few bags of cement appeared. Then my father rolled up his sleeves and gingerly laid the first brick. Straightforward enough the square piers; much less so, though, the curved walls between them. And positively treacherous the three courses of brick dentilling below the bird-bath. Weekend by weekend both my father's confidence and the fountain grew as he worked towards that ultimate challenge: the arch!

Now each radiating brick had to be carefully chosen, positioned, adjusted and inspected from a distance for geometric truth – the hallmark of the trade-tested 'bricky'. Slowly the graceful arch came to life until, with the laying of the keystone brick, it was complete. Finally, the stone cappings were tapped into position, the lion's head secured and a little rudimentary plumbing installed. Excitement mounted. Would it all work? My father turned on the tap and, faithful to the laws of physics, water began to gush. From the lion's mouth it poured into the bird-bath, and from there cascaded down to the pool below which, inch by inch, began to fill. So three hearty cheers for the architect-turned-bricklayer. Mr Churchill (another slightly better known 'bricky') would have been proud to shake him by the hand! All that was needed now were half-a-dozen goldfish from Woolworth's and a packet of ants' eggs.

24 The fountain finished.

With the brick path finished to the same exacting standard as the fountain, it was time for Butser's of Horndean to bring in a load of turves. Carefully they were laid and levelled and watered. What now? Well, speaking with the benefit of hindsight, 'what now?' amounted to 55 more years of lawn culture; dressing, fertilizing, sanding, weeding, de-mossing, de-moleing, rolling and mowing – as well as wondering what on earth to do with all the clippings! But that lay in the unfathomable future.

Now it was time for my parents to visit Barnham Nurseries with a long shopping list of trees and shrubs. Fragrance or foliage? Would it grow in our glutinous clay? How tall might it be in ten years' time? Other plants were brought down from our garden in London; green-fingered friends contributed roots and corms done up in brown paper and string. There was japonica for its jam, buddleia for the Painted Ladies and honeysuckle for its evening smell. And two beds full of lavender. Next, pink hydrangeas were planted on either side of the front door and a Dorothy Perkins rose bidden to buck up its ideas and beautify the wasteland* fence. Even my grandmother took to wandering around looking for something to lop off with her new secateurs.

Amongst this frondescence, I was allowed a little patch to call my own. In it I planted carrot, beetroot, parsnip and lettuce from seed packets promising results large, colourful and nutritious. What came up, though – after, it seemed, a lifetime – was only that on which the slugs, greenfly, whitefly, mildew and leafspot had made merry; that on which the eel-worm, thrips and mealy-bug had become fat. All I was left with was puny, deformed, perforated and inedible. My mother commiserated. Perhaps digging them up to see how the roots were getting on had, on reflection, been unwise!

Gradually, domestic life during holidays at Idlewylde settled into as predictable a pattern as two young boys, with their capacity for creating chaos out of order, would permit. Monday was wash day with its standing

---

* The 'wasteland' was a building plot on the east side of our bungalow which, on account of its triangular shape, was regarded as unsaleable. For years it was our football ground, cricket pitch and the nerve centre of our defence system against the marauding Billy Gill and his gang from West Avenue. In 1953 my father bought it to extend our garden. Today it lies under a new bungalow.

25 Until 1997 the *Victoria Hotel* was a well-known West Bognor landmark. Like so many of the town's privately owned hotels, it has been replaced by flats.

orders, viz. a) no washing football boots in the sink, b) no frightening the life out of Joan with the white mice, and c) no chemistry set experiments until after she had gone. An oval tin bath was lifted onto the gas stove; there – bubbles rising – it spent half the morning heating up.

Joan's laundering technology pandered to no advance beyond a three-legged dolly for pummeling sheets and a corrugated zinc washboard for rubbing smalls and ditchy shirts. For the rest of the day it was a steamy montage of red hands, streaming windows, slippery floors, Sunlight soap (which stung the eyes something wicked), Reckitt's Blue and the enamel bowl of Robin starch. All this required the pinafored Joan to be kept well-tuned with a steady supply of cups of tea and digestive biscuits brought to her by my grandmother. If I was good, I was allowed to turn the handle of the Acme wringer and to let down the ceiling rack to take the socks.

Out in the garden, pegged to the washing line supported by a larch pole, sheets, pyjamas, shirts and female unmentionables danced in the breeze while we ate our lunch of cold mutton, pickles and bubble-and-squeak with bread-and-butter pudding to follow. The rest of the afternoon was taken up with ironing in which Nana joined; flat irons placed on the gas stove and held with a bit of cloth still recognisable as my pramhood hat. For the small price of saying 'please', I was allowed a sizzling spit upon their scorching undersides.

Although most of Aldwick's medieval past had long lain under the lostness of time, one of its legacies hung on into the 'thirties in the local mode of drainage: the insalubrious cesspit! They were emptied twice a year by the Chichester RDC's gulper at 5s. a go. At Idlewylde, its six-monthly visit was declared a red letter day. A large pipe was run out from the tanker to our subterranean thunderbox at the bottom of the garden, an operation accompanied by a rich and unmistakable effluvia. Germs, as usual, weighed heavily on my mother's mind … 'don't touch the pipe, dear … all right, you couldn't help it, but now go and wash your hands'. Then the tanker made a sucking noise … smacked its lips and looked for more. Meanwhile, my mother was searching frantically for her purse and two sixpences for tips. But citizens stronger on initiative than conscience could have saved themselves the 5s. by cutting a hole in the bottom of the pit. And explained the prodigious size of some of our neighbour's tomatoes and marrows!

With the spring came another landmark of the domestic year. The annual visit of Mr Rawlins, the chimney sweep. Prior to the arrival of his pony and trap, drugget and dust sheets were laid over the carpet and furniture. Prayerfully, he would fall to his knees in front of the fireplace. A canvas screen was fixed across the opening; next, the spiky brush was screwed to bamboo poles. Then Mr Rawlins started pushing and shoving. This was the signal for Roger and me to rush out into the garden to watch; my extrovert brother danced a jig of ecstatic expectation ... any second now ... 'Look, look – there it is'! Momentarily the spiky brush wavered in the air above the chimney pot, disappeared, re-appeared ... then disappeared for good. Little bits of soot tumbled down the roof tiles. It was all over for another year.

Inside, Mr Rawlins shovelled the result of his labours into a black, sooty bag; and jolly small beer it was compared with what used to come out of the tall chimneys at Isleworth. 'Mother, can we have an apple for the chimney-sweep's horse?' But where would Mr Rawlins have been without some coal? So, each September, the grimy-faced coalman and his horse and cart used to deliver 15 cwt of Bottrill's Bright Burning Coal – at 1s. 6d. a sack – which he thundered into the timber fuel bin from whence it bequeathed its smell to the sideway for the next 12 months. 'Mother, you know those old crusts? Could we have them for the coalman's horse?'

On most days when we were at Idlewylde, Roger and I used to find some excuse to call upon Mrs Duffin at her Slated Barn Stores in Aldwick Road; perhaps a small culinary need of my mother's. More often, though, it was sweets. The loose door handle and the tinkling brass bell bade us enter; the W.D. & H.O. Wills' mat reminded us to wipe our feet. Inside the low-ceilinged shop the prevailing smells were of rising damp, lamb stew and paraffin. Pinned to the match-boarded walls were a Red Rover timetable, jumble sale notices and advertisements for Black Cat cigarettes, John Bull tyres and Pratts High Test petrol. Above the counter the light from a single electric bulb served only to accentuate the surrounding gloom. On the shelves lay a few dusty groceries, a basket of new-laid eggs and bottles of sweets. The best things, like chocolate and nougat bars, she kept under a glass lid which served as the counter. Over the shop window the Valor oil-stove drew a curtain of condensation.

Commercial pressure not being a feature at the Slated Barn Stores, our deliberations were unhurried as we pondered difficult choices ... those? ... or the ones next to them? ... or why not some of each? The contract was sealed. From under her shawl, arthritic fingers winced her eyes as she removed the bottle tops. Next, the aniseed balls and acid drops plinked into the brass pan; the little 2 oz. weight rose up to meet them. Then the sweets were fumbled into a paper bag and the coin exchanged. 'Wasn't it windy? ... was our gran's cold any better? ... and close the door, there's a good boy.'

Thumbing through some old copies of the *Portsmouth Evening News* a short time ago, I came across these lines which took me back to an event of 1929 only a shade less noteworthy than our moving down to Bognor.

THE SCHNEIDER TROPHY
If these pronounce it 'Schneider'
and those will have it 'Schneeder'
A BBC decider
must satisfy the reader ... etc.

J. Widgery
(*Portsmouth Evening News*, September 1929)

26 The Schneider Trophy, 1929. F/O H.R.D. Waghorn prepares to take off in the winning Supermarine S6.

That year, grubby pencil drawings of seaplanes with go-faster lines in their wake whizzed across the backs of my school exercise books. It was the Schneider Trophy. Suddenly all roads led to Gosport and Southsea as two million people were expected to make their way to the Solent to watch the World's Greatest Air Race. The nation's honour was at stake.

So, on 7 September 1929, we piled into the Citroen on our way to Southsea to watch the great spectacle. Our route took us past the forts on Portsdown Hill above Portsmouth Harbour. 'Palmerston's Folly'* shouted my father above the noise of wind and engine. 'Folly'? It sounded treasonable! How could a fort full of guns which belonged to us – the English – be anything but an Indisputably Good Thing? The term 'Folly' puzzled me; it sounded, well, not quite 'Rule Britannia'!

At last we arrived at a Southsea *en fête* for the occasion. Flags and bunting fluttered over a total congealment of motor cars and a *mêlée* of newsvendors, purveyors of hot pies and programme sellers shouting their wares for the benefit of the tide of spectators making their way to the various vantage points.

Having staked ourselves a place on the crowded beach, we settled down to await the race. To fill in time I went for a paddle. Suddenly, I heard my father shout, 'Look, there's one coming.' I raised my eyes to see a racer enveloped in an hysterical whine getting larger and larger as it sped towards me. Mesmerised, I must have stumbled ... backwards, into the sea with a resounding splash. Panic! My father had to dash into the water, empty his son of Solent and carry him to dry land. Shock and ignominy were gradually stemmed by a brisk rubbing down, but not before the little wretch had exacted an almost open cheque for ice-cream as being the only medicament capable of restoring his equanimity so that he might enjoy the rest of the scream-past of the Greatest Air Race in the World!

For those with a bent for aeronautical history, we saw a Supermarine S6, flown by Flying Officer H.R.D. Waghorn, win the contest at an average speed of 328.63 m.p.h. A few days later another machine of the same type,

* During the 1860s, when Lord Palmerston was Prime Minister, it was believed in British military circles that the Emperor Louis Napoleon III might attempt to avenge Waterloo by making a landing on the Sussex coast. Had the French been able to take Portsdown Hill their guns would have had command of Portsmouth Dockyard. The purpose of the Forts was, therefore, to discourage such an attack from the north. But a large body of opinion believed the French had no such intentions and considered the whole exercise a waste of money. It was also difficult for the popular mind to grasp why the guns didn't point towards the Solent. Hence 'Palmerston's Folly'.

flown by Flying Officer A.H. Orlebar, raised the world air-speed record to 357 m.p.h. It was to come about that this gallant officer's young cousin, Jean Hazelrigg, was one day to become a neighbour of ours in South Avenue. Reflected glory of this kind didn't often come our way. So, when she arrived, we hastily bent the rules of our hitherto all-male society to admit a young lady who must surely have been kissed by the Fastest Man in the World!

What we couldn't have known, though, was that within a few years Supermarine's Chief Designer, the legendary R.J. Mitchell, would draw upon the experience he had gained in designing the S6s to develop a fast, single-seat, eight-gun fighter which first flew in 1936: the Spitfire. In the spring of 1931 I can remember excitement of a different kind, this time closer to Bognor – rather too close, a lot of residents thought. For suddenly there arrived on the Owers' horizon a large warship moored bows-on to the town and not the sort of thing to escape notice. After a few weeks there was the sound of heavy gunfire which rattled the windows and shook the town. Some said they had seen smoke coming from the warship. Of course, it turned out to be a 'target'.

Disturbed by the noise, a number of residents complained to Bognor Council who, in turn, sent their plaint to Whitehall. On 18 June they received a letter from the Secretary to the Admiralty. After apologising for the inconvenience caused to the populace by the bombardment, he went on to explain that in the event of the ship being sunk, it was important that this happened in shallow water so she might the more easily be inspected and eventually raised. After the exercise, he said, he hoped to get £50,000 for her as scrap. The Admiralty, he added unctuously, was constantly aware of its obligation to get the best deal on the taxpayers' behalf. Hence the choice of the Owers Bank.

She turned out to be the old dreadnought *Emperor of India*, a vessel of some 25,000 tons built in 1914 and a veteran of Jutland. The whole thing

27 HMS *Emperor of India*, 'sunk' off Bognor in 1931.

was veiled in secrecy although, according to the *Portsmouth Evening News*, the guns being tested were known to be of 'the Krupp type … and fired a shell weighing nearly a ton'. The ship boasting all this advanced ordnance was, in fact, another Jutland veteran, HMS *Iron Duke*, the *Emperor*'s sister ship and Admiral Jellicoe's flagship during that engagement. Only recently had she been re-gunned for her unsisterly role. With her bottom so near the sea-bed, the *Emperor* offered no great spectacle when, late in May, she was 'sunk' after the town had received another shaking. For a long time afterwards her silhouette remained a fixture on the horizon until, one day, she disappeared just as suddenly as she had arrived, on her way, presumably, to Cox & Danks, the ship-breakers, in exchange for the £50,000 due to the taxpayers.

* * *

'Isn't it absolutely wonderful; the whole world in my bedroom,' I once heard my mother exclaim as she fiddled with the tuning dial of our new Detex portable wireless on the bed by her side. Well, it must have seemed a notable advance over the 'cats whisker' contraption on which, only a few years earlier, my parents had donned earphones to 'listen in' to 2LO broadcasting from Alexandra Palace before it became the BBC in 1923. If it wasn't too late I was allowed to listen in my pyjamas. Putting up with the deadly 'chamber music' of the Griller String Quartet was the price of waiting for something funny to come on: you know, Stainless Steven, Claude Dampier or Wee Georgie Wood – or, better still, the Western Brothers with their drawling catchphrase, 'Hello, cads'.

'Saturday night Music Hall' was another favourite. Curled up on her bed, I can recall listening to the voices of Stanley Baldwin, Yvonne Arnaud, the actress, and Bernard Shaw. In October 1930 we heard of the crash of the British airship R101 near Beauvais in France. And in February 1933 the main news was the destruction by fire of the Reichstag in Berlin. The end of the BBC's 9 p.m. 'Second General News' was the signal for me to return to my own bed. Then, on 19 January 1936, the family huddled round the portable to hear the sombre voice of the BBC announcer telling us that the life of King George V was drawing to a close at Sandringham. Within a few hours he was dead. 'God Save the nice new King Edward VIII', waiting to swap his cloth cap for the Crown of England, with the prospect of 'Reigning o'er us' for many years to come. Well, I believe that's what most folk thought.

5

The Paradise Rocks

An historic conflagration. And getting the milk out of cows.

And so the beaches and countryside around Aldwick became our oyster, awaiting to be opened under balmy summer skies, in the teeth of sou'westerly gales that threatened to blow the blackbirds inside out, and during depressions of incalculable depth when it rained for days on end and tested our waterproofness to the limit.

On most summer days – if it wasn't raining – we used to set off to Aldwick Beach accompanied by our maid, Joan. It was an excursion not without hazard. Beside our bungalow, the rotting railway-sleeper bridge was intent on up-ending us into the ditch, and the tottering stile was only for those with a bold heart and a sense of balance. And there still remained Mr Crockett's cows with their penchant for sitting on the footpath to chew their cud, each recumbent beast requiring respectful circumambulation. For, to tell the truth, we weren't yet all that familiar with cows.

But soon we were climbing over the other end stile, next to the clematis drape of Almora's fence. Then, Fish Lane crossed, the imperious gates to Aldwick Place skirted, the beach-ball bounced, the brother barged (and the retaliatory swipe ducked), suddenly we found ourselves enveloped in Dark Lane's leafy nave, its green canopy impenetrable to all but the most determined shafts of sunlight. Overhead, the arching elms echoed to the querulous cawing of hundreds of rooks, hurling insults at each other as they pinched bits of their neighbour's nests in the annual riot of raising the next generation of *corvus frugilegus*.

Passing the white-painted gates to Paradise, and with the smell of the sea in our nostrils, we rounded a slow bend and there, in front of us – beyond the little sand-gardens with their breakwater fences – sparkled, beckoning, the English Channel. So there we were, two small boys – and Joan – burdened down with the all the customary beach paraphernalia, including a well-patched pink inner-tube and the yellow-and-red beach-ball. In the wicker basket lay our picnic lunch which, as if obedient to some ancient covenant, had always to include Shippam's bloater-paste sand-wiches. Somewhere beneath the Parfrement's Pasties, the Lyon's Kup Cakes and the Thermos lay our literary nourishment of the day: the tuppenny *Rainbow* for him, the *Hotspur* for me and *True Romantic Stories* for her. In front of us stretched a whole day on the beach; to explore, bathe, paddle, put the wind up the resident shrimps and to demolish the picnic.

Now, to generations of children the main attraction of Aldwick Beach had long been the 'Rocks' – not, of course, the Barn Rocks which lie out at sea, but those very playable-upon boulders piled up against the sea-wall of

28 The gates to Paradise in Dark Lane, about 1935.

Paradise, from which this chapter draws its title. Of course, had we been asked how long those rocks had rested there like that (bearing in mind our deplorable lack of the most elementary geomorphology), my brother and I would have assuredly put our last ha'pennies on ... well, since the Beginning of Time ... at least. And, serve us right, we'd have lost our coin. For really, they were just a pile of impostors! Thus, not for the first time we tripped, unknowingly, over a little bit of Aldwick's history.

Around 1805, to the west of the seaward end of Dark Lane, lay an attractive garden overlooking the sea. Recently planted with a wide variety of trees, it belonged to Sir Thomas Brooke Pechell, Bt, one of Bognor's first Town Commissioners. In it he had built a long, romantic-looking thatched cottage *ornée*, veranda-ed and made charming by its supporting pillars clad in 'jessamines and honeysuckles'. Less thatchy, though, its name: the rather suburban-sounding Aldwick Villa. More to the front of his mind just then, however, was the alarming rate at which his garden was disappearing into the English Channel. It was a common enough problem on this part of the coast. As *Chamber's Guide* says, 'Bognor struggles bravely to keep itself from slipping into the sea.' A *Times* report of a great storm in 1820 paints an even more vivid picture: 'At Aldwick, Felpham and Bognor so much damage is done that it cannot be ascertained ... properties which were defended at high water by walls of rock of immense size could not withstand the tempest. Pieces of rock, some weighing 5 cwt. were torn up and carried a great distance.'

How was Pechell to save his garden? The Barn Rocks, visible at low tide, must have suggested the solution. Spared the need to look over his shoulder for lurking snoopers from the Planning Department, the Crown Estates, the Min of Ag and Fish, born-again Environmentalists or English Nature (who have since scheduled the Bognor Rocks as an SSSI), the resourceful Sir Thomas arranged to have taken from the sea a large number of suitably sized boulders which were moved* to the beach in front of his crumbling garden. And there, over time, they came to form a sturdy breakwater which, together with a new timber groyne further west (within my own memory it bore Pechell's Huguenot name), seems to have greatly improved the garden's prospects of survival. But that was not quite all of this rocky pile's history.

By the beginning of the 19th century Aldwick's coastal strip had become an enclave of gentry living in fine houses built in spacious grounds and was regarded as a smarter place to live than any of Hotham's developments in the town. At Aldwick Villa Sir Thomas would have had some distinguished neighbours. Richard Dally, in his *Guide* of 1828 (updated in 1838), lists them.

> On the margin of the sea, threatened by its inroads, stands in succession [from east to west]:
>
> Mrs Esdaile in a pretty house of true gothic architecture which combines elegance with comfort; but the devouring elements threaten its total destruction unless some overwhelming spirit should direct its waves to another quarter less prejudicial. [It must have stood just west of the Nyewood Lane ditch, the boundary between Bognor and the tything of Aldwick, on what is now the beach.]
>
> The property belonging to Sir Simon Clarke Bt. [Aldwick Place; then comes Dark Lane, followed by]
>
> The picturesque and unique cottage of Sir Thomas Brooke Pechell [Aldwick Villa].
>
> The villa built by the Countess of Newburgh after an Italian model. [Known then as the Pavilion, it was lived in at the time by the Rev. Henry Raikes, a Hellenist of note and a Bognor curate. Later it became Craigweil House and was run for some time by the Stocker family as a lunatic asylum. It became a household name when its last owner, Sir Arthur Du Cros (Dunlop Tyres), placed it at the disposal of King George V for his convalescence in 1929.]
>
> Barn Rocks built by the late Alderman Newnham, sometime the property of Sir Edward Colebrook and now of Mr Clarke. [Late in the 19th century Colebrook House was built adjoining Barn Rocks; it was demolished in 1934.]

* The late Martin Venables told me that at low tide the selected boulder was lashed to some sort of raft. As the sea level rose the boulder was lifted clear of the sea bed and towed to its new location below the disintegrating sea-wall, from where it was manoeuvered into position and released at the next low tide.

> West Cottage [later House] belonging to and occupied by Mrs Newnham.

Presumably she was the widow of the Alderman, late of Barn Rocks. Later, both A.E. Knox, the ornithologist, and Sir Beerbohm Tree, the London actor-manager, stayed at the Cottage (a smaller dwelling) during the the 'thirties. Eventually West House became the home of the Duchess of Rutland, her actress daughter and her diplomatic son-in-law – the Duff-Coopers.

By the end of the 19th century Aldwick Villa had been through the hands of various owners, among them Captain Sykes (1838) and the Reverend Thomas Scutt (1850), and, in about 1896, it had become the home of the Reverend Edward Croxton Johnson and his wife – and cousin – Emily, the daughter of Sir Henry Shiffner of Combe Hall near Lewes, and head of a great landowning family in those parts. 'Emmie' was a practised hostess and it wasn't long before the Johnsons became a fulcrum of the local gentry society which we can guess included such luminaries as the Stockers at Craigweil House, Mr and Mrs Symes from Barn Rocks, Beerbohm Tree at West Cottage and, of course, the vicar of Pagham, the Rev. S.H. Nobbs-Rawdon.

Meanwhile, the godly (if equivocally employed) Edward managed to persuade his father – also a Reverend – to stump up the funds to build a small chapel, complete with its own organ,* in the Villa's grounds to serve the spiritual needs of the little fishing community which in those days was settled on Aldwick Beach.

Sadly, in 1902, the Reverend Johnson departed this life and his body was cremated at Brookwood, near Guildford, a quite early example of this form of corporeal disposal. Tended by her six servants, however, Emmie continued to live on in her cherished home. And one can but envy her. For picture that beach on a hazy June morning in the early days of the last century: the sweep of the Channel bounded only by Bognor's Pier in the east and by Selsey Bill in the west; Emmie, mistress of the deserted strand; the white-laced waves and mewing gulls; even the footmarks in the sand, her own. And a Paradise Lane (otherwise Dark Lane or Lover's Lane) in which the presence of a motor car would have given rise to the wildest speculation in the snug bar at the *Ship* inn. And as for an ice-cream barrow – well, perish the thought!

In about 1904 Emily Croxton Johnson, perhaps to mark a break with the sadness of her recent past, decided to rename her house and its secluded grounds after the adjoining lane. Thus Paradise it became. And indeed, at times, it must have seemed only a scant less celestial than the real thing – quite apart from being a rather jollier name than Aldwick Villa. But, in the early hours of 18 April 1909, a terrible disaster befell Emily when the smell of burning proved to be a fire in the roof of her thickly thatched house. Urgently she made a call to the Bognor Volunteer Fire Brigade on her recently installed telephone. It came through to Captain Wood in his apartment over the Post Office in the Arcade, where he pursued his other role as that of Bognor's Postmaster. One can imagine the events which ensued.

---

* The chapel organ ended its days in the Masonic Hall at Bognor. In 1974 it was replaced with one from Pagham church.

29 Bognor Volunteer Fire Brigade answers a call. The Officer with his back to the camera is Captain Wood, who was in charge at the Paradise blaze.

Wood immediately phoned Tom Field, the job-master in Waterloo Square. Quickly, Tom threw on his clothes; soon he was running along the High Street holding the two fire engine horses. In Leading Fireman James Walwin's flat, over his hairdressing saloon, next door to the Fire Station, the electric bell sounded. Within seconds Walwin was through the inter-connecting door which led into the recreation room above the appliances. He picked up the wall-phone receiver; Wood's voice, 'Fire at Paradise – all speed!' Walwin was well rehearsed. His first action was to telephone the alarm to the firemen at their homes.*

Next, he threw open the Fire Station doors. Very soon Captain Wood was assisting Field to harness the two horses which helped absorb the slothful minutes as, on foot and bicycle, the volunteers made their way to the station. Meanwhile the Shand Mason had been pulled outside into the road and a taper applied to the oily cotton-waste in the box. Quickly, working clothes were exchanged for uniforms; leather thigh-boots pulled on; brass helmets donned. There was a shout of readiness. Suddenly the silence of the High Street was shattered as pump and horses clattered off, the post-horn blowing, on their long westward journey. And what a gallant sight they must have made, the volunteers hanging on to the rocking Shand Mason – its chimney belching smoke and flames – as they galloped along those rough, unlit Aldwick roads towards the bright orange beacon burning at the foot of Paradise Lane!

Yet, even with every sinew strained, by the time the Fire Brigade arrived at the conflagration the best part of half-an-hour had passed since Mrs Croxton Johnson had made her phone call. 'With praiseworthy celerity', wrote the *Bognor Observer*, 'a hose was connected to a hydrant outside as they set to put out the flames which were beginning to get a dangerous

* As early as 1904 the National Telephone Company had installed an inter-communication system enabling the fire brigade volunteers to be contacted by phone.

hold. Soon portions of the roof gave way and the flames shot up in the air testifying that the efforts of the firemen were none too soon.' But 'none too soon' proved to be the understatement of the night. For, in spite of 'a thousand feet of hose' and the firemen's strenuous endeavours, not to mention the efforts of Mr Stocker's private fire brigade from Craigweil House, the fight was already lost.

By next morning all that was left were the smoking ruins, out of which towered the fairy tale chimney stacks gaunt against the rookery elms as they looked down upon a chastened Emily Johnson helping to move her salvaged belongings into her father-in-law's now unused seaman's chapel. To

30 Paradise before the fire.

31 The ruins of Paradise smoulder in the early morning hours.

rub salt into the wound, a few weeks later she received a bill for the Fire Brigade's services. In their minutes dated 28 May 1909 is the entry: 'Paradise Aldwick Fire. That the claim for the Fire Brigade's attendance be made up and sent to Mrs Johnson at once.' It cost her £30 7s. 5d.

After the little chapel had been altered it became Emily's home. But the surviving walls of the house were left to become an ivy-covered ruin, a fitting repository for her bittersweet memories of Paradise.

In 1993 I met Mrs Belinda Suchanek, Mrs Croxton Johnson's niece. As a small child she remembered being taken to Paradise on one or two occasions, the last being with her mother, 'after Aunt Emmie's death, to rescue the family silver from the trustees'. She could recall the great lady faintly, although her chief memory was playing 'in the beach hut at the top of the shingle'. Mr Roy Suter, whose father was chauffeur to the Stockers at Craigweil House for many years, told me that Mrs Croxton Johnson used to have regular deliveries of fish (lobsters?) brought to her by sea from Selsey by Frederick Barnes, coxswain of the lifeboat. It entailed a round trip of nine miles in a rowing boat. In early 1929 she took her usual holiday at the *Hôtel Hermitage* at Monte Carlo. While there she developed pneumonia and died on 11 February with the British Consul at her bedside.

Shortly afterwards Paradise was sold to Mr D.F. Dalrymple, a company promoter, who cleared the site of buildings to make way for a large house designed in the Moorish style yet retaining the original name. During the early days of the war it was purchased for £50,000 by Mr Michael Hillman, a South African entrepreneur and owner of the Duchess Theatre in Catherine Street in the West End. After his death it changed hands again, and in about 1944 it became the home of William Webber, a retired farmer, and his wife, Alberta. It was they who renamed the house Strange Garden. In about 1962 it was converted into flats.

In the early hours of 30 December 1912 a maritime drama of some note took place at Aldwick when the square-rigged *Carnot*, outward bound from Calais for St Malo with a cargo of jute-bagged cement and 110 barrels of salted herrings, was driven by a fierce storm on to Emily's beach, west of Pechell's groyne. When Mrs Johnson came out of her house that stormy night she must have been mildly surprised to find herself looking up at the tattered sails and rigging of the 96 ton ship. Mercifully, its master, Captain Bailbed, his crew of six and the ship's dog were saved, and after the seamen had been given dry clothes and treated to a performance of *Babes in the Wood* at the Kursaal, Aldwick's *grande dame* had the crew to tea at Paradise.

Attempts to refloat the ship by the Littlehampton tug *Jumna* having failed, the *Carnot* gradually became a total wreck, still smoking from the herrings cooked in the heat generated by the setting cement. Eventually, much of the ship's remains were auctioned off. But what of the the lumpy jute bags of solidified cement strewn all over the beach? Well, where more convenient a place to throw them than onto Sir Thomas Pechell's rocky breakwater?

Of course, had my brother and I been aware of the history of this pile of boulders, it would have explained why so many of them had those funny sacking marks on them. Also, we might have been a ha'penny better off!

32 The two-masted barque *Carnot* hard aground on Aldwick Beach, 30 December 1912.

So, that morning, it was to the Paradise Rocks we made a bee-line. Among the limpet-encrusted boulders and the *Carnot's* jute-inscribed lumps of cement, Roger and I were soon trawling our way through their treasury of red sea anemones, sun-baked starfish, shrimps, sea urchins, little sideways-crabs, stranded jellyfish and fronds of bladderwrack. Amongst the nooks and crannies, infinitely diverse of colour and contortion, huddled tiny shells rubbing shoulders with unworldly gastropods, pelecypods and egg-cases of the lesser spotted dogfish. And on top of this pageant of natural life, there awaited our acquisitive instincts an array of highly collectable lobster-pots, Grimsby fish-boxes and cork floats – and occasionally the greatly prized glass ones – to say nothing of half a ship's lifebelt. And what of those foreign-looking palm-husks, surely wave-borne from some far off South Sea atoll? One day we discovered among the rocks a harvest of floating oranges – hundreds of them!

All that was left was for us to spend half-an-hour the other side of Pechell's groyne digging for pieces-of-eight and priceless artefacts around those tilted timbers which we were convinced were the topmasts of a Spanish galleon (in fact, the remains of the old *Carnot's* hull), until our labours were put at naught by the returning tide.

So that was the panorama of Aldwick Beach in the 'thirties: paddling in the lugworm craters, hide-and-seek amongst the Rocks of Paradise; king-of-the-castle proclaimed from their highest pinnacles, grazed knees, peeling backs, molten ice-cream trickling down sunburnt arms and sandy sausage-rolls smelling of sun-tan lotion. And overhead the rustle of our 'Atlanta' kite. With unseemly haste the hours sped by.

From time to time excitement gripped us when we heard the distant throb of aircraft engines heralding the approach of a brace of those silvery old dowagers of the maritime skies, the Supermarine 'Southampton' flying-boats from Calshot. As the great biplanes flew just above the sea on their majestic progress along the south coast beaches, we used to wave frantically to the little figures in their open cockpits … and then, one day, a diminutive hand returned our greeting – and made a story which even complete strangers had to be treated to!

Another summer sound on Aldwick's strand was the reverberatory thud of guns from the 'Rule Britannia' warships practicing in the Solent. And if it wasn't the guns, it was the mournful 'aaawoomph' from the Owers' foghorn as a pearly sea mist closed in around us. Then the restive Channel became a sheet of glass as the shouts of invisible children and barking dogs bounced off the sea-wall of Paradise. But it was never long before the sou'west wind strode in to bully away the the mist and make the white horses dance to its boisterous tune before beckoning over a grey apron of rain from somewhere behind the Selsey lifeboat shed.

And so our little expedition came to an end as we packed up our things and set off home like lines of refugees with beach towels over our heads to beat the rain. As we wended our way back under the quarrelling rooks of Dark Lane, it was the custom of the country to bring happiness to the ears of the old and crotchety by beating a last-post tattoo with our beach spades along the iron railings of Aldwick Grange.

Close by the Paradise Rocks was to be found that other diadem of Aldwick Beach, its famous, rusty, 20-inch iron drainpipe! Alas, drainpipes are not well known for their poetic inspiration, but at least the one at Aldwick was held in great affection by generations of young holiday makers. And not only on account of its rewarding resonance when whacked with a spade, or because it required a breath taking balancing act to walk its length in sandalled feet. For Aldwick's drainpipe only came into its own when the tide receded. Then the local ditches united to gush mightily from its downturned maw, to sculpt the sand into an intricate delta of channels and rivulets demanding to be dammed, diverted, jumped over – and fallen into. But, try as we would, our sandy dykes and barrages were never equal to the primitive urge of the waters of the Hundred of Aldwick to return to the restless sea. The pipe is still there, but now made ugly by another generation.

It would never do, however, to give the impression that we lived the whole of our young lives untroubled of heart, under a perpetual cavalcade of cloudless summer days. Such partisan memories expunge those sullen, grey afternoons spent splashing around in a choppy sea so much warmer than the bitter wind blowing above it; when our bodies shivered uncontrollably in the lee of a well-meaning but ineffectual breakwater as we dried chapped skin with damp, cold towels made cruelly abrasive by the clinging sand. There were tears compelled by the loss of 1s. 6d. worth of personal treasure among the labyrinthine rocks. Our red-and-yellow beach-ball more than once found itself the subject of grave questions of custody, accompanied by punitive threats, while three squares of Cadbury's Milk divided between two gave rise to nice questions of seniority and ugly ones of privilege.

Nor were pain and suffering unknown. Barnacles had an absent-minded trick of drawing blood long after they had been stroked; broken glass bottles could lead to a trail of gory footprints in the wet sand. Then there was the occasion when I was bitten by a deranged octopus lurking amongst Barn Rocks and remained unconvinced by my mother's assurance that it was merely a peevish jellyfish. Well, something punctured the boy, requiring him to be carted off home with a swollen leg followed by bed, physic and prayers.

Drama, too, had its place. Indelible, still, the memory of Auntie Dolly's choice of Aldwick Beach for the unveiling of her new, hand-knitted bathing dress. But seconds later there were panic-stricken screams as the water-logged costume unveiled itself below her knees! Our eyes were bidden turn landwards while my mother undertook the delicate task of Auntie D's retrieval. But it was sobering when, in September 1933, a 15-year-old Doctor Barnardo's boy was drowned amongst Barn Rocks.

During the 'thirties, our beach remained largely aloof from the spreading commercialism of Bognor's esplanades. Yet, I can remember two folk who carried on a little innocent business at the end of Dark Lane. One was the florid-faced owner of a dented *cor-anglais* whose forté was a continuous performance of the 'Londonderry Air'. The other was the Antarctic Ice-Cream Company's tricycling ice-cream salesman. Amongst the children he was a great favourite, allowing them to sit on the seat, tinkle the bell and turning a blind eye when they looked inside the *sancta sanctorum* where he kept the steaming blocks of ice, the tubs and choc-ices.

* * *

Had Justice been on her toes, my parent's horticultural zeal should have been rewarded with a garden and lawns putting to shame the Chelsea Flower Show. Instead, they had to come to terms with the disagreeable fact that they had begotten two young sons strangely gifted in their capacity to pillage and lay waste all that was beautiful, verdant and floriferous. So, for the next few years, dreams of nurturing their own little Sissinghurst had to be shelved as my brother and I dedicated ourselves to transforming their lovesome thing into a mere adjunct to our lives of meadow, ditch and beach.

Against a background of painted tin buckets, sand spades and bouncy, pink inner-tubes, Fairy cycles leant crazily against deckchairs occupied by clockwork lorries, Yo-Yos and half-made Meccano models. Yachts sailed among the startled goldfish and a bowl of watersnails rested uncertainly on a Saxa salt box vacated by an injured sparrow lately interred among the antirrhinums. Gradually the scorched lawn and the grey-green lavender disappeared beneath a multi-coloured patchwork of beach towels, bathing costumes, Joan's pinafores and freshly Blanco'd plimsols drying in the sun.

Everywhere lay evidence of our specialist's eye for the detritus of the Channel's draining-board, fronds of bladderwrack hanging limply from the sea-sculptures of silver driftwood. The garden was the last resting place of a rowing boat's rudder, a bleached lavatory seat, half a municipal deckchair and a skeletal tope – each speaking of triumphant journeys home from Aldwick Beach. Only a telegram announcing the imminent arrival of one of the Hampstead aunts had any hope of restoring order.

33 Aldwick Beach, *c.*1937. On the left is the famous land drain still with its down-turned maw. The bathing hut at the top of the shingle was the Rank family's gift to the Barnardo's boys at Margaret House.

Then, before we knew what had happened, the holiday visitors had faded away and the *cor-anglais* player and the Antarctic ice-cream man had fled, taking the blue skies with them; bathing dresses were consigned to the linen cupboard and the pink inner-tube to the garden shed. Suddenly we found ourselves wrapped in winter gear, sharing the beach with muffled-up figures exercising their dogs. In the snow-laden sky the herring gulls glided to attention as a Siberian easterly propelled us homewards along the sands after a visit to Goodacre's toyshop for a signal box for my Hornby railway.

* * *

A trade not much carried on in our suburb of west London was getting the milk out of cows. So the day we stumbled on Aldwick Farm* we were resolved to find out a bit more about how it was done. From within the gloom of their primitive milking shed, I daresay the cowmen paid little attention to two innocent-looking fair-haired boys standing at a respectful distance from the half-open stable door below the swallow-nested eaves. Perhaps it failed to excite their curiosity that every time they looked up the two innocents had moved a little closer.

Suddenly it was too late! We were inside their manurey cavern asking questions. 'What's that stuff, please?' inquired a finger pointing to a pail of cattle-cake; or 'how did she hurt herself?', indicating a lacerated udder being anointed with something pink and Germoleney. The cowman pouring a lemonade bottle of green medicament down a bovine throat was asked to account for his ways. So was the milker who squirted the first few teatsful from a bursting udder onto the disintegrating floor instead of into his bucket. To our barrage of questions, Mr Crockett's men showed tolerance

* The history of Aldwick Farm is covered at great length in Lindsay Fleming's *History of Pagham in Sussex.*

beyond the call of duty. So that must have been when we decided to throw in our lot with the workaday lives of the owners of those clean, pink hands, hands which so effortlessly brought forth the thin needles of milk from distended udders to fill their buckets with creamy heads like glasses of advertisment-Guinness. 'Could we help, please?'

And so it came about that on many holiday afternoons Roger and I gave selflessly of our services to Aldwick Farm as we 'helped' stagger with the pails of cattle-cake, 'helped' sweep the dung channel and squirted the rubber hosepipe in all directions. We chatted up the cows and learned their names scrawled in chalk above their stalls – Beryl, Zoe, Annie and Diana. Our 'help' found its way into the dairy, where milk flowed from the cooler to fill the heavy churns, churns resistant to our attempts to roll them along on their lower rims – an art which came so easily to Mr Crockett's men. Then, one day, I was placed upon a stool with my head tucked into the heaving flank of a Guernsey shorthorn cross and invited to get the stuff out. But my fingers spoke the wrong language; less than a tumblerful. And most of that down my leg: '… er's mak'n' it faster than you's gittin' it ait,' grunted the cowman who became my friend.

Naturally, such help deserved the occasional breather. Close at hand beckoned the cobwebby twilight of the Great Thatched Barn, where our good intentions quickly degenerated into horseplay among the cliffs of sweet-smelling hay. And when that palled, another diversion awaited us just outside the farm: to clamber up into the 'hollow oak' (no matter that it was an ancient elm) which, at different times, served as a machine-gun post or our Secret Service H.Q., besides being one of Tarzan's few tree-houses to have overlooked the Red Rover bus route. Yet, even for this short respite I daresay the cowkeepers of Aldwick were thankful. But show us the gate? To their eternal credit, never!

Milking over, we returned to the yard for the pay-off to our labours. With hedgesticks and dung-covered wellies as our badges of authority, we joined in driving the cows back to their pastures, whacking, thwacking and shouting Beryl and her friends out of the weedy ditches on the road to Chichester* – as well as savouring their lofty disregard for the traffic piling up behind them. In the autumn, the horse and cart taking Mr Gray's tamarisk huts to winter storage in Hewart's Barn in Rose Green Road was continually getting caught up behind the cows. It was on this route that we used to pass a little Dickensian hovel on the eastern verge of the road north of the Duck Pond and nearly opposite the footpath to Rose Green. This was called Willow Tree Cottage, built inconveniently close to the road, with a long, narrow strip of garden and lived in by a nice old chap whom I once helped catch an injured mallard. I think his name was Charlie Freeman. The cottage was demolished – or pushed over – just before the war. Now even the site has disappeared under Margaret Close.

At last, the five-barred gate was fastened in the wake of the emptied herd. Then, smiting the thistles as we went, we returned to trawl for frogspawn in its season or to seek a precarious balancing act amongst a prostrate elm's

* I had never heard of the Lower Bognor Road before the last war. Like Lindsay Fleming, we called it the 'road to Chichester'. Where, incidentally, is this Lower Bognor?

34 Willow Tree Cottage on the eastern verge of 'the road to Chichester'.

fractured boughs, allowing us to spy upon the moorhens skulking in their underworld of writhing roots. And never a voice to say 'Don't!'

But great changes were in store for this manurey quarter of Aldwick. For, unknown to us, the days of Mr Crockett's dark milking shed were numbered. What was now mud would soon be concrete; drain would vanquish puddle, and uncouth floor would be rendered smooth; bent roof timbers and broken tiles were shortly to be re-born as an asbestos and patent-glazed roof, covering a revolutionary and up-to-date milking parlour in which the cows would be asked to give of their milk to the most advanced electrical innovation. For recently a certain Mr Rowland Rank had purchased 'A Gentleman's Dairy and Stock Farm' at Aldwick.

* * *

'Aspects of Health; The Great Wen or Bognor? Discuss'. One day my mother and I fell to talking about this thought-provoking subject and the reasons she gave for coming to Bognor were unexpected. It wasn't entirely a sentimental return to the scene of her childhood holidays at the Debt House in the early days of the century. Neither was it the shamefulness of speculation. Nor did we know any Jones's with whom to keep up. No, the reason was more prosaic: tuberculosis.

Both my mother and grandmother had lived on the periphery of that terrible Victorian scourge. Mercifully our family had been spared it, but they had seen friends and acquaintances wither and die of its malice. The best medical advice for those with 'weak chests' was a move to the seaside. Great benefits were claimed, and the 'magical' recuperative and health-giving properties of the sea air had long been received wisdom. In this respect the south coast enjoyed a specially good press, as shown by this excerpt from *Bognor as a Health Resort*, written in 1904 by Dr H.C.L. Morris, the town's Medical Officer of Health:

> The sun's rays are of primary importance to the human constitution.
> Without the sun we become depressed and disinclined for work, and
> our mental and bodily energies become lessened. What is of greater

account to the invalid than sunshine? The winter visitor escaping from the fog and smoke of London is surprised to find Bognor bathed in sunshine, and quickly feels the invigorating effects of it. Our average sunshine for the last seven years is 1,886 hours and I cannot find this has been exceeded by any other place in the United Kingdom. This is something to boast of, and in itself is sufficient to stamp our Bognor climate as remarkable.

In 1928, coal-smoke still poured from millions of chimneys across London. Day after day its skies remained opaque and its winters bred the yellow pea-soup fogs. The sooty buildings showed it and so did my father's collars. His work looked as if it would tie us to London for many years. All this – and her dread of TB – greatly concerned my mother and strengthened her determination that her children should spend as much as possible of their growing years by the sea. History and geography pointed at Bognor. And that was why my parents entered into a long period of self-denial in order that they might build Idlewylde for us. So the sight of those sickly children from Bognor's convalescent homes soaking up the sun as they lay on their wheel-beds on the Esplanade – not to mention the choice of Craig-weil House at Aldwick to cure an ailing King – must have seemed like seals of approval upon their aspirations.

By the time I was nudged into the National Census statistics, a revolution had overtaken child-rearing. Eschewed, now, the cosseted, over-gowned infant condemned to its bottle of Nestlés milk in an unventilated Victorian coal-fired nursery. Instead, 20th-century baby was to be raised in the Great Outdoors. Well, that was what all the best books on baby-rearing said – and my mother must have gone through them with a tooth-comb. So, as soon as it was decent, I was banished to the garden in a slab-sided pram with the leaf-springs of a Leyland truck and a hood like a marquee and – according to my mother – left there summer and winter to endure pouring rain, driven snow and gale-force winds until darkness fell. The chance of succumbing to a handful of TB germs must have been as naught compared with the risk of my early demise at the hands of the British weather system!

My mother held strong views on most things, but on children's shoes in particular. Many of the foot ailments of later years, she declared, were due to their constant incarceration in unsuitable shoes during childhood. So, on arrival for our summer holidays at Aldwick, we kicked off our footwear on the loggia and for the rest of the holidays went unshod: barefooted on the beach, in the village, on the buses and even when shopping in the town, where we must have attracted pitying glances from passers-by, convinced they were witnessing the stark reality of the Depression. Only when playing in the fields – the bees and thistles being unaware of her theories – were we allowed to have our shoes back on. So, at the end of the holiday, the soles of our feet were as leathery as our shoes!

So that is why my brothers and I owe our mother – and Bognor's ozone – a debt of gratitude for years of rude health and bunionless feet.

6

A Trip Round the Shops

And All Things Bright and Beautiful!

In spite of the post-First World War building boom which was beginning to lard the surrounding countryside with houses and bungalows, Aldwick village, in 1929, remained relatively unscathed. Mr Rowland Rank's new Aldwick Place barely counted, as it was near the sea and invisible through its wrought-iron gates. More prominent was the Pearce's house, Orchards (later Fleurs, Aldwick Street; now Wick Cottage), both a newcomer and an arresting example of 20th-century lamb dressed up as 15th-century mutton. Post-war, too, was Charlie Tooze's 1920s sub-post office (Aldwick Street; now a private house), late of Hurst Cottage. But by far the most obtrusive *arrivistes* in the village were the new shops in Tudor Buildings, broad-shouldered and disarmingly infelicitous, an exercise in North Circular Road Mediaeval. And it was from under their creosoted deceit, at No. 3, that Mr and Mrs George Gates ran the village stores (Aldwick Stores, Tudor Buildings; now a removals firm).

Whilst perhaps not rating a heritage plaque, there is no harm in mentioning that it was here that I first went shopping on my own, refrained from folding my mother's list into a paper dart, paid Mrs Gates in assorted florins, bobs and tanners, and wrapped the change in a grubby handkerchief before threading my way back through Mr Crockett's herd of Guernsey shorthorn crosses to maternal approbation for not having eaten half the chocolate biscuits during the journey.

Soon, Gates' could count me a regular. Each day the choicest comestibles were delivered to their store by motor vans with starting-handles, unpacked, checked, placed by ladder upon high shelves, by ladder taken down again, dusted, examined, pondered upon, sliced, counted, weighed out, re-packed, recorded in indelible pencil and sold under pendant fly-papers in vexatiously small amounts. To assist their customers, no trouble was too great for Mr and Mrs Gates. Aldwick's store was also a renowned forum for local gossip. Before an expectant hush, all commercial transactions came to a halt as a valued customer's description of their recent operation in the Memorial Hospital got to the juicy bit which had invariably created medical history. Mum's blow-by-blow account of the daughter's wedding reception at Leslies' Restaurant was accorded the same respect. For funerals, voices were draped in black.

And when Mr Gates wasn't bustling behind the counter or outside swiping at the autumn wasps on the fruit and veg-piled forecourt, he was out in his small Morris van delivering orders in our Outback of puddled roads around Aldwick Gardens and Rose Green, where he conducted the financial side of his business from a leather pouch slung round his neck.

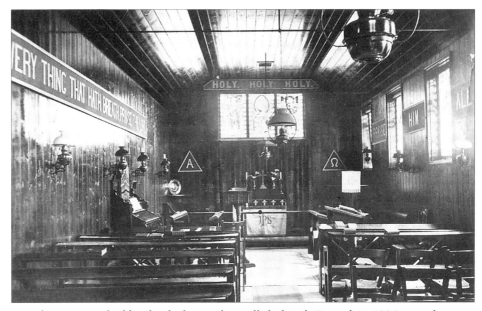

35 The interior of Aldwick's little wooden-walled chapel. Erected in 1906 to replace an earlier 'iron church', it was demolished in the early 'thirties when it became too dilapidated and the new St Richard's Church in Gossamer Lane was being planned.

Next door to the Gates, Mr and Mrs Roberts went in for newspapers (No. 2; now a newsagent and sub-post office), Four Square tobacco, Kensitas cigarettes (silk flags with twenties) and – closer to our hearts – Fry's Five-Centred chocolate bars and gobstoppers. And, in its season, Lyon's ice-cream. Outside, a revolving stand of Judge's postcards upset the shrimping nets and beach spades among the sand-shoes and rubber rings each time it was turned.

Between Roberts' paper shop and Kent and Parson's garage (Aldwick Motors, Aldwick Street; still a garage) – By Appointment puncture repairers to the Alford bikes – stood Pippins, the village café (1 Tudor Buildings, Aldwick Street; now a hairdressers). At Auntie Dolly weekends, she and my mother might have been found languorously draped over its wicker chairs, sipping their café au lait and chatting shamelessly of extra-sensory perception and Malthusian theories of population.

Although sharply conscious of it having nothing whatever to do with shopping, it would be a missed opportunity if, while we are in the village, we didn't take a look at one of its more curious buildings, Aldwick's little church dating from 1906. Timber-clad and roofed in iron sheets, it stood opposite Hurst Cottage on the grounds of what had once been Aldwick Lodge, at that time the home of the Seth-Smith family. In the 1930s, Miss Clear ran the Sunday School and Miss Suter did the flowers. In winter, it enjoyed the Christian virtue of being bitterly cold as well as having a leaky roof and holes opening up in the floor.

Yet, in defiance of its construction, I have heard it sometimes called the 'Tin Tab', which is surely an echo from an earlier place of worship. Let Kelly's *Sussex Directory* of 1887 shed some light: '[At Aldwick] there is an

36 The holiday season. A bustling London Road viewed from under the Arcade in about 1935. Timothy White's, Staley's and Pink's the grocers are all clearly visible. Today this is a shopping precinct.

37 E.H. Isted's shop in London Road.

iron church with sittings for 120 persons erected at the cost of Baron Grant whose seat is at Aldwick Place ... the Baron [*sic*] Rocks are off the coast at this point.'

In an interview with the *Bognor Observer* in March 1957, Miss Daisy Tooze, the postmistress at Aldwick, stated that she remembered well the 'iron church' as it had been built in the garden of Hurst Cottage, where she was born and where her father, Charlie Tooze, had opened the village's first post office in the early 1900s.

At any rate, clutching my godmother's prayer book, I used to be taken sporadically to Aldwick's little church by my mother, to sing in a high voice 'All Things Bright and Beautiful' and pray with remorse for petty sins – with an added PS asking Him if He could kindly arrange for a repeat performance of that memorable morning when hailstones as big as marbles had fallen on its metal roof, rendering all but inaudible the preacher's godly message. Even as I put my penny in the collecting bowl, the writing was on the chapel's wooden walls. For already there were rumours of a more substantial church at Aldwick, soon to be built in Gossamer Lane.

But back to shopping. At Idlewylde, our summer days continued to be spent on the beach living in and out of the sea like young seals, prying into the secret ways of nature in our territory of fields, ditches and hayricks, or getting under the cowmen's feet at Aldwick Farm. Yet, over this honeyed life, awaiting parental whim, hung the Sword of Damocles. Shopping! Nor do I mean the praiseworthy kind that followed in the wake of birthdays and Christmases and ended up at Burgess' Bazaar (a toyshop in Waterloo Square; now a computer store) or Goodacre's (a toyshop on the Esplanade; now part of the Place St Maur). Oh, no! I refer to the deadly serious sort of victualling in which one is dragged round the town by an elder with a shopping list.

'Oh, must I go?' 'Yes dear, Nana needs you to carry her basket,' exclaimed my mother. 'But I've got a blister on my heel.' 'That, dear, was last week. Now go and comb your hair – and put on your shoes in case it rains.' Oh, luckless boy! 'One and a half to the Arcade,' said my grandmother sweetly, a quarter-of-an-hour later, as she handed the bus conductor 3d. I just hoped it wasn't going to be those awful cushion covers all over again.

Shopping with my grandmother seemed inseparable from visits to the Public Library. It had just been moved from the Lyon Street School and was now under the old Water Tower (Water Tower Building, London Road; now shops), where it had been opened in 1930 after some well-chosen words from the Sussex author and journalist, S.P.B. Mais. So, while she changed her books (a Baroness Orczy for an Ian Hay; an Edgar Wallace thriller for something a shade less harrowing by Francis Brett Young), I used to pass the time thumbing through the current issue of Arthur Mee's *Children's Newspaper* – in its day, an incomparable publication – or turning over a few pages of the *Illustrated London News*.

Her literary tastes satisfied, we returned to an animated London Road blooming with holiday makers pouring from the railway station and choked with slow-moving traffic as we began our meandering progress through the shops. Nearby Isted's (corn chandlers, 22 London Road; now an opticians) could usually look forward to a visit from my grandmother: 2 oz. of ginger beer yeast, a packet of ant-killer and bag of locust-beans for her deserving grandson. Needs such as Epsom Salts, Gibb's Solid Dentifrice or a new head for the O'Cedar mop pointed us towards Timothy White's (chemist, 42 High Street; now a building society and a travel agent) – recent suppliers of our first rubber hot-water bottle. Then it was on to 'Style, Taste and Economy' at Mace's Gallery (house furnishers; now womenswear) at 25 London Road for a runner for the dining table. And more intense discussion about those dreaded cushion covers!

The Home and Colonial (41 London Road; now a drapers) and World's Stores (grocers, 15 High Street; now a hair and beauty salon) were two well-known multiples, seldom off my grandmother's list, which – for some reason – still remind me of Bird's Custard and boiled Empire prunes. Another hardy perennial was Pink's (No. 5) in London Road – also a grocer (now a record store). A sure sign that one of the Hampstead Aunts lay in the offing was a visit to Osborne's (baker's, 47 High Street; now an amusement arcade) for 'fancies' and a Dundee cake – otherwise it was the fallow of current buns and Chelseas. Then, if Nana suddenly remembered my father was coming for the weekend, I was lugged along – waving aside the advancing street photographer – as we made for the great sides of Sussex beef that swung in Harnett's butcher's department in their London Road shop (No. 14/16; now a chemist); three-quarters of a pound of rump steak and a few saveloys. And while we were there, why not pop over the road to MacFisheries (fishmonger, 7 London Road; now a building society) – if we could find a gap in the solid barrier of parked bicycles – for a pair of kippers for our late tea? In 1935 we noticed a rather splendid new grocers had opened up at No. 31: Sainsbury's (now womenswear).

A shop that enjoyed a semi-permanency on my grandmother's itinerary was Staley's (1 London Road; now Seasons, still a women's outfitters) opposite the Arcade in the High Street. Well, a chap could do worse than spend half-an-hour watching their overhead 'whizzers' – you know, those containers running on wires which used to whisk the customer's money across the ceiling to some far-off counting house before they came zinging back with the change. It was also to those whizzers that I looked to divert my eyes from my grandmother's bravura performance when she purchased her under-garments; the holding up to public view of all kinds of articles of dubious purpose in order to study colour, quality and fol-de-rolls, and to snap the elastic parts.

If, on the hastily contrived grounds that 'we hadn't time', Nana showed a granite-like imperviousness to my innocent suggestion that she might care to join me in a turn down York Road for a quick glance at Goodacre's toy-shop window, it was odds-on that she had in mind a new pair of shoes. Then the morning was as good as written-off, as the floor of Dutton and Thorogood (3 London Road; now a health food shop) became knee-deep in empty shoe boxes as she worked her way through their stockroom. And if she couldn't find her broad fitting there – merciful heavens! – there was the certainty of a repeat performance at Stead and Simpson's (35 London Road; now a travel agency) – if not an encore at Freeman, Hardy and Willis in the

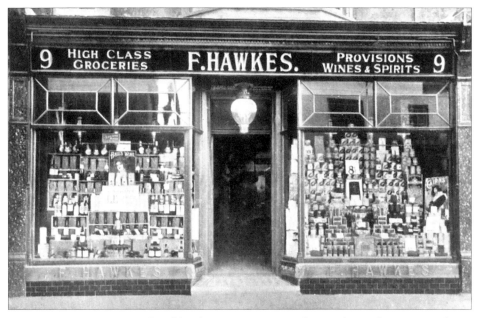

38 Dressing a grocer's window like this was an art. Hawkes in the High Street is where Wonnie once did so much of her shopping.

Arcade (No. 2; still a shoe shop). My reproachful yawn comes from hours of practice in lady's shoe shops!

In those days, we seemed to live in perpetual thrall to the Bognor Regis Gas and Electricity Company. This used to entail the long walk to their showrooms in Argyle Road (now flats), a shrine dedicated to New World gas-stoves and Ascot geysers, until, in 1936 – when Town Gas still had that suicidal fume – it was re-offered to the ebullient Mr Therm. After passing the time of day with the cashier, my grandmother used to write out a cheque in her copperplate hand while I built card houses with the gas-fire brochures.

From Argyle House it was only a few steps to Mr Geoffrey Wood, watch-maker and jeweller, in his cosy and clock-filled shop at 33 The Steyne – little changed, it seemed, since 'Est 1896' – to have a decrepit alarm clock awoken from its own long sleep. (33 The Steyne is now flats.) Next, Mant's the pork butcher in West Street (No. 3 Goodwood Place, currently vacant), where sawdust covered the floor and festoons of the better class of sausage and pig in all its guises of pink dismemberment covered everything else. Two mouth-watering pork pies and half a pound of streaky bacon added to the weight of the slave's basket. Then, from Mant's, it was back to Webster and Webb's in the High Street (stationers, No. 61/65; now estate agents and an optician) for a copy of *Weldon's Weekly* (for cuttings of my mother's sketches) and, while she was there, had they one of those little pipette things for filling her Swan fountain pen? Oh yes, and some Stephen's ink.

39 In the early 'thirties Hansford's new premises in London Road was one of the most eye-catching shops in the district. Access to the Public Library in Sudley Road was via a passage to the right of the showcases.

Our shopping trip was drawing to a close. With a bit of luck, our last stop would be the Bijou café in York Road (since demolished); a coffee for Nana and a strawberry ice-cream and a wafer for her drooping basket-carrier. Ten minutes later, with her on the lower deck and me on top in one of the front seats, we were on board a No. 50 Southdown bus on our way to Slated Barn.

However to see shopping as an art form, it was really necessary to observe my grandmother in action when the family was down in full strength, augmented perhaps by our embonpoint Aunt Kate from South Wales. Then Nana was called upon to victual the family at institutional level. For this she required the use of my father and his car to take her to Buckle and Clidero's door in the High Street (grocers, No. 23; now an off-licence). A fine display of deference ensued as the manager showed her to a cane chair from which she could conduct her business in comfort. And I could fidget on one leg with plenty of time to ponder how it was possible to spend ten minutes contemplating the c.v. of a tin of sardines. For every item had to be discussed at length embracing aspects of quality, quantity and price; each considered decision was then solemnly noted down in a duplicate book by means of a stubby pencil that required constant licking to make any sort of mark.

Tate and Lyle's 'gran.' was weighed out from a sack, poured into a blue paper bag and bumped three times upon the counter before it was folded and closed. Encores followed for the semolina and tapioca. Next, a pound and a half of English butter (slightly salted) was scooped from a mountainous feature and cowed into half-pound portions with corrugated wooden spatulas – oh, sweet-remembered, splodgy sound! Then it was time for a short entr'acte to touch upon the iniquitous/glorious weather we were suffering/enjoying.

Play was resumed with a pound of New Zealand cheddar being garotted from its parent drum by a sinister wire loop; for the want of anything else, not unexciting in its way. Then 12 oz. each of Osborne and Garibaldi biscuits were rehoused in paper bags from a terrace of Huntley and Palmer's glass-roofed tins. Negotiations followed in respect of 'Peterkin' peas, a tin of Fray Bentos corned beef and four cubes of Foster Clarke's dehydrated oxtail soup. Oh yes – she nearly forgot – and a tin of 'Sailor' salmon. One by one the items were crossed off my grandmother's list.

40 Mr Joscelyn Hansford out for a spin in his new Allday and Onions tourer in 1914.

At last came the *coup de grace*, the high-point of the expedition. After sharpening a long, homicidal-looking knife on the steel tied round his waist, the manager, with surgical precision, pared the requisite number of slices of sweet Wiltshire ham onto a piece of greaseproof paper and placed it upon the Avery scales for financial reckoning. And think of it: not a sheet of plastic in the shop!

To complete the order, a bottle of Gilbey's Invalid Port was tucked into the corner of one of the cardboard boxes. Half-an-hour after my grandmother had entered the shop, the completed order was carried out by a youth in a long white apron and deposited in the back of the waiting Citroen, un-hampered by yellow lines. The best place to appreciate my grandmother's mode of shopping is at Tesco's checkout, as one fights a losing battle between stuffing an avalanche of purchases into plastic bags with one hand while searching wildly for the Connect card with the other!

Compared with Nana's victualling expeditions, being taken shopping by my mother was an altogether more rigorous experience. For one thing, it wasn't just shopping. Haircuts at Campbell's saloon in the railway station got included, too. 'But I only had it done the other day,' I protested. 'No dear, that was six weeks ago – it looks an absolute mane.' Then there were those 'it's for your own good' things. How well I remember that 'surprise' appointment – but only to me, I may say – she made with Mr Sams the dentist, whose surgery and gurgling spitoon were at Bedford House in the High Street (now a building society). 'Open wider, there's a good chap' … and suddenly, as if by foul magic, in his hand was the dreaded drill. But that's what 'it's for your own good' jolly well meant!

On another occasion, I was dressed in my most comely gear and carted off to have my photograph taken by the artistic Richard N. Haile at his 'Sign of the Ikon' studio in Lennox Street (now an estate agent). Oh, but the preceding palaver: brilliantine, combs, flannels and scrubbing brushes. Really, it might have been Cruft's! Yet, although the results delighted my mother, to tell the truth, they came as a bit of a shock to me. Did I look like that, honestly?

Quite often our wanderings were in quest of raiment; to Herbert Mell's, in Linden Road (No. 3, menswear; now stationers and insurance brokers) for a 2s. 6d. pair of short, grey-flannel trousers was a familiar slog. So were the intermittent visits to Baker's in London Road (No. 17; now a health food shop) for a new mac, my mother being more sensitive to a few patches and choc-ice stains than her son. The trouble was it meant being 'tried on'. And to being 'tried on' I had a pathological aversion. Baker's, though, had one redeeming feature: their double mirrors. Quickly I discovered that if one stood just so, it was possible to see hundreds of oneself disappearing into infinity … infinity … inf … 'Wake up, dear – and *do* try and pay attention. Now, do you think it fits you?' It was a question which always foxed me. For apart from being a shade cleaner, it always looked exactly like the one I had just taken off. '… 's alright, I s'pose,' I would respond graciously, hoping that it would be enough to bring to an end the whole disagreeable business of being 'tried on'. Why my mother didn't simply dress me at jumble sales just points to the blindness of maternal love!

In 1936 a wave of civic pride swept through the town when word got out that we were soon to be gilded by a new branch of Marks and Spencer's to be built on part of the site of Ivy Lodge in London Road (No. 4; now Little-woods). Just think of it; Bognor, a 'Nothing Over Five Shillings' town! It was like being made 'Regis' all over again but twice as useful. As soon as it was opened, the sweetly perfumed stores with its polished maple floor was placed firmly on my mother's visiting list. Gradually, Cardinal Wolsey underwear was vanquished by St Michael as he hovered over more and more of my wardrobe. My first wrist-watch, too, came from Bognor's Marks: five bob.

But when she cast her professional eyes over the outstanding value offered by their mass-produced women's clothes, my mother was only too aware that one day it would mark the end of the exclusiveness of a fashion market upon which her reputation had been built. Even so, she would agree that M&S's skirts and blouses, together with Smith's Corona typewriters, had achieved more for women's independence than any of the shenanigans got up to by Mrs Emmeline Pankhurst and her Suffragettes.

For a long time the name over the art shop (Gough Bros, art shop, 71 High Street; now a gift shop), tucked away in what, long ago, was called Little High Street, puzzled me: how ought it be pronounced? So I sought that source of all enlightenment: 'Gough's dear,' she replied crisply. 'But,' I responded vexatiously, 'why not like in "plough" or as in "rough"?' There was a long silence. Then she-who-bore-me spake thus: 'Dear child, whilst the absurdities of English pronunciation deserve of long and profitless discussion, you will observe how your mother is up to her neck trying to finish off this sketch of a lady in a flowing tulle gown in order to catch the last post to London. So, for the moment, frankly, I am quite impervious to what you call them – Gow-Guff-or-Goff! Now, off with you and leave me in peace – and shut the door! And comb your hair!' So, that was how the new multi-hyphenated name for Bognor's art shop found its way into the family's lexicon and is the way we speak of it to this day.

41 Percy Stubbs' grocery shop and the Victoria Park Post Office at the corner of Charlwood Street in West Bognor. Today, its exuberant advertising painted out, it is Smith's, the dispensing chemists.

42 Wilmott's West End Garage, c.1933. The rear part of the building was formed from one of White and Thompson's flying boat erection sheds brought over from Middleton.

Not far from Bognor's art shop was Cleeve's the chemists, at 60 High Street (now NatWest Bank). Coming out of their shop one morning, my mother put her hand on my head and screwed it towards Reynolds' showrooms on the other side of the road. 'That is Lady Diana Cooper, the well-known actress, and her little boy – but don't stare dear, it's terribly rude.' Of course, 'the little boy' grew up to become the 2nd Viscount Norwich, better known to those TV viewers and radio listeners who have been enthralled by his historical documentaries and music programmes as John Julius Norwich. In those days the Duff-Cooper's spent part of their scintillating lives at West House at the end of Barrack Lane.

And while indulging in a little harmless name dropping, I should mention having seen Charles Laughton and his actress-wife, Elsa Lanchester, strolling by the tamarisk hedge at Aldwick, Jack Hulbert and Cicely Courtneidge putting pennies into the stamp machine outside the High Street Post Office and Middleton's Charlie Kunz, of syncopation fame, having tea at Leslies' Popular Restaurant. Oh yes, and Chesney Allen in a beach-wrap at a party on the shingle near Aldwick Hundred at Craigweil. That a well-known Yankee prize-fighter wrote in my autograph book 'Maxie Baer, your pal' doesn't really count, as that was at the London Zoo. But it all hints at the star-studded company I kept in those days!

Geography dictated that we should do a lot of our shopping in West Bognor which, in the 'thirties, had still the feel of a small village community. It was the scene of one of my earliest memories when my mother bought me a celluloid windmill from Cumming's (stationers, 4/5 The Parade; No. 5 is now a fish and chip shop), at the time I was minded to cut a dash among the local beach-society on the sands at the end of Nyewood Lane. I can also remember her shopping next door,

LESLIES'

Popular Cafe

& Restaurant

33, 35, 37 HIGH ST.
BOGNOR REGIS

Largest and Leading Caterers in the district

Officially Appointed by R.A.C.

CARS PERMITTED TO STAND

43 Advertisement for Leslies' Restaurant.

at Anthea's, the greengrocers (3 The Parade; now an insurance brokers) which had the eccentric notion of selling eggs by weight.

In West Bognor, as elsewhere in the country, most of the shops were family businesses. If it said 'J.G. Ragless, Fishmonger and Dealer in Game' (2 The Parade, now DIY) on the fascia, one could rest assured that Mr Joe was inside, filleting his plaice or trussing-up a few pheasants. So it was with Edwin Thorpe, the chemist, dispensing physic from his pharmacy in Aldwick Road (now a print shop); Mr Targett cutting up lamb chops at 1 The Parade (now a pottery shop); or, indeed, Abe Bradbury, the tobacconist, weighing out his ounces of Dark Virginia Returns (71 Aldwick Road, currently vacant).

With the introduction in 1935 of one of the new Belisha crossings in Aldwick Road, pedestrians suddenly found they were able to extend a statutory right to bring traffic to a shuddering halt as they smugly strolled across the road to the The Broadway, where they might have found Mr L.J. Wade the jeweller (9 The Broadway; now an estate agent), trying to stuff a bit more tick into my mother's gold Asprey watch, while enjoying the aroma of freshly baked cottage loaves that seeped out of Colborn and Wingate's bakery at No. 8 (now a video shop). Other shops on that side of the road were Robert's, the stationers (5 The Broadway; now a betting shop), and Achille-Serre (dyers and cleaners, 2b The Broadway; now an engravers) where my mother had the habit of arriving to pick up her curtains cleaned and dyed into a state of colourful respectability without the all-important half of her ticket.

Another port of call in the Broadway was at Miss Elsie Cripps' little sweetshop (2a The Broadway; now a chiropractor) for a topping-up of our reserves of pear drops and Packer's Chocolate Crispets. Poor Elsie could not have known that she was destined to be killed by a bomb which fell in Annandale Avenue on 11 April 1941. Back on the south side of Aldwick Road stood the boldly arched façade of Norman Wilmott's West End Garage (No. 65; now a car showroom) into which he had moved in 1922 after leaving the old Fire Station in Waterloo Square where, in the closing years of Queen Victoria's reign, he had started his success story by hiring and selling bicycles. Gazing enviously through their showroom window at £399-worth of gleaming 2-litre, Weymann-bodied Rover or at young Bernard Wilmott's 12 hp saloon (in which he and his co-driver, Ken Croxford, had taken part in the 1936 Monte Carlo Rally) was recognised therapy for a lad condemned to a morning's parental shopping in West Bognor.

Another remnant of our 1930s world was H.R. Pennicott's (outfitters, 73/75 The Broadway; now a furniture shop), whose forebears had tilled the soil of Pagham and Lagness since the 1740s, until his branch of the family took to the millinery and women's outfitting trade during the First World War at premises in York Road. During the 'twenties they spread out to West Bognor, where their shop stood to the west of Wilmott's Garage. But when it was over-built by Tom Tregear's Blackmill Building in 1930, they found themselves re-jigged in one of the smartest double-fronted premises in Aldwick Road. Just before the last war Pennicott's sold my mother a green Jaeger coat which lasted her until clothing coupons had become only a memory in the post-war world. And I nearly forgot to mention my good friend, the late Mr George White, the ironmonger (83 The Broadway; vacant), to whose temple of nails, putty and fish-glue I was a regular pilgrim and whose contribution to my early cultural development cannot be overstated.

Lastly, we come to West Bognor's grocers, two of them, both on the north side of Aldwick Road. On the corner of Charlwood Street, where Smith's the chemists now dispense their NHS prescriptions, stood the premises of Percy Stubbs, High Class Grocer, his integrity underwritten by a squeaky wooden floor, a red coffee-grinder and an all-pervading smell of gorgonzola and dog-biscuits which spread selflessly into the contiguous cul-de-sac of the Victoria Park Post and Telegraph Office. He could also boast a bus-stop named after him; 'Stubbs's Corner please', we used to say, as we handed the bus conductor our pennies.

44 Targett's delivery van in about 1925. The driver's name is Andrew Court.

Yet, it is the other grocer, whose premises were be found further west, next to the Bailey Convalescent Home (Aldwick Road; now a retirement hotel), who shall detain us a little longer. For one glance at his shop, with its glazed arcade and sumptuous window displays, was enough to conclude that here was a business built up by no run-of-the-mill proprietor. So even my most skeletal album of West Bognor recollections cannot remain inattentive to Thos. Tregear (grocer and butcher, 84 Aldwick Road, now a convenience store), the entrepreneurial and far-sighted patrician, without whose aspirations and achievements, as the next chapter shows, the town would have been the poorer.

So, over the years, my mother, often with her two (and, later, three) sons in tow, became a familiar sight among West Bognor's little community of traders and shopkeepers. Generous with their credit, swift to our doorstep on their delivery bikes and assiduous to lift their trilbys to her in the street, they would inquire after our Nana's rheumatism, speak favourably of her offspring and exchange opinions on the prevailing weather pattern. And that, my mother would have confided to the reader, was a privilege not afforded to her anywhere she shopped in London.

The changing trading pattern of shops in Bognor

The 51 shops in Bognor (this excludes the first three non-shops in our list) patronised by our family in the 1930s is a very individual sample, but it reveals the great changes that have occurred in their trading pattern over 65 years. Of the 51 shops, 43 had changed their trades, with eight continuing wholly or partly in the same one. These eight comprise two garage/cars and one each of chainstore, convenience store (but replacing a family grocer), stationer/newsagent, shoes, womenswear and the Victoria Park Post Office, which continues to trade under the same name in premises still recognisable from the 1930s.

None remain of eight family grocers, three butchers, two bakers, two cafés, two fishmongers, two menswear, two sweetshops, two toyshops and two watchmakers, and also lost are one each of corn chandler, dentist, dry cleaner, greengrocer, general clothier, library, photographer and utility. Even Gough ('Gow-Guff-or-Goff'), the art shop in the High Street, and George White, the ironmongers in Aldwick Road, have recently ceased trading. Only one remains of three shoe shops, but while three chemist, three stationers/newsagents and one furniture have opened in other premises in our sample; and while one womenswear continues, two others have opened.

Trades newly represented in our sample include three estate agents, three building societies, two hairdressers/beauty, two travel agents, and one each of amusement arcade, bank chiropractor, draper, engraver, fish and chips, gifts, insurance broker, off-licence, optician, pottery, records/CDs, removals and retirement hotel, together with a number of trades unheard of in the 1930s: betting shop, computers, DIY, health foods, print shop and video.

Four premises are converted for flats or other use, one is demolished, and three are currently vacant. Because of shops combining or dividing and problems of definition there may be minor inconsistencies in these figures.

7

Tregear's

The story of a family firm

During the 1930s the Silver Queen buses,* 'Scratcher' Mather's sandy etchings on the beach, the pleasure boat *Bluebird* chugging its way to and from Craigweil House, and the name 'Tregear' were all synonymous with Bognor Regis. Walk where one would, in Station or London Road, or on either side of Aldwick Road in West Bognor, at Pagham or in Felpham – one was never far from the patronymic TREGEAR displayed above their grocery and butcher's windows or from the fascias over their estate agent's offices. Flag-boards bearing their signature flew wherever land and buildings were bought or sold. And it was all the work of proprietor Thos. Tregear.

Yet, how did a name born of Cornwall's rufous soil come to stake a claim on Bognor's yellow clay? Part of the answer, of course, has to lie in the wretched condition of the Cornish tin and copper mining industries, brought about by the collapse of prices in the latter years of the 19th century. No less gloomy was the agricultural scene in this 'fourth part of Great Britaine' as the new steam-operated ships, many of them refrigerated, began filling the nation's larder with the produce of prairie and pampas. The result was an outflow of tens of thousands of miners, farm labourers and folk dependent on their wage packets, who now sought employment in Scotland, Wales and in the outposts of the Empire. But one family from St Just chose to travel less adventurously and was content to cross the Tamar into Devon; yet, even here, they seem to have run into trouble.

Around 1880, before the laws of England discouraged this sort of thing, we find Thomas Tregear's schoolteacher father, William, his wife and 12 children, thrown out of their home and left to wander the streets of Averton Gifford, near Kingsbridge. The reason? The schoolteacher's appointment lay in the gift of a peppery and despotic Squire, and he'd got wind that William had been writing around seeking another post. This would teach the teacher a lesson, impudent fellow!

However, William's attempt to better himself seems not to have gone unrewarded. For he is next to be found as the headmaster of a school in East Meon in Hampshire on a salary of £130 a year, with his son, Thomas, apprenticed to a grocer in Southsea. And it was while young Thos. (as he became known) was in those parts he met and paid court to a comely young lady 'in service' by the name of Elizabeth Refoy, whose parents lived in Bognor.

* The Silver Queen bus service, running between Bognor and the Eastergate area, was started by a Mr Walling in 1919. By the 1930s so popular was the route that on some evenings there were as many as five 'last' buses from Bognor! The route was sold to the Southdown Motor Services Ltd in 1944.

That this young Methodist came to our town in order to ask for his beloved's hand is as much conjecture as the hunch that his entrepreneurial instincts had already told him the grocery trade was the thing to support a wife. Nor is it beyond the bounds of reason to suppose that, while he was in Bognor, he spent a little time looking round the district, sizing up the competition and inquiring of the local wholesalers' terms, as well as weighing up the 'carriage trade' against the proleteriat. Perhaps Thos. also lent an ear to the salutary tale of the collapse, ten years earlier, of Arthur Smith's grandiose Victoria Park Estate scheme in West Bognor. Yet, it must have seemed clear to him that the town's westward growth was only a matter of time. It was the niche for which he was looking. In the meantime, he kept his eyes open for a tent in which an under-capitalised young man and his equally young wife might one day rest their weary heads. What is not conjecture, though, is that on 17 May 1892 Thomas and Elizabeth were married at the Methodist church in Southsea.

From all accounts, not much more than a tent was their first home and front-room shop at Bognor: some tumbledown farm buildings in Nyewood Lane on the north-west corner of what was shortly to become its junction with Shelley Road. To draw attention to his enterprise – and with no advertising control regulations of which to fall foul – Thomas had painted on the roof in large white letters, the words 'Nyewood Stores'. The year was still 1892 and he was two-and-twenty.

In spite of the shop's sequestered location, business was brisk. So much so that they had to take on another pair of hands, a youth by the name of Billy Allen. Soon the Tregears' capacity for hard work and the attention they paid to their customers' needs was rewarded with a balance sheet in the black: £20 profit in the first year and £50 in the second.* With the passing years Tom's capital grew. Eventually he was in a position to look for premises more prominent to the public eye. In about 1900 he bought a couple of plots of land next door to the Princess Mary Home in Aldwick Road. And in less than a year he was ensconced in a brand new shop with, above it, a flat for his growing family, Reg, Tom junior and Marion, with three more to come: Jack, Phil and Peter. To his new home he put a name with the ring of substance, Penrith House.

It was a courageous step. For on the other side of the road there lay only a cornfield – once Bognor's racecourse and cricket field – and all that separated his shop from the sea. Casting his eyes beyond the newly built Arthur Home in Aldwick Road towards the distant trees of Aldwick village, they would have encountered only meadowland, a scene he would have shared with my mother during her first visit to Bognor in 1904; pretty to her, profitless to him.

With the Nyewood Supply Stores in such an exposed position, Tom soon encountered a vexing problem. During the summer his premises became ferociously hot, while in winter the violent Channel gales were prone to mistake the shop's roller-blinds for the sails of a ship. So he arranged to have

* In 1996 I met Thos. Tregear's daughter, Mrs Marion Sleeman, then in her 97th year. She told me that in spite of these healthy figures, her father was haunted throughout his life by the fear of bankruptcy which, in those days, was a condition cloaked in shame.

45 Penrith House, 1904. Tregear's new premises in Aldwick Road are already enhanced by a glazed canopy.

erected over part of his forecourt a glazed canopy supported on slender cast-iron columns. It proved a brainwave. For not only did it protect his window displays and shelter the customers, but it also imparted an air of distinction to his premises. It was as good as a trademark!

To begin with, Tom divided his shop into three; the groceries department in the west, the family butchers in the east and, between them, a fish counter managed by a young lad by the name of Joe Ragless and assisted by Billy Allen. Twice a month, Tom used to make his way to Barnham market to buy sheep and cattle which he then drove, foot and hoof, back to Aldwick where they were penned in a field in Victoria Drive. Meanwhile, he bought a slaughterhouse in Gravit's Lane and, in 1905, opened another grocery shop at 10 Station Road. Thos.' eyes were now set firmly on his ultimate ambition, to become the town's grocer and butcher *sans pareil*; indeed, nothing less than Bognor's equivalent of Fortnum and Mason, catering for the needs of the growing influx of 'carriage trade', though it can hardly have escaped his notice that more and more of the carriages now had petrol engines!

While all this was happening, not far away, Tom's nephew, an aspiring young builder by the name of Herbert Seymour, had begun covering the local cornfields with rows of houses, a sight which, no doubt, warmed the cockles of Thos.'s heart as he watched Richmond Avenue and Tennyson and Shelley Roads grow into existence, each house and family a potential customer in his ledger.

Back in his Aldwick Road shop, it used sometimes to cross Thos.'s mind how much more profitable his enterprise would be if his growing list of well-to-do credit customers didn't choose to close down their houses for most of the year. So, in a spirit of enlightened self-interest, he set about encouraging them to enter into the 'furnished lettings' business.* What was more, he promised their owners to find them 'the right sort' of tenant. At first, the headquarters of his embryonic West End House Agency was a desk in the butchery department run by his book-keeper, a Mrs Booth who, it turned out, showed an unusual aptitude for dealing with furnished lettings. Soon the little sideline began to overflow the boundaries of its desk.

Two inter-related events in 1912 were to influence the future shape of Tom's business. The first stemmed from the purchase of the eastern end of the cornfield nearly opposite his shop by the local builder, Mr Leonard Booker. Booker's plan was to build on it a parade of shops incorporating a glazed canopy at pavement level. Already his architect, James Worrell of West Street, was at work on the drawings.

The second concerned young Joe Ragless, who was showing signs of restiveness. For it turned out that Thomas wasn't the only one in Aldwick Road to be fired with ambition. This Ragless lad, too, it transpired, dreamed one day of becoming his own master. By 1913, on the other side of Aldwick Road, Mr Booker's shops were about to come on the market. Perhaps it was lucky that fishmongering was not a trade that Thomas took to with much relish. At all events, he not only released Joe Ragless from his employ, but gave the lad a measure of assistance in setting up his business under Booker's new glazed canopy. And a canopy of such cast-iron splendour that one is tempted to believe Joe may have felt it outshone the one he had just left!

With the fish department gone, there was more room for the House Agency 'desk' which had meanwhile grown into a counter. With the assistance of Billy Allen, Tom was now able to reorganise his stores for the two trades he knew best, butchery and groceries, yet the truth was that more and more his mind was becoming preoccupied by his house-letting business.

By 1914 he had realised his dream of being Bognor's pre-eminent grocer. With pride, he claimed that he held more lines, allowed more generous credit and employed more staff than any of his competitors. At the same time, with an eye to succession on the house-letting side, he had his eldest son, Reg, articled to a firm of surveyors at Southsea. Then, in that fateful August, Tom's *annus mirabilis* came to an abrupt end with the outbreak of the First World War. Almost immediately Tregear's had to surrender four of their five horses to the Army's horse lines in Waterloo Square. As soon as they were old enough, Reg and Tom junior volunteered for the Sussex Yeomanry – with the Gallipolli landings their prospect.

* As early as the 18th century, 'house agencies' were often departments of firms associated with quite different trades. At Bognor, Charles Knowles, besides dealing in furniture and funerals, were estate agents and valuers. Reynolds in the High Street pursued much the same line. Mr Mace was another furnisher who ran a property department. A curiosity was Lewis Peacock, whose property business was run alongside his taxi firm. Webster Webb, the stationers, also dealt in property. Grocers in particular appear to have found it a profitable sideline. Buckle and Clidero, Leverett and Frye, F. Hawkes and Percy Stubbs in Aldwick Road all gave it a try. But none developed their estate agency departments as successfully as Thomas Tregear.

Gradually, General Kitchener's 'Your Country Needs You' exhortation reduced Tom's staff to a skeleton. Nevertheless, well before the national scheme for food rationing came into force in 1918, Tom had instituted his own arrangement to ensure fair play among his customers for goods in short supply. Slowly those four ghastly years dragged by until, at last, on 11 November 1918, the Armistice was signed. We can only guess the relief felt by the devout Thomas Tregear as he thanked his Maker for the safe delivery of his two sons from the recent carnage. But now it was down to business again.

First he articled Philip, his fourth-born, to a firm of surveyors and auctioneers at Eastbourne. Next he applied his mind to two problems: one was that the Aldwick Road shop could no longer accommodate his burgeoning house-letting business. The other was his wish to give Reg a decent start in life. In London Road, at No. 10, a moribund estate agent's office was on the market. Short of a lavatory, it was going cheap. Clearly, it could solve both problems. So Tom bought it.

Soon, Tregear's name was on the fascia and his two sons, Tom-the-Younger and Jack,* were put to work inside keeping the show going with interminable cups of tea and a primitive index system, pending the day that Reg could take his finals of the Auctioneers and Estate Agent's Institute and claim the manager's chair. Meanwhile, for calls of nature, a hasty path had to beaten to Newton's, the ironmongers on the other side of London Road! In 1920 Reg Tregear became a fully fledged member of the AEAI and duly took command of the London Road office.

At Aldwick Road the post-1918 shape of West Bognor was beginning to unfold. The old cornfield over which Tom had looked for all those years had long disappeared behind The Parade and other commercial and residential developments. Now opposite his stores was Wilmott's West End Garage, full of Rover motor cars. It wasn't the cars that interested Tom, though, but the piece of land that lay west of their premises. In 1922 he bought it, and shortly afterwards his nephew, Bert Seymour – by now one of Bognor's major building contractors – began erecting a pair of single-storey shops separated by an arched passageway.

As soon as they were ready Thomas put young Jack to run the Aldwick Road stores and promoted the middle-aged Billy Allen to manage the Station Road branch. Now he and Mrs Booth were free to move themselves and their property card index across the road to become the West Bognor office of Tregear and Sons, Valuers and Estate Agents. Meanwhile the second shop was let and became the West End Café.

By 1926 Edwin Thorp's allotments on the north side of Aldwick Road lay buried under the shops of The Broadway, a spectacular essay in the nailed-on Feudal style, an architecture close to the hearts of the property-developing classes. Westwards from Tom's old rival, Percy Stubbs, who had gone into the house-letting business too, nearly all the original villas on the

---

* Young Tom eventually found his feet studying under Professor Harold Laski at the London School of Economics before forging an academic future for himself in Hong Kong and China. More predictably, the late Jack Tregear went on to a distinguished surveying career in the Ministry of Works, besides being of the greatest assistance to the author in writing this chapter!

46 The Parade, West Bognor not long after it had been built by Leonard Booker in 1912. The unifying effect of the glazed arcade on a group of diversely designed shopfronts is notable.

north side of Aldwick Road had given up the battle for residential gentility and had become either shops or boarding houses.

But Tom's energies were still far from spent. In 1929, now with an option on the shop site to the east of Tregear's office, then occupied by H.R. Pennicott's the outfitters, he instructed Bert Seymour to commence the incorporation of his single-storey estate agency and the café into a new and much enlarged three-storey edifice to be known as Blackmill Building – only the arched passage and Pennicott's new, double-fronted shop being left to explain the riddle to a later generation of architectural historians!

The following year, it was the turn of Thos. Tregear's Grocery and Butcher's Shop for a facelift. Soon Bert Seymour was at work again, banging in beams and taking out walls. Perhaps Tom was still piqued at being out-arcaded by Booker. At all events, the existing shelter was demolished and replaced by a far grander construction covering the whole of his forecourt. It had green-tinted glass and richly decorated columns supporting a shapely fascia bearing the Tregear name in bronze classical letters. The Parade couldn't hold a candle to it!*

The late 'twenties marked the apogee of Tregear's Stores; their smartly tiled stall-risers, the distinguished arcade, the sumptuous window displays,

* It is quite deplorable that both these delightful glass arcades have been allowed to deteriorate to the extent that one has disappeared and The Parade looks likely to follow it.

cornucopian shelves and the smell of freshly roasted coffee that spilled over the forecourt all contributed to the enhancement of a West Bognor that had become an established and prosperous commercial centre. And that was how I remember it when I first set my un-sandalled feet on West Bognor's pavements after we came to live at Aldwick in 1929.

These must have been among Tom's happiest years, watching his six children making their way in life. Reg was successfully running the estate agency and enjoyed his hour of fame when he received the royal command to auction some of Her Majesty Queen Mary's expensive trinkets at one of Mrs Ricardo's fetes in aid of Pagham church. Tom must have been just as proud when Reg, a gifted musician, was appointed organist at the Methodist church, where in due course his evening recitals became a popular tradition.

As they entered the 'thirties, with their flag-boards flying in nearly every thoroughfare in the district, Tregear's had become one of the largest and most respected firms of valuers and estate agents in the town. Reg had also started developing in his own right. Already he owned Central Buildings in London Road, built to the design of Stanley Hennell FRIBA, whose offices were over Osborne's, the bakers in the High Street, and other schemes were under way. So, in spite of the enervating effect of the slump, the future must have seemed full of promise. It was all an object lesson in how 'tall oaks from little acorns grow'.

Although Tom never sought political office, his far-sighted views and business acumen benefited a wide spectrum of local organisations. Where he believed the town's best interest to be at stake he was fearless in speaking out with a voice which was heeded by the Council's Great and Good. As early as 1905 he opposed the placing of Bognor's sewage outfall at what he considered an inadequate distance from the beach. He was as acerbic in his opposition to building the new Town Hall in 'the backwater' of Clarence Road in 1929 as he was in favour of turning the Brooklands at Felpham into a municipal park a few years later. As a founder member of the Bognor Bowling Club, Tom was instrumental in persuading the Council to allocate part of Waterloo Square – hitherto used for penning sheep and cattle awaiting slaughter in the nearby abattoirs – for much-needed bowling greens. Marine Park Gardens in West Bognor was another town improvement for which he campaigned ceaselessly. In 1936 his castigation of the Bognor Regis Ratepayer's Association for opposing the Bathing Pool scheme opposite Colebrook Terrace, heartened many of his fellow citizens – even though it was not enough to sway the outcome.

The affairs of Bognor's Methodist church also accounted for a lot of Thos. Tregear's time. In 1924, when it was decided to build a new church in the High Street, they must have been grateful for his treasurership and sage advice in what was a considerable financial undertaking. And it was in that role he was often called upon to greet Joseph Rank, the miller – old 'Holy Joe', the arch-Methodist from Hull – who could always be relied upon to leave a sovereign in the collecting plate. Later, Tom was appointed Sunday School Superintendent, a position he held for many years.

Then, early in 1932, the Tregear family received disquieting news: Reg had become seriously ill. Slowly he deteriorated until, in September 1933,

47 Thos. Tregear, entrepreneur.

he died at the tragically early age of thirty-eight. Tom was devastated, but at least he could look to his youngest son, Phil – now a qualified surveyor and auctioneer – to take over the London Road office and, eventually, the whole business. But perfidious fate had not yet done with poor Tom. For slowly it was becoming clear that the sun that had shone so benignly – at least until recently – upon Tregear's the Estate Agents, now showed every sign of setting upon Thos. Tregear the Grocer and Butcher. For even in the early 'thirties the pattern of food retailing had begun to change significantly as the 'multiples' became more aggressive, with forms of marketing not easily matched by the smaller grocer.

And not only that. For Thomas's 'carriage folk' had long been in retreat from the onslaught of less exclusive families staying for their annual fortnight's holiday in the town's hotels and boarding houses. Those who chose to stay in furnished lettings tended to remain loyal to the same multiples that they used in their home towns. In the summer the influx of cars bringing thousands of families laden with picnic hamper and Thermos – not to mention the 'ruinous trippers' down from London on third-class returns – added hardly a penny to Tregear's weekly takings. Yet lowering his standards – standards which had not always been as profitable as they might have been – was not within Tom's nature. But perhaps the deciding factor was that there was no family successor with any interest in the grocery and butchery trades.

So it was not only the effects of advancing years, the anxieties of the slump and the tragically early death of his eldest son which eventually persuaded Tom the time had come to divest himself of his stores. The first to go was the butchery department, sold to Leonard Ley in 1933. Then, late in 1936, Cullen's purchased the grocery businesses in West Bognor and Station Road. And it was in the latter shop, where the elderly Billy Allen had been retained as manager, that there occurred a poignant turn of events which resulted in his sending a letter to the press.

It began with a short paragraph in the *Bognor Observer* of 13 May 1936 to the effect that Mr Allen was about to retire. The following week Billy had this dignified valediction printed in the same paper:

> Mr W.H. Allen, late of Thomas Tregear Ltd. of Station Road would like to correct the statement published in last week's Bognor Observer. He has not retired but has had his services terminated by Thomas Tregear's successors. It has been a great wrench, the severing of ties of a quarter of a century and he feels it is his duty to publickly [sic] thank the many kind friends who have given him their support during all those years. Coming from the Aldwick shop in 1911 (where he and Mr Ragless, now the fishmonger of West Bognor worked successfully together for Mr Tregear) he made new friends and also retained the

48 Tregear's new estate agency office in Aldwick Road, 1922. In 1929 it was over-built by the present Blackmill Building.

confidence of old ones, and it is to one and all of these, dating from 1895 to 1936, he tenders his most grateful thanks.

Under Phil Tregear's guiding hand, the estate agency continued to grow as the country climbed out of the slump. In 1937, to cope with the flood of houses being built in the Bognor district, they added an office at King's Beach, Pagham, to their existing branches at Middleton and Felpham. During the 'thirties, Tregear's were involved in many well-publicised property transactions: the Crescent shop development in Nyewood Lane, the Water Tower Buildings in London Road and the Odeon shops not far away.

1937 was also the year that millions heard for the first time, through their fret-fronted wireless sets, the Fuhrer's rasping voice. The Sudetenland, Mussolini and the sinister Axis; inexorably the clouds of war were gathering over Europe. After Mr Chamberlain's fateful broadcast, on 3 September 1939, estate agents enjoyed a flurry of activity as Londoners, fearful of a rain of bombs on their city, sought the safety of the south coast. Seven months later another flurry accompanied their precipitate departure as the Wehrmacht and Luftwaffe drew up their battle lines on the other side of the Channel and the country girded itself for imminent invasion.

But after that sun and bomb-soaked summer in which schoolboys and housewives learned how to make Molotov cocktails and much of Bognor was designated a Defence Area, the traditional work of estate agents slowly dried up. Now it was a matter of survival. Phil took a part-time job with the District Valuer's office at Havant, where he was involved in war-damage work as well as preparing 'a schedule of existing condition' of Bognor Pier before the Navy took it over and re-named it HMS *St Barbara*. But there wasn't much gravy in that – nor in anything else. In fact, Phil once confided to me that that there were times when he thought of closing the office.

Nevertheless, with the end of hostilities, Tregear's were quick to face the challenges of a post-war property market, which the majority of estate agents had every reason to believe would be simply a re-run of their pre-war experience. But by the 1960s they had good cause to change their minds. As people struggled to get into 'bricks and mortar', 'Chez Nous' became regarded no longer as merely a home and shelter, but as a wealth-creating device bought with easy money and increasing in value daily as the economy succumbed to the distortions of inflation. Soon, estate agents were having to deal with 'gazumping' and discontented clients caught up in a 'chain of buyers' as they sought their dream of a bungalow in Bognor's rapidly growing coastal suburbia.

Then, with the 'seventies, backed by the banks and insurance companies, a new breed of mega-estate agencies began prowling the High Streets seeking small family firms whom they might devour. It was now a large business, and for many estate agents an uncomfortable time of mergers, amalgamations and uneasy liasons. Phil dipped his toe in its muddy waters for a short time … and couldn't wait to get out. By 1972 he had had enough. On his 70th birthday he retired and his partner, Peter Hickman RN, DSC, took over. But within a few years the compelling need for rationalisation again asserted itself. In 1980 Tregear's became associated with Phillip Barrett, the Felpham estate agent. Sadly, two years later, Peter died suddenly. And within a few months the trading name of Tregear had vanished from the public's eye for ever.

Thomas, who had started it all from those tumbledown premises in Nyewood Lane in Queen Victoria's reign, lived to see his town change out of all recognition – although only the purblind would have considered it for the better. He died at Southsea in his 92nd year in 1962. But at least he was spared the knowledge that his mighty oak held no title to immortality.

8

Journeys down Stane Street

and a ghost in galoshes!

'Bognor' now commenced from the moment we left our house in Isleworth for the long twisting journey down to our bungalow, with Nana, her Abergelly puddings and Aldwick Beach and the roar of the shingle caught in the undertow.

It is those hundreds of night-time drives, often in winter, I remember best. At about half-past seven on most Friday nights my father used to start the Citroen so it could 'warm up'. Then he'd lock the front door of the house, get into the car and engage bottom gear ... it was the first slight movement of the wheels that nearly always caused my mother to utter an anguished cry, 'Oh, my dears, did I turn the gas off?' Or had she bolted the french windows in the breakfast-room? Or she'd forgotten to bring the skirt my grandmother had promised to lengthen. To get away first go was an unusual thing. But, at last, enveloped in the blue haze of my father's Abdulla 777 cigarettes and fortified with a bag of Nuthall's Mintoes and a block of Rowntree's Motoring Chocolate (not forgetting the half-potato for de-misting the windscreen), we made our way to Twickenham and Teddington where we bade farewell to the red London trams before heading for Bushy Park and the new by-passes skirting Leatherhead and Dorking.

Beyond the *Burford Bridge Hotel* and the Holmwoods, N and S, the lamps of civilisation began gradually to flicker out until, by the time we had passed the little flurry of lights of the *Red Lion* at Ockley Green – decreed by my father to be our half-way mark – we had entered a velvet-black envelope sparsely dotted with the pallid lights of isolated mansions, cottages and farm houses. In the course of those journeys my brother and I became familiar with every twist and turn of the route, every village, farm and hamlet, their road signs, pubs and bridges – especially that wicked little hump-backed bridge at Slinfold over which we regularly left our tummies. Half asleep at the back of the car, we had only to raise an eyelid to pinpoint our exact position – more often than not to find we hadn't got even as far as half-way Ockley.

Some of the signposts whetted the imagination; how could that one near Billingshurst pointing to 'Gay Street' fail to conjure up a picture of roistering country swains and bewitching damsels dancing in a flower-strewn lane? Another, near Rowhook, directing road users to 'Friday Street' was shrouded in mystery – what was it used for on the other six days? And surely the folk of 'Adversane' were of more than common clay. By these clues did we measure the distance still to go before my mother claimed she could smell the sea which might have been anywhere after Hardham.

In winter, we often seemed to have the A29 to ourselves for mile after mile. In the unheated cars of those days, especially tourers like ours with draughty celluloid side-screens, it could be bitterly cold. My father had to wear a motoring coat and fur-lined gloves while the rest of us dressed like Arctic explorers. We tried hot-water bottles, but by Dorking they only made us colder.

In the early 1930s street lights were few; suicidal road junctions often rated only a single, seedy electric light bulb; 'cat's-eyes' were awaiting invention. Other hazards were unlit bicycles and straying animals. My father put his car into a ditch at Ockley trying to avoid some loose thoroughbreds in thick fog, and didn't get pulled out by a cart-horse until close on midnight. Pelting rain seemed to invite punctures.

By now we were running past Oakwood Farm with its verdant ditches, tailor-made for that time-honoured cry, 'Dad, can we stop – I feel sick.' My brother had yet to make up his mind. 'Oh, if only they'd get it over together', groaned my mother. Equilibrium restored, we pressed on to Denne Bridge where a hollow moan from the back seat replaced the usually loyal 'Hurrah' when my father announced we had crossed the border into West Sussex.

Onwards purred the Citroen; headlamps cleaving the dark night; taking account of the telegraph poles and the looping wires ... the looping wires; the spiralling leaves ... and the looping wires and flying things with silvery wings, then, suddenly, the slant of rain. Our pencil beams lit up the eyes of the farm cats, pried on the stoats, winked at the rats, leered at the rabbits and gave warning to all the other ditchfolk bent on those ill-considered dashes in front of our wheels. More than once dazzled barn owls sought martyrdom against our windscreen; foxes were as common as badgers were rare – apart from that show-off at Fair Mile Bottom which once posed for a few moments before escaping into the gloom. That we never ran over a hedgehog was due only to my father's eternal vigilance.

That much of our journey followed the path of one of the great road-building triumphs of our Roman predecessors was something on which, as Mr Weller might have put it, our knowledge was more peculiar than extensive. So the Second Alignment of that great trans-Wealden agger, dealt with so attentively (if, at times, less than accurately) by Hilaire Belloc, in his book *The Stane Street*, became 'The Straight Bit', and thus it remained until we were old enough to pay Roman roads more respect.

At last we arrived at the sharp left turn at Roman Gate which, as usual, tumbled the back-seat passengers into all-of-a-heap as we rejoined the other leg of our famous 'Straight Bit'. With the speedometer nudging sixty, we were quickly over the Arun's bridge at Alfoldean. But Dad, take care for we are fast approaching Slinfold's little switchback bridge over the Southern Railway's Horsham-Guildford branch line which even so never failed ... whoops! ... to take us by surprise.

Minutes later, looking – according to my mother – as if the Black Death still hadn't finished with it, Five Oaks came and went. Then, in no time, we were running past the ancient tea shoppes and *Ye Olde Six Bells Inn* of a shuttered Billingshurst, sharing half-a-dozen electric light bulbs with even fewer of its shadowy citizens repairing to their homes for an early night.

49 Looking north along a car-less Stane Street at Billingshurst in about 1936.

Onwards, southerly; past silent farms in manurey shrouds; past net-curtained aspidistras and china cats; past five-barred gates, with insomniac cows breathing sweet steam; past ancient trees and mysterious turnings, glimpses of seed-drills, ploughs and two-wheeled carts all awaiting dawn and another day of work. Slowly the miles unwound, overprinted by malodorous whiffs of spread muck, and by fleeting signs for Pratts and Spratts, for Wills Gold Leaf and Lipton's tea. From the rear seat came a wan voice: 'Mother, can I have a Mintoe?' But now Roger had decided that it was his turn to be sick.

With that little contretemps behind us, it wasn't long before our head-lamps picked out the Pulborough sign. Soon we were coasting down Church Hill towards its single yellowy street lamp which marked the sharp right turn towards the bridge, as into view came the tile-hung gables of the *Swan Hotel*. If, by chance, a deep depression happened to be stationery over West Sussex, that was where we used to get our first glimpse of Pulborough's Great Watery Spectacular! For then the overburdened Arun and Rother rivers reached up to nearly the tops of the old four-arched bridge as their waters began their inexorable march across the valley's floor, submerging the fence-posts, chasing the sheep to the higher ground and inviting our lights to dazzle the galleon-swans tacking across the water-meadows where store cattle had grazed only the week before.

If it didn't look too deep, my father used to chance his arm, sometimes putting back the hood so we could more easily watch the milky-brown water swirling between the wheels. The bow-wave of a Southdown single-decker bearing down on us from the opposite direction called for murmured invocations on behalf of our highly strung distributor. If, though, it had become too hazardous to get across, then the Pulborough bobby, in his waterproof cape, used to lean his bike against the wall at the bottom of the hill, and wave us to a halt with his red bull's-eye lamp and advise my father to go round Fittleworth way.

50 Pulborough Bridge from the south, looking towards the *Swan Hotel*. Until the present A29 road bridge was built to the left of the picture, just before the last war, it carried the main road to Bognor.

51 The Arun and Rother overwhelm Pulborough's causeway.

On an autumn night the reflections on the water of a full moon playing hide-and-seek behind a tracery of scudding clouds was enough to transform the inundated Arun valley into the stuff of poetry. Since 1936, though, a new bridge and a raised causeway has knocked that kind of sport out of the journey. After my father had tested the brakes with his usual punc-tiliousness, we pressed on through the night and Domesday's Hardham and serpentine Coldwaltham, where our beams impaled cloth-capped men with mongrels held on binder-twine as they left the *Labouring Man* to trudge the mugwort verges back to tied cottages smelling of rising damp and paraffin.

With Watersfield getting nearer, excitement began to mount. Might we see her tonight? For 'her' was surely a witch! Well, a strange old woman bizarrely clad in a hooded red cloak and wearing a man's heavy boots. She lurked in the ditches near the village common, and used to jump out and pull faces at the passing cars. In time she disappeared. My father thought she might have jumped out at one swiftly moving car too many! Anyway, in time we forgot all about her. Sixty years passed.

Then, quite recently, I happened to be leafing idly through Sandra Saer's delightful little book, *Coldwaltham; a Story of Three Hamlets*, and there she was! Our red-cloaked old witch! Apparently she was a well-known and completely harmless character by the name of Trottie Woods 'who used to milk two cows she kept in the Brooks'. A letter from someone who knew her says, 'Trottie was not so daft as she made out ... and did you know five hundred safety-pins were found in her clothes when Nurse laid her out? And – they say – £40 in gold sovereigns stuck on candle-ends.' Now, that is the stuff of which your true Sussex eccentric is made!

With Trottie behind us, our next landmark was Bury Hill where, late on a Friday night, we sometimes passed clerkly men from the City pushing their bicycles up its winding steep. With some weekend call of duty or pleasure on our part of the coast, they had left their London offices after work. One of them we knew, Ted Brown, who lived near us and worked in the Square Mile during the week. Pennies must have mattered. Anyway, be claimed, given fair weather, he could be with his wife at Aldwick before midnight. Once, when the hill was caught in torrential rain, we picked up a bedraggled Ted, tied his bike on the back of the car and somehow squeezed him in amongst us.

Rain was one thing but three unexpected inches of snow on the hill was quite another. If it hadn't been for some muscular Council workmen on that January night we'd have become stuck. But it was a lesson quickly learned. The next day my father went off and bought a set of snow-chains! If the moon which had cast its silvery spell on Pulborough's flooded acres was still on duty at Bury, it could transform Pepper's Amberley chalk pits and the Arun valley into an impressive panorama, a scene improved upon only by the red glow and lighted carriages of a steam train, timed to dash through Amberley station a few minutes after the real one we shall shortly meet.

Ever onwards we sped; Whiteways, Fair Mile Bottom – the scene of our encounter with that extrovert badger – then the sharp turns right and left at *Ball's Hut* which brought us to the conifer-lined Fontwell Straight. A mile further on and our headlamps picked up the recumbent lion on the War

52 The tail-end of the lion couchant war memorial at Eastergate. It was unveiled by the Duke of Richmond in December 1920 and is the work of the sculptor G.F. Morris Harding. The road to Bognor branches to the right.

Memorial at Eastergate, deemed to mark the beginning of friendly territory. Not long afterwards, a flickering red light in the middle of the road at Woodgate showed the level-crossing was closed, heralding the imminent approach of a steam train. Hurrah! Monotonous pleading bent the parental will; Roger and I were allowed out of the car into the cold night to see it go by. 'Be careful, dears; and don't climb on the gate.' Mothers – honestly!

Already we could hear the train ... and now we could see it! An 'Up' from Chichester, the locomotive's orange fire reflected on the billowing steam. Nearer and nearer, faster and faster, it pounded towards us ... until with a ground-quaking flurry of thrashing piston-rods, whirling spokes and a deafening roar, engine and train charged through the old 'Bognor' station and between the crossing gates, a split-second glimpse of driver and fireman silhouetted against the white-hot glare from the open fire-box, blurred images of passengers seen through hurtling windows. In the wake of the red light on the last coach, a confetti of leaves and spent bus tickets chased after the train as it clacketty-clacked into the night. Over the level-crossing descended a pall of sulphurous smoke.

In the nearby signal box, bells tinkled as the shirt-and-braces signalman pulled and pushed the giant levers. More bells; more levers. Now his hands gripped the big iron wheel. Hesitantly, the white gates opened; one by one, the cars started to bump across the glistening rails. In the distance the clacketty-clacks could still be heard ... just. Soon we were passing the Shripney sign where another familiar sight awaited us, the watery-yellow headlamps of the last Silver Queen bus returning from Bognor with its load of country folk, anonymous behind windows opaque with condensation.

53 Wade's clock in York Road by which we used to measure the time of our arrival in Bognor. This fine building was pulled down in the 'sixties.

Nearly home! And to confirm it we could see looming up before us the Bognor Gas and Electricity Company's monumental new gas-holder,* already a source of pride to this young night-traveller. How many other towns, I used to think, could boast such an imposing feature to mark their northern portal? At last we found ourselves in a nearly deserted Bognor. In York Road, Wade the jeweller's bracket-clock† showed it to be a few minutes before ten. A street lamp's glow fell upon a Pier Cinema billboard: 'Mother, could we …?' 'We'll see, dear.'

By now we were driving along a darkened and shuttered Esplanade, past Sait's Tea Garden, the Southdown Motor Company's little offices by the *Beach Hotel* and Billy Butlin's Dodgems at the end of Lennox Street. If a brisk sou'wester had ganged up with a high tide, we could look forward to a spectacular end to our journey. That was when my father used to stop the car near the Pier, where it rocked in the wind as the sea-spray slashed across its windscreen, while we watched the petulant white-topped waves colliding and exploding against the sea-wall opposite the *Royal Hotel*; a roaring, primordial scene to which our headlamps added a touch of the theatrical.

---

* The waterless gas-holder at Shripney was commissioned in December 1933. It held one million cu. ft. of gas and stood 150 ft. high with a diameter of 100 ft. In 1942 a crippled German bomber flew into it leaving a great hole in its side. The holder was demolished in 1989.

† After the building's demolition in the 1960s the clock was saved and is now on the Clock Walk mall, High Street.

54 Rough seas opposite the *Royal Hotel*. At night, lit by headlamps, it was an even more primordial sight.

Except for a forlorn street lamp at Hammonds Corner in Aldwick Road, the last part of our journey was completed through utter darkness until we glimpsed the welcoming light left burning in my grandmother's bedroom window. In the bungalow's drive, four figures eased themselves stiffly out of the car, stretched their limbs and inhaled deep draughts of fresh sea air. 'Like wine', exclaimed my mother. Meanwhile, young Roger had rushed to the front doorbell to let Nana know of our arrival. Soon we were engulfed in a fusillade of hugs and kisses.

In front of a blazing coal fire, it was time for a re-run of the events of the journey; the unfolding of news from the Great Wen and family tittle to be tattled over tea served in Woolworth's cups and ham sandwiches cut with Doré hallmarked silver knives. In our bedroom, stone hot-water bottles warmed the beds of two young boys barely able to keep awake.

Once we were safely in bed, it was quite on the cards that conversation in the living room would turn to the supernatural … or, at least, to South Avenue's peripatetic ghost! It began in 1930 when my very level-headed grandmother was living in the bungalow on her own. One autumn dusk she was quite sure she saw walking past her bedroom window a strange-looking fellow – a seaman, she thought – wearing old-fashioned clothes and sea-boots. She was intrigued enough to go outside into the road to have a second look. But he'd gone, disappeared into thin air, which was strange because in those days the bungalow was in the middle of a field. There were no other houses; no other hiding place. Vainly, she awaited his return. Understandably, she was a trifle apprehensive and told my parents of her strange experience when the family came down the following weekend. She was half-convinced that she had seen a ghost!

Of course, my father pooh-poohed the whole thing. Her old sea-dog – or whoever he was – had probably pushed his way through the hedge at the end of the road and gone on his way across the fields. Soon my parents forgot about it. But not Nana. Although rather deaf, my grandmother used to claim there were certain sounds she could 'feel' rather than hear. And, apparently, ghosts in sea-boots was one of them. At any rate, from time to time she used to tell my parents of her having 'felt' the sound of heavy footsteps outside the back door – usually around midnight.

A few years later – after South Avenue had filled with bungalows – my mother happened to be staying at Aldwick with Nana. Late one night, while she was reading in bed, she suddenly heard the sound of footsteps 'like dragging sea-boots', first from outside in the front garden and then from the public footpath to the village which, in those days, ran quite close to the bungalow. Then they stopped abruptly. She woke my grandmother and together – rather bravely! – they walked round the bungalow with a torch. Nothing!

Shortly afterwards, my mother happened to relate her experience to our next door neighbour. To her surprise, Miss Morgan expressed relief that she had not been imagining things! For she, too, had heard these strange footsteps. Her description tallied with a man 'in heavy sea-boots'. Once or twice more my grandmother or Miss Morgan claimed they had heard our nocturnal visitor. But at last 'he' – or 'it' – disappeared. Or so we thought.

The war came and went. We boys had grown up and Nana had died many years earlier. Then, one moonlight night, late in 1950, when both my parents were in bed, my mother heard a sound which caused her to sit bolt upright! It was those still-remembered sea-boots! My father heard them, too. They seemed to come from the road. With commendable *sang froid* they whispered a stratagem to take this – well, whatever it was – by surprise! My mother crept to the front door, my father to the back. Simultaneously, they flung open both doors and peered outside. But, alas – or perhaps just as well! – they beheld no glowing apparition, no bodiless pair of seaman's boots nor any other vaporous thing. Just a douche of cold night air. They looked over the fence and even walked a few yards along the road in their dressing-gowns. Again, nothing.

And that was really the last we heard of Aldwick's incorporeal seaman. Perhaps, finally, he'd taken umbrage at forever being jumped out at.* Some years later my mother was reading Lindsay Fleming's *History of Pagham in Sussex* and was intrigued to come across a short paragraph in which he relates the singular experience which befell Mrs Emily Croxton Johnson at Paradise in Dark Lane. Apparently, while she was trimming a hat, she had cause to look up and was astonished to find herself peering at … the ghost of a sailor! Well, what are we to make of these spectral sea-boots that came to tease us? Or, more to the point, how many ghosts lived between Dark

---

* This story of Aldwick's ghost(s) appeared in a shortened form when my mother gave an interview to a *Bognor Regis Post* reporter in about 1956.

Lane and South Avenue? One – or two? My mother must have been thinking in the singular when she wrote:

> On through the night tramps the sailor of Aldwick;
> Keeping a tryst that is never to be.
> Looking for one who has gone on before him;
> Seeking a cottage that lay by the sea.
>
> DMA

It was upon Stane Street – a little south of Five Oaks on the A29 – that my father had the the pleasure of meeting the Queen of England. It happened in this way. One afternoon, in the spring of 1929, he was driving the Singer on his way to Aldwick when, at a place where the Council were repairing the road, a policeman waved him into the verge. Nothing sinister; Queen Mary's car, taking her back to London from Craigweil, was due to pass by.

Quite soon the Queen's unnumbered maroon Daimler came into sight … and that was the moment Murphy's Law arranged for the shafts of a tar-boiler to fall down, slap in the path of the royal progress. Her Majesty's car drew to a dignified halt exactly opposite my father and only a few feet away from him! For such an eventuality he was ill-prepared. What book of etiquette offers guidance on how a Loyal Subject should honour his Queen from a sitting position in a car surrounded by roadworks? The steering wheel precluded a bow, his lack of uniform a salute. Then the obvious occurred to him. He raised his trilby! The ice was broken; the Queen let fall upon her Loyal Subject a regal smile. Then they were on their respective ways, one to forget about it before she reached Dorking, the other to remember the occasion for the rest of his life!

9

New Neighbours

and Roger tries out the Dame School

For a long time the family lived in splendid isolation, the only bungalow in an unmade-up South Avenue. Then, one day, some men came to hammer white stakes into the field next door. And within a few weeks builders were at work digging out the foundations for some new bungalows. When they disappeared at weekends we quickly discovered there was no better place for games of cops and robbers – and all its variants – than the piles of sand, bricks, unsteady scaffold-poles and water-logged trenches of a half-completed 'mod bung in slct nbhd'.

On the men's return, the sound of the bricklayer's trowel brought the faithful apprentice to his side … 'Can I have a go, please?' Alas, the mortar slid off the trowel; the brick leaned ominously and daylight showed through the joints. Clearly, some of those bungalows were not as well-built as their owners might have fondly imagined! But soon the growing walls left the yellow clay behind, and within a short space of time they were ready for their Marley-tiled roofs and rising-sun front doors. Then, a few weeks later, up went the estate agent's flag-boards. And the next thing we knew was that we were surrounded by a lot of new pebbledash neighbours.

Living as we did on the rim of civilization, my brother and I were deeply touched by the sight of these elderly, retired strangers arriving in Aldwick Gardens; friendless, wretched from their travels and quite untuned to the Aldwick outback, its traditions, customs and protocols. So, with youthful earnestness, we were resolved to help them make a go of their new lives in South Ave.

The first intimation of the Good News that awaited these unsuspecting couples was usually when, unannounced, we called upon them just as the removal men had started unloading their pantechnicon and the newcomers were frantically trying to remember where everything was meant to go. Indeed, it was at such moments of crisis that we were wont to offer our 'help'.

Thus, between carrying in the trouser-press and the Harry Hall barometer, we were able to divulge how they could buy their Tizer and sarsaparilla from the Aerated Water Company's lorry which lurched along South Avenue on Saturday mornings; we insisted they make a mental note of the time of the last Red Rover bus from West Bognor, and recommended Mr Bartholomew at the bottom of the road for re-charging their wireless batteries. And we bet they didn't know they could pick up bottles of milk from Aldwick Farm until half-past four in the afternoon.

Eventually the removal men collected their tips and departed. But it must have been a great relief to these disoriented incomers to see that we showed no signs of following them. Perhaps – quite inadvertently – we gave the impression that we wouldn't mind being invited to a glass of Robinson's Barley and to demolish a plateful of their Custard Crèmes while we carried on with laying the foundations on which these innocents might yet come to live a fulfilling life at Aldwick.

Sitting on their packing cases with our mouths full of biscuits, we were able to instruct them on how to blow a bird's egg, the advisability of picking the dewy horse-mushrooms in the footpath field before 6 a.m. and the undoubted superiority of the large, glossy blackberries that grew in Yeoman's Acre. Our counsel flowed unstoppably: the best ditches for catching newts, how to tell a Hawker Fury fighter from a Demon bomber and where they could buy gobstoppers.

Within our remit lay the state of the tide on Aldwick Beach and a little help on the best kind of seaweed for telling the weather. We touched lightly on the crustiness of Colborn and Wingate's Coburg loaves; the name of the paper boy; we plugged Mrs Duffin for her paraffin, Mr Burchfell for shoe repairs and Mrs Gates, over in the village, for broken biscuits. Unstintingly, we offered an up-to-date commentary on the forthcoming attractions at the Pier and the Picturedrome cinemas with the date of the Pavilion Dog Show thrown in for good measure. And while we were there, would they care to see a demonstration of our Dinky Toy racers on their freshly laid linoleum?

At last they'd had enough. Wasn't our mother expecting us back for lunch? … perhaps we might care to call again after they had settled in … shouldn't we be down on the beach in such lovely weather? The sighs of relief as our worn-out neighbours closed the door behind us must have been audible! So why these oppressed newcomers didn't rise up and sue our parents on the grounds of their offspring's nuisance, invasion of privacy, pedagoguery and the detrimental effect we were having on the value of their bungalows, remains a mystery.

On the contrary, within a few months – and much to our parents' surprise – we had accumulated a whole retinue of elderly and forbearing friends extending from one end of our puddly road to the other: the Misses Warren at Thelma, Mr and Mrs Bowtell at Medina and Milverton's next-door Miss Morgan; there were the Barkers, the Hazleriggs, the Marshes of Little Clandeboye, not to mention the kindly Mr and Mrs May whose house remained nameless due to its not being even finished. It was a poor morning that didn't find us stuck into 'tenses', 'elevenses' and 'twelveses', seated in some neighbour's kitchen in exchange for a demonstration of glider-catapulting in their back garden. Neither did it prevent them giving us rides in their motor cars, nor from taking our photos with their Brownies.

Opposite Thomas Tregear's arcaded grocery business in Aldwick Road, the jovial Mr George White had opened his ironmongery shop not long after we came to to live at Aldwick. It coincided with an upward nudge in my pocket money and the licence to travel unaccompanied to West Bognor. Invariably, I celebrated my new-found independence by paying a bare-footed call upon Mr George, with whom I shared a common interest: nails. In fact, according to my mother, my early cultural development appears to have mainly evolved around nails. It was she who reminded me of the resultant catalogue of hand-wrought artefacts, still memorable for their lack of self-conciousness, absence of superficial decoration and refreshing freedom from the thrall of accurate measurement.

Unbridled sawing, hammering (and bandaging) brought forth a series of bridges, railway stations, coffins for sparrows and a tortoise's sarcophagus. Pencil-boxes were produced on the same line as coffins but distinguished therefrom by their hinged lids and the application of my initials in gold transfers. A little putty helped keep the pencils in. Nor should go unrecorded that scaled-down Mappin Terrace tailored to the smaller beast – in this case a hedgehog – which ungratefully absconded before it was finished.

But all paled when measured against my *chef d'oeuvre*, the Great Silver Fort of 1933. From the rude joist-ends, pieces of purlin and off-cut skirting-boards donated by the nearby building sites, and six ounces of three-inch wire nails weighed out by Mr White himself, there arose on the floor of the loggia – where it was most easily tripped over – this famous Military Construction. It boasted castellated ramparts and towers; there were slits for arrows and/or boiling oil, and a portcullis with brass hinges. With pride, I viewed the informality of its component parts, the subtlety of its leaning entrance gate and the teasing out-of-plumbness of its buttresses. So it was rather disappointing – and no fault of Mr White's – that when my mother came to test its table-crushing weight, it caused her to exclaim with unusual vehemence that it was quite the most unlovesome thing she had

55 Looking east along Goodman Drive (now Marine Drive West) in about 1935. The GPO telephone kiosk must have been a quite recent arrival. Famous for its ice-cream, the Marine Café is on the left. The building opposite the second lamp-post is the *Mill Hotel*, which was partly destroyed by a bomb in the last war.

ever clapped eyes upon and summarily banned it from entering the house. The silver paint that took a twelvemonth to dry didn't help either.

More nails, four-inch ones, provided both masts and 16-inch guns for a long line of men-of-war, hewn intuitively from off-cuts of 4 x 4 roof purlins, which, when launched in the goldfish pond or upon South Avenue's puddled lakes and inlets, invariably developed incurable lists to port or starboard as well as filling our hands with splinters. Mr White's nails also played a seminal role in securing the spindles and wheels of an extended range of home-built carts in which my brother's felicitous imitation of a horse's neigh condemned him to hours of pulling me round the garden path. With a bit of luck the wheels used to stay on until lunch-time – unless we were rash enough to venture out among the fissures, crevices and flinty crags of South Avenue, in which case their life could be measured in minutes.

But it was the groping for mastery over those simple materials which was the important thing, quite apart from the satisfaction of standing back to admire (uncritically) something one had created with one's own hands. Factory-made things may have looked more polished, but they lacked the essential satisfaction of wresting the whatever-it-was from the raw material, as well as the feel of nails, saw, hammer, chisel, splinters, a little blood and the occasional finger-stall – not to mention the resinous smell of sawdust and the ever-popular aroma of boiling fish-glue! So, in direct contrast to his aversion for dropping coin in the begging bowl if he thought it was for something out of a factory, my father exhibited a never-failing willingness to stump up the cash for the raw materials needed for anything we made with our hands, for which I am eternally grateful.

With the rising sap of May, ice-cream equities began to surge as word got around that our car had passed the Shripney gas-holder. In those days, when ice-cream was still an occasional treat and not merely part of the national diet, utmost bliss could be defined as consuming anything – pink or white – stuck on top of a cornet or slithering around in a Sheffield-plated bowl. Well, not quite anything. For the fact was that our first and undying loyalty lay with the Antarctic Ice-Cream and Cold Storage Co. Ltd, of Waterloo Square, behind whose walls the father of a friend of ours, Dennis by name, enjoyed a position of profit.

It came about that this young Dennis had acquired a nepotistic lien on a white-enamelled pail full of broken, hideously deformed, inside-out choc-ices which stood by the factory door. From time to time he would invite his friends – amongst whom my brother and I were proud to be counted – to gather round this sticky morass, from whence he generously doled out its viscid contents. And thus did we eat of Antarctic ice-cream until it threatened to come forth from our nostrils and became loathsome in our sight – if only until the next day!

Another source for serious ice-cream was the Marine Café (now the *Waverley* pub and restaurant) at the bottom of Nyewood Lane. There, it could be inhaled as well as eaten. From under their glazed canopy, my mother used to order her cryptic glass of 'milk-and-a-dash-of-coffee'. But, for my brother and I, it was the hard stuff: a double strawberry ice, trickled over with a crimson unguent.

Then, after suggestions regarding a second helping had been neatly blocked by my mother's ever-ready mantra, 'It'll only spoil your appetites, dear,' the bill was paid and we set off home. If the tide was in, we used to wander along to watch the workmen putting the finishing touches to the newly emerging Marine Park Gardens, or to call on the Gray's Huts fishermen for a half-pint of Bognor prawns.

Another of our ice-cream meccas was Sait's Tea Garden on the East Parade; '40% real cream', claimed management. It arrived in electro-plated bowls with two wafers and the added luxury of a linen napkin. At 4d. a time, it lay on the brink of parental means. At Saits, though, it had to be shared with the wasps; a sharp yell and my mother had to rush off to Timothy White's for some healing salve for her boy! At the top end of the ice-cream market stood Leslie's Popular Restaurant in the High Street. The sweet aroma of toast and coffee, its smartly dressed waitresses and wood-panelled walls all smacked of the carriage trade. So did their prices. Wicked, we thought, 6d. for a mere double scoop! So we only wiped our feet on their mat for birthdays or to impress the Hampstead Aunts. And that was at the heavy cost of being well hosed-down and our hair savagely combed and marinated in Anzora. School blazers, too. Otherwise, our only hope of getting into Leslie's was if my grandmother's bunion played her up after she had dragged us through Mace's and Reynolds' in her perpetual quest for cushion covers. On the Esplanade we used to meet our old tricycling acquaintances from London: Messrs Wall's of Acton and 'Eldorado' of somewhere slightly obscure. Their coming was heralded by a decorous tinkle on the bell and they seldom ventured into the rough puddles of Aldwick Gardens. But when they did, 1d. for a triangular Snofrute might just be mustered if the two farthings and a ha'penny could be disentangled from among the marbles, Yo-Yo and the speedboat key down amongst the pocket fluff.

So, I daresay no passer-by would have looked twice at a boy, in a pale blue shirt, sitting on the shingle by the Aldwick tamarisk hedge on a soft pearly morning in the late summer of 1932; a lad with a sagging strawberry cornet in one hand and turning the pages of *The Adventures of Huckleberry Finn* with the other. A chap oblivious to the passing strings of riding-school horses; unseeing of the beach show staging being erected on the sands nearby; deaf even to the Avro roaring overhead pulling its Bile-Beans banner. From beyond the horizon came the *basso profundo* 'aahwooomphs' of the Owers fog-horn as it tried to drown out 'Tea for Two' played on a *cor-anglais* two breakwaters away, but I expect that I was only half-hearing of those, too, what with all that bliss: the strawberry cone, old *Huckleberry* and Sussex's James Langridge's 104 against Kent.

When my father returned to London with the car the family had to make shift with the buses. In those days there were two companies that served Aldwick: the Southdown Motor Services, whose Tilling-Stevens single-deckers went to Barrack Lane, and the Red Rover,* a small private

---

* Mr Tate started the Red Rover company in July 1922. When the service was sold to the Southdown Motor Company in October 1932 there was a condition that required the continuance of the children's 1d. return fare between Pagham and Sefter School. For many years this was honoured by Southdown.

concern owned by Mr George Tate, the coal merchant, whose drivers and conductors were more renowned for their courtesy than his dark-maroon 16-seat vehicles were for their springs. From a garage in Havelock Close, they ran the Felpham-Pagham route – with a return trip to Chichester each weekday. One of their traditions was stopping anywhere on the road to put down and pick up passengers. Another was the gallantry they extended to my grandmother; when pouring rain turned our road into a quagmire, they used to divert from their scheduled route along Aldwick Road and instead drive up into Aldwick Gardens, nearly to our bungalow, in order that she wouldn't get her shoes muddy. I can picture her now, in her cherry-trimmed hat, being helped onto dry land by a respectful conductor. Today he'd get the sack for such a charitable action!

Although the Southdown buses were more modern than the Red Rovers, in the early 'thirties many of the former still had open upper-decks. With the close of the frog-spawning season, it was something which exercised our imaginations and led to an interesting diversion. First, though, it meant a visit to my mother's store cupboard where she kept the haricot beans. In the Bottom Field, opposite Mrs Duffin's stores, stood the Rackhamesque elm, its giant limbs stretching across Aldwick Road. Below it was a bus-stop. Soon we were lying quietly along one of the branches. When the bus arrived we found ourselves only a few feet above an array of bald heads, Marcel waves and summer hats. Then, as the bus moved off, we released a sprinkling of haricot beans among the passengers. Just what ensued, we had no idea. Panic? Calls for sal volatile? A cry for counselling? Did anyone question why haricot beans should have fallen from an elm tree in mid-July? I only hope we didn't mentally scar for life any of those innocent holidaymakers!

56 The conductor of a Red Rover bus stops for a chat at the end of Sea Lane, Pagham. This is quite an early photograph, probably about 1925.

Of course, in those Politically Incorrect days the Law and Order lobby would have liked to see us caught red-handed and our ears soundly boxed. But as the only witness to our little escapade was Lillian Crockett's Shetland pony in the field below – and perhaps Mrs Duffin, looking through her shop door ... but, then, the reader will recall what valuable customers of hers we were!

And here is the story of a bus and a troubled conscience. Occasionally, I was expected to perform Good Works for my mother. Not infrequently it was an errand to West Bognor, often to Joe Ragless' shop in the Parade for herrings in the days when the 'silver darlings' cost only 3d. a time. It had long been the established custom that on these excursions I should receive an honorarium of 2d. for myself and 1d. for one way on the bus. This presented me with an early moral dilemma. For not only did I usually need 2d. worth of nails from Mr White, but I also suffered an uncommon craving for pear-drops. Conscience told me that the 1d. was really for the bus. However, a little lateral thinking (at which I was better in those days) soon persuaded me that, providing I got safely to West Bognor, then whether the bus company or I profited by the penny was of only academic interest. Anyway, I hoped it would be okay with God. Guiltily, I refrained from getting on the bus when it got to the Slated Barn. The moment it left, I set off trotting in its wake to the next bus-stop at Hammonds Corner ... and then to the next ... and the next. By the time I had got as far as Arthur's Home in Aldwick Road I felt the penny had fulfilled its purpose and, with reprehensible ease, shed my moral burden. After calling at Miss Elsie Cripps' sweetshop in the Broadway, to exchange the troublesome coin for two ounces of giant pear-drops, I made my way to Joe Ragless's, and from there to Mr George White. Earnest in the service of my mother, and with a carrier-bag full of herrings, a pocket bulging nails and a mouthful of pear-drops, I returned home along the beach conquering each breakwater as I came.

1932 was a memorable year in other ways. For not only was my mother hectically busy in her London studio, but she had also let it be known that my brother and I might expect an addition to our family in the quite near future. Meantime, she remained at Isleworth while my grandmother and Ellen Williams – our new maid from Rose Green – continued to look after us at Aldwick. It was all veiled in mystery. But at last Nana received a telephone call from my father breaking the news that we now had a new brother.

A week later, carrying a blue bundle, and to the accompaniment of much female cooing and murmurs of 'how like his father', my mother arrived back at at Aldwick. Apparently this one was to be called Julian. After he had been decanted into his cot, I was allowed a closer look. This time I knew what to expect: bald, unironed, leaking all round and surrounded with gripe water, Bengers and tins of talcum, Julian at six days looked as unpromising as had Roger. Bowling us leg-breaks on the wasteland looked a long way off. Although, to tell the truth, I felt a sneaking pride in being seen wheeling him across to the village in his new pram.

Julian's arrival prompted some family rearrangement. So it was decided that Roger should stay with our grandmother at Aldwick and, for a few terms, attend the village school at 7th Cottage, run by the late headmistress of Sefter School, Miss Edith Clear. Each term-time morning, my brother – now Aldwick Farm-trained to be fearless of cows – used to weave his way among the puzzled beasts, as he crossed the dewy footpath field that separated our home from Aldwick village. Soon he was merged with the local *jeunesse* clutching their precious half-made raffia mats, raggy dolls and glass marbles (the stripy kind wrapped in grubby hankies), as they skipped, dawdled and scuffed their way down the long garden path that led to Miss Clear's seat of learning. For a description of its single, low-ceilinged classroom I have to thank Roger. Stone-floored, he says, and smelling of cheese, mid-morning cocoa, rising damp and, in winter, of camphorated oil. The only other feature in the room he could recall was a black-tongued cockatoo, which gave out ear-splitting screeches.

Miss Clear's curriculum included teaching her pupils to read with the help of gaily coloured ABC books and to write (particularly pothooks) on slates with squeaky slate pencils. In pursuit of numeracy, they recited their multiplication tables in sing-song unison and furrowed their little brows trying to grasp the mysteries of short division, explained with the aid of an abacus (for, in those days, teachers taught the hard way). When winter drew her icy patterns on the window panes, he tells me, Miss Clear used to move her pupils to the cosy warmth of her kitchen, where a large iron kettle murmured on a black-leaded range.

It was while my seven-year-old brother was attending the village school, it was found, to the family's shame, that he had been dabbling in an unacceptable enterprise. Each day, on his way to 7th Cottage, Roger used to call upon Mr Roberts, proprietor of the village sweetshop, to buy a 1d. chocolate wafer biscuit for break. One day he noticed a clematis looped over the fence of Almora, Mrs Firminger's house, next to the footpath. Being a sweet-natured child (he assures me) he picked one of the flowers and presented it to Mr Roberts. Much affected by this cherubic gesture, the kindly Mr Roberts responded open-handedly with a Sharp's toffee. Obviously this was a profitable practice to be made full use of, and so it was until it came to the ears of Miss Clear, who saw it as verging on blackmail rather than charming spontaneity and brought the career of a promising young conman to an abrupt end.

With the arrival of the winter holiday, it became the custom to deposit me with Nana and Roger at Aldwick, our parents and little Julian coming down just for occasional weekends. Scarved, gloved and double-socked, Roger and I spent a lot of our time scouring the deserted, wind-swept beach for flotsam and jetsam to lug home for Nana to admire and my father to burn in the incinerator come the summer, six months later.

Between kicking our soggy, half-inflated football about on the wasteland next to the bungalow, skirmishing with Billy Gill and his gang from West Avenue, a few visits to nearly empty cinemas and completing a large jigsaw puzzle of a steamship called the *St Julien*, we still found time to follow closely the fortunes of a deep trench which moved slowly along Aldwick Road, where the Bognor Regis Water Company was laying a new water main.

57 A solid-tyred Tilling-Stevens open-top-decker, on the Southdown 31 service, prepares to leave Worthing for the bumpy ride to Bognor in the 1920s.

Then there were the customary calls on Aldwick Farm for a little winter cow-thwacking and a climb up into the 'hollow oak' to see the world from a different angle. And while we were in those parts, it would have been perverse had we not tested the Duck Pond's icy surface over its shallow depths to see whether it would bear our weights. Thus, by the time we arrived home – after a numbing five minutes trying to get my brother's greasy Fairy cycle chain back on – both of us were stiff with cold and fairly waterlogged.

To restore our flagging circulations, Ellen or my grandmother used to make us mugs of cocoa while we sat round the fire toasting crumpets and listening to *The Wind in the Willows* and the catchy music of Roger Quilter, introduced by Uncle Mac, on Children's Hour from Daventry. At last, thawed out, it was Lott's Chemistry time for me and reading-aloud time for Roger – *Stalky and Co*, it being his turn for Kipling.

So, by the time the effluvia from my experiment had seeped through the bungalow and we had had our supper, played a game or two of dominos for matchstick stakes and had a go on the bagatelle board, the mantlepiece clock was creeping inexorably towards our bedtime. It was at such junctures, with the wind soughing in the chimney, that my grandmother, sitting in her armchair in front of the flickering coal fire, her ear-trumpet by her side and a ball of wool on her lap, would complain bitterly of the draught from the French doors ('would one of us be a dear and fetch her shawl from the bedroom?'), while she darned our socks on a boxwood mushroom. And that was the moment, to stave off the finality of bed, we were wont to chant that time-honoured cry: 'Oh, Nana, please tell us a story.'

Well, she'd consider it if we were very good and went to bed without the usual pillow fight; and if I didn't tie the ends of my brother's pyjama legs into knots; and if I cleaned up the kitchen after my malodorous chemistry experiments. Also, we were both to promise not to abandon our bicycles on the garden path for her to fall over.

Nana could draw upon an inexhaustible fund of stories – although, of course, none were about Bognor. Yet, I feel honour bound at least to mention them. One, I remember, was how she had gone skating and eaten hot chestnuts on the Thames at Hammersmith during the great freeze-up of 1894. Then, a few years later, in 1901, she recalled paying her last respects to Queen Victoria as the funeral train passed through Acton station on its way to Windsor. Nana had seen barefooted children begging at Shepherds Bush and watched a dancing bear on Turnham Green. Still fresh in her mind were memories of crossing-sweepers and going for rides in Hyde Park in Aunt Clara's carriage before anyone had heard of motor cars. She could even remember, as a girl, travelling on Brunel's 7ft.-gauge Great Western Railway when she went to stay with her aunt at Aylesbury.

A spine-chilling story she used to tell was of a German airship* which she had seen caught in the searchlights over Potters Bar in Hertfordshire when she was staying with her cousin, Winifred, during the Gotha raids on London in 1916. Suddenly it burst into a great orange ball of flame, broke in two and slowly fell to earth near Cuffley. 'Oh, my dears, those poor men; it doesn't bear thinking about – after all they couldn't help being Germans.' But by far my favourite story was about an heroic street-cat – or rather a roof-moggy – which my grandmother, as a little girl, had seen crawl four times across the parapet of a burning warehouse in the City to rescue its kittens. She claimed there was not a dry eye amongst the onlookers at this feat of feline heroism. The effect on me was just the same!

And there were many other tales, such as that of their new puppy: Nana began to find little pools on the kitchen floor, there was gentle chiding, and the pools were wiped up; the pools continued and the discipline became firmer. Its nose was pushed into a pool and it was given a smack, but nothing seemed to work. At last she confided to their maid that these continual little pools meant the puppy would have to go. 'Oh, ma'am', replied the maid, ' I'm so sorry, but that's me filling up my hot-water bottle.'

Two brief glances she gave us of our grandfather: the first was of him crossing Richmond Bridge on the top of a bus and being astonished to see his spaniel Music trotting over the same bridge on some affair of his own and five miles from home. In those days dogs (and children) were so much freer to roam on roads that had none of today's traffic hazards. And there was his teasing witticism, spoken lovingly to Nana as they went past the church where they had been married, that it was the church he had gone into once too often!

But real life had to break in, and the next thing I remember was being loaded into my father's car for the bleak Sunday night journey back to a new school term, with its doleful horizon of French infinitives, those insufferable Corn Laws and keeping goal for the Third XI on bitterly cold Wednesday afternoons.

---

* This was the German airship L.11 which crashed at Cuffley, Herts on 3 September 1916 after being shot down by Lt. Leefe Robinson RFC, for which he was awarded the VC.

10

Voyages of Exploration

and a 'flapper' next door!

When I was still in short trousers and our London suburb's nights began at four, it was easy to get the impression that time had changed down to bottom gear on its way to Christmas and my April birthday – quite unlike its pushy eagerness to get to those back-to-school dates, exams and appointments with the dentist's drill. Yet, somehow, the days congealed into weeks, and the weeks – forming a quorum – took to fancying themselves as months until, at last, they fell off the end of the calendar to make way for another upstart-year. I felt, though, that somehow they resented leaving.

Then, quite suddenly, we found ourselves going to bed when it was still daylight. From the candled chestnuts that lined our road, the blackbirds and thrushes diligently practised their scales in preparation for the forthcoming season. Something was stirring; from whence the sniff of seaweed from the Paradise Rocks? the scent of new-mown hay in Yeoman's Acre? and that hint of the urinous bouquet which invested Aldwick Farm? From the back of the throat arose remembrance of Nana's summer puddings and strawberry ice-cream in plated bowls. Summer was 'icumen in'. Shortly, our weekend visits to Bognor would be resumed with a purpose.

But if one had only recently opened the car door and disposed of one's last meal at the foot of the Watersfield signpost, a swaggering entry into one's territory was liable to a heavy discount. Parental recommendation was strongly in favour of an early night for a condition so enfeebled. Predictably, a good long sleep rallied the sinews and raised the spirits; once again I was in restless mood, ready for my brother to join me in a reconnaissance of our territory's boundaries to see how this Mr Rowland Rank was getting on.

Over at Aldwick Farm big changes had been effected. Mr Crockett's medieval milking shed had disappeared to make way for a well-lit modern milking parlour in which Alfa-Laval electric milking machines did the work of those pink and practised hands. Now to each beast – *vache-chic* – a metal yoke; even a drinking fountain. New, too, was a dairy white-tiled with hygiene. In a pen built to the specification of the Maginot Line, now resided, ring-in-nose and fearful of aspect, a walloping great Redpoll bull whose name was William. If the cowkeepers of Aldwick had thought they were rid of us at last, they had another think coming! Inspired by these new surroundings, we were quickly back under their new roof, 'helping' with renewed enthusiasm, sweeping the dung channel, wheeling the smart new metal wheelbarrow, and wondering why these new-fangled electric cups didn't keep falling off the creature's udders. But this time our labours attracted an unexpected reward.

When milking was over and we had whacked and thwacked the last dawdling shorthorn cross back to its evening pasture, Ginger, the under-cowman, used to harness the light horse to the milk-cart and load up the churns. Then we climbed on board and soon were clip-clopping down Aldwick Road, under the Rackhamesque elm and past the pile of purply mangold-wurzels by the gate of Hammond's Barn, on our way to the Chichester Dairies bottling depot in Charlwood Street. After the milk churns had been dropped off and Ginger had lit a fag and passed the time of day with his gumbooted friends, we came to the reason for our journey. On the way back he used to allow us to hold the reins – and do a little geeing-up – until, all too soon, we were arrived at Mrs Duffin's Stores, where we clocked off our working day. After reassuring Ginger of our continuing loyalty on the morrow, we ran home full of our afternoon's exploits.

Another of my agricultural acquaintances, collarless, gaitered, wes'ketted, a cigarette permanently welded to his lower lip, was the cow-man who 'did' for the Aldwick Farm heifers in their milieu of blancmangy mud and sparrow-chirp at Hammond's Barn. So, when ennui weighed heavily at Idlewylde, I wasn't above offering him a little of my free time for any diversion that might add to the common welfare. One day he announced that such a post had just become vacant – on the other handle of the mangold-wurzel crusher. It was hard work, even though he did most of it. Outside, the leggy beasts, with their pubescent udders and fashion-plate eyelashes, waited, pictures of bovine patience – that is, until they caught sight of my friend and me carrying the old tin bath containing the stuff. Immediately, they were transformed into a riotous mob of shoving, barging heavy-breathers as they fought to get their wet noses into the trough. And here is a tip: heifers, in their unguarded moments, are rather partial to Fruit Pastilles – just the black sort, which I didn't like.

As a *quid pro quo*, my friend used to turn a blind eye as I clambered up to the top of the straw bales for a little Tarzan practice on the hoisting rope which hung from a sturdy beam. But swinging wasn't without its risks, a little blood about the knees. Consequently, my arrival home was not always greeted with unalloyed joy by my mother. 'My dear child, do you really have to get quite so close to those cows? Now wash your hands and face and fetch me the iodine from the medicine chest … and comb your hair!'

Fifty-five years after my encounter with the mangold-wurzels and my agricultural friend in Hammond's Barn, Mrs Rowland Rank and her son John generously presented the building to the Bognor Regis Lions' Club who raised over £150,000 to convert it into a magnificently equipped community centre – the Rowland Rank Centre. In this admirable enterprise, the 'little boy' on the other handle of the mangold-wurzel crusher of 1934 played a backstage role, being appointed by John Rank to keep a watching brief on the project on behalf of his family. The architect was Dennis Boyt RIBA, Alex Sayers and Partners acted as building consultants, and Middleton Building Co. Ltd was the contractor. But it was their foreman Colin Killick on whose shoulders fell the burden of getting everything right on the site. And of course, when the Centre opened on 11 January 1989, the result was brilliant!

58 Still with plenty of plots for sale, the Bay Estate *c*.1932.

In our quarter of West London, the streets were becoming ever busier with motor traffic. It was 1932; no 30 m.p.h. speed limit, no Belisha crossings, no driving tests nor MOTs. Traffic lights were few and far between. It was the era of ill-adjusted cable-brakes, bald tyres and 'one for the road'. To cross a busy street meant having to make a dash for it; even for children coming home from school. Consequently, the accident figures were horrendous. So, when not at school, our enforced presence at meal-times served to assure our mother that neither of us had suffered an accident under the wheels of a motor car. To both my parents, the roads were of gnawing concern; heartfelt, their daily benediction, '... and be careful of the roads, dears', as we left the house.

But at Aldwick, for most of the year, the roads were fairly quiet and the local rush hours easily overlooked. At any rate, it was enough to mollify my mother's fears about motor cars. So the tradition of 'home for lunch' became gradually more honoured in the breach than in the observance until, finally, it was waived. If we wished to go off 'exploring' for most of the day she would let us have a pocketful of sandwiches and a good-for-the-teeth apple. Wine gums were up to us.

At last, those laggardly months relented, my April birthday arrived and I found myself the proud owner of a Norman 'boys' bicycle (Gamage's, £4), larger than a Fairy cycle but smaller than a man's. So, when I wasn't polishing its every spoke and mudguards, we were able to explore the Great Unknown which lay beyond the inchoate puddles of South Avenue. But as I was expected to keep an eye on this brother of mine – still underpowered with his Fairy cycle – the speed and range of our convoy rested upon when I judged his legs were about to fall off!

In the early 'thirties the north side of our part of Aldwick Road, where Westmeads sprawls today, marked the beginning of a vista of rural Sussex with fields as far as the eye could see. A short cycle ride took us to half-a-dozen working farms – Aldwick, Crimsham, Morrels, Rookery, Lagness and Chalcraft. It was commonplace to see lines of farmworkers hoeing mangolds and turnips and lifting potatoes by hand in a fieldscape dotted with scarecrows. Horses were still used for pulling carts, ploughs and reapers as they fought a losing battle against the iron-wheeled Fordsons. With the harvest came the threshing machines pulled by smoking traction engines – and still more men in flat caps. In profusion, hay and straw stacks stood out against the horizon.

Also, the roads and lanes were narrower then and looked still narrower as the summer brambles and convolvulus encroached upon their tarmac surfaces. The fields were smaller and more numerous. There were more hedges, elms and rooks. Verges and ditches were wider and deeper; farmers still employed a lot of men with bil'uks and grafters for hedging and ditching. In Hook Lane at Nyetimber I remember watching a labourer scything a grassy verge, pausing every now and then to sharpen his blade with the *zwee-wee, zwee-wee* of a whetstone. The sound carried a long way.

Thus, it was along these quiet lanes that threaded the countryside around our part of Sussex – and on which we were as likely to meet a horse-drawn Ransome and Marles winnower and side-rake as we were a car or a lorry – that our little two-bicycle convoy (with me in front) must have been a familiar sight. With pockets full of sandwiches, we pedalled speculatively, each trip a lottery, with destinations unpremeditated and road maps unknown. That was how we discovered Sefter School, the duck pond at the Manor Farm at Merston, as well as Pagham Beach and the watercress beds at Vinnetrow Farm, beyond the *Walnut Tree Inn* at Runcton.

It is difficult to believe, now, that we could find ourselves among the thatched cottages of a still-rural Rose Green, with no Grosvenor Gardens, and could peep into Hewart's Barn, only to find it full of Mr Gray's bathing huts. And that we could come upon William Adame's sail-less Nyetimber Mill (1859) in Pagham Road, its door boarded up and sealed with brambles. Even our first venture down Barrack Lane proved to be quite eventful. That was when we discovered the Coastguards Cottages and, just round the corner, the Arcadie tea shack, where the 55 Southdown buses used to turn round and a glass of lemonade made from yellow crystals cost a ha'penny.

A short distance beyond the tea shack we came across some flint pillars on which were inscribed the words, 'The Bay Estate'. One glimpse beyond them showed that if 'the rich' lived anywhere it must be here; the well-upholstered denizens of those famous Ways: Manor, Fair and Bye. Respectfully, we turned in among them and for the first time saw palm trees growing by an English roadside. Half an hour later, after watching some thatchers Norfolk-reeding a dormered roof and having inspected the Estate's directory of variegated architectural styles, garnished with the occasional Alvis, Daimler or Humber Snipe, we returned to Barrack Lane. And there we came across a sight even more demanding of our attention

For on the beach at the end of the road we spotted a lot of men with shovels filling metal trucks with shingle* which were then pulled by a horse up the beach on narrow-gauge rails to where carts and lorries awaited

---

* Known locally as 'beach', it was a mixture of salty sea-sand and shingle. When gauged with cement it made an inferior kind of concrete much used in the foundations and oversites in the new houses springing up all over this area.

loading. Unknown to us, though, was that this was the undertaking set up by the Duff Coopers' *éminence-grise* butler, the enterprising Mr Holbrook. In her *Autobiography*, Lady Diana Cooper says a little more about him:

> … Duff's Napoleonic manservant … the pompous scoundrel Holbrook … who wearied us with his importance and long words … he even made us several hundreds of pounds by forming the Holbrook-Cooper Company for transporting shingle from Bognor beach to waiting lorries on the road. The Company's office was a tin hut on the beach and its stock-in-trade an old white horse and some trucks. The deeds and agreements had green tapes and red seals. His profits were double ours. We always rather hated him, and were not sorry the Admiralty* daunted him. He rightly left us when it came to an end. He took his pension and came to dust.

As we cycled round our district, its villages, farms, road junctions and landmarks became imprinted on our minds. One day my brother and I came across a sign announcing that we were in 'Nyetimber'. Outside the *Lamb Inn* – then a watering hole for the working man, not the smart restaurant it has since become – we stopped to survey this latest addition to our geographical lexicon. Unavoidably our gaze fell upon a contemplative-looking Clydesdale standing outside a low building with a stable door which opened into blackness. All around, awaiting repair, were rusting ploughs, mowers and harrows. A forge!

Letting fall our bikes among the docks and dandelions, and squeezing past a family of tetchy geese, we went to look inside. Apart from a small flickering fire it was pitch black. Then, as our eyes became accustomed to the smokey gloom, we perceived the blacksmith holding a pair of tongs. 'Might we watch?'

'Yes,' nodded the perspiring Mr William Christian, for it was that renowned farrier to whom we were speaking, 'providing we didn't get in his way'. With his grimy hands he was about to make another horseshoe. Striding to the huge leather bellows, he began to pump. Instantly the fire roared to an angry white heat; showers of sparks lit up the cobwebby forge. Then into the fire he put a half-made shoe. More bellows and more sparks. Next, Mr C. tonged the glowing iron from fire to anvil. This was what we were waiting for! Now he attacked it with a tattoo of hammer-blows bounced back and forth from anvil to red-hot shoe. Then, on the other side, the same. Oh, blissful, clangy sound! Slowly the rude iron began to match the shape stored in his farrier-mind as he wrested the shoe with hammer, tongs, punches and all those other implements whose purposes are known only to blacksmiths.

Outside, in the daylight, the Clydesdale roan towered above us. 'Might I hold its bridle?' Mr C. nodded. Somehow, it seemed a privilege to be so close to that velvety nose, those yellow teeth and soft brown eyes. Only a touch, and a gruff 'c'mon', was needed to make the horse raise a hoof the size of a dinner-plate for our farrier to hold upon his leather apron. The old shoe was removed and fell to the ground; careful paring and rasping prepared

* Sir Alfred Duff Cooper was First Lord of the Admiralty 1937-38.

59 The forge at Nyetimber in the early 1900s.

60 William Christian, master blacksmith and farrier of Nyetimber.

61 The *Royal Oak* at Lagness before it was replaced by the present building in about 1930. The shed on the left is a forge worked at one time by William Christian, the Nyetimber farrier.

the 'frog' (one learns these terms, consorting with blacksmiths), before Mr Christian disappeared back into the forge. Soon he returned holding the incandescent shoe in his tongs. Now came the exciting bit. As he placed it carefully against the hoof, up billowed a little cloud of acrid smoke as it burned into the horny tissue.

And before we had found an answer to why the horse didn't scream with pain, our farrier had driven in the last of the seven nails. Picking up a piece of straw, William Christian measured the next hoof – it was all he needed to set about making another shoe. Really, it was worth a round of applause! But, of course, it all took much longer than just writing about it.

Five thousand feet below the three little Hawker Furies from Tangmere, performing their crescent dives, the gander stretched his neck, honked and led his family fastidiously between our bicycles. The time had come to take our leave of Mr Christian. But not before we had assured him he could look forward to soon seeing us again. Then, full of yet another new experience, we cycled off, past Pooley and Tooze's butcher's shop and the *Bear Inn* before turning into Nyetimber Lane and setting course for home.

One autumn morning the sight of a cloud of wheeling black-headed gulls drew us to one of the Rookery Farm fields near Sefter School, where the pushy Fordson tractors were still held at shaft's length by working horses. As ploughing rated highly on our schedule of free entertainment, and since gull-cry, hoof-thud and chain-clink were music to our ears, my brother and I hunkered down on the headland grass among the scented nosebags, and the ploughman's haversack and coat, to watch a pair of Suffolk Punches at work on this clover ley. After a little while a large Humber drew in through the gate and out got a tall, patriarchal-looking man with a short beard. He wore a cape over his shoulders, leather gaiters, a Norfolk hat and carried a shepherd's crook. If it flashed through my mind, as he strode across the furrows to speak to his ploughman, that I might be looking at some latter-day St John the Baptist, at least I was aiming in the right direction.

For this distinguished-looking figure, who was to become so familiar to us in the years before the war as he walked the fields of Rookery Farm, was John Maxwell Aylwin, whose religious convictions had led him to become College-trained in preparation for a long period of arduous missionary work in Paraguay. At the turn of the century he had returned to till the soil in a part of Sussex his forebears had farmed since 1590. In 1906 he married Lottie Stay, a fine-looking woman of Singleton farming stock. Just after the war I renewed my acquaintance with him and he divulged how he judged a field of wheat to be ready for reaping; and still he was using horses. John Aylwin died in 1949. He rests in Pagham churchyard in an unmarked grave as is the custom among the Plymouth Brethren.

It was in those same parts, a few weeks later, that we came across something else to tempt our inquisitive natures. One late summer afternoon, pedalling our way along Pagham Road, a little south of the *Royal Oak* at Lagness, we spied an overgrown footpath. Where might it lead? To find out we abandoned our bikes in the ditch. The brambles presented a painful barrier; our woolly sleeves were wretched ever after, but at last we found ourselves standing on a little brick bridge above a pellucid stream. At the far end was a squeaky gate operated by an iron weight. Might this be the Pagham Rife which we'd heard of but never found?

Along its banks reed-beds rustled in the wind, and waterweeds waved their sinuous patterns under the clear water. In the low-lying meadows beyond the bridge red bullocks grazed knee-deep amongst the long grass, silvery in the afternoon light. The sky was full of birds – and by now I could distinguish quite a few: mallard, heron, shelduck and lapwing – although many of the LBJs (little brown jobs, in the trade!) still resisted recognition.

We leaned over the parapet, remained still and gazed expectantly along its winding course of sparkling ripples skimmed by the flight of swallows. After a little while we were rewarded with the sapphire flash of a far-off kingfisher; then the sight of a water rat trailing its wake to the other bank. In the shadow of the bridge* we spied a shoal of sticklebacks. The blue dragonflies hovering around deserved more than the small mention we gave them. Over our heads flew a pair of fluting waders which I advised my brother were redshanks – well, I was pretty sure that's what they were! Then, suddenly breaking the riparian peace, 'Look! Look! A Duck!', shouted Roger, pointing at something with large webbed toes swimming, submerged, under the bridge. Swiftly came the informed response, 'Idiot, that's not a duck – its a dabchick,' showing that my *British Birds* had not gone unread. Meanwhile, unused to such controversy, the subject had hurriedly sought refuge among the reeds.

Soon we'd had enough of keeping still. Here was the sort of stream for which A.A. Milne had invented Pooh-sticks. Twigs abounded; two at a time we chucked them into the upstream water and then rushed to the bridge to see whose stick came first past the downstream parapet. The score wavered to and fro. But Pooh-sticks destroys the young brain's sense of time. We had failed to notice how low the sun had dropped; it was why we were growing hungry. Hadn't we promised not to be late? Through the brambles we retraced our steps. The journey home, pedalled *allegro molto* to beat the sinking sun, was enough to have made Roger's legs seize up! To my mother's question of what we had been doing with ourselves all the afternoon, 'Oh, we found a bridge' seemed to cover it adequately. But to those peaceful water-meadows at Bowley Farm I was to return time and time again – and still do when my diary allows.

'At Pagham Beach will be found a bungalow town which has grown into great popularity during the past few years with those who prefer an uncon-ventional holiday' (*Bognor Regis Town Guide*, 1930). The road simply came to an end. That was how we discovered Pagham Beach; Sea Lane (Adames Lane, not that long ago) still a single track. But when we saw in front of us that collection of railway-carriage bungalows, we knew we were looking at something requiring our reconnaissance in depth. Wheeling our bikes along the pebbly roads and paths, we set off to examine more closely Pagham's casual Left-Bank-on-Sea architecture and to inhale the heady whiff of not just 'the unconventional', but of the most admirably eccentric!

---

* On the Sussex River Authority's maps (1957) it is referred to as Bullen Bridge. It also figures on an 1847 Plan of North Mundham Parish. In Lindsay Fleming's *History of Pagham* the track leading to it is shown as Bullen Lane.

62 Mr Charlie Tooze (of Pooley and Tooze, the Nyetimber butchers, and post master at Aldwick) is shown here in shirtsleeves outside his shop next to the *Bear Inn*, *c*.1925.

Continuing our way amongst the jacked-up first-class composites and third-class suburbans, with their asbestos- and felt-clad extensions, annexes and indeterminable excrescences, it soon became clear that the natives of Pagham Beach not only displayed an uninhibited flare for concocting their impromptu dwellings but, when it came to naming them, enjoyed unusual gifts of euphony; Bide-a-wee, Happy Go Lucky, Linga-Longa, Dolce far Niente – even Yo-Ho, being among the less exceptional. Just think of living in a room with a window labelled 'No Smoking' – and opened and closed with a leather strap! And what price entering Chez Nous through a front door with a window engraved 'Ladies Only'? Even their puddles could learn nothing from those in our road at home.

Gradually we began to absorb the flavour of life on Pagham Beach. Out of driftwood garages grinned waspish AC three-wheelers showing the place they'd won in Pagham hearts. No less observable those tokens of her maritime roots; all around us dinghies, rowing boats, rubber sea-horses and rusty anchors lay stranded among the stones and sea-kale clumps; fishing rods leaned against corrugated porches, and prawning nets teetered on oil-drum water-butts. Like lines of sails, the washing fluttered in the afternoon breeze. With ungrudging admiration we regarded the lobster pots and painted rocks that served to mark out gardens embellished with coloured gnomes and concrete herons fishing in dried-up ponds. The further we wandered, the more envious we became of Pagham's youth.

Fancy waking up to find the English Channel in front of you and the Lagoon behind; a muddy harbour full of birds at one end of your road and an ice-cream stall standing at the other. Surely here were the Elysian Fields over-egged! Well, we had to admit it; Aldwick Gardens couldn't hold a candle to Pagham Beach. A little more exploring and a visit to the ice-cream counter of the Beach Café, which mopped up the last of our pocket money, meant the time had come to bid au revoir – but certainly not goodbye – to this eccentric south coast garland. So, feeling like a couple of explorers who had just discovered a Lost City in central Africa, we pedalled off, past the rookery at Mant's Farm – its field still awaiting the new *King's Beach Hotel* – and along the cornfield road which instinct told us led to the Bay Estate. And a much quicker way back to our humdrum South Avenue than the route by which we'd come. But we were to return to Pagham Beach, time and time again.

In fact, it was on one of these later visits – by now it must have been about 1937 – and while we were eating our sandwiches by the coot-spattered Lagoon, my brother and I heard a monotonous bang-bang-banging which suggested we had not yet drunk all of Pagham's heady pleasures. It was a pile-driver at work. Now, pile-drivers – like new Odeons – we rated as 'good things'. So, our sandwiches finished, we set off to investigate. The sound drew us along the track to the mouth of the Harbour. And there, within a lunar-looking landscape of shingle banks, peninsulas, isthmuses and swirling tide-race we could see a crane with a steam 'dolly' ferociously hammering in sheet-piles. It seemed an undertaking not without merit and well worth our attention for a quarter of an hour or so – relieved with a little stone-skimming – before we were off to seek further diversions.

It wasn't until some months later, while exploring around Church Norton, that we came across the sheet piling again. But now it lay in disarray, pushed over into drunken shapes by the onslaught of storms and the weight of stones.* Yet, as far as I can recall, we never once asked ourselves what had been the real purpose of this gratuitous – and clearly, expensive – entertainment. Which was very remiss of us because it was, in fact, a fascinating story.

In 1935, Mr A.W. Thornton, lord of the manor of Selsey and the owner of Pagham Harbour and much other land in those parts – at Aldwick, too – was faced with the disquieting knowledge that the railway-carriage bunga-lows and the Lagoon stood quite soon to be engulfed by the sea. And to prevent this calamity was going to cost him a lot of money.

At a meeting with the Board of Trade officials held at the Masonic Hall in Bognor in November of that year, his engineers, Howard Humphrey and Partners of Victoria Street, SW1, explained how the harbour's mouth had been created at the Church Norton end of the shingle bank at the time of the 1910 inundation. Since then, though, it had been gradually moving eastwards 'at the mean rate of 91 feet per annum'. It now threatened the existence of the Pagham Beach bungalows and the Lagoon. The plan, therefore, was to seal off the existing mouth with a double row of steel sheet-piles and re-open a new mouth roughly in the position of the 1910 breach. Eventually, they thought that it might be possible, by means of

---

* The collapsed piling resulted in a long-running High Court action between Mr Thornton and the contractors, the Demolition and Construction Co. Ltd.

63 Pagham Harbour: the new mouth showing the collapsed sheet piling after the severe storms of March and April 1937.

sluice gates, to make the harbour once again non-tidal. On behalf of Mr Thornton, his engineers were now formally seeking the Board's consent to carry out the work. But it was a solution more easily propounded than achieved.

From the *Bognor Regis Observer* 25 January 1939:

> Engineers and sea defence contractors have been busily engaged at Pagham Harbour for over two years, but the exact purpose of carrying out this work has been kept secret.* ... Several attempts have been made to close the original harbour mouth but tremendous sea backed by terrific gales swept all before them, twisting the steel interlocking piles into every conceivable shape. Eventually it was decided to erect a wooden gantry across the mouth with sheet-piling on either side and the centre filled with shingle. This has so far stood up.

Meanwhile, 800 yards further west, it was a race against time and winter tides to complete the new mouth. Already its sheet-piling had suffered severe damage from the great winter storms in March and April 1937. Another problem was the twenty foot high bed of shingle, caused by the mill-race nature of the main channel, which was threatening to erode Pagham Beach. But just as the pile of shingle had been removed and the earlier damage to the steel piles repaired, another storm in October ruined the new gantry at the Church Norton side of the mouth.

Nevertheless, in spite of these setbacks, by late 1938 the new opening had been established, thereby ensuring a more certain future for Pagham's shacky architecture and the nearby Lagoon. And it was about then that Mr

---

* There seems little doubt that the 'secrecy' which attended this operation was due to Thornton's intention one day to seek an aeronautical future for Pagham Harbour.

64 The author (right) and his brother, Roger, resting between 'explorations'.

Thornton's sharp ears picked up a sound very much like the approach of an Imperial Airways flying boat! But to discover more about his curious illlusion, the reader will need to wait until Chapter 18.

There is a postscript to Pagham Harbour's peripatetic mouth. In 1957 fierce storms again breached the protective shingle bank. The sea came close to the top of the dyke. Subsequently, by means of more sheet-piling, a 'hardened' entrance was formed by the River Board in a position roughly halfway between the 1910 mouth and Pagham Beach. And there it remains to this day.

From time to time, the sight of a column of brown smoke rising into the sky above Pagham Beach used to warm the hearts of two young connoiseurs of accidental combustion. Usually it meant that one of the railway-carriage bungalows was ablaze. A few minutes later we would hear the fire engine's bell as it left the old High Street Fire Station. Hastily, we grabbed our bikes and cycled down to Aldwick Road to await the Leyland Escape come tearing past, with Second Officer Leslie Walwin* ringing the bell, and the rest of the volunteer crew hanging on for dear life. Then we followed the fire engine as fast as we could using the spillages from its water tank to guide us. But by the time we had pedalled to the scene of the fire, in spite of the fire brigade's 'prompt attention', what was left of the late railway carriage hardly seemed worth looking at!

In 1936 our elderly next-door neighbour, Miss Morgan, put the sale of her bungalow in the hands of Gentle and Green, the estate agents, and flicked the talcum dust of South Avenue from her shoes for the last time. After a few weeks a Pickford's van arrived outside the empty bungalow

---

* According to the late Leslie Walwin, in 1937 it took about twelve minutes to get to Pagham from the old High Street Fire Station. But after a barrier was erected at the west end of the Fairway, on the Bay Estate, the longer Nyetimber Lane route added another three minutes to the journey. Apparently, given a clear road, the Leyland could top 60 m.p.h.

bearing the tea-boxed chattels and three-piece suite of our new neighbour. Soon it was around that her name was Miss Pullen. So, after allowing her the statutory 24 hours settling-in time, my brother and I made it our business to present our visiting card at her back door. Gratifyingly, we were soon seated at her kitchen table dealing with the last of a Victoria sponge and a flagon of fizzy lemonade. And that was when it dawned on us that we now had a well-above-average next-door neighbour.

For Miss Ruth Pullen proved to be a go-ahead ex-flapper of the 'twenties. Of indeterminate years, she was friendly and humorous. It was she who introduced us to the sight of a lady in long trousers, with a bottle of Gordon's gin on the kitchen table and a shilling-in-the-slot cigarette machine in her living room. But her greatest asset stood outside in the drive, a Wolsey Hornet racing car with a fish-tail exhaust, leather bonnet-strap and its race number painted on the doors. And it had done the Monte Carlo Rally! Nirvana having arrived, it was only a day or two before we felt in a position to ask our new neighbour whether we might be allowed the privilege of washing her car. 'Of course you can – and jolly decent of you, too.'

With frenzied zeal we set about lathering, leathering and Karpol-ing the little racer. At the end of half an hour it looked quite spanking. Of course, with a mother like ours, the scurvy notion of 'reward' was not allowed even to enter our heads – well, hardly. But we needn't have worried. 'You chaps care for a spin?' 'Gosh, yes – not half!' Cramped in the passenger seat, with Roger on my lap, we were soon roaring down Aldwick Road, with the wind in our hair and the exhaust's *vroom-vroom* in our ears, with the prospect of a a short pit-stop at Sait's Tea Garden for a top-up of ice-cream.

Neither was Miss Pullen above allowing us a lien on her many friends. One of these was her Morris Oxford cousin, Gerald, who shared his car with Carl and Dmitri, a pair of imperious-looking borzois that took an immediate shine to these two brothers. Basking in the reflected glory of these canine aristos, we were allowed to hold them on the lead when Mr Gerald took them down to Aldwick Beach for a gallop and a roll in anything unspeakable they could find. Meanwhile, we looked for those tell-tale signs of envy in the eyes of our mongrel-owning friends. My mother, not one to miss noting how much more socially enhanced her sons appeared in Carl and Dmitri's up-market presence, made good use of her black-and-white Agfa.

From time to time Miss Pullen's standing in our community was raised in surprising ways. As, for instance, when an aeroplane circled low over her bungalow waggling its wings. It was merely her cousin showing that he hadn't forgotten her birthday, but such a performance above South Avenue had never been heard of before! And, in our eyes, it made Miss Ruth Pullen more admirable than ever.

Then, one spring, she introduced us to her two nephews, Ian and Peter Bailey, who had come to stay with her. They were about our own age and proved lively and agreeable companions. Thereafter, we looked forward to their visits to join our beach-days, meet our friends, share our one-pad cricket on the wasteland and to fool with the frog-spawn in its season. So you will see how Miss Pullen, and her little Wolsley Hornet, won their place in Bognor's crown, beside the Duck Pond, the Leyland fire engine and the Shripney gas-holder – not to mention all the other jewels that glittered in our pre-war days!

'Have you both got hankies? ... and your money? ... and an apple each? ... and cleaned your teeth? Now, don't eat your sandwiches the moment you get into Bognor. And be careful of the traffic. And do remember to comb your hair occasionally. Off you go, dears, and have a lovely day – and try not to be home too late.' Equipped by our mother as if for global navigation, we set off. Opposite Goodacre's toyshop on the Esplanade, Roger and I clambered on board the leathery-smelling Silver Queen bus. 'Two halves to Aldingbourne, please.' For on this prayed-for sunny morning we were bound for Tangmere aerodrome. Alighting at our destination, our instinct for survival led us quickly to the village stores for a short re-victualling stop: Smith's crisps, a bottle of Pink's lemonade and twopenn'orth of aniseed balls to supplement our apples and liver sausage sandwiches. Soon, we were trudging the dusty verge towards the aerodrome.

Our vantage point by the perimeter fence reached, we threw ourselves down among the cow parsley and bumble bees to await events. Before us, with its back cloth of the South Downs and Halnaker Mill, sprawled the airfield's verdant acres caressed by the shadows of passing clouds and sweetened with the call of skylarks. Outside the far-off hangers stood six Hawker Furies bearing the famous black-and-white chequerboard heraldry of No. 43 Squadron.

'Look!' cried my brother excitedly, 'there's a Hawker Demon.' 'You ass, that's not a Demon; it's a Hart – no gun in the rear cockpit ... but look over there, Rog – that's the Gloster Gauntlet we saw yesterday ... and the one

65 A Silver Queen Dennis 'E', PO 186 on the Slindon service, waits opposite Goodacre's toyshop on the Esplanade. The last buses of the evening carried a postbox on the front (as here) so that folk in the country districts could catch the late mail from Bognor.

66 No. 43 Squadron's Hawker Furies flying north of Chichester. The Lavant Straight from where it leaves Stane Street (A285) can be clearly seen. Part of Goodwood House lies near the top of the right-hand margin.

behind it looks like a Vildebeest from Thorney. And there's a Westland Wallace – see it?' But my brother's gaze had been drawn to a passing aircraft in the sky. 'Mike – isn't that one of those new Avro Ansons? ... d'you think it's going to land?' And thus did the two aeronautical experts pass their time.

After a while we heard the sound of the fighters' engines being run-up on the tarmac. The windsock wavered auspiciously nor'west. With luck they might take off in our direction. To fill in time, crisps were crunched and concertina'd sandwiches munched; bees shoo-ed off and the bluebottles and horse-flies dispatched to a more respectable afterlife. Next, we unscrewed the lemonade, with elder brother getting first slurp – for such was the shape of our democracy. Then we shared out what were left of the aniseed balls.

Meanwhile, things were happening on the aerodrome. Diminutive in the distance, two flights of Furys had taxied their way to the far end of the grass runway and were turning into the wind. For a while … silence. Then came the rumble of throttles being opened-up. Imperceptibly, the six aircraft began to move. Slowly at first, but with gathering momentum, they sped towards us … quicker and quicker … up came their tails … onwards they raced, ever faster … until, suddenly, the neat little biplanes seemed to spring from the Tangmere turf, their Rolls-Royce Kestrels lifting them effortlessly skywards … and now our up-turned eyes were filled with Hawker Furies roaring overhead, wheels spinning; bracing wires and propeller arcs glinting in the sun; their chequerboard heraldry inviting us to touch it.

As they banked and thundered towards Chichester, we were treated to an unforgettable picture of those six elegant fighters and their leather-helmeted pilots – young chaps, unknowing that one day they would be called to write their own valiant chapter in these same skies – 'The Few'.

Not always was the weather on our side. Meteorological depressions had a mean habit of letting us board the Silver Queen before announcing their presence. Sometimes they seemed to follow the bus. Often we reached the rain-swept airfield just as flying was abandoned for the day. By the time we had retraced our steps through the downpour to Aldingbourne we were already soaking wet. And in front of us, still, the long, sodden walk from Butlin's. Sometimes, what used to turn up on my mother's doorstep was enough to have made a social worker weep!

* * *

During the long summer days of July and August, when the scents of late hay and lavender lay upon the air, the peace of Aldwick Gardens was liable to the challenge of the sound of bugles: the Boys Brigade. They used to pitch their tents in the field opposite the Duck Pond, and as the night drew on we could see their camp fires flickering and hear them singing. But their speciality was Sunday morning Church Parades. As soon as we got wind of them lining up in Aldwick Road, we were quick to join the crowd of onlookers. Smartly dressed in their black uniforms, pipe-clayed belts and jaunty pill-box hats, these lads – many from very poor homes – presented a stirring sight as they set off towards the Methodist church in the High Street, headed by the youthful mace-bearer twirling and tossing his symbol of office, followed by the colour guard, flag-bearer and the silver band – bugles, fifes, kettle drums and a big bass drum. To hear those bugle calls again, the reader should put on a CD of Benjamin Britten's *Noye's Flood.* They occur in the section on the Arrival of the Animals.

Other uniformed visitors, less innocent, used also to find their way to Aldwick – bearing arms! Units of the Territorial Army frequently held their summer camps behind Hammond's Barn (now the Rowland Rank Centre). Once they brought with them a menacing-looking 3.7 inch anti-aircraft gun and sound-detectors. Often they drilled in the field opposite the barn. I daresay the *Ship* didn't do badly out of them either. Apparently, the arrival of this mass of 'licentious soldiery' caused some of the local matrons to lock up their daughters – well, at any rate, my Aunt Bertha warned my pretty little cousin Elizabeth not to speak to anything wearing puttees and a peaked hat!

11

The Empire Expects

In Balfour's day, according to my mother, Hampstead was full of blazers, and old school ties going about their stiff-upper-lipped business of inheriting the British Empire and playing cricket. Her cousin, Graham, sounds like one of them: schooled at Chigwell, Army Captain, Boer War Medal and all that. When she was still quite young he once dropped her the hint that should she ever bear a son, the boy could only hope properly to serve the Empire if he could ride a horse and swim a river. Just what her cousin got up to on the banks of the Modder at Ladysmith is veiled in mystery, but apparently a bit of riding and swimming – and his stiff upper lip – all came in useful.

At our school, though, there was no truck with swimming. Cricket and soccer, yes. Even 'fives' – a plebeian version of squash; no racquet, but a heavy leather glove. All were claimed to hone the lad's character. But not swimming. Whether the little dears sank or swam was a matter for parental discretion. So, with maternal sagacity, my mother took her two sons on the 'No Spitting' tram to the chlorinated Municipal Baths at Treaty Road in Hounslow.

Under its glass roof, echoing to the screams and shouts of dripping children and the splash of divers swooping off the top board, we changed into our reach-me-down swimming costumes behind the slatted doors of cubicles smelling of decaying towels. Soon we were at my mother's side where she awaited us at what was laughingly termed 'the shallow end'.

Unable to swim a stroke herself, she was about to teach us the art. In more enlightened times such a notion would have been enough to have brought out on strike every card-carrying swimming instructor in Middlesex! From an article in a Boy Scouts manual, we had already practised the breast stroke while lying across a narrow bed with my mother's hand under our chins, so freeing our limbs to practice the movements. And much more ache-inducing than doing it in the water, I recall. In fact, her secret was a canvas belt attached to a length of rope; the belt went under our armpits while she held the rope and shouted instructions and encouragement from dry land.

I daresay we taught ourselves really. But the rope gave us the confidence to let our feet part company with the reassuring tiles beneath. After a few lessons – and the ingestion of a measure or two of chlorinated water – we felt able to dispense with the canvas belt. During the ensuing weeks Roger and I practiced our passable breast strokes and inelegant crawls; we learned to float and tread water until we felt brave enough to venture down to the deep end for belly-flops off the lower spring-board. Soon the curling breakers on Aldwick Beach would behold us, if not in awe, at least no longer with contempt.

But before doing anything foolhardy, let us harken to Dr Morris, Bognor's Medical Officer of Health in 1904, who took seriously the whole business of sea bathing:

> The first bathe should not be of long duration, for even the most vigorous constitutions may suffer from depression if the immersion is lengthy. After the bather has dressed, his condition will afford an excellent idea as to whether his exposure has done him good or harm. If he has benefitted he will feel warm, exhilarated and ready for any muscular exertion. This condition should last all day. If ill resulted he feels chilly and sick, his head aches, there is a sense of langour and disinclination for exercise and a loss of appetite which continues for the rest of the day.
>
> No one ought to bathe until three hours after meals and even the strongest should not bathe before breakfast without having taken some warm milk and a biscuit.

Reading that, it is a wonder that any of my mother's sons survived beyond their first bathe!

Next, it was To Horse. The saga unfolded at the Marine Riding School in the mews nearly opposite The White Tower in Aldwick Road. The mews is still there but no longer echoes to the sound of horse's hooves, just exhaust pipes and slamming car doors. But first a history lesson.

On the stables wall hung a brass bell inscribed 'HMS *Bellerophon*', the name of the ship which, in 1815, took the prisoner Napoleon Bonaparte from Rochefort to Plymouth on the first stage of his journey to perpetual confinement on St Helena. That this particular bell had come from a small eponymous Great War vessel was not the sort of impediment my mother would have allowed to stand in the the way of a good story about one of her Doré relations, a Captain Bennett who had been appointed to a position of command in one of the British regiments charged with ensuring the ex-Emperor's secure incarceration. During his tour of duty, Bennett became acquainted with 'Boney' (who generally had an aversion to British officers), and occasionally took sherry with him when they played a kind of bezique in his bleak prison-house, Longwood. At least once he called upon the Bennetts at their home and gave the Captain's lady 'a sweeping bow'.

When 'le petit monstre' died, in 1821, the rude, native coffins were considered unworthy of a person still awesome even as a corpse. Oak it had to be. But this species was unknown on the island. So Captain Bennett's great oak dining table was cut up and used for the purpose. And it was in this coffin the Emperor's embalmed remains, clad in his green Field Mar-shall's uniform, lay until, in 1840, *La Belle Poule* arrived with some crack French morticians to decant Boney into a more upmarket casket, before returning him to France for eventual interment at Les Invalides in Paris.

As a child, my mother used to tell us how she had met Captain Bennett's daughter – by then a Mrs Owen of great age, lying on a couch – who had been present when Napoleon's coffin was carried on board the ship and had helped embroider the French flag which covered it. My mother could also remember being allowed to hold a cup and saucer which had belonged to Napoleon and which had come into the possession of a branch of the Dorés. I had heard these stories when I was very small and for a long time was under the impression that Napoleon was some kind of delinquent uncle!

But back to that first riding lesson. Our Master of Horse – and Secretary of the Bognor branch of the Legion of Frontiersmen – was Captain Frank Harding, who broke the ice with a joke about what would happen if the rider tried to mount a horse in the manner of getting on a bike. Although the ergonomic details escape me now, I think it resulted in the rider ending up saddled, but facing the tail. Next he explained the leathery purpose of snaffle, head collar, cantle and girth. Then he introduced us to our mounts. Mine answered – metaphorically speaking – to the name of 'Beau', Roger's to that of 'Belle'.

But it was only when we started practising mounting and dismounting that I realised what an enormous thing a horse was; how far away the ground suddenly looked. As an insurance policy I stroked Beau obsequiously

67 At the Marine Riding School in Aldwick Road. The author is furthest from his mother's camera.

and murmured 'dear horse' into his ears, while imploring my mother down below to stuff the thing with sugar cubes! At last, securely moored to Captain Harding by lead reins, we crunched off into Aldwick Road.

Vanity immediately beset me. For, secretly, I wouldn't have minded an hour's stroll through the town on the off-chance that someone I knew might see me mounted on such a fine steed. The Captain's plans, however, prevailed and soon we were carefully clip-clopping down the ramp opposite the Marine Café at the end of Nyewood Lane.

And that was when the trouble started. That was when I might have been excused for questioning the horse's slot in the Great Scheme of Things. As we began to trot it quickly became clear that here was a creature totally unsuited to carrying human flesh; tent poles, yes; the regimental washing, perhaps – even demijohns of snake oil. But not a boy. A trotting Beau, I discovered, had little in common with a walking one; suddenly its backbone seemed to be connected to the wrong legs. 'Move with the horse', shouted the good Captain, oblivious of the poor thing's wretched deformity. At the end of that first, bumpy lesson certain parts of me were exceedingly tender!

It took a few more excursions down the ramp before I discovered the secret of how to avoid those uncomfortable collisions. Gradually, though, I began to get the hang of it. My morale began to rise; I found myself enjoying the sensation of being at one with the movements of a horse. And a horse which no longer looked so unnervingly large. In time we took to cantering and eventually there came that memorable morning when the lead was slipped and I found myself the sole – if slightly uncertain – custodian of dear old Beau who, it turned out, harboured nothing but compassion for me, tempered only by an irresistible urge to get back to his stable as soon as the hour was up lest that awful kid start talking all that tripe about the one-ness of horse and rider again!

Afterwards it was along to the Marine Café for our daily fix of straw-berry ice-creams and my mother's 'milk and a dash'. That was when we used to see the motor horse-boxes parked at the end of Nyewood Lane bringing well-polished race-horses, *chic* in their chequered blankets, for a therapeutic paddle in the Aldwick shallows. Heads tossing contentedly, they used to stroll their way along the water's edge until – like a spring uncoiling – one of them would break into a headlong gallop through the wavelets. In a halo of spray, tail streaming to the wind, horse and crouching stable-girl would disappear across the corrugated sand in the direction of the Pier. Now, why didn't I learnt to ride like that?

At Easter, the smell of linseed oil being applied to my great-uncle's cricket bat – the cudgelly sort, of a size suited to the late 20 stone W.G. Grace – heralded the beginning of our cricket season. Our wasteland play-ground next to Idlewylde had its grass sickled, its molehills removed, the ravages of the football season filled in and the *Ship's* empty whisky bottles shown the dustbin. Next, a petition was laid before mother to borrow the garden roller and her Meltonian shoe whitener for marking out the crease. And while we were at it, was there any chance of 6d. for a new 'compo' cricket ball from Woolworth's?

Our cricket was one-ended-one-pad stuff with bail-less stumps. Fixtures were spontaneous; the rules simple. Batting order was decided by who 'bags-ed' first. A knock into Mrs Prior's garden was four-and-out; hits into the ditch near the wasp's nest were restricted to a ceiling of six runs and cousin Elizabeth was allowed to be out twice. Scores were kept in the head, their accuracy often the subject of lively debate.

When batting, Don Bradman was our model; long-hop off-drives and swipes to leg with the one pad on the ground the vogue. Any sign of defensive play was branded as immoral, punishable by bouncers, the accuracy of which, in length and line, were in the inverse ratio to the energy expended in their delivery. Maiden overs were unheard of. Fielding was – well, simply not batting; first slip for my suicidal brother and deep-mid-on for the more contemplative Arthur Marsh, with me bowling what purported to be leg-breaks from the rolled-up pullover end. With the sight of the Aerated Water Company's lorry lurching down South Avenue rattling its

68 Another of Bognor's pre-war core of private boarding-houses which has disappeared, The Arlington at the corner of Norfolk Square, with The White Tower in the background. A doctor's surgery now stands in its place.

crates of Tizer, it was customary to declare an open-ended refreshment interval while pockets were dredged for pennies.

Thus, throughout the holiday, the wasteland was the scene of great cricketing triumphs and debacles; of argued rules and disputed scores as, gradually, the pitch lost its grass and our ball its paint. Play frequently ground to a halt to allow safe passage along the footpath for nervous-looking visitors in beach-wraps. Banged shins, batsmen's thumb and wasp stings, were all part of the wasteland's legacy.

And yet we had only to cycle – no hands, of course! – to the Bognor Cricket Club in Hawthorn Road to see the amateur game played at its best. Ah! what it was to lie on one's back under the swooping swallows and just wallow in the smell of freshly mown grass and the crack of ball on bat, the earnest 'howzats', the cheeky singles, and the lazy ripples of applause from spectators slumped in deckchairs while their children practiced cartwheels in the rough; the clink of Pavilion tea cups told the time. Now and again I helped with the scoreboard, which rated a couple of shortbreads and a glass of lemon squash at the tea interval. Bognor's giants in those days were Ireland, Ayris, Jennings and Colonel Byrne.

Not only was 1938 the last year of peace, it was also England's turn to host the Australians in the battle for the Ashes. And it was during that August that word got around that Johnny Walker Whisky (alias the Distiller's Company) had erected a large scoreboard in the grounds of the Pavilion, claiming it to be the cutting edge of modern communications technology. For 3d. we could sit in front of what was not only a scoreboard

69 An early autumn stroll in West Street at its Chapel Street junction, with the Steyne in the background. The poster announces that *Babes in the Wood* is playing at the Pier Theatre. The date could be anywhere between 1912 and 1916.

but incorporated a diagram depicting the Test Match ground, in this case the Oval. On either side of it appeared the names of those great masters of the game: Hutton, Bradman, Sutcliffe, McCabe *et al.* Above the contraption strode a nine-foot-high figure of Johnny Walker himself. Then, through loudspeakers, the voice of – I believe – Howard Marshall, gave a commentary on the game while at the same time a white 'ball' on the screen moved to wherever in the ground it had been hit and the two 'batsmen' – red and yellow discs – 'ran' between the wickets.

But the most exciting bit came when one of the batsmen reached a landmark score. Then Johnny Walker stiffly raised his top hat; once for a fifty and twice for a century. At a time when we were barely aware of what a television set looked like, exposure to this kind of electronic wizardry – while eating a 3d. Mars Bar – had to be counted as temporal bliss of a pretty high order, even if we were not there for Len Hutton's record-breaking innings of 364 runs. But England's victory came as no surprise to those folk who, the previous week, had watched him and Hedley Verity practising on Aldwick Beach during their stay at the *Victoria Hotel* in West Bognor.

12

Bognorum, impudens et nobilis

Of toys, slot-machines – and that lion again!

Apart from the extravagances of Christmas and birthdays, for the most part we found our pleasures on our own doorstep, borrowed them from nature or procured them at small cost. However, there were occasional and welcome windfalls. Indulgent godparents, the Hampstead aunts or uncles of Alford stem could all look forward to the spiritual satisfaction that came from slipping these model(!) children the odd half-crown. And by persuading us to play such out-of-character roles, one might say they got a bargain!

So, from time to time, Roger and I found ourselves faced with *embarras de richesse* and with the siren voice of Bognor's *dolce vita* throbbing in our ears. Invariably our downward path commenced amongst the careworn slot-machines on Bognor's Pier, where seediness and excitement were to be found in felicitous combination. The machines were in the charge of 'Management', marked out from lesser men by his fawn coat and a leather pouch slung round his neck from which he exchanged our sixpences for coppers. 'Management', though, needed careful watching since we discovered he had eyes in the back of his head the moment we thumped the machines when they failed to work. Sternly, he would bid us stand aside so that he could exact his own more authoritative kind of retribution – usually in the form of a sort of karate kick taken on the run. Often it was too much for the thing. Bits fell off inside. Defunct!

By tradition, it was the Football Match which claimed our first pennies; cloned players dressed in knitted jerseys, kicking in aimless unison at a ball wandering around in touch on the other side of the field. Then the penny gave out. I never remember either of us scoring a goal. Next, the Horse Race; wild-eyed jockeys riding gravity-defying thoroughbreds, condemned to proceed only in fits and starts to an inconclusive finish, no matter how furiously the little brass wheel was turned. Then it was on to the Yacht Race, where the same dubious technology ensured the same equivocal result. For another penny we could shoot at Cats Sitting on a Wall, or make a little ball whizz round a spiral maze before disappearing through a hole in the middle. There was a Haunted House with ghosts and skeletons although, to my way of thinking, the best was a felon being hanged on a gallows, with a smirking priest looking on to see fair play for his soul.

Other machines were simply money down the drain – like the wand-waving Wizard who told tuppeny fortunes of such powerful banality they made even us cringe. Anyway, for 1s. 6d. we could have had them told by the 'Universally Acclaimed Professor Alva, late of the Crystal Palace', the palmist who, for as long as I can remember, did the tarots and crystal ball on Bognor Pier. According to my mother, our Aunt Kate once gave him a try and looked pretty thoughtful for a long time afterwards! Now all that remained was for us to get caught out by that actionable swindle, the chromium-plated crane with its grab cunningly engineered to pick up only Liquorice All-Sorts instead of one of the more valuable gifts which littered its dusty floor. Yet, never once did experience triumph over hope. Our only reward was those revolting All-Sorts.

The slot machines, though, were only a cash crop amongst the Pier's other diversions. Threepence at the turnstile, and we could find ourselves rubbing shoulders with the anglers. That was when we discovered there was more to lifting a fish from the ocean than met the eye. Sometimes three rods were needed. It required supporting echelons of haversacks and shopping baskets out of which spilled tins of bait – gentles, lug-worms and fish-heads. Spread around each angler were spare reels, scales, kitchen knives, Thermos flasks and sandwiches. Waterproof capes, woolly hats and gum-boots were *de rigeur* on Bognor Pier. Required reading was the *Angling Times*.

What first struck us, though, was how many of the fishers seemed sound asleep, hunched up in deck chairs. It was only then that the purpose of the little bells attached to the tops of their rods by clothes pegs revealed itself – one small tinkle and the recumbent figure hurled itself from its chair, firmly grasped the rod and wound it in expectantly. Often it was only a crab. But if it was a silvery fish the owner of the rod waxed jubilant while his less fortunate brethren ground their teeth as they offered him their congratulations.

In due course, my brother and I decided to take a shot at fishing ourselves. A frame and line, with all the paternosters, hooks, weights and things, cost us 9d. each at Burgess's Bazaar. Bait was lug-worms forked from Aldwick Beach in pouring rain. But that was the easy part. Casting proved the problem. It soon became clear that the centrifugal or 'bolas' method was charged with inherent dangers. A circum-gyratory assemblage of wickedly barbed hooks, brass rods and lead sinkers hissing through the air at high velocity, had the immediate effect of clearing a sizeable area of the Pier of one's fellow anglers, suddenly intent on self-preservation. If released too early it rocketted skywards on one side of the overhead telephone wire and returned via the other. This used to cause great excitement amongst both fishers and passers-by. Often it coincided with the sudden appearance, *bombasto furioso*, of 'Management', who enjoyed special telepathic gifts for incidents of this kind. Since one was left holding the frame, convincing excuses were hard to come by and only a penknife could restore an uneasy status quo.

If, on the other hand, the thing was let go a shade too late, the whole seething mass was apt to wrap itself round the Pier's railings in an abstraction of knots so complex as to defy unravelling. As a sizeable chunk of our time was devoted to repairing the ravages of one or other of these emergencies, the actual time spent fishing was quite short, our haul modest. Roger did once pull in a red mullet, but my catch included the fish with those abominable spikes which left a nasty wound on my hand. Besides, I

70 The Esplanade in its heyday with the 'ruinous trippers' down in force! The entrance to Butlin's Zoo and Aquarium was under the lath-and-plaster 'Alps' to the left of Tipper's restaurant. Further left, beyond Cotswold Crescent, the white-painted building is where Billy B. ran his Dodgem set-up at the end of Lennox Street. There seems curiously little traffic about.

always felt a bit beastly about the poor worms. Then, one day I forgot to tie the frame to the railings while casting – and the whole caboodle described a graceful arc into the sea. At low water I went back, but found not so much as a lead weight in the wet sand. Perhaps someone else had taken up fishing.

With the tide nearly full, Bognor's high divers became the focus of attraction. Big crowds gathered on the Pier and along the Prom to watch. In the early 'twenties it was the famous one-armed 'Professor' Quinn; in 1927 his place was taken by the fearless 'Professor' Davenport (with so many 'Professors' the Pier must have resembled a University Common Room!). Madge Goodall was a celebrated lady diver of the late 'twenties. But in our day they were a couple dressed in reach-me-down costumes, performing swallow dives, double somersaults and a variety of novelty routines culminating in the man plunging into the sea on a bicycle. A round of applause and pennies thrown into a bucket were their reward.

Another attraction used to be the Pierrot show at the little sea-end Pavilion, where Roger still remembers us watching a conjuror mix flour, eggs and water in his top hat and then take out of it half-a-dozen freshly baked buns which he threw to the children. Well, if it wasn't magic it was the next best thing!

Not far away, Albe Ide's speedboat, *Miss Bognor Regis*, burbled her deep-throated exhaust as passengers gingerly made their way down the iron stairs for the next high-speed soaking; 40 knots into a stiff breeze could be jolly wet in spite of the rubber aprons provided. So, if we wished to get rid of the whole of our inheritance at one fell swoop, a 2s. 6d. speedboat trip was the way to do it. Speedboats were also the passion of Mrs Victor Bruce, the well-known flyer, and motorist, who raced ACs at Brooklands. I remember her two boats, *Sez You* and *Dinky*, doing trips from the Pier. The other speed-boat forever associated with Bognor was *Miss Magic* which came on the scene a few years before the last war and was also run by Albe Ide.

Both *Miss Bognor Regis* and *Miss Magic* were owned by Sir Ronald Gunter, who ran the Tythe Barn Club on the Bay Estate. Both boats were leased to Albe Ide. Built in America and equipped with a Chrysler straight-eight engine, *Miss Bognor Regis* was powerful and, in 1930, she broke the Dover-Calais-Dover speed record. In the following year Sir Ronald, in spite of a heavy handicap, participated successfully in the National Speed Boat Trails at Southsea; Albe Ide was known to have run her at 48 knots. In about 1934 Sir Ronald and some friends used *Miss Bognor Regis* for water ski-ing, the skier being towed off the beach into the water! Albe eventually became the owner of *Miss Magic*, a Chriscraft boat with a straight-eight engine also built in America. She was last seen a few years ago by his son, Peter Ide, laid-up in a deteriorating state in a garage at North Bersted.

Tired of the Pier, only a few steps brought us to the nautical world of the Bognor fishermen below the *Beach Hotel*; the Raglesses, Welfares, Fellicks and Kents. I can still remember the terrible tragedy which struck this little community in the winter of 1936 when the two Tom Kents – father and son – were drowned among the Bognor Rocks in mountainous seas.

In the summer a few of the fishermen turned their hands to the pleasure-trip business. The best-known boats were Jack Shelley's *Silver Spray* and 'Bassy' Ragless's *Bluebird* (more of which in Chapter 20). At only a shilling a go they were more affordable – and drier – than speedboats. Sweet was the anticipation of adventure on the choppy main as my brother and I waited for the *Silver Spray* to fill with trippers, precariously picking their way over the ricketty landing stage. But at last we were under way, setting a course past the head of the Pier, with the *Rock Gardens Hotel* coming up on our starb'd bow. And how perverse it would have been not to have soaked one's sleeve up to the elbow in the lumpy waves as the boat chugged its way past Gray's bathing huts and Aldwick Place, *en route* to Craigweil House.

Our land legs regained, it was time for that mysterious magnet to draw us to the end of Lennox Street, where the old Olympian Gardens had surrendered to Billy Butlin's electric Dodgems in 1930. Soon we were enjoying five minutes of anarchic bumping and bashing, with our three-pences collected by a lad jumping from car to car. Next it was on to the fountain of coloured ping-pong balls – catching enough of which in a little wire cage at the end of a stick to win a prize permanently eluded us. From

71 The *Silver Spray* chugs home after another voyage to Craigweil House.

there it was no distance to the candy floss stall for an untidy nest of the pink stuff which tickled the nose and stuck to the hair. Clearly, we hadn't inherited my mother's inhibition about eating in public!

Further east sprawled Butlin's Zoo with its enigmatic collection of shop-soiled animals of veldt and forest, weeping out their lives under an inappropriate massif of lath-and-plaster 'Alps'. By the entrance stood a large, black African wearing a topee and dressed in white tropicals. On his shoulder rested a red macaw. Butlin had a sure touch for this sort of thing. Publicity was his strong suit. But in July 1933 it seemed as if it might be his undoing. 'Dad, do you think it might come to drink at the Duck Pond?' I asked as we drove down to Bognor one evening in that same July. 'It' was a lion. And somewhere near the town, Billy Butlin had carelessly mislaid the beast while it was on its way to his new Zoo on the Esplanade. It was still free. Earlier, my father had been on the phone to my grandmother; if she felt nervous she should stay indoors until we got down.

The story had started in the *News Chronicle*. 'Great Lion Hunt; holiday makers armed with rifles,' ran the headline. But now it was in all the papers. The only thing that was clear was the lion's name: Rex; all else was confusion. Mr Butlin's manager had called at the Police Station offering to supply 'a man able to tackle lions', but the Police had expressed surprise and pointed out that no one had yet reported a lion lost. 'However', said Inspector Cozens, gravely, 'it is the duty of anyone owning an escaped lion to report it.'

Of course, 'Nyetimber man eaten by lion' would have made a circulation manager's day! Within hours, the cream of Fleet Street's reporters were flooding into Bognor. 'Where was it last seen?' asked the reporter from the paper whose headlines later claimed it to be 'a forest-bred lion on the prowl'. 'Climping; seen by five people,' replied Mr Butlin – and he'd offered a reward

72 The Waterloo Square garden laid out to delight in about 1936.

of £50 for its apprehension. 'No, it was quite safe unless interfered with.' But might not the lion regard the 'twenty men armed with fishing nets' looking for him as being interfered with? Mr Butlin didn't think so; it was very tame, but better not to pet it. The *Evening Standard* was sympathetic towards Rex; he had fallen out of his cage … a great shock for a lion … and there was reason to believe he had chased after the lorry to get back in.

But Butlin and Co. could have saved themselves the trouble of hunting the beast at Climping. For everyone else was looking for it miles away – near Pagham. At least, that was where the press corps was. And no wonder. For – horror! – the mauled carcass of a sheep had just been discovered there in a field. The news spread like wildfire. Worried parents kept their children indoors; a Rose Green school-teacher claimed her class was in a state of terror; there were reports of a jodhpurred Billy Butlin and his lion-tamer – both late of Climping – having been seen in the fields near Sefter School, carrying nets borrowed from the Bognor fishermen. 'Lion hunt by moon-light', cried the *News Chronicle*; 'its tracks have been found and Major Conran, with his loaded gun and an iron bar, is waiting for it to return to the carcass.'

At last we arrived at the bungalow to find the drive gates tightly closed. 'Because of the lion,' explained my grandmother. But surely it was at Pagham? 'Yes, dears – but one can never tell' – quick on their paws, lions. Climping one day, Rose Green the next, perhaps Aldwick Gardens tonight. No! her eldest grandson certainly could not go looking for it in Yeoman's Acre tomorrow; not one inch beyond Mrs Duffin's Stores until it was caught! However, unbeknown to the general public, the truth had at last emerged. The report had been a mischievous hoax started by a journalist with an address in Bognor whose father – also a journalist – happened to be

on the staff of the *News Chronicle*. His accomplice, who had planted the
the dead sheep, was a small Pagham farmer. There was no lion.

But, up till then, Butlin seems to have genuinely believed it might have
been his own beast which had escaped. Remote from the day-to-day running
of his Skegness menagerie, it was only when he got through to his headquarters on the phone that he was reassured the lion didn't exist!

Now he was in a quandary. If the public got to know the lion was only
a phantom, inevitably they would draw the worst conclusion – that it was
he, the notorious publicity-seeker, who was the hoaxer. What Billy Butlin
needed more than anything else at that moment was a real lion; a lion
safely behind bars to convince the press, public and the police that the panic
was over. So he made another telephone call. This time to a circus in
Maidstone.

Eventually, and much to the relief of the folk of Pagham and Nyetimber,
rumours began to circulate that what the *Evening Star* claimed to be a 'two
year-old native of the Nairobi jungle' had been caught. The *Morning Post*
filled in the details: 'Lion pays friendly call; found eating tomatoes at
Craigweil Country Club by Mr Ramella who said, its keeper led it away like
a pet.' 'Vegetarian lion captured,' sniggered the *West Sussex Gazette*. '350 lb
lion found exhausted in field near Pagham,' added the *Portsmouth Evening
News*, and then went on: 'after it had knocked Mr Skerrit over, Mr Butlin
ran forward and threw a net over the lion'. But the *Star* wasn't to be
outdone: Mr Skerrit had told *their* reporter that 'it leapt out of some bushes,
knocked me down and stood over me'.

The next day Mr Butlin announced Rex had been examined by a vet and
found only to be tired and exhausted. He was now in his cage and had gone
to sleep. But the *Evening Standard* remained sceptical and refused to believe
it had been captured at all! 'Rex was nothing to do with another lion earlier
re-captured at Craigweil.' Suddenly, Nyetimber was infested with lions! The
truth had been more prosaic. In the early hours of the morning, after a long
cross-country journey from Maidstone, a bored and rather elderly lion had
suddenly found itself behind bars in a darkened Esplanade Zoo, where, for
the benefit of the *Evening Star* reporter, 'it roared loudly at the loss of its
recent freedom'.

When the Esplanade Zoo was opened a few days later, the king of beast's
cage was conspicuously empty. For the time being, Billy Butlin had evidently had his fill of lions! But the Law is a bit sniffy about frightening the
life out of the public besides wasting the time of the police. In December
1933 the Great Lion Hoax was re-enacted before Mr Justice Charles and a
jury at Lewes Crown Court. The defendants were W.E. Butlin, a menagerie
proprietor, his lion-tamer, Mr Skerrit, the Bognor journalist and the Pagham
farmer. In the event, the jury were prepared to believe there had been no
collusion between the journalist, Butlin and his lion-tamer. But they found
that the journalist and the farmer had intended to cause a public mischief.
In passing judgment, Mr Justice Charles fined the hapless journalist £30, and
added, 'I hope your father will deal with you.' The farmer's fine was £10.

For the press it had been a field day; circulation figures had soared. Which
just went to show how the truth should never be allowed to get in the way

of a good story! In fact, the only paper to emerge unstained was the *Bognor Regis Post*, which washed its hands of the whole 'escaped lion' nonsense. But to this 'silly-season' story there was a more significant aspect. For, as Gerard Young points out in his *History of Bognor Regis*, in the public mind it was the Great Lion Hoax of 1933 which irrevocably linked Bognor Regis with the name of Billy Butlin. And the full repercussion of this had yet to be felt.

Phantom lions or not, the shameful truth was that my brother and I were unrepentant Butlin *aficionados*. It was on his part of the Esplanade that we might often have been found, shoeless, guzzling Snofrutes as we strolled a shiftless path past Cleeves shacky photographic shop and Tippers Tea Rooms; past the the animated sideshows and the stalls selling McGill's saucy postcards. And all around us, the seductive cacaphony from the piping roundabouts, the Ghost Train's screams and the *thuddity-dud-dud* of the captive punch ball. To which, of course, had to be added the usual sort of Public-on-Holiday buzz.

And smells, too. In these the Esplanade was rich, the spectrum wide. From the ammonia taint of Butlin's Zoo to the sweet aroma of freshly roasted coffee at Sait's sunken-garden café; waftings of strawberry and vanilla mixed with the cloy of popcorn roasting and candy floss spinning. And then there were the not-so-easy-to-describe ones – like *Daily Mirrors* stuck in racks, windmills made of celluloid, and shiny rubber sea-horses. And that curious electrical smell that only Dodgems make. Across the road, our noses were arrested by smells appointed by the sea and all it touched: tarry lobster pots and greasy winch, salt-edged tarpaulins and fishing nets; lug-worms shrivelled in the sun, hempen rope and varnished boats. Other smells were brought ashore by Billy Welfare's wet and sparkling catch; codling, plaice and Dover sole. And green, encrusted crabs with barely-moving claws in white enamelled pails. But as for that fearful pong, fondly imagined by visitors to be 'ozone', well, as we all know, that was just tons of seaweed rotting on the sands!

Thus, South Avenue's two tousle-haired vagabonds – hardly a credit to their mother – continued on their meandering way home. And as they paused now and then to pick from the gutter some collectable-looking Aldershot and District bus ticket or matchbox top new to them, a passer-by would have been hard put to distinguish them from the street-bred kids from Beckton, Forest Gate or Mile End Road, as, democratically, all of us stocked up our impressionable young minds with memories of the sights, sounds and smells of a seaside funfair. And I am sure such childhood recollections of Bognor's Butlin's are still given an occasional airing in those places by people who have been drawing their Old Age Pensions for much longer than they care to admit!

By now our dusty feet had passed Queen Victoria's drinking fountain in Waterloo Square and were padding the Promenade between the Pier and West Street, where Butlin's jollity gave way to the architectural probity of the genteel Steyne, the charm of *Lansdowne House* and the grandeur of the *Royal Norfolk Hotel*.

By 'Ossy' Bridges' slipway, at the end of West Street, a forest of newspaper placards rustled in the wind, their messages aimed at the holiday

73 'Professor' Davenport about to risk his neck on Bognor Pier in 1927.

crowds: 'The *Daily Mail* Man in Bognor To-Day!' Spotting him while in possession of a copy of the *Mail* could be worth a fiver, a lot of money in those days. The *Daily Sketch* was into Sandcastle Building Contests; the *Express* offered Community Singing on the beach, and the *News Chronicle* had the brainwave of teaching children how to swim. Other placards hinted at fortunes to be made on the horses at Goodwood and Fontwell. Nearly all the papers did Holiday Crossword competitions; yet others gave away bicycles. But, in 1937, history was made with the appearance on the beach, below the *Royal Hotel*, of the 'Daily Mirror Eight', a bevy of shapely young ladies who performed callisthenics to music relayed from a silver coach.

Soon we were lost among the phalanxes of deckchairs filled with perspiring British Legion husbands dressed in their Sunday bests, their other halves clad in C&A prints, stockinged in twisted lisle and fanning themselves with *Mirrors* or *Tit Bits*. Meanwhile, driven by the incoming tide, the beach hordes were making their way up the wooden staircases onto the overcrowded promenade where they were greeted by the sandwich-board man's sombre message, 'Repent ye for the End of the World is Nigh.' Down on the sands, a skeleton audience watched the waves fingering the guy ropes of Mr Punch's little booth, where his alter ego was urgently whacking the long-suffering Judy ... 'that's the way to do it'. Ho, ho – how we always laughed at that!

Not far away, between groynes 20 and 21 (at £30 a season, the most expensive pitch on the Esplanade), Bognor's Clown wiped the greasepaint from his face as he waited for the tide to uncover enough of his sea-washed stage to start his routine for the umpteenth time that season. In the next groyne, only the lower part of London Bridge was left to remind the passing throng of the ephemerality of 'Sandscratcher' Mather's latest masterpiece.

From the Western Bandstand, the *William Tell* Overture drifted across the sea to merge with the roar of the old Avro passing overhead, pulling its *News of the World* banner; a harassed nursemaid scolded her charges; the Antarctic ice-cream man tinkled his bell; a moustachioed beach inspector marched past self-importantly, and scores of visitors glanced at their watches so as not to miss the London train. In Aldwick Road, the 55 Southdown bus growled past on its way to Barrack Lane. It was a scene in which we had played a walk-on part a hundred times.

Our pockets bare except for 2d., it was a toss-up: heads, a couple more Wall's Snofrutes; tails, the luxury of a bus ride back to Aldwick Gardens. Since these two brothers' capacity to spend pocket money so exceeded their parents willingness to stump up with it, near-insolvency was our normal condition. So, finding free entertainment became our trade, making it possible for us to spend a whole afternoon in metropolitan Bognor on 2d. each. And quite often on nothing at all!

All the diversions I have listed – Punch and Judy, our Sandscratcher's latest creation, and Bognor's Clown – as well as Duggie Campbell's beach show – could look forward to our non-contributory presence in their audience. A gawping stroll through Butlin's cost nothing. Neither did messing around in the pools below the Pier, or chatting up the billy goats and Mr Neil's donkeys. Helping the fishermen heave one of their boats up on to the shingle showed a generosity of spirit contrasting with our financial frailty. If we sat on the grass, we could listen to half-an-hour of music from the Western Bandstand at no cost. And Burgess' Bazaar or Goodacre's in York Road were always available for a little premature Christmas window-shopping. In 1935 I remember whiling away part of an afternoon looking at a huge model of the liner *Queen Mary* with revolving propellers which suddenly appeared in Lewis's furnishing shop window in London Road.

Municipal drainage trenches, road tarring and pile-driving for the Pier's new landing stage were all costless time-fillers. If the doors were open, we could always peep inside the High Street Fire Station with the hope of being allowed to sit in the driver's seat of the Leyland Escape. Calls of nature were met courtesy of the new Southdown bus station, gratis and freshly aromatic. And, when all else failed, what better than to emulate our Uncle Gilbert thirty years earlier, by seeking envelopment in the delicious, oily-smelling steam from the chimneys of the Southern Railway locomotives as they puffed under the bridge at the level crossing? But we had one trick up our sleeves that our uncle hadn't – putting a spare halfpenny on the railway line so that the first train that came along turned it into a sort of thinnish penny! How we did it without being spotted by the nearby signalman remains a trade secret, but it involved dropping a hanky near one of the shiny running rails!

74 Looking east along the High Street in about 1931: Timothy Whites, Leslies' Café, and Osborne's Tea Rooms – those friendly ghosts from yesteryear.

When we had squeezed the last ounce of free entertainment out of the town – and if the tide was low – we trawled the rockpools back to Aldwick in the hope of finding some luggable-home piece of flotsam. In winter, when the Duck Pond flooded over Aldwick Road, there was half-a-morning's fun to be had watching the cars and buses ploughing through its muddy waters – always in the hope that one of them might become stuck! My mother, I know, never feared for our safety. Truly, it was an age of innocence.

Toys! That word so redolent of one's short-trousered days! It is the early hours of that Christmas morning *c.*1932. Through the eiderdown, a gentle weight upon my legs ... I lean down in the cold air ... my fingers touch a box ... What might it be? ... lead soldiers? ... a chemistry set? ... something for my railway? Excitedly, I draw it towards me ... then tear away the paper wrappings ... Gosh! For just discernible in the pre-dawn gloom I can read that magic word, 'Meccano'! Quickly, on with the electric light, off with the lid! And, behold, in front of me a sumptuous array of green metal bars shiny red plates patterned with little holes. I can see rows of brass wheels and bundles of mysterious-looking brackets – not to mention four wheels with rubber tyres; even a screwdriver and a spanner. By half-past seven I was able to awake my father and show him a windmilly thing I'd made. Frank Hornby had invented a winner!

Some of the larger models took many hours – with overtime spent on hands and knees searching for miniscule nuts and bolts that constantly strayed beneath cushions and armchairs; the Hoover bag was a last resort. Gantries, cranes, motor cars and bridges; over the years all were screwed and spannered together. Plastic was never the same.

After Christmas, postal and money orders from the Hampstead Aunts, grandparents and my French Riviera-dwelling godmother were cashed at Mrs Duffin's stores. With unholy thoughts of material acquisition wrapped in tissue paper, our next port-of-call was Burgess' Bazaar at the corner of Manor Place in Waterloo Square – where, as the reader will recall, my mother bought her doll in 1904. And what a cornucopia of toys it was! Shelves groaned under boxes of Meccano and Hornby trains ('British toys for British boys'), sagged under Lott's Chemistry Sets, Ubilda and Kliptiko. There were pogo-sticks, hoops and punch balls. Covetously, our eyes ranged over the products of Messrs Wells and Lines Bros, over the wares of Mettoy and Chad Valley. Appetites were whetted by regiments of Britten's lead soldiers, by 'self-guiding' roller-skates and brass-boilered Marklin steam engines (tut tut! a German *spielwaren* for a German *junge* – but impeccably made). At different Christmases and birthdays we carried away the Progress Toy Company's gyroscopes, 'Diana' air rifles, Bulldog printing sets, clock-work fire engines and painted tin railway engines that threw out sparks from their funnels. Alas, their working parts were no match for salt and sand; rust-locked machinery was a permanent feature of our toy chest.

Nor must I fail to mention the FROG, a model aeroplane with an elastically-driven propellor – although its acronym, for 'Flies Right Off the Ground', was an expression of hope rather than experience! But at 5s. it could be the subject of tortuous negotiations with parents who pleaded penury. For the rest of the year, though, our purchases were more modest; parts for our Hornby railway, 'Atlanta' kites at 1s. 3d. and sixpenny silver gliders. Oh yes, and endless red 'compo' cricket balls.

In 1934 we were in at the launch of the Dinky Toy cult. Real rubber tyres were their attraction and racing cars our favourites, with quite good like-nesses of Hotchkiss, Auto-Union and Mercedes-Benz. It wasn't long before my brother and I discovered the best race-tracks were to be modelled in sand on the sloping sea-wall opposite the Steyne. Gravity did the rest – given the odd push. But that was long before the accountants turned the top part of Bognor's beach into an unhappy imitation of the Chichester gravel pits.

Other toys we accumulated were Hornby Speedboats – with loseable keys – and a rubber-tracked army tank ('Travels 50 feet On One Winding!') which spent its short life climbing up and over *Gresham's English Dictionary* on the rug in front of the living-room fire. Yachts, too, quite good ones for 1s. 6d. After the Pavilion Boating Pool had been opened in April 1937, we – which now included our youngest brother Julian – sometimes took our boats there to share its ports and tideways with the paddler's splashy legs.

With the 'thirties came the various 'crazes': the Yo-Yo was the best known and in those days was to be found in nearly every schoolboy's – and girl's – satchel. Brilliantly simple, it came in various sizes: the '99', which

was made of tin, hummed and cost an unbelievable one guinea; the '66' and
'33' were of wood, silent, cheaper and thus more appealing to parents. I
remember a competition for Yo-Yo addicts being held at the Pavilion. A year
ot two later it was the turn of the 'Bif-bat' to hit the market – a rubber ball
attached by a length of elastic to a wooden bat – that's all, but it gave us
hours of fun. In my mother's day the 'craze' had been the gyroscopic
'Diabolo'.

Central to our younger days were lead soldiers and farm animals. And
what could be more mouth-watering than peeling back the tissue-paper of
a box containing a dozen red-jacketed Coldstream Guardsmen, under their
burnt-sultana busbies, marching with 'shouldered arms'? Farm animals may
not have had the charisma of soldiers, but had the advantage that they could
be collected singly; a chicken for a penny, a sitting-down sheep for 2d. or
the standing-up ones, 3d. A black-and-white Friesian would wring from us
6d. – the same as a milkmaid with two buckets on a yoke – while a shiny-
harnessed Clydesdale in a brown paper bag could deplete a wincing parent's
reserves by all of 1s. 3d. And, with a bit of luck, an unbalanced aunt might
be cajoled into parting with half-a-crown for a tipping farm-cart.

But farm animals suffered from their inherent passivity. It was difficult,
I mean, to imagine three sitting-down cows getting up and breaking into a
ground-trembling stampede. Somehow they seemed more for buying and
swopping than for playing with. Imagination-wise, soldiers had the edge.
And that was how, with a passable imitation of a Lewis gun in support of
my stiffly advancing Coldstream Guards, I could reduce my young brother's
mob of Hussars, medieval knights and a mercenary Arab to unconditional
surrendcr within minutes. And what better way to celebrate a great victory
than a bit of *oom-pah-pah* from the Band of the Royal Marines and their
leaden big bass drum, parading unsteadily on the ramparts of my mother's
tea trolley?

Alas, the hens and sheep were destined to be dug in round the rhubarb,
and when the cows and horses lost a leg or two, and most of their paint,
they were put out to grass in the OXO box reserved for orphan toys ... but
the rifleless soldiers remained bravely on duty, nearly up to the time a real
war overtook our short-trousered days.

The other toy shops in Bognor were Toyland in the Arcade and Goodacre's on the corner of York Road and the Esplanade. One day Toyland was
damaged by fire* and from the ensuing salvage sale I emerged triumphantly
bearing a slightly scorched model of the three-funnelled *Berengaria* costing
next to nothing, while my brother acquired a cut-price submarine which
underwent its diving trials in Mrs Gentle's water-butt.

---

* This was not the big fire of 5 November 1930, which destroyed a lot of the east side of the
Arcade, including Toyland, but a later and smaller conflagration in about 1934 which affected only
the toyshop.

Vale Nana

In September 1935 our dear Nana – she who had shared my bringing-up, combed my hair, kept me fragrant and read to me from *Chick's Own* – passed peacefully away at Idlewylde, her hand in my mother's until the end. Her heart. The family's grief can be imagined. So the bungalow, with its poignant memories, was locked up and we went back to London, not to return to Aldwick until the following spring.

Perhaps in an attempt to fill the gap left by our recent loss, a few weeks later my parents presented us with Judy, a liver-and-white springer spaniel puppy with an overwhelming instinct for fetching and carrying. To Judy, cushions, pyjama tops, face flannels, pieces of Meccano and little Julian's squeaky rubber duck all counted as pheasants! Any visitor would be eagerly presented with whatever Judy could find – usually, it seemed, some unwholesome item of dirty laundry. At Aldwick it was a perpetual chore, collecting the family's infrastructure from up and down South Avenue; even from halfway to the beach. And when she wasn't carrying, she was burying. Nothing was more precious to Judy than her collection of dry bones, each of which had to be energetically interred one day and vigorously disinterred for inspection the next from among the roots of what my mother used invariably to moan was some irreplaceable shrub.

But, of course, in time it was Judy herself who became irreplaceable.

75 Judy

13

Before the Picturedrome

Bognor's hitherto baleful reputation for its lack of entertainment facilities underwent a sea change in 1911, when William Tate's* Kursaal and the Pier Theatre were opened within a few months of one another.

The Pier Theatre's story began in 1908, opposite Waterloo Square, when Michael Shanly and his partner, Alfred Carter, relieved the Bognor Council of their rapidly disintegrating Victorian Pier, a transaction which cost them a nominal 10s. Often dubbed the 'Chair King', the entrepreneurial Shanly – domiciled at Felpham – had made a fortune out of hiring chairs in the royal parks (and at Bognor, too) as well as from a variety of enterprises in other holiday towns. And his wealth was about to come in pretty useful. For their moribund purchase was no snip, bringing with it the expensive legal obligation of rectifying years of Council neglect. Only the development possibilities of its shore-end adjoining the Parade made the Pier a worth-while proposition. And for such an exercise they required the services of an architect, preferably one with a knowledge of iron piers.

Over at Southsea they found George Edward Smith FRIBA, who, besides having designed the Portsmouth Municipal College, had also been res-ponsible for Southsea's South Parade Pier. Smith's proposal was for a 920-seat theatre with a well-equipped stage and a graceful dress circle balcony sweeping round three sides of the auditorium. Access to the new building was via an arcade of 12 shops leading off the Promenade. Above the shops his brief had included something still a novelty at the time: a purposely designed 600-seat 'Electric Theatre' equipped with 'the latest kinemato-graphic machinery'. Further seawards, at the same level, he planned an Al Fresco Roof Garden for summer use only. The contractors were Messrs W.H. Archer & Sons of Gravesend; the cost, £30,000. Meanwhile, the deteriorating Pier was let to Hepworth's Studios as a stage-set for making a slapstick picture called – well, what else? – *Painting the Pier!*

In Shanly and Carter's hands the new ciné culture was enthusiastically received. For almost as soon as contracts had been exchanged their assistant manager, the 'pushful and energetic' Mr Claude Flude, was put in charge of adapting the little sea-end Pavilion for showing 'Shanly's High Class Ani-mated Pictures' – although, as Mr Flude reminds us in a reminiscing article published in the *Bognor Regis Post* in November 1964, not until it was dark. For blacking-out the Pavilion's windows proved a constant problem.

Nevertheless, improvements were introduced and thus, from April 1909 – in between roller-skating sessions, 'confetti battles' and ladies egg-and-spoon races – the public began flocking to see films with titles such as

---

* For information on William Tate see the Appendix, p.307.

Love, Luck and Gasoline, Round the World in a Motor Car and *The Talisman*; 'hand-coloured' and an early example of a 'singing picture' in which a gramophone record was synchronised to match the movement of the person's lips – a technique not best known for its accuracy! On 4 January 1911 the little Pavilion cinema enjoyed something of a *coup* when they were able to show Pathé Gazette's pictures of the Sidney Street Siege* within 24 hours of them being taken. With seats at 3d., 6d. and 1s., these films proved highly popular; often it was difficult to get in. In the meantime, the new theatre facing Waterloo Square was nearing completion.

On Whit Saturday, 3 June 1911, Shanly and Carter opened their first-floor 'Electric Theatre' – 'the coolest theatre in town' – with a collection of 'Animated Pictures'. The *Observer's* reporter was much impressed: '... the animated pictures at the Pier Theatre are as well nigh perfect as anyone could wish ... there are crowded audiences at every performance ...' Seven weeks later – barely completed – the contractors handed over the rest of the main theatre. Following the obligatory Band Concert the previous evening, on Monday 14 August 1911, its stage was brought to life with a production of Louis Shipman's much-heralded comedy, *D' Arcy of the Guards*, while upstairs in the Picture Theatre patrons were treated to 'two Red Indian pictures', *The Chief's Daughter* and *The Trapper's Prize*. Outside, in the ozone-steeped Al Fresco Roof Garden, Grey's Concert Party turned an honest penny entertaining those members of the public unable to get into the other two halls.

On 10 September the Pier Orchestra accompanied the first Sunday programme of 'latest and best pictures' shimmering on the main theatre's screen. Soon they were followed by titled films, amongst them *The Price of Beauty*, *Foe to Richelieu* in October and the hand-coloured *Battle of Trafalgar* a few weeks later. Meanwhile, the 'Electric Theatre' upstairs was proving even more popular than its Pier-end predecessor. It, too, was regularly sold out; 'standing room only' became the norm. Patrons were advised to book in advance to see such cinematic treasures as *Lady Godiva*, *The Engineer's Daughter*, *Thrown to the Lions* and *The Still Alarm*, 'the greatest "fire" picture ever made!' By 1912 jerky black-and-white newsreels, changed twice a week, showed the Boat Race, the State Opening of Parliament and War in the Balkans. Then, in that same year, the Electric Theatre's name was changed to the less ambiguous one of the Pier Picture Theatre.

In 1909, with the success of his Arcade behind him, William Tate embarked upon his most ambitious project, the great Kursaal entertainment complex on the east side of York Road between the Esplanade and Belmont Street. The Kursaal began life in the Arcade Chambers office of Bognor architect William Tillott Barlow ARIBA, the designer of many local buildings, including Reynolds' Furniture Depository opposite the Picturedrome.

Barlow's scheme for the south end of the site comprised a roller-skating

* On 3 January 1911 three armed Russian anarchists barricaded themselves into a house in Sidney Street in the East End of London. The Scots Guards were called out and shots were exchanged, watched by the Home Secretary, Mr Winston Churchill. Later the building caught fire. Inside two charred bodies were found, but the notorious 'Peter Painter' was believed to have escaped.

76 The Pier Theatre, Bognor's first 'modern' cinema. Showing on this occasion is *The King of Jazz*, with Paul Whiteman and his Orchestra, which was doing the rounds in 1930. It is difficult to remember that the Pier and its theatre once looked like this!

rink on the first floor and, below it, a general purpose concert hall – one day to become famous as 'Pierrotland'. There was space also for a 'balconied tea-room'. The northern part of the complex was taken up with the Kursaal Theatre, approached through an arcade of shops which gave the illusion of being a continuation of Tate's earlier Arcade on the opposite side of Belmont Street. The first- and second-floor suite of rooms facing the sea, '46 feet long extending between the domes', had been let to the Unionists and Constitu-tional Club and was the first part of the new complex to be commissioned – at a ceremony performed in November 1910 by Club President, Lord Edmund Talbot MP. It was not until March 1911 that the skating rink was opened, when, to the approbation of the *Bognor Observer*, '300 skaters took to its maple floor' and inaugurated what was to become a long-lasting Bognor institution.

On Whit Monday, 5 June, preceded a day earlier with a concert given by the Royal Garrison Artillery Band, the new Theatre's curtain – emblazoned with the Bardic quotation, 'Come unto these yellow sands'* – rose for a stage performance of Arthur Benham's production of *Old Heidelberg*, a romantic comedy brought hot-foot from London's St James' stage. 'The theatre', reported the *Observer*, 'was in every way significantly equipped, presenting a brilliant spectacle, and every part of the house was packed.' A few days later, the covers were removed from the Kursaal's 'Patent, flicker-

* From Ariel's song, Act I, Scene II of *The Tempest.*

less, fireproof kinematograph' for screening its first programme of 'shorts', described as 'dramas, humorous and scenic' and including such titles as *Baptist thinks he was Bitten by a Mad Dog* and *Tweedledum is Late.*

With a few exceptions, such as the weekday showing of the Fleet Review, the Coronation of King George V in 1911 and *With our King and Queen through India* in 1912, film performances were generally restricted to Sundays. Otherwise, the Kursaal remained resolutely stage-orientated. *Oh, Susanna*, Shaw's *Candida* ('a mystery in Three Acts') and *The Merry Widow* all appeared in 1911; *Babes in the Wood* was staged at Christmas 1912, with the crew of the two-masted barque, *Carnot* – wrecked a few days earlier on Aldwick Beach – enjoying free seats amongst the audience. In 1913 theatregoers were treated to 'a pantomimical musical comedy' entitled *The Mormon's Honeymoon*, while 1914 was marked by the staging of *A Cigarette Maker's Romance* as well as the appearance on the theatre's boards of the great Sir Seymour Hicks. Indeed, seven years later, in 1921, the gifted young Lady Diana Cooper – not far from her Rutland roots at Craigweil – could have been found there playing the lead role in *The Naughty Young Wife*, straight from her London success.

In April 1919, six months after the Great War had ended, a curiously delayed streak of patriotism, the Kursaal's Germanic name was removed from the roof and re-christened the Theatre Royal, with the skating rink and Pierrotland becoming known as the Theatre Royal Building. And in this form it continued until the waning interest in roller-skating in the 'thirties forced it into a catalogue of entertainment roles – although Eric Ross' *Dazzle* was still playing Pierrotland when another war was declared in 1939.

After the war, the Theatre Royal building was refurbished to emerge in May 1947 as the Rex Entertainment Centre, its skating rink transformed into the famous Grand Ballroom and *Dazzle* still playing at what had now become the Rex Theatre.

However, by the 'seventies, Tate's old Kursaal found itself confronted by the planners from the Bognor Regis and Arun District Councils. In 1975 the Rex and Theatre Royal – the latter now reduced to Bingo – were deemed to be in the way of the latest version of Bognor's innumerable post-war seafront re-development schemes. Sentence to death by bulldozing and iron ball was the inevitable verdict. By the end of 1975 no vestige of either remained as plans were drawn up for building their less worthy successor.

Fending off the Kursaal's competition, the Pier Theatre continued to stage many successful plays, including Marie Corelli's *The Sorrows of Satan* (1911), *The Merchant of Venice* during a Shakespeare week in October 1912 and Victor Hugo's *Les Miserables* in May of the following year. And yet it was the vaudeville turns which stuck in the mind of Mr Flude, who reminds us that Harry Tate, George Robey – 'the Prime Minister of Mirth' – Little Tich and Vesta Tilley all at different times took their bows in front of the Pier's curtain – as, too, did Roy Beaver 'in some Extraordinary Feats of Legerdemain', not to mention the cast of *Uncle Tom's Cabin*, serio-comic and 'with real negroes!'

Although the Pier began, like its York Road neighbour, by showing films in its theatre auditorium mainly on Sundays, such was the demand for the longer and more prestigious 'star' pictures – distributed by Itala, Edison, Pathé Frères *et al* – that performances increasingly spilled over into other days of the week. So the sight of the projector's beams dancing through the cigarette-smoke-laden air gradually became part of peoples lives as they watched the un-reeling of such spectacles as *Charge of the Light Brigade*, 'with special effects' provided by the local Territorials, Pathé's hand-coloured drama *A Beautiful Traitor*, and Max Reinhardt's masterpiece *The Miracle*, an 8,000-footer 'augmented with choir and organ!' In May 1914 the term 'cartoon' first appeared in a Pier advertisment.

Then, in August, Pathé newsreels began screening 'the crisis' and, later, the great military events of the First World War; those ghastly battles such as Ypres, the Marne, the Somme. Yet, even the war failed to dampen the public's insatiable appetite for 'the movies'. By September 1914 more films were being shown in the main auditorium than in the little Picture Theatre upstairs. According to Claude Flude, the following month the Pier's directors let it be known that 'in order to save clashing with the Theatre Royal' they had decided to move away from stage productions and henceforth would concentrate mainly on showing 'moving pictures'. The little picture theatre upstairs was relegated to become the Pier Hall, destined for strolling players. Thus, more by chance than design, the Pier Theatre became Bognor's first, major, 'modern' cinema.

In July 1936 the Pier Theatre's name was changed to the more factual one of the Pier Cinema, which continued showing films until, during the 1950s, it entered upon a period of decline which was to prove terminal. Unlit for most of the year, it came to life only for short summer seasons with a return to the vaudcville tradition of its youth: Bernard Delfont's *Show Time*, *The Front Page Lovelies* of 1953, and Skiffle and Talent Contests in 1957, interspersed with the sporadic stage appearances of 'Cheerful' Charlie Chester, Tommy Fields and Elsie and Doris Waters. Changing its name back to 'theatre' in 1956 did nothing to revive its fortunes. Implacably, television, bingo and the Esplanade Theatre eroded the viability of a building with over a thousand seats to fill. The end came with more of a whimper than a bang on 30 August 1959, when the curtain fell for the last time on an unremarkablc talent competition.

The little 'Electric Theatre' of 1911 was reincarnated as the Roof Garden Theatre in 1937, and after the war it became the home of the brilliantly talented Phoenix Players Repertory Company and their producer Ian Stewart. Who can forget those inspired performances by Lydia Jaeger, June Flavell, Donovan Ubsdell and John Cabot, which brought pleasure to thousands, including the author, during those days of rationing and electricity blackouts in post-war Britain?

In 1908 the only purposely designed entertainment building of any size in Bognor, apart from the Olympian Gardens and the little Pier Pavilion (we can forget the Victoria Hall in London Road, more often the venue for Reynolds' auctions than for any work of theatrical endeavour), was the rather leaden-sounding New Assembly Rooms dominating the corner of Canada Grove and Linden Road. Completed in 1886, this rather stylish building with its lantern-like facade was the work of Arthur Smith, another

Bognor architect, whose work included the all-but-still-born Victoria Park Estate scheme of the 1870s, the Board School in Lyon Street and the *Royal Pier Hotel*. His scheme was for two halls: a large auditorium and a smaller general purpose room with the former seating 800 persons on a level floor which boasted a stage and facilities for giving magic-lantern shows. Sumptuously finished internally, the cost was £4,500.

On 8 June 1886 the new Assembly Rooms were opened by the Earl of March 'before a crowded and fashionable audience comprising most of the élite of Bognor'. Soon it became a popular venue for dances, variety acts, exhibitions and the occasional visit by the Poole Brothers' travelling 'myriographic film shows'. In 1911 the building was given the slightly brighter name of the Queen's Hall in honour of Queen Mary, the recently crowned King's consort

During the years which followed, in addition to its staple diet of whist drives, melodramas, roller-skating and the annual Bognor event of the Primrose League Tea Party – not forgetting the appearance of Mark Hambourgh at the piano – the Queen's Hall enjoyed a few piquant occasions. On 18 May 1912 it was the setting for a noisy protest against the 'Disestablishment and Disendowment of the Church in Four Welsh Dioceses'. Beneath its roof in December 1913 the Balham Operatic Society presented Pinero's *Floradora* to an enthusiastic gathering of Bognor's opera buffs. In January of the following year a cinematograph-aided lecture entitled 'Port Sunlight and the Prosperity of Sharing' no doubt warmed the cockles of a few Fabian hearts.

Altruism was displayed by the Queen's Hall management. In 1912 the proceeds from a film show were donated to a Mrs Roe, widow of a drowned local fisherman. And in the following year another 'benefit' was staged 'to help Bognor's Clown, who had been seriously ill and unable to work'.

During the Great War the Queen's Hall served loyally, if briefly, as a barracks. By 1919 change was in the air. The Hall, now owned by P.D. Stoneham, an Eastbourne architect, was given a silver screen, a fire-proof projectionist's box, a ramped floor – and yet another name, the rather modish 'Picturedrome'. On 5 June, to the accompaniment of its in-house orchestra, the new cinema was declared open by Mr James Fleming of Aldwick Grange (father of Lindsay Fleming, the author of *History of Pagham in Sussex*). And, with that, the screen lit up to Hepworth Studio's *Boundary House*, starring Alma Taylor, one of Cecil Hepworth's 'discoveries'. Neither was the new management lacking in the altruism of its predecessor; the day's takings were donated to the War Memorial Hospital of which James Fleming had long been the benefactor. And so, at the end of that eventful day, Bognor found itself raised to the rank of a two-cinema town.

Since it became a cinema the Picturedrome has had a number of different managements: in 1922 it was taken over by Shanly and Carter of the Pier Theatre; and since the Second World War it has worn the logos of a number of cinema chains and undergone much adaptation to keep up with the ever-changing state of ciné technology. Yet, as proclaimed by its Art Deco name over the entrance porch, it remains, miraculously, 'The Picturedrome' to this day.

14

'Isn't this where we came in?'

It now requires a conscious effort to recall the magic world opened up to us by the 'movies' in the pre-television 'twenties and 'thirties. When the family first came to Bognor it contained the Pier Theatre and the Picture-drome. One of the earliest films I remember being taken to was something starring Jackie Coogan, black-and-white, silent with subtitles, and augmented with a piano. The cinema I've forgotten but it must have been during our holiday at Forrabury in 1928.

However, big changes were afoot. In September of the following year the Pier Theatre announced the imminent arrival of Bognor's first 'talkie', Western Electric's film *The Perfect Alibi*, a '100% talking, singing and dancing thriller', starring Mae Busch, a pal of Rudolf Valentino's. To meet the expected rush, the Pier booking office opened at 10.30 in the morning. From Canada Grove came the strangled cry of a lost cause: 'The Picture-drome for silent films!'

At the Pier, 'talkie' versions of *Showboat*, *The Four Feathers* starring William Powell and Fay Wray, and *The Leatherneck* with William Boyd quickly followed. Curiously, though, there is no sign of the Pier ever having screened Al Jolson in *The Singing Fool*, one of the first 'talkies' to be distributed in this country. At all events, within a short time, the silent 'main feature' had been consigned to the waste-bin of celluloid history.

Our visits to the 'flicks', hitherto strictly rationed in London due to my parent's doubts about their suitability, now became less harshly regarded as my mother discovered the sweetness of a life freed for a few hours from the noisy exuberance and cooped-up energy of her two sons – especially during periods of rainy westerly depressions. Usually we were taken by our maid, Joan, a *Picturegoer*-carrying film fan to whom these outings were among her more precious perks.

So, 'talkie' or silent film, I can still recall that feeling of pleasurable anticipation as we shuffled down the sloping auditorium floor, treading in the little pools of light from the usherette's torch before settling in our seats to await the flickering trademarks of Paramount, Gainsborough or MGM's roaring lion (*Ars gratia Artis* must have been a lot of people's first brush with Latin) and our first glimpse of the kiss-curl and darkly-shadowed eyes of the studio's favourite heroine/femme fatale and their brilliantined, chain-smoking hero.

In fact, it was the shenanigans got up to by these femmes fatales that prompted my mother to issue Joan with an Edict of Suitability. Utterly proscribed were Greta Garbo, Gloria Swanson and Mae West. So, too, were James Cagney, Charles Boyer and – for reasons less clear – George Formby.

On the other hand, the 'deemed to satisfy' supplement included anything starring Charlie Chaplin, Buster Keaton or Laurel and Hardy, and went on to include the clock-hanging Harold Lloyd, the Will Hay Gang and the Mack Sennet 'shorts'. And all cartoons. Custard-pie stuff had my mother's blessing!

Unfortunately, though, Joan's proclivities lay in precisely the opposite direction. 'A' certificate films promising heavy-duty embraces, unrequited love, the whiff of risk with a hint of White Slave traffic thrown in to her were the main reason for going to the cinema. In consequence, Roger and I were quite often condemned to sit through long, fidgety afternoons, sustained only by 2 oz. of Sharp's toffees, as some torrid and incomprehensible three-reel weepie – things like *The Scarlet Woman*, *Coquette* or *Madam X* – unwound in front of our semi-comatose eyes. Some of the things we saw would certainly not have met with my mother's approval. But we never split on Joan, honestly.

In fact, our innocence was in far safer hands with Frances, our Aunt Bertha's maid, who shared our own love of knockabout films. She was a Geordie girl with a large heart and a powerful belly laugh. Quite unfunny things used to start her off. It was like sitting next to a time bomb! She was at her most devastating when we shared a nearly empty Picturedrome with half a dozen other patrons. Suddenly Frances would erupt into paroxysms of Tyneside guffaws which used to cause the undemonstrative natives to crane their necks in our direction, in case they could be of any assistance. Meanwhile we used to shrink down in our seats and pretend she was nothing to do with us!

Of Bognor's two cinemas, the Pier, I think, was my favourite, if only because of the hint of adventure that came from watching a film from a seat – well, a kind of red velveteen tourniquet – only a few feet above a demented sea sloshing around the frail-looking supports. Given enough on the Beaufort scale, it could be quite exciting: the whole place shook, the emergency doors banged open, curtains ballooned, broken glass tinkled and Mr Flude, the manager, came out looking slightly anxious. Often it was better than the film itself!

At the end of the performance we emerged from the darkness of the auditorium into blinding daylight, to be greeted with the roar of a blustering sou'wester, an angry sea, rattling signs and the complaining calls of herring gulls poised motionless over the silent slot machines. It was as if Æolus and Poseidon were trying to upstage the silver screen, and only bettered by the bit where old Ollie's trousers had fallen down in the last reel! Then Joan made us link arms as we bent to the boisterous wind and struggled towards the bus-stop by the Western Bandstand.

Yet, of all those miles of flickering acetate I must have seen in the early 'thirties, my mind retains little, just snatches of cowboys leaping off railway carriage roofs, the Keystone Cops dashing around in Model 'T' Fords, *Mickey Mouse* and *Felix* in black-and-white, or Tom Walls leaping over a sofa with a cup of tea in his hand in one of the Aldwych Farces. Better the newsreels. There I can still rustle up images of a pipe-smoking Stanley Baldwin leaning out of a railway carriage window, the ex-Kaiser sawing logs during his exile at Doorn in Holland and the launch of Cunard No. 534 –

the *Queen Mary* – on Clydeside. Also a terrible coalmining disaster at Gresford Colliery in 1934.

If *King Kong* deserves a mention it is only because of my triumphant cry that I could see the stitching down his hairy back … 'hush, dear, you mustn't spoil it for other people,' my mother had whispered, reprovingly. Another film deserving of immortality for all the wrong reasons was *Sanders of the River,* starring Leslie Banks and Paul Robeson, which my brother and I saw in about 1935. Thereafter, armed with broom-stick assegais and dustbin-lid shields, we spent many happy, blood-curdling hours trying to impale each other, with bonus marks awarded for dramatic death throes and the Old King's last gurgled chants!

In the days of 'continuous performances' it seemed almost mandatory to arrive in the middle of the main feature. Seeing the end of it separated from the beginning by the *The Three Stooges* and a *Silly Symphony* we took in our uncritical stride. Half-time was signalled by the house lights coming on and the smokers lighting up as we watched the yellowy, jingle-free adverts. The regular ones in those days were for Targett's the butchers, Thorpe's the chemists in West Bognor, and the electrical engineers Rowbotham and Pinnock. Others were Hansford's, Tregear's the grocers and Captain Seagrim's Riding Stables at Slindon. Lastly came the clips for 'forthcoming attractions', their subliminal contents duly noted.

An hour and a half later, one of us would mutter those time-worn words, 'Isn't this where we came in?' Then, after searching under our seats for the remains of the wine-gums and the usual missing glove, we excused ourselves past half-a-dozen rather cross-looking members of the audience as we made our way out into the daylight and the long walk home – so often, it seemed, in pouring rain.

1933 marked a notable ciné occasion in Bognor when Miss E.L. Carter's Albany House School for Girls in London Road was knocked down and a

PICTUREDROME
[OPPOSITE STATION]
FOR SILENT FILMS

Monday, Sept. 16th for 3 days
Continuous from 2.45
CHARLIE MURRAY
in the laughter film
THE HEAD MAN
also Ian Hunter & Louise Prussing in
THE THOROUGHBRED
A Thrilling Drama of the Turf

Thursday, Friday, Saturday
NANCY CARROL & RICHARD ARLEN
in
MANHATTAN COCKTAIL
and Full Supporting Programme

Sunday, Sept. 22nd at 8
Patricia Allon & Rolla Norman in
THE RULING PASSION

PIER THEATRE
BOGNOR REGIS

Monday, September 16th for 7 Days
(Sunday 22nd at 8 only).   Continuous from 10.30

The Management beg to announce that the Theatre has now been equipped with the latest and most efficient apparatus for the presentation of
TALKIES
This apparatus supplied and fitted by the Western Electric Co., Ltd., is the same as that in use at all the Leading London Cinemas.

Monday, September 16th for 7 Days
SEE AND HEAR
A 100% Talking, Singing and Dancing Dramatic Thriller
THE PERFECT ALIBI
with CHESTER MORRIS, PAT O'MALLEY and MAE BUSCH
Supported by
Pathe Sound Magazine and Silent Programme

Prices *(including tax)* : 9d. 1/3, 1/6, 2/- & 2/4.   Boxes 9/4 for Four

77 The end of the beginning … and the beginning of the future: advertisements for silent films and 'talkies'.

78 The Odeon Theatre in London Road; in 1934 the last word in modern cinemas.

new Odeon cinema* began to go up. Since we regarded all new Odeons as 'good things' we watched Bognor's grow with warm anticipation.

At a gala performance on Saturday 14 July 1934 attended by Oscar Deutch, the head of Odeon Cinemas and Fred Perry, the All-England tennis champion, Captain H.C. Pocock RN, Chairman of the Council – who had cornered the market in this sort of thing – cut the metaphorical tape and let loose an evening in which the speeches and general jollification took precedence over the showing of some 'shorts' and then the main film, *It's a Cop*, starring the effervescent Sydney Howard. One visit to Bognor's new, perfumed cinema deluxe with its streamlined auditorium, comfortable seats, hand-picked usherettes and a uniformed doorman was quite enough for us swiftly to relegate the Pier and the Picturedrome to the second division.

Although the town now had three cinemas, with two and a half thousand seats between them serving a population of some 18,500, it only narrowly escaped getting two more. In 1933 Mr Harry Humphry's Little Pavilion site on the north-west corner of Waterloo Square had come on the market and immediately attracted the attention of the cinema chains. In June of that year Cinema Services applied to the Council for consent to build on it a 1,202-seater which would have made it by far the largest cinema in the town. However, after a bumpy journey at the hands of the

---

* The Odeon's architects were Whinney, Son and Austen Hall, a well-known London firm of cinema architects. W.F. Blay Ltd, also of London, were the contractors. The cost was about £14,000.

Chichester magistrates to do with building lines, road widening and traffic hazards, it was dropped in 1935.

Undeterred, in the following year Union Cinemas instructed Robert Cromie, an eminent cinema architect – the Regals at Bexleyheath and Beckenham were his – to have another shot at Humphry's site. The result was the Rex, a more modest 980-seat scheme embodying every 'lavish luxury'. Yet, although it received Bognor Council's consent, Cromie's plans still had to face the rigours of the Magistrates' Court at Chichester, where it met a similar fate to its predecessor. Appearing as a witness for the objectors, the manager of the Pier Theatre and the Picturedrome, Mr Flude, in a rare moment of impartial observation, considered a fourth cinema in Bognor quite unnecessary! Refusing the application, the magistrates not only appeared to agree with him, but made heavy weather of the cost of employing two police constables to control the traffic. Today the site is occupied by flats.

In developers' minds, too, cinemas were regarded as gold mines. A year earlier, in October 1935, a Mr S.G. Sloggett came up with a scheme. His plan was to demolish the *Royal Norfolk Hotel* and build on the site a cinema deluxe plus some shops facing West Street, together with a ten-storey block of flats and a salt-water bathing pool overlooking the sea. Yet in spite of receiving the Council's uncritical blessing, it too – mercifully – sank without trace.

In fact, Bognor had to wait until the second year of the war before it got its fourth cinema. With the acting profession rushing off to join ENSA, the khaki audiences mainly unappreciative of straight theatre, and the lure of Hollywood insatiable, the Theatre Royal – formerly William Tate's Kursaal – at last threw in its thespian sponge. By then in the hands of Harold T.A. Philpot, a Midlands-based cinema proprietor with a house at Bognor, it was

79 The Olympian Gardens at the end of Lennox Street, here a backdrop to a departing Southdown excursion in about 1925.

given a decorative facelift and installed with 'high-intensity projectors and the Western Electric Sound System' to emerge as 'a new Cinema de-luxe in which only the very best films, regardless of cost, were to be expected'. After a few apposite words from the comedian Sydney Howard, it opened on 3 November 1941 with *The Road to Zanzibar* staring Bob Hope, Bing Crosby and Dorothy Lamour. And that was just what the troops were stamping for!

Thus, one is aware of having lived through a large part of the golden age of a medium which, in the space of little more than a quarter of a century, completely changed the leisure habits of much of the western world. Going to the cinema – or 'the flicks' – became a constituent part of social habits. And it was quite difficult to be far from a billboard that didn't proclaim the coming to town of one or other of the reigning Hollywood gods and god-desses – Douglas Fairbanks, Ronald Coleman, Garbo, Myrna Loy, Clark Gable *et al* – even Zazu Pitts a feather-brained and rather lovable smaller goddess.

Apart from the cinemas and the big Pavilion off West Street, the only other entertainment establishment I remember at Bognor was the old Olympian Gardens where, in 1930, my mother took me to see the comedian, Leonard Henry (even then well-known to BBC audiences), who was appearing in his *Little Show.* In the late 19th century there had stood at the south-west end of Lennox Street a site known locally as the 'coal wharf', once the depository for coal brought to Bognor by brigs from the north-east ports which unloaded their cargo on the nearby beach. In 1900 – now redundant – it was purchased by the well-known impresario, Wallis Arthur, who, after fencing it in and partly covering it with a canvas awning, named it, rather grandly, the Olympian Gardens. Arthur's speciality was 'Sopranos, Baritones, Comedians, Conjurors and Pianist'. For years his was Bognor's main venue for 'Al Fresco' entertainment; many up-and-coming stars sharpened their talents on its boards, among them Gertrude Lawrence, Gillie Potter and Milton Hayes.

Around 1911, by which time Wade and Glusten, the Bognor architects, had arranged for the Gardens to receive a more substantial roof, a sloping floor and 'incandescent lights', Wallis Arthur took a short-lived – but doomed – shot at showing films. In spite of this setback, his niche in 'concerts which have helped in the making of Bognor' continued to earn him popularity throughout the 'twenties. *The Opeiros* was in 1924 and *Cabaret Kittens* in 1927. But for Wallis Arthur the writing was on the wall. For in 1930 the Council refused to renew his licence on the grounds of the theatre's tinder-box construction. The last curtain-fall of the *Little Show* also spelt the end for the gimcracky Olympian Gardens.

And, with that, the Juggernaut began to stir. If anyone abhorred a vacuum more than nature – especially on Bognor's Esplanade – it was Mr William Butlin. Soon his foot was in the door. The screams and shouts from the new owner's electric Dodgems lay only months away.

But, as my brother and I sat under those flickering beams, chewing our Trebor Fruit Salads whilst watching that film – what was its name? the funny one starring Flanagan and Allen and Alistair Sim – we were totally unaware of being surrounded by the bricks-and-mortar of quite recent cinematographic history.

15

Beyond our Rubicon

A close-up of nature and winter's icy hand

One September morning, under a hazy sky with a watery sun slowly recovering after dreary days of early autumn rain, Aldwick Gardens' two intrepid explorers, their pockets bulging sandwiches, a piece of Dundee cake and an apple, climbed the gate of the Bottom Field intent on a major adventure. For we were off to discover what uncharted countryside lay beyond the hedges of Chalcraft Lane, a territory as strange to us as the Empty Quarter. Might we even get as far as those distant purple Downs?

Soon we were walking through the clover and the long grass, the sort that glosses wellies with last night's dew. Some fields were newly ploughed and over these we bumped and jumped, kicking off the furrow tops as we went. And when we came to stubble – the scrunchy sort of stubble – we scuffed through that as well. And, of course, we thwacked the hare's tables with our hedgesticks and trod in all the cow-pats where they lay upon our path.

Then came a short interval while the two explorers carried out an autopsy on a very dead rook which had met its Maker in a water-trough. Soon we spied a straw-pile meant for thatching hayricks – but it looked equally good for us to bounce upon. And when we'd tired of bouncing – then what? Ah yes, it comes back to me – we set course for the tadpole pond where the magpies chattered in the wind-bent alders that surrounded its dark and sodden edge. And we felt a need to know just how deep it was. Exactly! It responded by filling our wellies with black and stagnant ooze.

Onwards we squelched, tracing the line of the hedges; whitethorn, blackthorn, mixed with painful bramble, and busy with flocks of corn bunting, twittering, fidgety, sweeping away and sweeping back. As we approached rabbits would stop feeding and sit bolt upright before slowly bob-tailing it into their burrows. Next we came across an abandoned seed-drill needing careful examination, with each of us having a go at sitting in its rusty seat. And that was when we noticed, not far away, an inviting looking field gate. Climbing over it we found ourselves in Chalcraft Lane. Our Rubicon. For beyond its tarry ribbon lay a countryside as yet untrodden by our wellies, its fescue, vetch and foxglove heads unsmitten by our hedgesticks; its gates and ditches yet unclimbed; its barbed-wire fences inviting our impalement.

Soon we were navigating a course of random chance and wilful speculation; to inspect an old bird's nest here, a late slow-worm there and a flamboyant toadstool in quite the opposite direction. And a rabbit's burrow in another. I remember that because we put our ears to a hole to listen for its inhabitant; hadn't we heard that rabbits thumped the ground with their back legs at the approach of human danger? And did they? I forget, to tell the truth. But, in any case, by that time we'd found an old horseshoe embedded in the clay which took a lot of getting out. High above us, six Hawker Furys from Tangmere roared across the sky, a sky on the verge of having second thoughts.

In his *History of Pagham* Lindsay Fleming shows that quite a lot of our wanderings south of Chalcraft Lane and east of the Lower Bognor Road were over land once well-treed and known as Haywards Coppice. This may have accounted for the very mature trees which used to grow beside the ditches in those parts. It now lies under the Westmeads Estate.

Not far from where we dropped the horseshoe we came across a rabbit in a snare – dead; still warm; garroted by that wicked noose and caked in frantic mud. Nor was it the first we'd found. What's more, we knew the boy, his pockets full of brassy loops. Should we get some ourselves? Did Isted's sell them? But from somewhere a mother's voice said firmly, 'No!'

Onwards we trudged, mud congealed between our toes. Partridges burst out of the headland grass and whirred away knee-high – yet never far – while the superstitious wood pigeons clapped their wings and banked abruptly so as not to cross our path. Further on, we came by a late-summer bumble bee, laden down with loot, disappearing into a hole. Might he come out again? We gave him thirty seconds; he wasn't in the mood. Boredom prevailed and soon we were on the tramp again. But it brings to my mind a poem about a bumble bee written by our mother:

> Handsome fellow!
> Banded body, black and yellow,
> Full of boomings, deep and mellow
> Like the low notes of a 'cello.
>
> Clumsy, furry, triple jointed.
> Legs so delicately pointed,
> Brow with shining black anointed.
>
> Tiny wings! It's not surprising
> Science – ever patronising,
> Rather doubts your power of rising!
>
> DMA

A little further on our eyes fell upon some velvety sloes the other side of a barbed-wire fence and a quaggy mire. Upon such challenges we thrived; a measure of blood and half-a-pint of algae in our already ooze-logged wellies was a cost no higher than expected. But when we tried to eat them – ughhh! – they drew our mouths and we had to spit them out. In a broad ditch, a field and a half away, a hunch-backed heron, intent on spearing frogs, spotted the two intruders with that part of his eye reserved for survival. *Kaaa* he complained, and launched his crooked neck into the still air, awakening half-a-dozen head-under-wing snipe. Up they rocketted, zig-zagging their way to a safer stand. In the meantime we had discovered some juicy, clustered blackberries; soon our hands, mouths and cuffs were stained purple.

Skirting the prudent heron's ditch, we came to a meadow where our path was blocked by a herd of cows awaiting milking. As we dropped off the five-barred gate, a hundred inquisitive eyes etched the shape of these intruders on their minds. The bolder moved warily nearer for a closer look, necks outstretched, nostrils flared, ears and eyes joined in caution. But by now the two of us had learned something of the ways of cows. Clapping our hands, we advanced towards them uttering the cowman's mantra, 'c'mon, c'mon, aye-aye-aye', that we had learned at Aldwick Farm. Uneasy at our temerity, the beasts began to back away, heads tossing, threads of saliva glinting in the air, lungs pumping the smell of chewed grass as they licked their flanks in disbelief. A few stood their ground uneasily, then lumberingly changed their minds. Two small boys and fifty large cows. Now we were engulfed in a restless sea of flanks and horns, an horizon of pendulous udders and swollen teats, a forest of forelegs, hinderlegs and cloven hooves squelching the glutinous mud. Yard by yard we edged our way through the herd until, at last, we found ourselves in the meadow beyond and were able to resume our inconstant path – trailed by half-a-dozen beasts, quite unable to detach themselves from such a spectacular carry-on!

80 Cows – but from an earlier era. A.R. Dresser's picture of a herd of friesians being driven past the *Royal Hotel* in the 1890s. It is a scene which would have been familiar well into the 'twenties. For whom does the flag fly at half-mast?

Before long our tummies began to murmur 'food'. So, by a ditch widened by the recent rain, we paused, rubbed our nettle stings with dock leaves, removed the burrs from our socks and were soon polishing off the sandwiches and pieces of fractured cake, while we shared our hoarded scraps of knowledge. Beside us, across the reflections of the clouds, the water-skaters and the upside-down water boatmen (they swim on their backs, did you know?) scudded away their miniscule lives; a line of little whirlpools betrayed a frog acting out its food-chain role. But what we were really looking for were those orange-bellied crested newts.

On such expeditions, it was a point of honour to catch at least one or two. How? Well, like this. First, I used to lie with my head overhanging the ditch, hands cupped just above the surface. Then I waited … and waited … until, suddenly, there appeared that tell-tale string of tiny bubbles and a flash of orange amongst the feathery waterplants. Then, with a mighty splash, hands were plunged deep into the water – and that was generally the moment I remembered that I had not rolled up the sleeves of my jersey! At any rate, with a bit of luck, there it was – in my palms a wriggling and very surprised-looking crested newt. With no jam jar, it was only possible to wonder at the perfection of its put-togetherness as it crawled over my lap and hands, before I returned it to its native pool where it would have an unlikely yarn for its young ones – or, at least, for those of them that it hadn't eaten – for newts are the most frightful cannibals!

But now the sky would have us warned. For not only did the Downs look even further off than when we started but they had changed colour to a sullen grey. Meanwhile, just ahead of us, seeking voles, a kestrel hovered, sideslipped and hovered again. But that was the trouble with the country-side; there was so much to distract the explorers from their need to hasten. So it must have been just after we had ignored the sight of a flock of restless goldfinches attacking the tops of a clump of thistles on the grounds of over-familiarity, that we heard from the next field an unornamented voice. 'Git-back,' it said. Then, 'whoa'.

Peering through the hedge, we could see a horse and a two-wheeled cart engaged in tipping a load of manure to add to an orderly pattern of piles that covered a field of stubble. It was a common sight before the fields became marinated in nitrates. After it had been spread, the neighbourhood could look forward to becoming enveloped in an agricultural smell that could be cut with a knife. And it was just there, while sitting quietly watching the horse and manure cart, that our attempt to reach the road suffered another set-back. A faint rustling and a slight movement in the hedge-grass; for a little while we could see nothing; then, suddenly, there it was – the glossy, chestnut head and shoulders and white underparts of a beady-eyed stoat standing on its back legs, looking from side to side and sometimes turning its head backwards to inspect the world astern. For a full half-minute we hardly dared breathe! Then there was an explosion in the undergrowth as discretion got the upper hand of valour – and it was gone. But not before it had impressed an image on my mind clear enough to last a lifetime.

By now we had come to a five-barred gate from where we spied those familiar Scots pines marking Crimsham Farm – and the road back to Aldwick. Nor should we tarry, for overhead flocks of lapwings were flying low against a background of advancing grey clouds. Already, the nettles were beginning to curtsey to the raindrops. Only two fields to go. But now a ditch with a pair of water rats in residence wilfully interrupted our progress; in this way another quarter-of-an-hour evaporated as we watched them doodling in the green algae. Then a further five minutes went adrift while we examined some murky little pellets we found under a stunted oak. An owl. Not beautiful, but pocketable.

At last we reached the farm, layered in its smells of hay, steaming dung, cattle-cake and overtones of diesel. 'Git back … whoa,' said the unornamented voice we had heard earlier, as it unharnessed its horse. We offered shy 'hellos' to men in gumboots carrying buckets of crushed mangolds, wheeling barrows and forking straw. To their barricaded bull, we offered words of peace. About our feet scuttled red-wattled cockerels intent on seeing us off their premises.

With pockets richer in wine-gums than in useful coin to offer to the conductor of a 59 bus, we set off on the long serpentine walk back to Aldwick, a walk we shared with the swallows swooping across our path as they gorged themselves for that mysterious journey south. In the distance a flight of mute swans became momentarily silhouetted against a blood-red gap in the clouds as they traced the Pagham Rife. On Lagness Farm an early barn owl flew buoyantly along the hedgerow patterns. Was it, we wondered, the owner of those murky pellets?

With that rain-on-warm-tar smell in our nostrils, we continued our homeward trek – or, at least, we would have – had we not come across a sight which was another temptation, a milk bottle floating insolently in a rain-pocked ditch. War! Nearby a thoughtful County Council had tipped an arsenal of roadstones. But, before we could report 'Enemy bottle sunk, Sir', another ten minutes had to be added to our ever-lengthening time-sheet. In fact, we might as well have torn it up! For just near Trafalgar Cottage, we spotted something which touched us to the quick, a land-drain blocked with straw. A rescue plan was evolved. Five minutes later, heedless of the drizzle, we were able to admire our handiwork as hundreds of gallons of yellow landwater cascaded onwards into the surcharged ditch. It was just then, to add insult to injury, that a 59 bus tore past, covering us in spray.

So, by the time my brother and I had got to Morell's Farm, not only were we drag-of-foot and on the verge of starvation, but we were about to get well and truly drenched. For now the rain had begun to hiss down like stair-rods. And we both had blisters. It was at that moment that good fortune came from behind to smile on us. An approaching motor car slowed down and stopped. Through the rain-flecked windows peered one of the two elderly Miss Warrens of South Avenue. What a bit of luck! Paid-up members of our territory, too! And how nice for them to be able to repay us for all those demonstrations we had given them with our Dinky toys on their new linoleum. Miss Ethel beckoned us into the leathery-smelling Morris Cowley … but would we mind first wiping our feet on the grass.

On Idlewylde's loggia we removed our wellies, emptied them of their unsavoury contents and let ourselves in. 'Oh, there you are – and absolutely soaking,' groaned my mother. 'Where've you been all day?' We were tired. My reply was synoptic: 'Oh, just messing around in the fields – and we saw a stoat ever so close to. And we found some owl pellets. And I've got a blister. Anything to eat?'

* * *

When we first came to live on our western edge of Bognor, in 1929, Aldwick was still surrounded by largely arable countryside. So with the onset of July and August the area became engulfed in a gradually rising tide of rippling barley, oats and wheat. Eagerly we awaited Lammas Day and the coming of the harvesters to the meadow behind our bungalow.

Then, early one morning, we heard the voices of farm labourers, the clink of chains and the sound of horse's hooves thudding the hard clay. Above the hedge we caught a glimpse of revolving flails. Excitedly, Rog and I leapt the stile and ran to the field. 'Could we help?' Soon we were at work in the wake of the chattering reaper, picking up the spewed sheaves and building them into those nearly forgotten stooks. For much of the day we contributed our efforts – with the occasional breather for feeding the horses with crusts of bread – until, much too quickly, the sun lay red upon the horizon.

At last the horses, tired from hours of summer reaping, were unhooked from their machine and led off for their nosebag supper. The one remaining farm labourer swigged the bottom inch from his Thermos, lit another cork-tipped Star and set off on his bike to his cabbage-bordered garden path at Rose Green. And that was when we and the rooks and the rabbits found ourselves the sole inheritors of those tram-lines of crackly stubble and the pheasant's evening call. Then the long-shadowed stooks became a backdrop for epic tales of cowboys armed with cap pistols in pursuit of short-trousered Injuns who were expected to die bravely in defence of their wheatsheaf wigwams. That is, until the rising autumn mist brought our mother hastening to the stile to complain that it was way past our supper-time and we were to come in immediately. 'Oh, mother, honestly; must we? Can't we have just five more minutes – please?'

During those harvest weeks, cart-horses pulling four-wheeled farm-carts, bearing the names of the local farming families – the Crocketts, Rusbridges, Aylwins and the Smarts of Pryor's Farm – were still commonly encountered on the straw-strewn roads around Aldwick. A ride on top of a soft bed of cornsheaves was the recognised reward for a few hours of unsolicited help with a pitchfork – not forgetting to duck when the cart went under the Rackhamesque elm opposite Mrs Duffin's Slated Barn Stores!

* * *

One afternoon a large traction engine with a red-coloured threshing machine and a water-cart in tow pulled into the meadow opposite Hammonds Barn – near where *The Martlets* pub stands today. Within a few minutes a dozen small boys and girls, amongst whom my brother and I could be numbered, appeared out of thin air and gathered expectantly around the boiling Leviathan. Very soon a pulley-belt was placed to connect the threshing machine to the traction engine's flywheel. Water was poured into the boiler and the fire-box trimmed with coal. With due seriousness, the man in the cloth cap tapped the water gauge and opened the damper. A squirt of oil fell upon a glistening piston rod and the safety valve hissed impatiently.

Now came the moment for which we had waited. With careful deliberation, Cloth Cap moved a lever slowly forward. With a jerk the belt tightened; then, almost imperceptibly, it began to move. Suddenly, with a

81 The photographer has his back to Fish Lane in this picture, taken looking towards Aldwick Gardens during the harvest of about 1933. The meadow now lies under Aldwick Felds.

82 Although this scene is from somewhere nearer the Downs, it is typical of threshing throughout the country before the combines took over.

great clatter the threshing machine burst into vibrating life. That was our signal! Soon we were in amongst the clouds of flying chaff, where sunburnt men with tattoed arms laboured with their burnished pitchforks to assuage the roaring beast's insatiable appetite for sheaves of wheat tossed down from red-and-blue farm carts. From under the avalanche of tumbling straw, the new rick began to grow; from the rear of the machine, torrents of golden grain cascaded into jute sacks as tall as ourselves.

The threshers proved to be as generous as they had been tolerant, for half-way through that hot afternoon one of them wiped the top of a bottle of White's lemonade with a red rag and handed it to me and Roger to finish off its lukewarm remains. But that was merely the wage temporal; our reward spiritual lay in being part of that animated scene, surrounded by a smell concocted from flying wheat-chaff, horse-dung, Woodbines, coal-smoke and honest sweat, and to consort with horses wearing straw hats and with men in collarless shirts and waistcoats shiny from their work.

When we got home, my mother took one look at her dust-encrusted sons and uttered that single, dread word: 'Bath!'

* * *

One late autumn afternoon, by our woggly stile, I was drawn to the sight of a man in an oil-stained trilby in charge of a Fordson tractor pulling a three-furrow plough. He was tinkering with the engine. What unimaginable power must lie behind those huge iron wheels, I thought, as I ran my fingers over the cold, smooth mould-boards. Here was the promise of the sort of entertainment close to my heart. Imagine, then, the scene as this agricultural Brunhilde roared up and down the footpath meadow, drawing in its wake all the cataclysmic drama of a Wagnerian opera; the song of the plough as it folded over the ribbons of damp-smelling earth; the supporting chorus of a hundred ill-tempered black-headed gulls, and the domestic upheaval suffered by a myriad juicy worms – the whole extravaganza played out under the clouds of blue smoke pouring from the tractor's straining engine.

So, if my mother mislaid me that afternoon it was because I was otherwise engaged, trotting up and down the furrows in my clay-bound wellies behind this growling monster, hidden from the world by an undulating filigree of screaming gulls. Personally, I found it a richly reward-ing experience, one which could only have been improved by the descent from the clouds of Sir Thomas Beecham conducting a mighty orchestra!

In 1934 Aldwick Gardens – as a thoroughfare – bore an uncanny resem-blance to Mother Earth as she must have appeared early in her history! No other unmade road in the district could compare with its dust and bumps, or puddles and deep tracks, according to season. To my parents they they were a constant source of complaints. Perversely, though, it was just this implacable un-made-up-ness which so endeared it to both of us. Indeed, it was with acute anguish that, from time to time, we used to observe the Council's workmen attempting to fill in the best and deepest puddles. Fortunately, the Highway Department's repairs were well-known for their transience, and the reader will be relieved to learn that our road suffered no lasting good at their hands. So, as the end of summer yielded to the first days of autumn, and the garden began to smell of dead chrysanthemums, and the clogged-up mower was put away for the last time, it was with relish that we watched the white, dusty moonscape of Aldwick Gardens gradually dissolve into an amorphous emulsification of wallowy sloughs, lochs and peninsulas, their waters calling us to float upon them our Hornby speed-boats and listing timber-built battleships.

Other diversions offered themselves. In the wake of heavy precipitations, it was our custom to stand in the the road's deeper troughs to see how close to the tops of our wellies we could tempt the water before it poured over their rims. It also helped to fill in time as we waited for a car or delivery van to roll through the puddlescape and spew out water in spectacular green fans as they passed. Which of us dared stand nearest the inundation? Misjudgment of speed or distance could result in an icy douche and a bedraggled retreat home for a change of clothing and a little homily from my mother upon how sure she was that our friends were much better-behaved and less messy than we were!

But at last the clocks were put back an hour and the excitement of the harvest-home and Brunhilde's dramatic ploughing receded into memory, leaving only Guy Fawkes Night to relieve the tedium of the autumn term and the slow-motion run-up to Christmas. With a modest bonfire, we used to celebrate 'the Fifth' at Aldwick on the nearest Saturday night to the actual date. By then we had accumulated a sizeable arsenal of golden rain, catherine wheels, volcanoes, bangers, roman candles, squibs and the flat-topped sort of rockets. But the larger rockets with conical noses we regarded as being beyond our reach. Then, one year, my father treated us to just a single, large and expensive red-nosed rocket bought from Goodacre's.

That evening, as our guy flickered terminally among the embers and the penultimate firework gasped its last spark, the super-rocket was taken from its box and stuck into the milk bottle. Authoritatively, my father lit its blue paper with a match and retired in accordance with the instructions. There was an expectant hush. But all the rocket did was to splutter once or twice and then appear to go out. My father demanded a wax taper. But where were they? Everyone thought they were in a different place. So we all went indoors to look. The moment the family's back was turned, from out in the garden there came a mighty 'swoosh'! Quickly we all poured back through the French windows – just in time to see a trail of blue smoke parallel with the ground and a few desultory sparks descending over the hedge at the bottom of the garden. A few yards beyond lay guttering the remains of our expensive red-nosed rocket!

With studied lethargy the weeks dragged by until, at last, the school piled into Hall for the usual interminable end-of-term speeches and a few carols. Then the Headmaster wished us all a Happy Yuletide, we gave him three cheers and with that we broke up. The next evening we travelled down to find a Bognor festooned in municipal electric light bulbs for a Christmas I best remember not only for the electric Hornby railway engine and its three brown-and-cream coaches my parents gave me, but also for the unseasonally mild weather which allowed the family to eat its turkey on the loggia table bathed in a low, afternoon sun.

But the warm spell was short-lived. Only a few days into the New Year, the afternoon sky over Aldwick gradually changed to that yellowy-grey colour that heralds snow. Even before Stephen King-Hall's talk on Children's Hour had come to an end, the first small flakes had begun to fall upon a rapidly freezing countryside. The next morning we awoke to a strange silence and a curiously diffuse light which fell upon the bedroom walls. Still in our pyjamas, we went to the window, wiped away the condensation and peered out at a garden mantled in snow. Instead of having to be prised from our beds, we dressed with uncharacteristic alacrity. Breakfast quickly over, we donned our coats, gloves, scarves and woolly hats and opened the back door – only for the cold air to take away our breath as we gazed out at a road dazzlingly white, marked only by the hoof and wandering wheel-marks of Chichester Dairy's horse-drawn milk-float.

Soon, with Judy gambolling around in the first snow she'd ever seen, we were sliding and snowballing our way to the fields beyond Yeoman's Acre, where the snow lay in a white network upon the trees and transformed the hedgerows into white bolsters of sculptural ingenuity. On the ground our wellies added alien characters to the notepad on which the birds and animals had scribbled a hundred messages. We also performed a good deed for the day. Finding the Aldwick Farm cows breathing cloudlets of incomprehension as they gazed blankly at their frozen trough, we climbed chivalrously on to it, stamped the ice into little bits, and left them drinking. But, to cows, showing gratitude is not easy.

So, as the Sussex countryside succumbed to that imperial freeze-up, Aldwick Gardens became our St Moritz, offering our friends and us an extensive programme of snowballing and ice-sliding on the frozen puddles which hastened the end of those leather shoes that had survived the summer. Our fingers in their wet woollen gloves and ears were reduced to constant numbness. Only periodic visits to our mother's kitchen for mugs of Bovril and a little thawing-out in front of the Valor oil-stove kept hypothermia at bay.

That year my father made us a toboggan. A suitable slope, though, was the problem. Aldwick had none. Dragging little Julian over the fields and across the village footpath soon palled. We demanded the Trundle. But hardly had we got there than the car became stuck in a snowdrift and by the time it had been dug out it was nearly dark. Then the thaw set in. A few years later, during that memorably bitter winter of 1939, our toboggan earned its keep for the first time by warming us as it blazed merrily on the living-room fire! Our winter sports exertions, though, weren't cheaply bought. Barked shins, lacerated hands, grazed knees and even what we firmly believed to be frostbite were borne with fortitude, but nothing happened with which my mother's DIY clinical skills, and the medical section of *Pears Cyclopedia*, couldn't cope.

Indeed, our medicine chest bore a marked resemblance to a Base Hospital: bandages of various widths and lengths, lint, iodine, camphorated oil and even splints; there were bottles of Gee's Linctus, Scott's Emulsion and Parish's Food, as well as copious supplies of cascara, Feenamint Aspirin and cotton wool; a styptic pencil stood by the razor to stem my father's weekend blood-letting. The museum section included an Edwardian chemist's unopened bottle of 'physic', aconite pills, a box of Dr Williams' Pills for Pale People and space for a tub of Gregory Powder. And that is not to mention obscure alleged cures for goitre, piles and bladder troubles. Should one of the Hampstead Aunts have faltered, *sal volatile* was close at hand.

Somewhere at the back of our Base Hospital there skulked a clinical thermometer, but for serious diagnosis my mother used to rely upon the back of her hand placed against the fevered brow. For a temperature or a sore throat the cure was standard: to bed with a hot-water bottle and a school sock wrapped round the throat fastened with a large safety pin. Then she spoon-fed us a crushed aspirin in strawberry jam, a cascara pill and a hot lemon drink. 'And say your prayers, dear.' Par was one day off school/ excused parental shopping. For years on end we never seemed to see our family doctor Dr Dudgeon. So what we'd have made of the NHS I cannot think, although I bet any group practice doctor would have been a bit more generous with the days off!

16

The Miller's Tale

At his Hanover Square office in the West End my father was inundated with work. The summer of 1936 found him involved with schemes for the Duke of Newcastle at Clumber Castle in the Dukeries, a large housing project on the Duke's estate near Dorking, as well as alterations to the house of a certain Mr Kemp, a name engraved on a million chocolate digestive biscuits. To add to the list, he had recently been commissioned to paint a large mural in the member's dining room at the newly opened Whipsnade Zoo. Little wonder, then, that he looked forward to the weekends for a short break with his family and a potter in the garden at Idlewylde.

Those Saturday afternoons I remember well; my father – surrounded with rolls of drawings – chatting with my mother on the loggia over a relaxing cup of tea. I can also recall how, on these occasions, they would often speak with unaffected pride at having achieved their long-held – if modest – dream of owning a roof by the sea at Aldwick.

We can be quite certain, however, that, indulging in this harmless sort of reverie wasn't the prerogative solely of Frank and Doris Alford. In fact, a case in point lay no further than two fields away from our garden gate on the other side of Fish Lane. For here lived another couple of about my parents' age. And as they sipped their gin-and-tonics on the York stone terrace of their new house, it would have been bordering on the perverse if they, too, had not found time, now and then, for a little self-congratulation at the way their own dreams had been so amply fulfilled – quite apart from having chosen to build Aldwick Place in one of the choicest spots on the Sussex coast. For, compared with that of my parents, Rowland and Margaret Rank's version of 'a roof by the sea' was absolutely Olympian!

So, as their visions and aspirations left such an indelible mark upon Aldwick before the Second World War, I thought it worth exploring the Ranks' story a little further. And to do that we need to start in East Yorkshire and learn something of his father.

Rowland's father was the great Joseph Rank. Born in Hull in 1854 of quite humble origins, Joseph was an East Riding Methodist and a miller; the order is important for his religion was central to his life. In 1875, with capital of £500 – left him by his father, also a miller – he acquired his first windmill, Waddingham's in Holderness Road in Hull. Yet he had no opinion of the vagaries of wind as a means of grinding corn. The future, he was convinced, lay with milling by power-driven machinery. But Waddingham's had its virtue; its income allowed him to get married. 'So on June 15th 1880, I took Emily Voase for better or for worse,' he wrote in his diary.

His next mill was the nearby West's, where engines drove the traditional stones. Its importance to Joseph was that it showed him mechanical rolling

83 If this photograph of the gates to Aldwick Place was taken before 1899 (the year of his death), Baron Grant may still have been in residence. The Prussian eagles were removed in the First World War and the cast-iron gates (spurned by Queen Victoria) were broken up to provide armaments in the Second.

could be made to pay. Scraping for capital, his sights were now firmly fixed on building his first fully mechanical modern mill. A few years later, in 1885, his determination was rewarded when the Alexander Mill in Williamson Road, where gas engines provided the power, came on stream – and proved to be 'the mill that made the money'.

Then, in the early 1890s, he opened the great Clarence Mill on Hull's waterfront – in its time, the most advanced flour-milling plant in the country – where steel rollers, worked by triple-expansion engines, resulted in a weekly sack output running into many thousands. With increasing wealth, he was now able to practice his deeply held religious convictions in the form of notable acts of philanthropy. The gifts he made to the Methodist Church were substantial and sustained. Foundation stones bearing his name are to be found all over Hull and, indeed, much further afield.

By 1925 he owned mechanically-operated mills – and flour mills are huge things, each one a landmark – in all the major shipping ports in Britain: London, Ipswich, Hull, Southampton, Liverpool and Glasgow; even at Belfast and Barry in South Wales. And along the cornice of each, inscribed in large, bold letters, ran the name of JOSEPH RANK LTD.

Although his firm no longer exists as an entity, the wealth he created continues to be distributed, through the Joseph Rank Benevolent Trust, to a great number of charitable organisations which – to pick but a few – include the YMCA, the Boy Scouts, Girl Guides and the Sail Training Association. Nor is this at the expense of the ex-employees of his once huge empire, who still benefit from the Trust in many diverse fields. Joseph's homespun philosophy can best be summed up in one of his favourite sayings, 'Make all you can, save all you can and give all you can.'

Emily and Joseph had three sons and four daughters. All the sons became millers. From an early date, the eldest, James Voase, was groomed to succeed his father as president of a firm which, by 1950, produced nearly a seventh of the nation's flour. Best known to the public, though, was his youngest son, Joseph – J. Arthur Rank (later Lord Rank of Sutton Scotney in the County of Hampshire), the Methodist Sunday school teacher and milling millionaire who, besides founding the giant Rank Organisation, with its studios at Pinewood, Denham and Elstree, managed also to collect, *en passant*, six hundred Gaumont, ABC and Odeon cinemas! Nor should we forget the Rank Charm School with its bevy of beauties, arm-in-arm with whom he had a penchant for being photographed!

But what of Joe's middle son, the publicity-shunning Rowland, the resident of Aldwick whose fields, ditches, trees, farm, barns and milk-cart my brother and I regarded as part of our very own territory during the 1930s? Rowland was born in 1885 and spent most of his younger days at the family home at Hull. Although his father held no opinion of formal public school education, he nevertheless sent his son to a good one, the Leys at Cambridge. But no university followed. Instead, on leaving school at 16, Rowland began a long apprenticeship in his father's mills where he was expected to take his share of floor-sweeping and sack-humping. Eventually he graduated to a stool in the Rank offices at Bankside House in Leadenhall Street, from where he learned the arcane art of purchasing grain on the Baltic Exchange.

Aldwick was already known to the Rank family. In 1900 Aldwick Place was a large, rambling, early Victorian, ivy-clad mansion overlooking its sea-wall at the end of Dark Lane. The first Aldwick Place had been built in the 1820s for Alexander Williams, a well-known Chichester wine merchant. How long he lived there is unclear, but in time he was followed by a

84 Aldwick village at about the time the Rank family stayed at Aldwick Place in 1900. Note the dovecote on the left of the *Ship Inn*'s wall. Although The Street is finished only in 'hoggin' (a mixture of stones, clay and sand), it has been obviously well maintained.

number of other occupants of substance; first a General Stuart then, around 1850, Sir Simon Clarke Bt, one of Bognor's Commissioners. It was he who carried out 'extensive works' on his property, which so impressed Richard Dally. They were probably to the sea-wall. The *Bognor Guide* of 1856 says this of the works:

> the great expenditure of the Baronet, the present proprietor, to preserve his favorite [*sic*] retreat from the sea, has been of most essential service to the poor of the neighbourhood and munificence and taste has been displayed in every improvement that has taken place on this estate under his superintendence.

A few years later the house was occupied by Benjamin Bond Cabell Esq., barrister and philanthropist, by whom it was described as a 'marine retreat'.

By the late 1880s Aldwick Place had became the home of Albert, Baron Grant, a man who trod a shadowy path in the world of money-lending before graduating to the equally opaque field of company promotion. And in this area his successes proved to be as brilliant as his failures were spectacular. As the *Daily Mail* put it, 'he had no prejudices and could float anything from a bathmat to a Republic'.

Born Ernst Lerch Gottheimer in Dublin in 1827, his Barony was a gift from the King of Italy, who also made him a Commander of the Order of St Maurice and Lazarre as a reward for completing and opening the Victor Emanuel Gallery in Milan. This 'Prince among Bankrupts' and his wife, Emily, enjoyed a larger-than-life existence, entertaining lavishly in the course of their social climb towards acceptance by the Establishment. And in this they seem to have met with some success, for in 1865 Albert was elected MP for Kidderminster as well as being appointed Deputy Lieutenant of Tower Hamlets. In the House of Commons he was well-known for his repartee and sharpness of wit.

Certainly the Baron's acts of philanthropy were real enough. After refurbishing the run-down area of Leicester Square he presented it to the nation – with the busts of John Hunter, Sir Joshua Reynolds, William Hogarth and a statue of Shakespeare thrown in – at the cost to himself of £30,000. He was cheered in the House when he announced he had purchased Landseer's portrait of Sir Walter Scott for the country after the Chancellor of the Exchequer, Sir Stafford Northcote, claimed the Government hadn't the money. He also launched the broadsheet *Echo*, which at ½d. was the cheapest paper on the streets at the time. Just how he collected a doctorate in law, though, is obscure. However, Albert Grant was also quite capable of sharp practice. In a poor part of Kensington that he intended to develop, he enticed the occupants of the houses 'out for a day in carriages' and, when they'd gone, removed the roofs from their houses!

Although at different times the Baron was immensely rich, he suffered the hazards of his trade by being periodically made bankrupt. Amongst his more spectacular failures was the English Crédit Foncier Bank and the collapse of the Lisbon Tramway. In consequence, he was endlessly engaged in lawsuits, often defending himself. Once, in court, he spoke for three days and was congratulated upon his eloquence by the judge.

Grant's speculation in property seems to have served him little better. To assuage his appetite for social advancement, he had the road leading to Kensington Palace widened at his own expense. In Kensington High Street he built a great mansion which he hoped to let to a royal personage; in fact, it was eventually demolished without ever having seen an occupant, the staircase ending its days at Madame Tussauds. No doubt it was in the same spirit that he offered Queen Victoria the gift of a pair of rather heavy-looking cast-iron gates for the entrance to Kensington Gardens. That Her Majesty declined them is well known, although whether she did so on aesthetic or social grounds (his dodgy title may not have amused her) remains unclear.

Instead, unabashed, he had them brought down to Aldwick Place where they were hung on brick pillars surmounted by stone urns and Prussian eagles. In 1904, according to *Heywood's Guide*, the gates were painted blue. Alas, in the name of patriotism, the eagles were removed during the First World War and the iron gates broken up for scrap during the Second. The Baron and his wife appear to have been quite popular figures locally. His donation of an 'iron chapel' to Aldwick village was mentioned in Chapter Six.

It was while enmeshed in bankruptcy proceedings for the third time that scythe-and-hour glass did for him at Aldwick on 30 August 1899. His wife died only a little more than two years later. At Pagham church, the inscription on the couple's tombstone reads: 'Albert, Baron Grant D.L. Born Dublin Dec 18 1827. Died at Aldwick Place 30 August 1899. Sometime MP for Kidderminster, and his devoted wife, Emily Isabella. Born June 8 1827. Died October 18 1901.'

Thereafter Aldwick Place fell into the hands of a Mr Jackson, a Londoner whose instincts led him to ventures in property speculation and accounted for many of the houses which still line Aldwick Avenue. Perhaps Jackson was in the 'holiday lets' business, too. At all events, it was arranged that Joseph Rank should rent Aldwick Place for that year's family holiday.

So, at the age of about 15, this was young Rowland's earliest glimpse of Aldwick's golden sands, the Barn Rocks, the pile of boulders below the wall of Aldwick Villa (the Paradise Rocks), the village with its *Ship Inn*, and Hurst Cottage, where Charlie Tooze was still a fly proprietor, not yet the postmaster. For the first time he must have heard the strident chorus from the rookery amongst Dark Lane's elms, and discovered the Duck Pond and Aldwick Farm when out walking with his brothers and sisters along those untarred and car-free country lanes. Unsurprisingly, all this rural charm was not lost on Joseph's middle son.

In a family firm headed by a patriarch of Joseph's cast, it was inevitable that as his sons became men – and men of character and ability – there should be some degree of paternal and filial manoeuvring while a new pecking order evolved. After all, in 1912, 'Holy Joe' (that's what they called him up in his native Yorkshire) was only in his late fifties and still hale and hearty, his role of Governing Director unchallengeable. James, the eldest son, was already Managing Director and J. Arthur's directorship only a matter of time.

Rowland, though, was something of an individualist. Already he had made it clear to his father that he would prefer to run his own ship. Perhaps this suited Joseph's plans. At all events, the opportunity arose for him to buy his son the old, run-down Mark Mayhew Mill at Battersea. First, though, it had to be altered and re-equipped. And it was in the middle of this complex operation that the dawn of 4 August 1914 brought with it Great Britain's declaration of war upon Germany. Rowland, already with a commission in the Territorials, was called to the Colours.

With characteristic generosity, Joseph undertook to complete the work and run the Mark Mayhew Mill pending his son's return from what most people believed would be a short military skirmish that 'would be over by Christmas'. Instead, Rowland, in his thirtieth summer, found himself enmeshed in the four blood-letting years of the First World War.

Transferred in due course to the Royal Field Artillery, Captain Rank was fortunate to serve for some time in England. Even doubly fortunate; for while his Trench Mortar Brigade was training in Shropshire in 1916, he met and paid court to Margaret McArthur, a noted Canadian society beauty who was visiting her military stepfather, stationed near Ellesmere. One day they visited the Swallow Falls near Betws-y-Coed where he proposed to her. But such was the noise of the crashing water, his message failed to reach her pretty ears! Back in the car, he tried again. This time, happily, Margaret got the gist and graciously consented to become his fiancée.

At the beginning of 1917 Rowland learned he was to be posted to the Western Front. They decided to get married. This raised a thorny issue. The stern old Joseph, whilst tolerant of wartime engagements, was adamantly opposed to khaki marriages. Secrecy had to be observed. And that was why they chose for their ceremony the obscure registry office at Whitchurch in Shropshire. Of course, it all came out in the end. But Margaret refused to be intimidated by her irascible old father-in-law and thus gained his respect, which in time ripened into great affection.

This romantic interlude behind him, barbarous reality soon found Rowland experiencing the misery, mud, stench and fear of the trenches. In June 1917 his Brigade was sucked into the Third Battle of Ypres, where a mighty bill was paid in the blood of both sides. The Germans used gas and Rowland received a near-fatal dose of it. With seared lungs, he was returned to Blighty to face a prolonged period of convalescence, interspersed with painful operations which continued long after the Armistice, and were made bearable only by his young wife's love and tenderness.

Rising above his disablement – although, we can guess, too soon – he threw himself into the task of taking control of the Mark Mayhew Mill, where much still remained to be done. But Rowland's slowly-healing lungs concerned his doctors. The London of those days, where they lived in a flat at No. 7 Park Lane, was still a smoky and foggy Victorian city. So, when his doctors advised him to spend as much time as possible near the sea, there was no difficulty in deciding where he and Margaret should go: it was to Aldwick.

Their first home was rented in Aldwick Avenue, The Wigwam belonging to a Mrs Wedgwood. From there Rowland, with Margaret by his side, was able to spend many hours walking on the beach and inhaling the curative Bognor air. In due course the Ranks made the acquaintance of that great

85 Aldwick Place. Built in the 1820s for Alexander Williams Esq., a Chichester wine merchant, it is shown here in its later guise as a boys' preparatory school in about 1914.

86 Aldwick Place, the home of Mr and Mrs Rowland Rank and their family. Completed in 1927, it had a comparatively short life, being demolished in the 1960s to make way for a private housing development.

character, Mrs Emily Croxton Johnson, Aldwick's *grande dame*, still holding court at Paradise where, it transpired, she had a small dwelling – The Cottage – which happened to be vacant. For whatever reason, the Ranks quit The Wigwam and moved into their new quarters at the end of Dark Lane.

They had a new neighbour. For Aldwick Place had changed hands and was now a small preparatory school run by Mr R.R. Frederick MA, whose brochure promised to meet the educational needs of 35 young boys dressed in bright red blazers and prepare them for their public schools or the Royal Navy. Strong on tradition, its pupils were condemned every morning, summer and winter, to run from the house to Baron Grant's iron gates and back again to earn their breakfast.

In 1991 I met the late Percy Cartwright (then aged 91), who, with his three brothers, was a pupil at Aldwick Place School during the First World War. Amongst his memories were doing physical jerks on the beach and seeing Norman Thompson's flying boats and RNAS 'blimps' passing up and down the coast. He could also remember one of the boys being told of his father's death in action on the Western Front. Apparently the school had one girl pupil. Her name was Elizabeth, the daughter of Sir Arthur Downes and a niece of General (later Field-Marshal and Viscount) Edmund Allenby. Her family lived at Summerlands in Aldwick Avenue. Percy was known as Cartwright Tertius, his brothers as Major, Minor and Quartus.

The avalanche of flour that flowed daily from the Battersea mill's chattering machinery now unlocked the door to whatever hopes and ambitions a man of Rowland Rank's mould might entertain. The future would have looked brighter had it not been for the legacy of Ypres; he was still not a fit man

By 1923 Rowland and Margaret's young family measured three: a son, Joseph, destined to become Chairman of the Rank empire after the Second World War, and two daughters, Margaret – called Peggy – and Patricia. Not surprisingly, they were beginning to find the little cottage a bit of a squeeze. It was time to look for a larger and more permanent home of their own. For some while they had been casting their eyes in the direction of Aldwick Place so, it must have seemed an act of providence that 1923 was the year Mr Frederick decided to move his gown of learning to a peg in a school at Climping. Thus did Aldwick Place come on the market and thus did the Ranks decide to buy it.

Margaret and Rowland now settled down to contemplate their acquisition and to work out how it might be turned into a family home. But slowly it began to dawn on them that its ivy-clad charm seemed more and more outweighed by its shortcomings: it was cold and draughty; there were a lot of rooms but few pleasant ones; the floors were on many incoherent levels; damp rose remorselessly from below and seeped down from above. What might have been eminently suitable as an expensive boarding school was not, on reflection, so easily converted to a liveable home. Only the site was beyond criticism. The problems must have suggested the solution. The old Aldwick Place would have to be pulled down and a new house take its place.

Percy Meredith FRIBA of Old Queen Street SW1 was the kind of architect who attracted commissions for specially fine houses on exceptionally beautiful sites which were expected to cost rather a lot of money. Meredith's brief sounds mouth-watering. Of course, it included all the usual things: a withdrawing room, and rooms for sitting, dining and sewing, as well as a study for Rowland; it required a generous number of bedrooms with an abundance of the usual offices; the kitchen was to be light and airy; there had to be a scullery, pantries and, of course, a wine

87 The Rank children call upon Mrs 'Emmie' Croxton Johnson. In the background are the ruins of Paradise. It is now the site of Strange Garden, originally a house and now a block of flats.

cellar. But, in fact, the brief had barely started! For it went on to include the incorporation in the design of an old oak and cedar staircase from Boling-broke House at Battersea, which John Rank remembers as 'smelling like pencil sharpenings'. Loggias facing south were a *sine qua non* and so were a gymnasium, tennis courts, and a thatched-roof squash court sunk partly below ground level. There had to be garages, loose-boxes for horses and a small range of kennels for greyhounds. Rowland also bred and raced pigeons, which pointed to the need for a pigeon-loft. And while Mr Meredith was at it, he might as well design a dovecote to house a flock of haughty pouters it was proposed should one day lounge around the new roofscape.

To gild the lily, Mr Morley Horder FRIBA, a well-known architect and landscaper who'd just finished altering and refurbishing Craigweil House for Sir Arthur du Cros, was earmarked to design the formal gardens, and Messrs Waterer's appointed to think up something for the water garden. Meanwhile the nine-hole golf-course in front of the house was placed in the hands of the legendary Mr Simpson, whose most recent triumph had been the golf-course at Le Touquet.

In due course Mr Meredith unrolled his drawings of the new Aldwick Place for his clients' approval. And one can picture their excitement as they tried to make head-and-tail of his scheme, just as one can imagine the amendments, alterations and second thoughts that followed. For with expensive houses and well-to-do clients it is ever so! But at last the scheme was agreed and, early in 1925, the contractors, Messrs James Longley Ltd of East Grinstead, were instructed to commence work on the site.

In the summer of 1927 – after the usual delays due to the architect and his client's changes of mind, not to mention the slothfulness of the ever-blameable sub-contractors – the removal vans turned up at Aldwick Place MkII and the Ranks moved in. It must have been a splendid house. But hardly the sort that ran itself. To service it required nine indoor staff including Mr Cox, the butler, and Mrs Darby, the housekeeper. There were also five gardeners who, when not rostered to tend the plants and manicure the golf-course, had to find time, twice a year, to change the fence that ran along the sea-wall: white-painted pallisading in summer and wattle hurdles for the winter.

Margaret Rank was a practised hostess and entertaining came easily to both her and Rowland. A glimpse at the old visitors' book shows the people of note who at different times were invited to Aldwick Place. Amongst the earliest were Lord and Lady Ashfield, he once Lord President of the Board of Trade in Lloyd George's wartime government. They were followed by former MP Lord Dewar of whisky fame and Humphrey Vernon, of Spillers Ltd. Another who signed was Wing Commander Maurice Baring, the journalist and writer who found time to come to Aldwick between being a war correspondent in China and writing a book on Sarah Bernhardt on Buck's behalf. On another page is the signature of Lord 'Beef' Tweedsmouth CMG, DSO, MVO, 3rd Baron and Lord-in-Waiting to His Majesty the King. Their neighbours from West House, the Duff Coopers and Lady Gladys' mother, the Duchess of Rutland, were other frequent droppers-in. So, of course, was Emily Croxton Johnson from Paradise.

88 Mrs Margaret Rank in 1915.

Early in 1926 Wyatt's, the Bognor estate agents, were instructed by Mr W.H.B Fletcher, lord of the manor of Aldwick, to offer for sale a sizeable portion of his vast estate which had once allowed him to ride a horse from Bognor nearly to Selsey on his own land. Part of it was at Aldwick and included 'A gentleman's Dairy and Stock Farm with 275 acres of arable and grazing'. The reason for the sale was a sad one. Fletcher's only surviving son, John, had been killed at Bethune in France. There was no one to inherit.

At the auction, held at the *Royal Norfolk Hotel* on 20 May, Mr Rowland Rank put in a successful bid and Aldwick Farm found itself on the books of the latest of a string of owners which had begun during the reign of the first Elizabeth. The next event of any importance in the Rank menage was when, in January 1930, *The Times* carried the announcement that Margaret Rank had been safely delivered of a second son, John; a blessing not only to his parents but also to this author, for without his help this chapter must have remained unwritten!

Away from the Battersea mill, Rowland Rank continued to enjoy the country pursuits he had followed as a young man in the East Riding. If he shunned the headlines of the national press, any 1930s copy of *Horse and Hound* would restore the balance. Within its pages his name occurs time after time. For RR's obsession was hare-coursing, admittedly a pastime which no longer enjoys much popular support. But in those days and in those circles he was a well-known and respected figure. For many years he was on the Standing Committee of the National Coursing Club and in 1926 was elected a Member.

In 1937, great was the rejoicing at Aldwick Place when his legendary Rotten Row ('the best greyhound of the century' according to the *Daily Mail*) won the Waterloo Cup. Other triumphs he enjoyed were the Southern Plate, the Altcar Centenary and Barbican Cup. Yet winning cups was only a means to an end: his preoccupation was the breeding and genetics of racing dogs. And in this field he was regarded as an authority. In the 'thirties his kennels at Aldwick Farm were among the most up-to-date in the country, and the sight of his kennelman, Mr Howe, exercising half-a-dozen blue-blooded greyhounds was a staple part of the Aldwick scene.

But already RR had begun to consider a quite different venture, a venture made possible by his purchase of Aldwick Farm. No doubt he turned to his brother, James, a noted bloodstock owner, for expert advice. Rowland's plan was to turn part of his land into a modern stud farm. And it was this enterprise which was to alter the face of much of Aldwick in the ten years before the last war.

By late 1931 the first signs of his plans began to appear. The fields to the north of Aldwick Place and the village (*our* fields, on to which Idlewylde abutted) were divided into paddocks and punctuated with stylish-looking loose-boxes. Next, thousands of yards of creosoted, pallisade fencing were erected, encircling the 'peninsula' bounded by Silverston Avenue, Aldwick Road and Fish Lane. This was followed by the planting of hundreds of young conifers* around the paddocks' perimeters. And for each sapling an augured hole. How well I remember those holes! For as soon as they began to appear in the paddock behind Idlewylde, we and our friends quickly invented an exciting new game as we crouched in our dug-outs, firing cap pistols and amiably hurling clods of clay at each other until, to our chagrin, the men returned to plant the trees!

In fact, it was the sight of so many conifers which prompted my mother to write to Mr Rank. She wondered whether, when they got opposite her garden, he might consider planting one or two trees of other species. His reply was both courteous and sympathetic. After thanking her for the interest she was taking in his enterprise, he suggested she should visit Barnham Nurseries and choose six young trees she liked, put them down to his account and he would see that they were planted opposite her bungalow. Years later, thanks to RR, our garden enjoyed a handsome backcloth of mature silver birches, a couple of Lombardy poplars and a copper beech. Also a crab apple which was one day to make its mark on our garden in a quite unexpected way, as the reader will learn in a 'The Story of a Seedling Apple', at the end of the book.

Meanwhile, at Aldwick Farm the contractors were busy adapting, re-modelling and adding to the old buildings. Opposite the Duck Pond a new farmhouse was being built for Farmer Crockett while, not far away, Penelope Cottage – the little bungalow which stands on what had once been Aldwick Green and the site of a military barracks at the time of the Napoleonic wars – was being overhauled and re-roofed for Mr Inns, the Ranks' greyhound trainer. Gradually, Rowland Rank's smart, pneumatic-tyred farm-carts, pulled by sturdy Percherons, became a familiar sight on local roads. Cows, though, were not really Rowland's cup of tea and the dairy side of the farm was leased to Chichester Dairies Ltd.

In the course of our meanderings in the fields, on the primrose banks of

---

* To this day, a lot of those windbreak conifers, now venerable in years and of massive girth, still survive in Aldwick Felds, although many fell victim to the severe gales of 1987 and '89.

the Sheepwash ditch, squelching around the Duck Pond's dank border, and from our hide-out in the 'hollow oak' outside the Great Barn at Aldwick Farm, Roger and I observed all these goings-on with deep interest. For one thing was clear: in future we should have to share our territory with Mr Rank!

89 Rowland Rank holds a brood mare by the head collar in one of the paddocks.

The philanthropy which marked old Joe's life sat easily on the shoulders of his sons. Rowland donated the old Aldwick Farmhouse, built by W.H.B. Fletcher in 1909, to Dr Barnardo's Home. Renamed after his wife, it became known as the Margaret Home.* Soon its little crocodile of boys, out for their afternoon walk in charge of their matron, Miss Fairban, became an integral strand of the Aldwick picture. It wasn't long before the Rank family established a special rapport with these Barnardo boys. Besides providing them with a beach hut at the end of Dark Lane, they laid on firework displays on Guy Fawkes Night and, during the summer, often stood treats with ice-cream tubs all round – which soon emptied our friendly Antarctic salesman's reserves! Rowland Rank also made handsome gifts to the Bognor Boys Club as well as allowing Aldwick Wednesday Football Club – admittedly, not much in the headlines nowadays – the use of the Bottom Field, opposite Mrs Duffin's store, for their home ground.

In 1933 a shock-wave ran through Aldwick Place; RR had suffered a heart attack. Lord Horder, the country's most eminent physician, was called to his bed. For a long time it was touch and go and Margaret was never far from her husband's side. But gradually Rowland's condition began to improve. He took to riding a bicycle for excercise. Not for the first time, Aldwick's benevolent climate and the clean sea-air joined forces with his own fierce determination to achieve a slow recovery. But it was a recovery ominously incomplete.

By the late 'thirties, Aldwick wore a markedly well-heeled appearance. And not a little of this was due to the works of Rowland Rank. From the West Car Park to the Duck Pond, from Penelope Cottage via Aldwick crossroads to Fish Lane, the windbreak trees were beginning to show above the sky line, and well-groomed brood mares with their leggy foals roamed the paddocks.

Resplendent in the Rank racing colours of red, navy blue and white, Aldwick Farm looked as smart as any model dairy in the land, and a clock could be set by the regularity with which the cows held up the ever-growing traffic on the road to Chichester. Its quiet, shaded water yet ungentrified, the Duck Pond continued to cast its spell over passers-by as they watched the swallows and the reflections of the bordering elms. In the village, visitors felt for their cameras when they saw Almora framed by its mature trees, with Baron Grant's fine wrought-iron gates in the background. While

* The Margaret Home failed to survive the property boom of the 'eighties; it was demolished to allow the building of an estate of red-tiled houses called Margaret Close.

90 Aldwick Farmhouse. The living quarters are to the left, the rest is a barn. Of early 18th-century origin, it is now a Grade II Listed building.

in Gossamer Lane – although, admittedly, nothing to do with Mr Rank – the new St Richard's Church cast its spiritual light over the surrounding district.

At Aldwick Place Margaret and 'Rowley' continued to entertain a cavalcade of people outstanding in their different ways. And none more so than old Joseph Rank himself, now in his eighties and still presiding over his company's board meetings. Invariably his visits to Aldwick allowed him time to attend Sunday morning service at the Methodist church in the High Street, where two of its stalwarts, Thomas Tregear, the Secretary, and Albert Seymour JP, in his role of Trustee, were waiting to greet him – and to bank the sizeable offering he was wont to leave in the plate. Some of the visitors bordered on the exotic. In August 1937 the Ranks welcomed Mia Macklin, the international ice-skater, for a long weekend during which she and young Joseph Rank had to be rescued from their broken-down motor boat in heavy seas. Not long afterwards, Françoise Gilot, a young law student and aspiring painter, enjoyed the relaxing facilities of Aldwick Place before bettering herself by becoming Pablo Picasso's mistress at the rue Grand Augustins in Paris.

By 1938 the sound of muffled war drums could be heard from the other side of the Channel as people listened uneasily on their wireless sets to Hitler's ranting voice staking out his territorial demands. In old Joseph's mind war was inevitable. Yet for a long time his advice to the government to accumulate grain supplies went unheeded. But at last the Whitehall penny dropped. Quietly, on the government's behalf, he was appointed to purchase secretly huge shipments of wheat for storing in silos all over the country.

Then, in that December, the alarm bells at Aldwick Place sounded with even greater urgency. Rowland had suffered a stroke. Once more Lord Horder hurried to his bedside; once again Margaret spent hours in anguished vigil. Gradually, though, he began to improve and by the early summer of 1939 there seemed cautious grounds for his recovery. But on 11 July he suffered a second stroke which this time proved fatal. He was only 53.

A few days later the funeral cortège, amongst the longest ever seen in the district, wound its way slowly towards the 13th-century church of beginnings and endings at Pagham, watched by hundreds of people who had come to pay their last respects to a man of whom no ill could be spoken. Inside the church, his friends from the worlds of business and sport filled every seat not already taken by the staff of the Battersea Mill. And it was a cruel irony that among the family mourners should have been his 85-year-old father, Joseph Rank, the man who had seen no future in windmills more than fifty years before and was now one of the greatest millers in the world. Rowland Rank rests in Pagham churchyard in a grave marked by a granite millstone.

For his broken-hearted widow, it must have been a time of grief and emptiness, only deepened when, two months later, she listened with the rest of the nation to the grim voice of Neville Chamberlain telling them that once more Britain was at war with Germany.

Yet perhaps this was a blessing in disguise. For soon, with consuming energy, Margaret was able to immerse herself in war work. Aldwick Place was turned over to entertaining servicemen, at first through the uneasy months of the 'Phoney War' and then, after 18 May 1940, with greater purpose as the fateful events in Europe began to unroll. In the first two years of the war many of the hard-pressed pilots from Tangmere and Westhampnett – Douglas Bader and Squadron Leader Peter Townsend among them – had the Rank family to thank for a few hours of respite, a glass or two of the hard stuff and the chance for some warm and friendly words with Margaret and her daughters. But as the war dragged on so the visitors book, scrawled with the signatures of RAF pilots, came to read more like a Roll of Honour.

One group of servicemen particularly close to Margaret's heart was the 1st Canadian Division who, by June 1940, had begun taking up their defence positions on the Sussex coast. Soon, Aldwick Place became their oasis of hospitality, doubly welcome for being run by one of their own country-women. Sadly, though, many of them were earmarked for the ill-fated Dieppe raid in August 1942 and were never to enjoy such precious moments again. Eventually, rationing, a shortage of alcohol and the steady depletion of staff put a brake on these hospitable activities. Instead, Aldwick Place became a WVS distribution depot where Margaret and her daughters helped in dispatching comforts to servicemen overseas. And so, from this exposed, front-line position on the south coast, they carried on their work throughout those long, bleak years when so much of the news seemed depressingly bad.

But at last, in June 1944, the Allies were ready to carry the war across the Channel. For weeks the Ranks, with the rest of Bognor, had a ringside seat as the components of the Mulberry Harbour were marshalled off the coastline. Then, in the early hours of the 6th, the whole town was wakened by the roar of the great fleet of troop-carrying aircraft, each with its green identification light, flying overhead on its way to Normandy. The invasion and the liberation of Europe had begun.

Eleven months later, on 8 May 1945, came the unconditional surrender of the German forces. The surge of thankfulness that swept across Britain was deeply felt at Aldwick Place where young Peggy was already a war widow. Fate was at her most malevolent when, seven months later, she decreed that those early days of peace should be marred by the evil legacy of war, and a tragedy occurred almost on the Ranks' doorstep. On the morning of 22 December 1945 Roy Suter was walking his dog on the beach when it galloped off ahead – only to come to an abrupt stop on the far side of a breakwater below Aldwick Place, where it had discovered a large spherical object covered in barnacles. The dog gave it a good sniff … and cocked his leg! But when Mr Suter got to the groyne he found himself looking at a stranded sea-mine. Nor was it the first to be washed up during the recent storms. Quickly he made his way to the Dark Lane cottage of his friend, Charlie Axtell, the gardener at Strange Garden. Charlie immediately phoned the Police who, in turn, alerted the Naval Mine Disposal Unit at Gosport. Not unduly concerned, the Ranks sat down for lunch with some friends.

Just after 2 o'clock in the afternoon the whole district was shaken by a huge explosion. On the beach lay dying 23-year-old Lt. Walter Prior RNVR, who had been attempting to defuse the mine. The Ranks and their friends rushed to the scene. For the young lieutenant they could do little but at least they were able to comfort the weeping WREN driver and two injured naval ratings, all of them in a deep state of shock. Roger still remembers the great noise made by the shingle as it cascaded back on to the beach and the shocked WREN driver walking back up Dark Lane. In time Margaret Rank made the acquaintance of the young lieutenant's father, the Reverend Clement Prior. It was tacitly agreed he should be allowed his dearest wish, to erect a memorial plaque to his son on the sea-wall opposite the place where he had met his death.

But all that was before her accountants brought Margaret disagreeable tidings which werc to have a profound effect on her and her family's future. For the arithmetic of Rowland's death duties and wartime income tax at 19s. 6d. in the £ pointed clearly to it becoming ruinous to continue running an establishment the size of Aldwick Place. The curtain was about to fall. In November 1946 it was sold to a new owner. Meanwhile Margaret, her widowed daughter, Peggy, and John had moved into Fleurs, a smaller house she had bought in the village nearly opposite the *Ship Inn*. After renaming it Wick Cottage, she made arrangements for one of the rooms to be converted into a photographic studio.

91 Tragedy on Aldwick beach. A police sergeant and other willing helpers tend the mortally wounded Lt. Walter Prior RN after the mine he was trying to defuse exploded.

Although she had long possessed a Leica given her by Rowland before the war, it was only now that Margaret began to take seriously her considerable talents as a photographer. Portraiture was her speciality, and her pictures – developed and enlarged by herself – had that professional touch which was to win her many awards both in this country and abroad, leading eventually to her election as a Member of the Royal Photographic Society.

While she was settling into Wick Cottage Margaret learned with sorrow of discord at Aldwick Place. For it transpired that deep in the new owner's soul there dwelt some inexplicable animus which was to deny the Reverend Prior the boon of fixing his son's plaque to the sea-wall. Fortunately, when news of this impasse reached the sympathetic ears of Mr and Mrs Webber, the new owners of Strange Garden, they willingly agreed to it being fixed on their own wall. And that is why the memorial to a young Naval officer, attempting to prevent danger to other lives on Aldwick Beach in 1945, is to be found at the end of Dark Lane* instead of on the sea-wall many yards to the east where he met his tragic end.

In the early 'fifties the Rank's old home was purchased by Mr Lindsay Fleming, the author of a three-volume *History of Pagham in Sussex.* A few years later, in 1961, a mere 34 years after it had been built, the house was

92 Our friendly Antarctic ice-cream man photographed with the Barnardo's boys from the Margaret Home on one of the Ranks' '3d. tubs all round' occasions.

demolished to make way for a development of modern dwellings with only the name of one of the new roads to remind the passer-by that here once stood the earlier and the later Aldwick Place.

In May 1962 Margaret Rank and her son John moved to the beautiful Regency house Sennicotts, near Chichester, once the home of the Bowes-Lyon family. On 27 February 1988 Margaret passed peacefully away in her 91st year, cared for by her son to the last. She was laid to rest next to her husband, Rowland, in the churchyard at Pagham. Although it is more than twenty years since a mooing cow was heard at Aldwick Farm, I am glad to say that its buildings still remain in the ownership of John Rank.

---

* The present bronze plaque was erected by the Aldwick Parish Council on 21 March 1987 to replace the original one which the ravages of the sea had made illegible.

17

A New Town Hall

Some notes on its builder. And the Campbells are coming!

'That, my boy', proclaimed my father as he pointed to the walls of the Town Hall – we'd called to pay the rates – 'is brickwork with a capital "B".' Well, there's no doubt that the use of two-inch silver-grey facing bricks laid in Flemish bond adds lustre to a building. And even more so when the work is carried out by brickies as skilled as those employed by H.W. Seymour, the contractor who built it in 1930.

(The use of capital letters to emphasise anything he considered of outstanding excellence was one of my father's quirks. On another occasion I can remember him drawing my attention to the green-glazed roof-tiles of a new, white-stuccoed house in King's Parade (it was years before I discovered that Sandmartin had been built for R.C. Sherriff, the author of *Journey's End* and that very Bognor story, *The Fortnight in September*): 'Now, that, old chap, is roof tiling with a capital "T"!' he had exclaimed. And it was the same with the new wall to Mr Rowland Rank's Aldwick Place in Fish Lane, which he rated as 'flintwork with a capital "F".' Thus, from an early age, I was expected to know good workmanship when I saw it. Architecture was seeping into my blood.)

In fact, I can just recall my father taking me with him when he went to look at the new Town Hall while it was still being built in Clarence Road, just after we first moved to Aldwick; it is a faded image now of scaffolding, red roofing tiles and the 'clock' lantern still incomplete. What completely escaped me then was why it had come to be built there and not on the site for which it was originally intended! Anyway, it created quite a commotion at the time!

But, first, a little background. Up until the late 1800s the old Local Board – the predecessors of the Urban District Council – had made shift with a quasi-Town Hall at W.K. Wonham's* Assembly Rooms in Sudley Road. Eventually, though, it became too small for their ever-growing administrative duties, the fate of many small Town Halls of those times.

In 1880 the old Jubilee Charity School stood on the north side of the High Street, just east of Fitzleet House; it had been built originally for 'educating fifty poor girls', had become surplus to requirements, and was put on the market. So the Board, looking for a site to build a new Town Hall, decided to buy it. But they had overlooked the aversion of Bognor's

---

* William Kimber Wonham and his father, Daniel, were Bognor's most prolific builder/developers in the early 1800s. Many of the houses on the west side of Waterloo Square are theirs; also the Rock Gardens Crescent, which became an hotel.

ratepayers to putting their hands in their pockets to pay for any proposal considered as desperately extravagant as this one, a trait in the town's psyche which was to cost it dear in the 1930s. Instead, Mr Stringfellow, the Council's Surveyor at the time, was reduced to merely converting the school into offices at the cost of £500. They were opened in 1882. Then, in 1894, the Local Board was redesignated the Bognor Urban District Council.

Thus, 1926 found Bognor UDC administering a town with a population of some 17,000 but still operating from the old ex-Jubilee School building – by then No. 68 High Street ('The Chamber') – to which had since been added the premises on either side plus a handful of departmental outposts in different parts of the High Street. Clearly, the time had come to contemplate once more that ultimate symbol of municipal virility, a new Town Hall.*

The first question the Special Purposes Committee had to address, though, was where to build it. Various alternatives were looked at: Claremont Place in West Street, Waterloo Square's Hothampton Place and the *Royal Clarence Hotel*† site on the Esplanade which the Council had recently purchased for a car park. But all had their disadvantages. (Of course, the best site of all would have been in the area opposite the railway station, had the Picturedrome cinema not got there first.)

At any rate, by a process of elimination, it was decided that Bognor's new Town Hall should rise upon the Council's existing High Street site, enlarged by taking in some small shops, which extended its eastern boundary to Bedford Street. Faced with the upheaval of the demolition of their existing offices, the Council looked around for temporary premises. In those days, between Staley's (now Bobby's) on the corner of London Road and the *Sussex Hotel* (recently renamed *The William Hardwicke*) stood Camden House. It was purchased, although first it had to be wired for electricity, a concession to the 20th century less surprising than it may seem when it is remembered that only in 1928 was electric lighting installed in London Road to replace the old gas lamps.

Meanwhile, Mr Draper – 'Ossy' Bridges'‡ successor as the town's Surveyor – had been in touch with the Royal Institute of British Architects with a view to arranging an architectural competition for the new building. In due course the President laid out the rules to be observed for this sort of exercise, and at the same time recommended that Mr Septimus Warwick FRIBA, a well-known London architect, should be appointed Assessor.

Among the perpetually work-starved members of the architectural profession, it proved a popular project; briefs and the competition rules were dispatched to 91 firms, including Percy Meredith, who had just finished designing Aldwick Place for the Rank family, and Stanley Hennell ARIBA, the Bognor architect with offices in the High Street. Soon, studio wastepaper baskets began to fill with screwed-up balls of discarded ideas as the competitors applied their minds and 2B pencils to the pursuit of those elusive

---

* Strictly speaking, only a Borough was allowed to call its headquarters a 'Town Hall'. At Bognor they were merely 'Council Offices'. But as most people used the former term, I have followed suit.
  † The Council had toyed with the idea of converting Samuel Beazley's *Royal Clarence Hotel* building into Council Offices as early as 1923.
  ‡ See Appendix, p.307.

93 Bognor's Council Offices in the High Street in about 1927.

ideals of beauty and fitness-for-purpose proper to a seaside Town Hall. Meanwhile, the old Council Offices were demolished.*

In July 1927 Septimus Warwick was able to report to the Council that, having inspected the resultant swathes of hopeful and hapless schemes submitted, he had no hesitation in declaring the design presented by Charles Cowles Voysey ARIBA to be the winner. The runners-up were Clayton and Black, a firm of Brighton architects. In the lottery of architectural competitions, Bognor could count itself fortunate. Charles Cowles Voysey, son of the even better known vernacular designer, Charles Voysey, was an inveterate competition winner with many municipal buildings to his credit. Only recently he had been awarded the White Rock Pavilion scheme at Hastings.

His design for Bognor's new Town Hall – set ten feet back from the High Street pavement line – showed a nicely proportioned and carefully detailed grey-brick building with stone surrounds to the main entrance and the balcony above, all in the uncontroversial neo-Classical idiom. The rear elevation facing on to Bedford Street West† was carefully fenestrated but was

* The old Council Office site was eventually sold to the Southdown Motor Company for £5,000 for their new Art Deco bus station which was opened in 1932 and demolished in 1994.

† John Street appears to have been temporarily renamed 'Bedford Street West' for the purpose of the competition, where it is referred to in the brief.

otherwise unexceptional. There was little room for parking. To fulfil the various accommodation requirements meant building on the whole length of the High Street frontage, thus giving it only this one significant façade. There was no view 'in the round', no 'presence'. Clearly the site was barely large enough for the scheme. However, Mother Nature was shortly to deal with these deficiencies.

Why the digging of 'trial-holes', to ascertain the suitability of the ground upon which the new Town Hall was to stand, was left until late in 1927 is a mystery. At any rate, it appears that only after Voysey had been appointed and the design approved did anyone attempt to find out! And that was when it was discovered the site was bedevilled by that well-known local geological bugbear, running sand. Since the scheme included a basement, it would have added greatly to the cost of the new building. It is also possible that it began to dawn on the Committee – prompted by Voysey – that, in any case, the current scheme was virtually incapable of future expansion. At all events, it was decided to look again at one of the sites they had earlier eschewed – the *Royal Clarence* 'car park'. Besides being geologically less troublesome, this was much larger than was needed simply for a Town Hall. There was space for other buildings. Soon references to a 'public library, a museum and a fire station' began to appear in the Council's minutes.

Thus, almost by accident, the notion of a civic building complex in Clarence Road began to evolve. Yet, would not your average Bognorian on top of the Southdown omnibus have considered the new site to be among the town's more notable backwaters? It promised a Town Hall without much town. Nevertheless, on 17 February 1928 the Council abandoned the High Street site in favour of the *Royal Clarence*. When the Council's decision became known, there was a tremendous furore! Most vociferous were the nearby traders, fearful of the competition which would result if more shops were built on the old Council Office site. That guardian of Bognor's conscience, Mr Tom Tregear, felt compelled to write to the *Bognor Observer*, '... the idea of building the new Town Hall in a back street has come to the ratepayers like a thunderclap. It was something the town will regret as long as it exists.'

But more to the point, what of Mr Cowles Voysey, left sitting on a winning design for a building on the wrong site? Well, he threw his hat in the air, I wouldn't wonder! For Clarence Road, from an architect's point of view, offered more breathing space for a building to be seen 'in the round'; four highly visible elevations. We can only suppose it was with pleasurable anticipation he returned to his drawing-board!

When the new version of the Town Hall was unveiled it revealed a shapely building with its front elevation splayed towards the intersection of Belmont Street and Clarence Road. The second-floor fenestration had been strengthened and the roof raised. To break the ridge line, a clock lantern had been added, which would have included a clock had not the Ministry of Health struck it out to help pay for the addition of an elaborate *porte-cochère* supported on stone columns (later changed to pairs of brick pillars) over the front entrance. Voysey had also taken the opportunity to increase the height of the Council Chamber and to get rid of the two rather

FRONT ELEVATION TO HIGH STREET

94 The High Street elevation of Charles Cowles Voysey's winning design for the new Town Hall as intended for the old Council Offices site. But the discovery of running sand where the building would stand precipitated a rapid change of plan.

95 The revised Town Hall design for the 'backwater' site in Clarence Road. Cowles Voysey must have welcomed the change to a larger site as it resulted in a more handsome design worthy of being shown at the Royal Academy Exhibition of 1928.

overpowering chimney stacks of his earlier scheme. The result was a distinguished yet unpretentious composition which – by now – bore little resemblance to the winning design! Yet, for virtually re-churning the whole scheme, Cowles Voysey's bill was remarkably modest: £100.

Soon, Bills of Quantities were dispatched to approved contractors. And when, a few weeks later, the bids were opened, Messrs H.W. Seymour Ltd of Bognor had submitted the lowest price of £18,000 5s. 5d. Of course, in those days, one got quite a lot of Town Hall for a one pound note!

Now came the question of laying the foundation stone, a ceremony dear to Urban District hearts. Who should perform it? Not far away, at Craigweil House, the Queen of England was still in residence. Respectfully, the Town Clerk wrote to her secretary, Sir Clive Wigram. Would she possibly? Sir Clive's reply was discouraging: he was sure the Council appreciated that Her Majesty was constantly being asked to do this sort of thing … a line had to be drawn, etc, etc.

So, wounds licked, the Council returned to earth and decided, instead, there should be two foundation stones, one laid by the Chairman of the Council, Canon J.A. Sacré, and the other by William Grice, its oldest member and headmaster of Colebrook School, which could number amongst its more illustrious *alumni* none other than H.W. Seymour himself. On 15 May 1929 the King Emperor, restored to health, his colourful rhetoric unimpaired, left Craigweil with the Queen bound for Windsor Castle. A week later, on the 22nd, the two foundation stones were 'laid in a business-like way', and the Canon and Mr Grice were presented with their suitably inscribed silver trowels.

We will now leave Herbert William Seymour in peace to get on with putting up his Town Hall. Yet who was this man who suddenly found himself responsible for the construction of Bognor's most important modern edifice? Well, for one thing the new Town Hall – although the most prestigious – was only one of many important projects with which his firm left their stamp on the emerging character of Bognor in the first thirty years of the century. When I was a boy, wherever there were piles of bricks, sand and scaffold poles, they seemed nearly always to be under the blue-and-cream board of 'H.W. Seymour Ltd, Builders'.

His father, Edward Seymour (occupation, gent), had come to Bognor from Cornwall in the 1870s. His only stock-in-trade appears to have been a parcel of meadow land at Aldwick, left him in the last will and testament of his father who, otherwise, had devoted himself to drinking most of the family's other assets, assets which had once included the land on which now stand St Martin-in-the-Fields and the Adelphi in London.

In 1881 Edward married Miss Clara Refoy, a local girl, whose sister, Ada, to everyone's confusion, had married Bognor's other well-known Seymour, Albert the stone mason, later a proprietor of the South Coast Steam Marble Works in Station Road, a JP and one of Bognor's leading public men. In 1883 Edward and Clara's first-born arrived, and so we meet Herbert

96 Albert Seymour.

William Seymour – as well as more confusion for, upon reaching his teens, Herbert was apprenticed by Edward to Albert at the latter's marble works.

Although his name appears only sporadically in this book, no register of the men who influenced the shape and fortunes of Bognor on either side of the turn of the century can claim to be complete without some mention of Albert Seymour. Unlike those other movers and formers of his time – William Tate, Thos. Tregear, Oswald Bridges, H.W. Seymour *et al* – who left their mark on the town in the form of buildings and enterprises, Albert Seymour's contribution was in the shape of hundreds of hand-cut memorial stones found in cemeteries all over Sussex. But to the people of Bognor he had much more to offer than that.

Albert was born of a quarry-owning family at Swanage in 1861. At the age of 23 he removed his Methodism and his stoneworking skills to Portsmouth where he met his wife, Ada Refoy, a Bognor girl in service there. Three years later in, 1887, they came to our town where he joined another Seymour – the ailing William Butler Seymour (their kinship is unclear), who had a marble works near *The White Horse* in Chichester Road. Soon Albert was running the firm.

When William died the works became his and Albert renamed the enterprise the South Coast Steam Marble Works; shortly afterwards he moved to new premises in Station Road where he continued producing gravestones until he retired in 1924. But it was in local affairs that Albert Seymour seems to have found ultimate fulfillment. And in this sphere – discounting the sustained and devoted service he gave his beloved Methodist Church – his record is remarkable.

In 1890, shortly after coming to Bognor, Albert Seymour was elected a member of the Bersted Parish Council of which he was Vice Chairman for five years; 1895 found him Chairman of the Bognor and Bersted branch of the British and Foreign Bible Society, President of the Free Church Council and a Trustee of the Methodist Church. By 1899 he was serving on the School Boards, the Board of the Lyon Street School and the Board of the Royal Sussex Hospital, besides being made a member of the Sunday Schools Council. To these duties could be added his chairmanships of Arthur's Home in Aldwick Road and, after the First World War, of the local branch of the League of Nations. In 1899 he was elected a Councillor. From then on, for the next 25 years – including the period in 1921-2 when he was Chairman of the Council – his name appears among those present in the Chamber, or attending one or other of the many Committees on which he served.

Albert Seymour was Chairman of the Band and Entertainments Committee and in 1921 he led the Council at the time they purchased Norman Thompson's aircraft hangar at Middleton (which was to become the Pavilion). He also played a seminal role in setting up Bognor's first Public Library in part of the Lyon Street School. He found time to to be a Steward of the Methodist Church for 38 years and run a Bible Class for 40, and, although a non-player, he was a founder member of the Bognor Golf Club. After he retired he was made a JP, with all the commitments that entailed. In fact, it is almost a relief to learn he found time for a few games of bowls with his many friends at the Bognor Bowling Club in Waterloo Square! He died in 1942 aged 81. No community could have been more diligently served by this industrious and public-spirited stonemason.

When Edward Seymour died the family land, which lay westwards from Nyewood Lane and behind the Victorian villas on the north side of Aldwick Road, passed to Herbert his son. By the time he had reached an age to act on his own behalf, the 20th century was upon the country, bringing in its wake that air of optimism which epitomised Edwardian England. It must have also seemed to him a proper time to marry. On 8 February 1904 he took as wife Ellen Kate Collins, the daughter of an old Bognor family. West Bognor at this time was growing rapidly and he judged his meadows to be ripe for development. Working from his office at Cucumber Farm in Nyewood Lane, Herbert – better known as 'Bert' – began hatching plans for developing what are now Shelley and Tennyson Roads and Richmond Avenue. Soon his houses were selling like hot cakes and within a few years he had amassed the capital necessary to sustain a successful building business. Next, he acquired larger premises in Crescent Road, 'with good stabling for horses'. By 1910 Seymour's the Builders were playing a major role in the jigsaw of Bognor's accelerating expansion.

Then, in 1914, came the upheaval of the First World War. Aeroplane propellers were in great demand and the skills of their joinery department enabled his firm to land a long-term government contract for making them in hundreds. Although fully occupied running the business, Bert Seymour's compassion for his fellow men found its outlet in regular voluntary work at Chichester's Graylingwell Hospital, where he spent many long nights bringing what comfort he could to the wounded soldiers invalided back from France. After 1918, as his firm picked up the threads of their building work, Bert Seymour became a familiar figure driving around the town in a giant Studebaker car he had bought from an American officer.

Unusually for a firm of general builders, it gradually became involved in civil engineering contracts. All over the country, tarmacadam roads were being replaced with reinforced concrete. At Bognor, Seymour's got their fair share, among them the High Street, Station, Sudley and London Roads as well as Collyer Avenue and the Upper Bognor Road. The eastwards extension of the promenade towards Felpham can be added to their ventures into civil engineering.

As contractors in the more traditional role, Seymour's were responsible for building the Congregational church in Linden Road – designed by Mr S.T. Hennel ARIBA – the extensions to Staley's in the High Street and the Mons Avenue council houses, as well as many residences in Marshall Avenue. They built the Fish Lane kennels and lodges at Aldwick Place for Rowland Rank, the miller, soon after Herbert William had completed Blackmill Building in West Bognor for Tom Tregear. Not all their jobs went smoothly; the Waterloo Square Lavatories nearly brought them to their knees when they struck that old enemy, running sand.

Outside the town their name-boards were to be seen on extensive housing schemes at Yapton and in Fontwell Avenue. I can remember clearly Seymour's erecting Reynolds' new showrooms, opened just as the war started and another of their landmark jobs. However, Bert Seymour's *chef d'oeuvre* – apart from the Town Hall – was the development of the West Marine Estate (the residual part of W.H.B. Fletcher's land after the Council had carved out of it what they needed for Marine Park Gardens), which transformed the appearance of Bognor's western fringe with the building of those avenues bearing themeless names – Selsey, Wessex, Princess and Silverston – as well as King's Parade, in which his best-known house, Sandmartin, was built for R.C. Sherriff.

Much of what I have written about Herbert William Seymour was gleaned from his daughter, Mrs Greta Blythe, who also told me how he looked forward to regular chatty evenings at Aldwick Manor with William Fletcher and Bognor's Medical Officer of Health, Dr H.C.L. Morris MD. All were men of wide interests and one can only suppose their conversation flowed easily as they devoted themselves – in Greta Blythe's words – 'to putting Bognor straight'. And, by the sound of it, getting through a fair amount of Mr Fletcher's brandy in the process! In fact, Greta herself was no stranger to Aldwick Manor, having been taken there from time to time by her father. She remembered meeting William's wife, Agnes, who showed her round her reptile collection: 'She was quite fearless of these scaly creatures; and used to pick them up and talk to them. But what shocked me was when she suddenly took a live mouse out of a box, banged the poor thing's head on the bench to kill it, then threw it to this huge snake!'

97 H.W. Seymour, master builder.

Bert Seymour had an abiding interest in the town's affairs. He was a founder of the Bognor Golf Club and one-time Chairman of the Bognor Gas and Electricity Undertaking. During the 'thirties he was elected to the Bognor Regis Council on which he served for ten years apart from a short period when, as one of 'the four men good and true', he broke his lance battling in support of the controversial Colebrook Terrace bathing pool in 1937. Of that, though, more in the next chapter. H.W. is remembered, too, for his collection of prints, drawings and photos of old Bognor, on which he collaborated with Mr Frank Reynolds, which remain an invaluable record of the town's history.

Like many men born towards the end of the 19th century, Seymour lived to see two world wars. During the blitz in the second he was appointed West Sussex Area Leader of the Mobile Labour Force, which entailed taking train-loads of building repair gangs from Bognor to the bomb-devastated areas of Croydon, Deptford and Portsmouth.

When he died, in 1959, his son Jim took over the running of the firm, and local historians will remember the skill it exercised in the restoration of the old Ice House in London Road and the rebuilding of Queen Victoria's jubilee drinking fountain in the Steyne in 1969. But the 'hot-house' environment of major construction contracts undertaken during a period of remorseless inflation, and the difficulties of obtaining first-class craftsmen, had, he once told me, 'knocked the fun out building'. Gradually the firm shrank in size. Then, sadly, at the age of only 64, Jim died in 1982. And within a short time the name of H.W. Seymour Ltd, Builders, disappeared, remembered only by those who had witnessed their heyday between the wars.

But back to the end of September 1930, and Mr Seymour has removed his builder's board from Bognor's completed Town Hall. A few days later, on 6 October, after a simple ceremony performed by Mrs Sacré – sadly marred by the illness of her husband and the recent death of William Grice – the new offices were declared open, as the Council girded its loins in preparation for the great municipal sagas of the future: the scourge of Billy Butlin, the Esplanade bathing pool, the new Winter Garden's Bandstand and the bogey of the Rose Green aerodrome.

After the First World War, that quaint English phenomenon, the nailed-on, creosoted, half-timbered *chez nous* spawned its way along the shores of the new concrete by-passes and arterial roads, raising its kin on nearly every available residential building habitat throughout the southern half of England. This eccentric Meccano set of inglenook fireplaces, two-centred arches, false oak beams and leaded window panes exerted on Kingston By-Pass Man in his little Austin Seven, plus-foured and mortgaged to the ears, a terrible fascination as he sought the imaginary manorial heritage to take his mind off his nine-to-five existence 'somewhere in the City'. Seeking retirement in the sun at Bognor, he was spoilt for choice; from the Bay Estate to Pevensey Road and from North Bersted to Marshall Avenue, houses and bungalows in the new genre rose from the native clay in democratic profusion.

As a child, long before I had the notion of becoming an architect, able to draw the Four Orders of Architecture from memory, I regarded building as merely part of the entertainment business: Punch and Judy opposite the Steyne in the morning; after lunch, call in and see how the stonemasons were getting on with the walls to the new church in Gossamer Lane, where there was neither a hard hat to be seen nor a radio to be heard! 'Could I help?' Or perhaps spend a few minutes watching the carpenters putting the roof on one of the houses on the Bay Estate. Wherever I called, my 'help' was available. I was a willing hostage to holes in the ground, working concrete mixers, scaffolding, cranes, bricklayers and the smell of boiling asphalt.

Aldwick was created 'A Conventional District', the preliminary stage before becoming a full ecclesiastical parish, early in 1931, with the Rev. C.H. Mosse appointed priest-in-charge. By then, however, the little timber chapel in the village had succumbed to the ravages of wet and dry rot and thus, for some years, services were held in Rose Green Church Hall. In 1932 it was decided Aldwick should have a new parish church built on the north side of Gossamer Lane on a site costing £500. Early in March 1933 Mrs H.R. Mosse dug the first spit and on 3 April – St Richard's Day – the Assistant Bishop of Chichester, the Rt. Rev. H.K. Southwell, performed the founda-tion-stone-laying ceremony. On 12 May 1934 St Richard's Church was consecrated by the Bishop of Chichester, the Rt. Rev. G.K.A. Bell DD, assisted by the Rev. G.G. Knox, the Vicar of Pagham. Exclusive of the oak screens, choir stalls, altar and the organ (£1,500), which were gifted, the cost of the new 400-seat church was £12,300, a considerable part of which was funded by the Rev. Mosse's parents. The Horsham architect of this strikingly handsome church was Gordon Troup FRIBA, a close relation of the Mosse family. The contractors were Chapman, Lowry and Puttick of Haslemere.

From Barrack Lane to Lion Road, from Grosvenor Gardens to Crescenta Walk, I became a participating voyeur, getting under the feet of the brick-layers, carpenters and plasterers as they went about their innocent business of covering the cornfields of Aldwick and Rose Green with 'desirable residences' to suit retired Kingston By-Pass Man's every taste, chequebook and intellectual deviation. And, from each excursion, the indelible legacy of paint, lime or grease on mac or woolly!

* * *

> Another feature of attraction to this delightful place will be a hand-some Pier with convenient approaches, affording a safe landing not only for Dieppe, Havre, Guernsey, and Jersey steam vessels but for passengers *from all over the world.*
> From the Bognor Improvement Company's prospectus, 1835.

Not all the building activity which caught my eye was on Bognor's mainland. One day in 1935 I noticed some pontoons and a steam crane floating off the Pier head. A few weeks later the monotonous bang-bang-banging of a piledriver echoed along the beach. It turned out to be a new landing stage for the paddle-steamers. The banging went on for months as the timber piles were driven through the sand into the London clay. At low tide the beach shook underfoot; below the Pier the sound was deafening. Month by month I watched it grow.

On 11 June 1936 the new landing stage* was decorated with flags and bunting. Predictably, Captain H.C. Pocock RN, Chairman of the Council, was there to open it, surrounded by the Town's Great and Good, which included Messrs Shanly and Carter, whose Pier it was, and Mr Oswald Bridges FRIBA, whose design it was. A military band from Chichester Barracks was in attendance. Out at sea, dressed overall, the white-funneled *Brighton Belle* closed the gathered throng. Soon, to the strains of *Sussex by the Sea*, there came a gentle bump of steamer against fender: bells clanged, mooring lines snaked, sea dogs shouted and the gangway was lowered. Amidst permutations of handshakes, the Council's Chairman, the Pier's directors and the ship's master exchanged pleasantries in the names of town, the new landing stage, the Pier company and the weather.

Now the speeches. Mr Shanly welcomed the gathering and appealed to them to support his new landing stage 'so that Campbell's would continue

---

* The landing stage was 109 ft. long by 19 ft. wide and a height of 29 ft. above the beach. The basic structure was formed in 14 ft. x 14 ft. British Columbian pine piles driven some 13 feet into the London clay. The contractors were Messrs Jackaman Ltd of Slough, Bucks.

to call here. You have got to come forward so that we can show other places on the South Coast that Bognor Regis is the best resort because you have such wonderful weather etc. etc.' (prolonged applause). Next it was the turn of the gallant Captain. 'Ladies and Gentlemen,' he announced, pithily, 'it is thirty years since a paddle-steamer called at this pier ... this is an epoch-making event for Bognor for the simple reason ... you are going to get the advantage of approaching Bognor from the sea which is a very different matter to approaching it by rail.' (Loud cheers from those who looked forward to coming to Bognor in future by boat!) He also hoped the extension to the landing stage would be completed soon, 'then we can call it "Port Bognor Regis"'! Now came the important part of the ceremony as Captain Pocock strode forward and broke the Union Jack to open the new landing stage. 'Like launching a ship', he chortled as if, given half a chance, he could do that too!

By then, all eyes had turned towards Bognor's high divers as they marked the occasion with their breathtaking routine. Now it was time for the visitors, with their cups of tea, to wander round and touch things with their hands and murmur how strong and good it all was. At last, they'd had enough. God Save the King! The Great and Good safely aboard, three hooter blasts echoed across the Esplanade as the *Brighton Belle*, her great paddles thrashing, eased away from the new landing stage and set a course eastwards for a municipal jolly in the direction of Littlehampton. Slowly, St John's spire and the Shripney gasholder began to recede into the distance.

A few weeks later my mother and I trod Bognor's new landing stage in earnest, when we boarded the paddle-steamer *Lorna Doone* on our way to Worthing for strawberry teas under a blue-and-white-striped awning dripping with summer rain. The journey back, alas, was on board the less-nautical 31 Southdown bus. But Bognor's landing stage wasn't destined for much of a life. The extension was never added. Barely four years later, during the invasion scare of 1940, the removal of three bays of the Pier cut it off from the mainland. Even its little fleet of visiting paddle-steamers was decimated at Dunkirk: the *Gracie Fields*, *Brighton Queen*, and *Brighton Belle*. And although the Pier became a Royal Navy gunnery school named HMS *St Barbara*, the Germans considered neither it nor the landing stage worth even a small bomb.

After the war the paddle-steamers continued to call at Bognor for a few years until, by the mid-'fifties, they gave up the struggle as the shiny Ford

98 An aerial view of Bognor showing the Pier and the new landing stage opened on 11 June 1936. Note the bathing huts to the left of the Pier. Some sort of entertainment appears to be going on between the most westerly groynes.

99 The Pier's little Pavilion collapses after a storm, 3 March 1965.

Consuls and the lure of the Costa Brava stole their trade. The *coup de grâce* came on 3 March 1965 when the little Pavilion at the end of the Pier fell into the sea, leaving the landing stage permanently marooned. From then on, it gently mouldered away with only the local cormorants prepared to put in a good word for it until, in January 1990, great storms reduced it to a dismal array of sticks. Soon even those were gone.

Yet, as I walked round it at low tide in 1936, it looked to me as if it would last for ever. I can guess what my father would have said; 'That, my lad, is Piling with a capital "P"!'

18

Nemesis on the Seafront

and a 'Brooklands' on the Brooks!

Every now and again there occurs in this part of Sussex a kind of 'spring rash' of airy-fairy schemes for developing the district, although in many cases the exact detail is of a kind of hazy, rosy mist ... and it is surprising the interest they arouse in those ... who listen to those schemes with rather pathetic credulity.

(Morton Swinburne, *Bognor Regis Post*, March 1939)

It is a thankless position to serve on the Council, for if they do not raise any scheme for the improvement of the town, the members are likely to be turned out at the next election, and if they do bring forward anything good for the benefit of the ratepayers, they are rejected at the poll also. So what is one to do?

(Captain H.C. Pocock OBE, JP, RN,
Chairman of the Bognor Regis Council, 29 April 1936)

Upon arrival at Idlewylde, after our Friday night journey from London, almost the first thing I used to do – pending the appearance of the ham sandwiches and the 'go-and-wash-your-hands' command – was to open the *Bognor Post* on the hearthrug and sate my appetite for natural history by reading 'A Countryman's Notebook'. At that late hour, though, concentration quickly flagged. Sleepily, I turned from the life-cycle of the warble fly to the prospect of Spencer Tracy and Jean Harlow, locked in each other's arms at the Picturedrome; then, over a page with a bleary glance at 'Found drunk in Waterloo Square', one more turn brought me back to the front page. And that was where, one Friday night in 1935, something caught my eye. I was gazing at the Council's proposal to build a bathing pool on the beach opposite Colebrook Terrace. Now, new bathing pools – like new Odeons – my brother and I counted as 'Good Things'. So we settled down to await the arrival of this promised landmark on the Esplanade and the day we might show off our inelegant belly-flops from the diving-board one up from the lowest. And we waited ... and waited ... and went on waiting!

In 1935 a glance over the Esplanade battlements would have revealed the outcome of the 'battle of the cabbage patch'* six years earlier. Billy Butlin, the unbridled importer of the meretricious and raucous horrors of

---

* The 'cabbage patch' was part of the old Cotswold Crescent site which had been used as allotments in the First World War. In 1925 the owners offered it to the Council, who rejected it on the grounds of cost. The short-sightedness of their decision came home to haunt them with the arrival on the Esplanade of Billy Butlin in 1929.

Skegness, was now the undisputed leader of the Bognor entertainment centre from Sait's Tea Garden to Lennox Street. Even worse. For ever since the 'escaped' lion saga of 1933, the town had had to endure the 'Butlin Regis' epithet; funny old name, what? Ha ha!

Yet, for this newly royal town all was not quite lost. For in the Town Hall there huddled a small cabal of councillors reflecting every shade of daringly innovative vision, suicidal political conviction and good old-fashioned *amour propre*; seekers after inspiration from among the sunlit municipal uplands of Worthing, Bournemouth and Hastings. Under the severe rod of the Chairman of the Council, Captain H.C. Pocock OBE, JP, RN it was known collectively as the Establishment and Town Improvement Committee; its purpose, to spawn an endless register of wondrously seductive – and mostly unpriced – schemes of imaginative improvement thought necessary to place Bognor's name firmly on the better kind of visitor's map.

100 Captain Pocock OBE, JP, RN, Chairman of the Bognor Regis Council during a large part of the 1930s.

And what glittering promises they were: illuminated fountains in Waterloo Square and Marine Gardens; the continuation of Goodman Drive (now Marine Drive West) to meet the Aldwick Road near the *Rock Gardens Hotel*; the refurbishment and/or demolition of the old Pavilion; new tennis courts in Victoria Road and more shelters on the Esplanade – not to mention extensions to the Town Hall, a new Fire Station, and a Library with a Bognor Regis Museum thrown in for good measure. And that took no account of the Council's huge drainage scheme costing £80,000. Nor, yet, was the Improvement Committee's quiver empty.

Because to this list had to be added the two most gleaming diadems of all: a new bathing pool in front of Colebrook Terrace and a Winter Gardens 'bandstand' opposite the *Royal Norfolk Hotel*. Alas, the rest of this chapter is the story of how the fate of these last two Town Hall dreams put paid to many of those glittering promises, ruined the political prospects of 'four men, good and true', and gave a final shove to Bognor's downhill slide towards Skegness. But, to begin a little nearer the beginning.

In September 1935 the long walk at low tide suffered by visitors and residents in search of a sea deep enough to wet above the ankles weighed heavily upon the Establishment and Town Improvement Committee's conscience. So did Bognor's lowly placing in the league of 'forward looking seaside resorts'. What the town needed was a something with a bit of 'class' to offset Mr Butlin's bawdy Esplanade amusement park. So the Council instructed Mr Draper, the Town's Engineer and Surveyor, to work out a scheme for building a bathing pool on the beach opposite Colebrook Terrace. Apart from one lone voice which expressed mild concern about the scouring effect it might have on the beach and Councillor Caiger's doubt whether a bathing pool lying derelict for eight months of the year could be said to constitute an improvement to the Esplanade, the proposal elicited little further discussion.

In due course Mr Draper's scheme was shown to the Committee. Briefly, it allowed for strengthening and raising the height of a couple of existing groynes opposite Colebrook Terrace, and then enclosing the area between them with a sea-wall built about 150 feet out from the promenade to form a bathing pool. It included a water-filtering plant, changing accommodation and a small café. The cost, he calculated, would be about £10,300. With that, the scheme was approved in principle and the Town Clerk asked to make an application for loan sanction to the Ministry of Health. And that proved to be the first stumbling block. For the Ministry demanded a hugely expensive water purification set-up. Nor were they satisfied with the strength of some of the concrete walls. Twelve feet under the diving boards would be better than ten. And were there enough lockers? They suggested Bognor take a look at a similar bathing pool at Margate. So, in October, a small Council posse including Mr Draper and Councillor H.W. Seymour – with his camera – were dispatched to cast their eyes over Margate's open-air bathing pool and to pick up what tips they could on how to run it.

We now meet H.C. White and Son of Victoria Street, London SW1 – an address in those days stiff with famous structural engineers – who had been appointed to prepare a revised scheme based on Mr Draper's layout but modified by the Ministry's requirements and whatever the Council had gleaned from their visit to Margate. In the middle of November 1935 White and Son presented their proposals. Although similar to Mr Draper's earlier layout, they had been rather less sanguine than he when it came to the amount of expensive reinforced concrete considered necessary to stand up to the onslaught of Channel storms. Then there was the additional cost of the purification plant. More lockers, too – over a thousand of them – not to mention deeper water under the diving boards. And it was all reflected in a revised estimate which had shot up to an alarming £43,000!

Undeterred, the Council sent off again to the Ministry of Health to request its permission to borrow this unexpectedly increased capital sum from the Westminster Property Co. Ltd 'at the rate of £3 2s. 6d. in the £100'. Mr Draper meanwhile was instructed to obtain eight tenders from suitable contractors. It was now that the Council caught the first whiff of trouble. For had they heeded the old Army maxim, that 'time spent on recon-naissance is seldom wasted', they might have discovered rather sooner than they did that between the Town Hall and the bathing pool – and indeed the whole of Bognor's New Jerusalem – there lay well marked with warning signs reading, 'The Bognor Regis Ratepayers Association'.

As it was, the Council appears to have become aware of this obstacle only when, immediately after the astronomical cost of Bognor's new pool had reached the newspapers, they found themselves staring down the muskets of Manley's Armed Irregulars recruited from centres of disaffection ranging from the cretonned lounges of the Bay Estate to the distempered parlours of Gravits Lane. And all in a high state of anti-pool dudgeon! Rapidly the Ratepayers convened 'Stop the Bathing Pool' meetings throughout the wards. At Aldwick's Parish Hall, the pro-pool Dr Clarke failed to persuade an audience, immune to semantics, that the bathing pool was really a 'luxury lido'. Implacably, they recorded their distaste for either. All the best towns may have had swimming pools, but it was clear that all the Ratepayers wanted for Bognor Regis was cheap drainage and clean drinking water.

On 4 February 1936, sharing the nation's grief for the death of King George V, the Council met again to review the bathing pool tenders. Soon they found themselves gazing, half in disbelief, at the lowest – a hair-raising £53,000, submitted by Higgs and Hill Ltd of London. However, gritting their teeth – and apparently impervious to the growing anti-pool opinion beyond Clarence Road – the Council approved both scheme and price and the Town Clerk was instructed to draw up a contract with Higgs and Hill, subject to Ministry of Health's approval of the latest figures.

That same evening, incensed at what they considered the Council's gross extravagance, the Ratepayers Association summoned a meeting at St Mary's Hall in Glamis Street. To Mr Eastland's question, 'Do Bognor's lovely sands need a bathing pool?' there was a loud and predictable cry of 'No!' Instead, a public meeting was demanded at which the scheme could be properly examined. And, with that, Manley's Irregulars dispersed to their bunkers to contemplate how they might exercise their vote when the four pro-pool members of the Town Improvement Committee came up for re-election on 6 April. 'I am sick and tired of trying to make improvements in Bognor,' complained Councillor Wallis. 'We shouldn't be guided by a few Ratepayers; we should do it off our own bat.'

Nevertheless, aware now that the Ratepayers meant business, the Council acceded to their request. On 12 March over a thousand – mostly anti-pool – citizens gathered in the cavernous interior of the Pavilion for the town's great folkmoot. Nothing like it had been known at Bognor before! Persuasively the Council put their case for the pool: the pathetic sight of visitors searching for the sea at low tide; keeping up with the seaside Jones's; and the many – if unquantifiable – advantages that would accrue to Bognor's traders. Mr Lyndsay, the Town Clerk, thought 'bathing in the sea would become old-fashioned once people discovered the advantages of swimming in bathing pools'. Councillor H.W. Seymour, chairman of the bathing pool sub-committee, then created a little *frisson* among the assembly when he challenged Mr Eastland of the Ratepayers to stand and fight him in the forthcoming election on the single issue of the bathing pool.

Yet just how little the Ratepayers had been swayed by the Council's case was only too clear from another thunderous 'No!' that greeted Mr Manley's question to the hall, 'Are you in favour of spending £53,000 on providing a new bathing pool for Bognor?' With growing confidence, the Ratepayers and their ilk awaited the Ministry of Health's inquiry, which was due to take place at the Pavilion on 25 May 1936. Such was the ferment occasioned by Bognor's *cause célèbre* in that early spring of 1936, that wherever public men and women got up to speak, it was almost certain that the subject on their lips would be the bathing pool. At the Town Hall, Captain Corbishley – a hard-centred Ratepayer – reflected the prevailing mood when he said, 'It has raised a storm of protest the length and breadth of Bognor Regis, Aldwick, Rose Green and Pagham. If the Council had purposely set out deliberately to irritate and annoy the people of the town, they couldn't have succeeded better than they had done with this wretched scheme.' He wanted it permanently dropped – and not least because 'it would fill this delectable little town with trippers'.

Even the usually non-partisan *Bognor Regis Post* was virulently anti-bathing pool. 'Write to the Ministry of Health and object,' it suggested to its readers. The *Observer*, too, was mildly against the scheme, although not above carrying a letter from that old war-horse, the pro-pool Thomas Tregear, whose pen was always ready to support any cause he considered to be in Bognor's best interest: '… one is at a loss to understand the attitude of the Ratepayers of Bognor. Each time any scheme for the attraction of visitors is brought forward they turn it down.'

Throughout 6 April business at the polling stations was brisk as Bognor's citizens delivered judgment on those councillors in favour of the scheme. Predictably, when the ballot papers were counted, nemesis! By handsome majorities the Ratepayer candidates swept the board, ousted those 'four men, good and true'* and altered the Council's political complexion for a long time to come. Of all the words of condolence of the victorious for the vanquished, the words of Councillor Eastland for Bert Seymour were, perhaps, the most heartfelt.

At last the day of the inquiry arrived and once more the Pavilion was filled with rebellious Ratepayers. At one table sat Mr Thomas Gates appearing for the Council; at the other was Mr H.A. Hill, the barrister representing the Ratepayers. But most eyes were on the table between, reserved for Mr W. Fyffe MInst.CE, the Ministry of Health's Inspector, in whose lap rested the fate of Bognor's bathing pool.

The preliminaries over, it was time for pertinent questions, hesitant answers and special pleading. Mr Hill to the Treasurer – 'Has the Council ever run a swimming pool before?' The Treasurer – 'Well, no. But they'd made a special study of those at Rhyll and Skegness.' Mr Hill – 'But did they not both show an annual loss?' Haplessly, the Treasurer could only nod. Mr Hill again – 'Would he confirm that in addition to the bathing pool, the Council had it in mind to spend £80,000 on a new sewerage scheme and great sum on a new bandstand?' That was so, explained the Treasurer, spiritedly, 'But if Bognor was to hold its own among other resorts in the country it had to spend money.' 'Maybe,' snorted Mr Hill, 'but you have to run the town for its citizens, not the whole of England.'

Mr Hill then turned to Captain Pocock, Chairman of the Council. Mr Hill – 'Have you heard of a newspaper called the *Bognor Regis Post*?' – 'Yes, I have.' Mr Hill again – 'Do you ever want to hear of it again?' 'No, I do not. Indeed, the opposition has been largely instituted by the press. I cannot understand the mentality of the people of Bognor, allowing themselves to be led by the nose like this,' replied the irascible old sea dog, undiplomatically.

* This was Captain Pocock's appellation for the pro-pool councillors, H.W. Seymour, C.E. Hudson, W. Silcock and Dr R.E. Clarke, who lost their seats to the Ratepayer candidates, Messrs J. Eastland, P. Pentland, R. Thompson and A. Blackwell.

101 Compared with its 1904 predecessor shown on page 11, the enlarged (1914) Western Bandstand was an altogether grander structure. Here, in the 'thirties, it awaits execution for being too draughty. In the background (right) can be seen the *Arlington Hotel*, the White Tower and, in the distance, the *Victoria Hotel.*

Finally, Mr Hill invited Mr Dugall Hancock, the Headmaster of Greenways School in Hawthorn Road, to say that he was against the pool because 'it would mean the loss of our glorious sands'. All day the lawyers for both sides earned their keep, putting the best/worst gloss on the enlightened/barmy notion of building a bathing pool on Bognor's front. Everything about it having been said, the town could only await the decision by His Majesty's Minister while its citizens filled in time tittle-tattling about that other *cause célèbre* of the hour, Mrs Wallis Simpson and our increasingly ambivalent young King.

On 13 July 1936 a letter from the Ministry of Health arrived at Bognor Town Hall. It read, 'The Minister has carefully considered the report of his Inspector but in view of the heavy expenditure involved (£53,000), the anticipated deficit and the strong and widespread opposition, he does not consider he would be justified in giving the sanction sought.' And thus, with a few well-chosen words of Ministry of Health prose, the plug was pulled on the town's bathing pool.

* * *

A long-ago occasion, perhaps, but the image – for some reason – still hangs around in my mind. It is the memory of a summer morning in, I suppose, 1928, while we were staying at Forrabury in Aldwick Road; the sun's milky disc peering through rolling banks of sea-mist; my mother wearing her green cloche hat, a string of amber beads around her neck and carrying a cream parasol; I in a floppy white hat and a blue shirt, with a copy of *Bubbles* stuffed in my trouser pocket. It was the day she took me with her to listen to the scarlet Military Band playing at the little Western Bandstand where, a quarter of a century earlier, she and her cousins had been amongst its earliest customers.

But hardly had the strains of 'In a Monastery Garden' begun to drift over the audience, than my eyes suddenly became rivetted on the horn player. And not merely on account of his dexterous fingering. No, no! It was in sheer fascination at the way, every now and then, he emptied the spit out of his horn! Little wonder, I thought, that band concerts were so popular. So, at the end of the performance, my enthusiastic applause wasn't so much for a bit more Sousa or Percy Grainger, but in hope of an encore from my spit-emptying hero! Saddled with a son so depraved, the only bright spot for my mother was being able to save 3d. by making me sit on the grass in the hope I would read my comic and remain silently uncritical – at least during the quiet parts.

From then onwards, though, visits to the Western Bandstand became a regular time-filler on our holiday agenda. Then, nine years later, on a Friday night in 1937, as we were driving past the *Royal Norfolk Hotel* at the end of our journey from London, there was a cry of consternation from my mother. 'My dear, look its disappeared – gone!' She was pointing at where, a week before, had stood the Western Bandstand. Eventually it seeped through to us. Apparently, in its place 'they' were going to erect a new 'Bandstand Enclosure'. When a caterpillar digger arrived and F.W. Hill's bricklayers began work I used to stop on my bicycle to see how they were getting on.

At last, in the middle of June 1937, it was opened by the new Chairman of the Council, Captain H.W.E. Thomas. A few days later my mother took me and my kilted Glaswegian cousin to an afternoon performance by the Bognor Regis Municipal Orchestra. Yet, funnily enough, as we sat within its all but roofless interior, I cannot recall its preying on my mind that the town had been shamefully short-changed with this mere apology for the gleaming diadem it had once been intended should grace the old boat pound site.

For, in 1935, 'Ossy' Bridge's Western Bandstand had stood accused by the Establishment and Town Improvement Committee of being both too small and too jolly draughty, even for the well-wrapped-up brass-band trade. It was 'a slur on Bognor's name'. Summarily, 'this rabbit hutch' was sentenced to demolition and resurrection in a form more reflective of the comfort-seeking 'thirties. On any day of the year at Eastbourne, Worthing and Bournemouth visitors could keep warm and dry while listening in comfort to Municipal Orchestras playing in draught-free Concert Halls and Sea Pavilions. So why not such a building for Bognor? And with the cost of hiring military bands becoming ever more exorbitant – the 2nd Hampshire's demanded £135 for a week by the sea – why not throw in a Municipal Orchestra, as well?

At Clarence Road – where talk of a Winter Gardens had been a staple of discussion for as long as anyone could remember – these ideas gradually took root. So, in June 1935, Mr Draper was instructed to prepare some sketch designs for a 'bandstand'* on the old boat pound site opposite the

---

* The old boat pound, owned by Major James of the *Royal Norfolk Hotel* and leased to the Council, enjoyed a covenant limiting its use to the erection of a 'bandstand'. With a wink and a nod, this term continued to be used in Town Hall circles although describing a quite different type of building. There is no reason to believe the Major was ever fooled by these semantics!

Royal Norfolk Hotel. In September H.C. White – whom we last met in connection with Bognor's swimming pool – were appointed engineers and their estimate awaited with interest. Meanwhile, it must have come as music to the Town Improvement Committee's ears when Mr Rivington, on behalf of the Bognor Regis Ratepayers, tacitly offered their support; 'I think the Ratepayers will be in favour of a bandstand. We believe in improvements with wise spending.'

When it was placed on show at the Town Hall the design proved to be for a striking, cream-coloured, all-weather concert hall disposed at right-angles across – and blocking – the Promenade, with a large part of the auditorium overhanging the beach. To get past it, pedestrians needed to return to Aldwick Road. There was no car park and the entrance hall was rather cramped. Of course, to the architectural *cognoscenti*, one thing was clear: this was yet another case of trying to squeeze too much building on to too small a site.

Nonetheless, the general layout passed the Council's muster. There was seating for 880 people in winter; in summer this could be increased to 2000 by means of glazed sliding screens on either side of the auditorium, taking advantage of the raised and curved promenades. Ice-cream and teas were to be served overlooking the sea. So, here at last, elegant and draught-free, with a 21-piece Municipal Orchestra tuning up on its stage, was the long-awaited Jewel in Bognor's Crown. But gleaming diadems don't come cheap. According to H.C. White's estimate, this one was going to cost £38,000.

The story of Bognor's bandstand was one of omens and auguries. The new building's gestation period had taken place under the 'old' Council, whose brainchild it really was. On the other hand, the go-ahead at the cost of £38,000 had been made, with barely a murmur, by the 'new' Ratepayer-dominated regime in July 1936 at the meeting following the bathing pool débâcle. But at least they could claim they were only its wet nurse, not its mother.

Across the chamber, though, the lack of car parking space caused concern. Might it not prejudice the granting of liquor and dance licences? What if the police banned parking in Aldwick Road? Other voices feared the noise of the wind and the waves would drown out the music; might not sea-weed come through the windows? Major James, the owner of the *Royal Norfolk*, wrote to the *Observer*: 'It is amazing for a town of 17,000 inhabitants to build a bandstand costing £38,000. Why encourage trippers of the cheapest class by spending this enormous amount? … they neither pay for it nor appreciate it.' And, of course, everyone knew of a better site for the new building: Waterloo Square, the Pier, the Pavilion Gardens, Clarence Road, even the west end of Marine Park Gardens, all had their advocates.

Then, on 22 September, the Town Hall was rocked by the news that Captain Pocock, the acerbic Chairman of the UDC, had resigned, piqued by what he claimed was the disloyalty of five councillors who had tried to shine a torch onto what they considered the less-than-transparent procedures of the Improvement Committee. However, a few days later, after the tremors had ceased, the less-controversial Captain H.W.E. Thomas, a Ratepayer to his fingertips, was elected the new Chairman of the Council.

102 The Pavilion; a favourite venue for dancing, stage, flower and dog shows – not to mention popular uprisings! Its steel structure was one of Norman Thompson's flying boat erection sheds from Middleton. In July 1948 it was damaged by fire and afterwards demolished. The Fitzleet car park now marks the spot.

103 What an ungrateful electorate got after £34,000 had been lopped off the cost of the grand Winter Gardens scheme. The new Western Bandstand Enclosure, completed in June 1937, awaits its landscaping.

Mindful of the charges of opacity levelled against the *ancien régime*, and with the salutary lesson of the bathing pool still fresh in their minds, the new Council decided to hold another great folkmoot – the second in seven months – 'for the Electorate's approval or disapproval of the scheme prior to the Ministry of Health's inquiry'. On 16 November all roads led once more to the Pavilion where the proposal to build Bognor's Winter Garden was put to the assembly. Hardly could the result have been less expected. For suddenly the Ratepayers Association described a complete volte-face and opposed the scheme tooth and nail! A little harmless culture, they cried, was one thing, but £38,000 to pay for it was quite another. And not even a car park. 'It was preposterous.'

In fact, apart from the members of the Committee, the Hotel and Boarding Houses Association and the Chamber of Commerce, voices in support of the bandstand were hard to find. Slightly nonplussed, Councillor Peerless – another Ratepayer – put forward the notion that the people really *did* want such a scheme, but they had had so long to think about it 'they had wobbled!' Councillor Blackwell, however, was much in favour of a concert hall because he believed 'young people would benefit from hearing "live" music instead of getting it through the wireless'. Another sensitive member hoped the music would not be of the 'hot cha-cha' type.

But remorselessly, resolution by resolution, amendment by amendment, the Winter Gardens bandstand, as originally envisaged, was reduced to an unrecognisable heap of ruins! After two and a half hours of scathing criticism, a forest of hands endorsed Mr Manley's motion, 'that having discussed and considered the proposed scheme … the meeting is of the opinion the Council should propose alternative schemes and alternative sites'.

Back at the Town Hall, the Improvement Committee and its officers hastily got scrubbed-up. Not, though, for meticulous surgery, but for panic-stricken butchery! On 9 March 1937, after a gory £34,000 had been hacked off the price, the Committee untied the tapes and tossed the unpromising £4,375-worth of remains to Bognor's undeserving electorate.

Thus, for the first time, the public saw what they were about to get in exchange for Bognor's doomed Jewel: a little low-walled, 'magnet-shaped' and largely roofless building squeezed on to the old boat pound site. The title read 'Western Band Enclosure, 1937'.

Yet, in spite of a large part of the audience having to take to its umbrellas when it rained, the new Enclosure enjoyed considerable popularity. It also fulfilled one of its extravagant predecessor's promises: it became the home – albeit summers-only – of the Bognor Regis Municipal Orchestra under the baton of its conductor, Mr Walter Collins, 'a child prodigy at eight' and late leader at the Bexhill De La Warr Pavilion. A composer as well, he wrote a little piece called *Pride of the South*, which Bognorians fondly believed to be their own signature tune, unaware that its earlier title had been the fist-clenching *Comrades All*.

But, in Bognor's south-west wind, the Enclosure soon met its match. Having spoiled the ship for a ha'porth of tar, the Council now had to face complaints about its draughtiness. By 1939 plans were afoot to cover the

104 The Pavilion boating pool was opened by the Marchioness of Cambridge on 12 April 1938, the event being recorded by Frank L'Alouette, perched with his camera at the top of the Fire Brigade's escape ladder.

open area with 'a canvas tent'. But before the scheme could reach fruition it was August 1939 and, suddenly, filling sandbags seemed more important. After the war, the Enclosure did get a roof – of asbestos sheets. It also got a new stage, a fireproof curtain, and a lick of paint to become the Esplanade Hall, Bognor's Centre for the Performing Arts. In this guise, and in spite of its many shortcomings, it brought pleasure to both audiences and players – especially to the Bognor Regis Amateur Theatrical Society, the BRATS, whose talented performances on its stage are still remembered. But with the arrival of the new Regis Centre the writing was on the wall. In about 1980 it was demolished. For a time part of the remains served as a café before becoming a contractor's yard and, latterly, a skateboard rink attached to an ornamental garden. *Sic transit gloria Bognori*!

However, to relieve the gloom of municipal frustration, in 1938 a single shaft of sunlight fell, not so much upon the Esplanade but a little further back in the Pavilion Gardens, where Mr Draper, the Town's Surveyor, had been touched with genius when he designed the new boating pool in the shape of the outline of England and marked with all her major ports.

On 12 April 1938 the Marchioness of Cambridge, accompanied by her daughter, the Lady Mary, was driven over from Three Ways, their house in Canon's Close, and in front of a gathering of Bognor's *crème de la crème* – apart, that is, from Mr Frank L'Alouette, the photographer, who had elected to spend the afternoon perched at the top of the Fire Brigade's 55 foot escape in order to record the event with his camera – she officially named the pool after HRH The Princess Elizabeth. To round off the occasion, the young

Lady Mary launched a model yacht which was last seen on a broad reach heading towards the Port of Blackpool on the other side of this tiny ocean.

* * *

And thus we come to that greatest of all Bognor sagas; the story of Billy Butlin's annexation of the Eastern Esplanade in the 1930s. Already secure with his 'Autocars' operation at the east end of the Esplanade, and proposing to build a Zoo on Davies' redundant garage site, Butlin had also purchased the old Olympian Gardens at the end of Lennox Street at the cost of £7,000. In 1931, needing an architect to design him a large 'amusement shelter', he judiciously sought the services of Mr Oswald Bridges FRIBA, Chairman of the Council. In due course he was issued with an annual – but, of course, rescindable – licence for the new building.

Early in 1934 Butlin made an application for an Interim Development Consent (viz Permanent Planning Permission) in respect of his amusement shelter. The Council, having had three years to repent allowing him on to the Esplanade in the first place, were this time resolved to adopt a tougher line. They refused not only to renew his licence on the grounds of the noise and disturbance that he created, but asked him also to remove his 'temporary' building. The reason given was that the land was earmarked 'for housing, hotels and boarding houses'. Further negotiations with a new design, incorporating the well-known stepped facade, having proved fruitless, Butlin, now thoroughly aggrieved, lodged an appeal with the Ministry of Health.

Faced with this proposition – and perhaps uncertain of the outcome of anything involving William B. – the Council decided, in June 1935, on one last bloodless trick to lure their bête noir from his Esplanade stronghold. East of Gloucester Road lay the 5½ acres of riverine Brooklands, home to a handful of redshank, resting gulls and Bognor's sewage works. It was a site, though, with a history hardly auspicious for developers. In 1842 Richard Clark, one of Bognor's early property men, went bankrupt, leaving four unfinished houses at Black Rock on its Gloucester Road edge. Forty years later, in 1881, two developers from London, Jean Severin Simon and Edward Meniere, prepared a scheme for a grandiose square with 'sixty houses and public buildings'. They even named its Avenues: Beatrice, Princess, Belle Vue and Brooklands. Alas, not a brick was laid.

So, in June 1935 – apart from the Council's sewage works and the town's redundant fever hospital, now converted for use as Colebrook House School's cricket pavilion – the Brooklands remained unsullied. It was upon this muddy canvas that the Council gave Mr Butlin a free hand to design himself a super-funfair. However, to these machinations there was one snag and one proviso: the snag was the Council didn't own the land and the proviso was that Butlin should stay his pending appeal.

The centrepiece of this grand amusement mecca proved to be 'a speed-way for petrol driven cars' requiring two bridges across the rife – a quite different sort of 'Brooklands' from the one most people had in mind! There was also a miniature railway, a 'monkey island', 'a Natural Zoo', sideshows and a number of 'amusement devices'. Not surprisingly, when the people of Felpham got to hear of the scheme there was uproar! There were cries of

105 Butlinland! By 1938 Billy B's conquest of the Esplanade was complete. The entrance to the Zoo was from under the lath-and-plaster 'Alps'; in the far distance, beyond Cotswold Terrace, can be seen his white-painted Dodgems building on the corner of Lennox Street. Strangely, there is not a car in sight!

'Bar Butlin from the Brooks!', 'Not East of the Rife!' A petition signed by 1,127 people opposed to Butlin's plans was sent to the Council. Commander C.R. Hudson OBE suggested that the land would be better 'laid out as gardens for posterity'. Tom Tregear thought so, too.

Faced with such vehement opposition – and much to the Felphamites relief – in November the Council advised Butlin's solicitors that the scheme they had encouraged him to submit was 'unacceptable'. Another seafront scheme was about to bite the dust! Whether or not Billy Butlin's face lit up when he received the news remains conjectural, but certainly the Council's decision played into his hands. Now the injured party, he set about re-instating his appeal on the Lennox Street site, his first love being Bognor's Esplanade.

At the Town Hall on 7 August 1936, the Ministry of Health's Inspector, Mr S. Beaufoy ARIBA, conducted an inquiry into Bognor Council's refusal to issue Mr Butlin with a planning consent for his Lennox Street property. The battle lines were clearly drawn. Butlin claimed he had 'put Bognor on the map', besides providing the public with amusements and – apart from the Council's three little shelters – the only free, undercover protection from bad weather on the Esplanade. His slogan 'When it's wet, it's dry at Butlin's' seemed to sum up his case. And, through no fault of his, the Council had prevented him from moving to the Brooks. As his solicitor said, 'Put not your trust in Princes – nor in the Bognor Urban District Council.' He also believed the opposition had been fanned by the *Bognor Regis Post*, 'which did everything it could to prevent development in Bognor'. For the Council's part, they could only fall back on that hoary old town-planning mantra, that Butlin's activities 'were injurious to the amenities and detrimental to the locality'.

A few weeks later the Minister delivered judgement. In synopsis, he found the alternative Brooklands site on to which Mr Butlin might have been moved was 'unavailable'. Neither did he think an 'amusement park' on the Esplanade would be all that injurious to the neighbourhood, especially as the Council couldn't point to a better place. Consequently, he allowed the appeal. And with that, he lowered the East Esplanade's crown on to William Butlin's brow to mark the start of a reign which, to Bognor's detriment, was to last for the next 25 years.

The calendar has turned to 1939, and a chance for the private sector to see if it could breathe a bit of life into Bognor's seafront torpor. In January, contemptuous of the Brooklands unpromising history, the entrepreneurial Mr F.T. Wonnacott of the *Carlton Hotel* unveiled an imaginative proposal, prepared by his Middleton architect, Mr E.A. Elson ARIBA, to build on them a Marina costing £100,000. Wonnacott's plan was to divert the meander in the Aldingbourne Rife to form an extensive 'locked yachting harbour with berths for hundreds of sailing boats and motor cruisers'. It even included facilities for commercial boat-building besides offering a wharf for local fishermen. A landing stage for paddle-steamers was also planned. Nearer Gloucester Road, Elson's drawings showed a Dance Pavilion and a covered swimming pool as well as a toddler's 'splash' and miniature golf course.

But the feature which would have had the most impact on Bognor's coastal scene was the construction of a large harbour created by building a sea-wall projecting some 500 feet southwards from the end of Gloucester Road. 'Why', asked the persuasive Mr Wonnacott, 'spend fifty thousand pounds on sea defences when, for another fifty thousand, Bognor could have itself a first-class Marina?' Certainly the Council, the Chamber of Commerce and the press welcomed it euphorically. Well, it had about it the ring of feasibility.

'There is a tide in the affairs of men, which taken at the flood leads on to fortune …' And so it might have been, had not Wonnacott's flood been staunched by the ever-lengthening shadow of the Third Reich.* Timing was his only fault. Like so many other entrepreneurial aspirations born of those last few months of peace, it sank without trace to join – less deservedly than most – Bognor's insatiable reliquary of lost causes; a reliquary still hungry for those with the temerity to try their hands at developing her post-war seafront!

Nor, just before the war – apart from the monstrous 376 ft. long Goodman Drive shelter which was mercifully dropped in favour of four smaller ones that 'let in the wind and kept out the sun' – were any further municipal seafront initiatives planned for the immediate future. For now it was time for the Council to buckle down to the imperative of ARP and getting the new Fire Station built in Clarence Road – in spite of the gloomy prognostication of Martin Swinburne, the editor of the *Bognor Regis Post*, that it was 'a waste of money, as the Brigade hadn't had a proper call for the last three months'.

* Ultimately, the Marina's fate proved to have a silver lining. For eight years later, in 1947, the wheel turned full circle when Bognor Council purchased the Brooklands which, eventually, proved a prize seductive enough to entice Butlin off the Esplanade in exchange for permitting him to develop the area as a holiday camp, which was opened in 1960.

19

The Bognor Sky

The Pioneers and a tribute to Norman Thompson
and John Porte, flying boat constructors

The time has come, the critic said, to talk of many things; of strength
of tail and fuselage; of chassis, struts and wings.

F.K. Turner 1911

I remember my father once telling me of the near-disbelief with which his
generation of schoolboys had greeted the news of Louis Bleriot's perilous
cross-Channel flight made on 25 July 1909. In September 1953 we caught
a fleeting glimpse of Squadron Leader Neville Duke's Tangmere-based
Hawker Hunter on its way to setting a new British air-speed record of 747
m.p.h. over the two-mile Rustington-Kingston Gorse measured course …
Little more than half a person's lifespan separated the two events. Aeronautical development during those intervening years, sadly propelled by war,
marked one of the great phases of man's innovative genius.

After 1909 Bognor's sky played host to a number of 'seat-of-the-pants'
aviators. The sound of a petrol-driven engine over the town was first heard
at 7 p.m. on 8 May 1911, when Graham Gilmour flew his Box Kite along
the front on his way – according to Sylvia Adams, the aeronautical
historian – to 'bomb' his Royal Naval brother at Fort Blockhouse with
oranges! Perhaps it was to show that not even a great Naval base was
immune from attack from the sky. My good friend, the late Martin
Venables – then a schoolboy – remembered the event vividly. Sadly, less than
a year later Gilmour crashed to his death in Richmond Deer Park, adding
yet another name to the long list of flyers who paid the ultimate price for
their intrusion into this imperfectly understood element.

A man who taught himself to fly – he was shown the controls of an
aeroplane in the morning and took off on his own in the afternoon – and
whose family owned Hendon Aerodrome, has to count as a founder-figure
of British aviation. He was Claude Grahame-White, the proprietor of a
fashionable flying school and a designer and constructor of aeroplanes. On
3 August 1912 he landed on the sea at Aldwick, allowing the townsfolk and
visitors their first close-up glimpse of a heavier-than-air machine. In fact it
was a single-pontoon Curtiss hydroplane belonging to Monsieur Louis
Paulhan, the well-known Belgian aviator, who had obtained a European
agency for Curtiss flying boats and, at that time, was based at Eastbourne.
As he was well acquainted with Grahame-White – having narrowly beaten
him in the 1910 *Daily Mail* London-Manchester Air Race – it seems highly

106 Bognor gets its first close look of a flying machine: Claude Graham-White's Paulhan-Curtiss single pontoon hydroplane at anchor off Gray's huts on 3 August 1912.

likely that on this occasion G-W was demonstrating the Paulhan-Curtiss on the Belgian's behalf, no doubt with a commission in mind!

In the *Brighton Gazette* of that date there is a report of his flight, which had started from Eastbourne with Cowes his final destination: '... he descended at Bognor on the way and settled in the water at the western end of the front near the Aldwick huts where a big crowd of visitors assembled to greet him'. Afterwards, 'with the help of some fishermen' (surely the Ide men), he had the Curtiss drawn up on the beach. During his short stay, Grahame-White allowed a few Bognor worthies to sit in the pilot's seat on the wing of his cockpit-less plane. Among them was a little girl who had to be lifted onto it by her father, H.W. Seymour, the builder. Now Mrs Greta Blythe, she it was who told me this.

Later in the day G-W had his hydroplane returned to the the sea, where a photographer was waiting to take its picture riding at anchor with the words *Daily Mail* clearly visible under the lower wing.* In the late afternoon the plane was seen 'to taxi nearly to Pagham where it took-off out to sea in a cloud of spray before disappearing over Selsey' on its way to Cowes where, the next day, 'Mr Grahame-White made a circuit of the Royal Yacht'.

On 26 May 1913 the town once more emptied of its citizens as they streamed down to the seafront to watch another aviation milestone, the first land plane to visit Bognor. It touched down on the beach just east of the Pier. This was Cecil and Eric Pashley's Clapham Junction-built Hewlett-Blondeau† – a machine with tail booms, four-wheeled undercarriage and seats for two passengers. Power was derived from a Gnome rotary pusher engine driving a two-bladed propeller. The occasion had been organised by Arthur Taylor, the landlord of the *Beach Hotel*, who, together with a

---

* The words 'Daily Mail' visible under the Paulhan-Curtiss's lower wing denote that the plane's owner was sponsored by Rothermere's paper to give public flying demonstrations.

† Virtually a Maurice Farman built under licence at their *Omnium* works near Clapham Junction station in London.

107 The first land plane to visit Bognor, the Pashley brothers' Hewlett-Blondeau biplane on the sands opposite Cotswold Terrace on 26 May 1913.

number of local businessmen, hoped to cash in on the new flying mania which was beginning to sweep the country.

Learning to fly on Somer monoplanes at Brooklands, both Cecil and Eric qualified as pilots in 1911. *Flight* refers to Eric's 'banking and *vols piqués*' at the nearby Hewlett-Blondeau flying school as being particularly thrilling! Shortly afterwards they started up their own flying school in a field near Bungalow Town Halt at Shoreham. But pleasure flights were the important part of their business – although at two guineas a time they sound quite expensive compared with the five shillings charged by Sir Alan Cobham in the 'thirties. Sadly, Eric was killed while flying a DH2 in France during the Great War.

In 1925 Cecil Pashley, together with F.G. Miles, the aircraft designer, founded what became the Southern Aero Club at Shoreham, where they kept a motley collection of Avro 504Ks, a Grahame-White Bantam and a Box Kite. After the war, one of Eric's pupils was Charles Purley, the founder of LEC Ltd at Bognor. Before he retired in the 'sixties, Cecil claimed to have spent nearly 20,000 hours in the air, either instructing or giving pleasure flights.

White and Thompson

When I suffered that restless childhood urge for excitement the sound of fire engine bells and a column of smoke on the horizon found me on my bicycle making quickly for the conflagration. So, on Christmas Day 1929, when we got wind of a large fire at Middleton's New City Holiday Club, I badgered my father to take me to the scene. The seat of the flames in this case was the club's dining hall, which had been used for storing bedding. In no time it had become a furnace. I can still remember the smell of burning, the spaghetti of hose pipes and the fire engines from Bognor and Littlehampton.

Outside stood piles of salvaged mattresses. But it wasn't until many years later that I learned that those scorched walls had once housed the dreams of men audacious enough to seek the conquest of the skies.

The early years of the 20th century were marked by a nascent aircraft industry struggling to its feet. Many entrepreneurs were induced to chance their wallets – and sometimes their lives – in a field dogged by uncertainty and strewn with perils. In making aeroplanes the prevailing design philosophy still lay somewhere between the Theorem of Three Moments and 'it looks about right'. But gradually the cabinet-maker's empiricism was giving way to the authority of the engineer's slide-rule. Just such a firm were White and Thompson, aeronautical engineers who, in 1909, set up in business at Middleton-on-Sea. Dr Douglas White, a man of means and financial probity, dealt with the money side while the incorruptible slide-rule was supplied by Norman Thompson, Harrow and Trinity College, Cambridge, who had started as an electrical engineer before opting for a new career in aviation influenced by the technical writings of F.W. Lanchester, the well-known motor engineer and aerodynamicist. Later, Lanchester was to become W&T's consultant.

But why choose to build their factory at Middleton, a seaside village renowned only for its absence of engineering tradition? One obvious clue was the landing ground. More space is required for flying and testing aircraft than for making them. Land, purchased or rented, was a cost to be avoided. In those days, beyond its breakwaters, Middleton beach at low tide presented a wide, uninterrupted sweep of firm sand. It was also on the line of the prevailing wind; flying could be carried on between tides. Moreover, it was rent-free. So that may have been their reason for coming to the seaside. But there may have been another for, as early as 1909, those aircraft designers who toyed with hydroplanes and flying boats saw water as the natural home of the flying machine. Perhaps Middleton allowed White and Thompson to hedge their bets.

Be that as it may, their first aeroplane was very much a land plane, a single-seat 'high-speed fighter'. Built in 1910 to Lanchester's design, it started life as a fuselage in the Daimler Company's factory at Coventry where it became known as 'The Grey Angel'. Later it was moved to Middleton. It appears to have been a highly experimental exercise. To begin with, the biplane wings – covered in 23 SWG aluminium – were mounted at the rear and the large rudder and elevators placed at the nose end. The fuselage was clad in thin steel sheet on an ash frame in the manner of a motor car of those days. Its four castoring wheels were another unusual feature. The power units were two side-by-side 50 hp Gnome rotary engines cross-belted in case of engine failure.

However, before the machine was completed, a combination of heavy storms and menacing tides replaced Middleton's smooth sand with a vista of ridges, pools and beds of clay, quite unsuitable for testing aeroplanes. Thus, when the day came to get No. 1 into the air, it was pursued by White and Thompson's employees armed with planks of wood to prevent the wheels sinking into the sand! Alas, gravity proved intolerant of all Lanchester's novelty. Without becoming airborne, the plane ran into the sea and overturned. Repaired, it still showed an implacable resistance to leaving the ground. Finis No. 1!

In fact, such was the cost of these experiments that the enterprise was soon on the verge of running out of Dr White's money. In 1912 a private company was registered under the name of White and Thompson Co. Ltd, formed 'for the purpose of producing aircraft on a commercial basis'. In 1913 their Aeroplane No. 2 (confusingly designated WT No.1) appeared. This was a side-by-side two-seater and more conventional for the period. The wings were fabric-covered; the rudder and elevator were in the traditional positions; it had a two-wheeled undercarriage and required a skid to keep the tail off the ground. One unusual feature, though, was the front-mounted ABC engine which drove a single three-bladed pusher propeller at the rear via a shaft through the length of the nacelle.

Thompson himself made the first flight. To everyone's relief No. 2 flew quite well. Later it was flown by a number of RNAS pilots including a certain Lt. John Porte who, when he wasn't teaching flying at Shoreham, acted as White and Thompson's test pilot. However, a few weeks later young Porte contrived to turn the machine over, damaging it badly. And the reason why it was never repaired will become apparent soon enough.

Although there was the end of W&T's second prototype, it marked only the beginning of their test pilot's remarkable career; a career which was one day to influence the decision to build quite a different sort of flying machine. And it is why Porte shares part of this chapter with the Middleton constructor. So, at this juncture, may be as well to expand a little further on the career of Lieutenant John Porte, the serving submarine officer with an obsession for flying and a flare for aeronautical design. Exactly where he learned his engineering skills is unclear; 'a gifted amateur' may be his best description. At any rate, in 1909, with the assistance of a brother officer, he

108 Norman Thompson stands by Aeroplane No. 2.

designed the curious stagger-winged Porte-Pirie glider which, after a few flights on Portsdown Hill, was abandoned there in pieces. Then, more calamitously, in 1911 he was diagnosed as having developed tuberculosis and discharged from the Navy.

Porte, though, seems to have responded to medical treatment. Having learned to fly in France, he became technical director of the (British) Deperdussin Aircraft Company at Hendon, where a lot of his time was taken up testing a prototype monoplane. It was after the firm collapsed, in 1913, that he again began to act on an *ad hoc* basis as White and Thompson's test pilot at Middleton. The attention of the aeronautical press was being drawn increasingly to the work being carried out on seaplanes at Hammondsport on the shore of Lake Keuka, New York State by Glen Curtiss, a well-known flier-turned-aircraft constructor. In 1912 he built and flew the world's first viable flying boat.

It so happened that John Porte was acquainted with a Captain Ernest Bass, a member of the well-known brewing family. Bass was a flying enthusiast who appears to have been taught by Curtiss to fly seaplanes on Lake Keuka. Curtiss had just produced a small two-seater single-engined flying boat, the 'F' boat. Besides ordering one for himself, Bass let Curtiss know that he thought there was a market for these machines in the UK. Not one to miss a sales opportunity, the American agreed to bring the crated 'F' boat to England by sea.

Just what prompted White and Thompson's venture into building flying boats at this point – except commercial nous – isn't clear, but the upshot was they appointed Ernest Bass to negotiate the manufacturing rights for making Curtiss flying boats under licence in the UK. It was a decision made possible only by their maritime site. It also explains why it was considered a waste of time repairing White and Thompson's second prototype that Porte had badly bent on Middleton beach a few months earlier.

In October 1913 the 'F' boat was erected and exhibited at Brighton, by Magnus Volk of Electric Railway fame, where it was housed in a large tent on the beach below Paston Place next to his new seaplane hangar. Inside was a notice which read:

Curtiss flying boats.
Exclusive Agency held by Capt. Ernest C. Bass
and Lt. J.C. Porte R.N.
H.Q. Royal Albion Hotel Brighton
Sole authorised repairers White and Thompson Ltd., Bognor.

On the 15th, Curtiss, Gordon England, Grahame-White, Thompson and Ernie Bass – besides a delegation of German naval experts – gathered to watch Curtiss's pilot, J.D. Cooper, undertake a series of demonstration flights, twenty of them in three days. The *Brighton Herald*'s reporter was much impressed. 'The Curtiss made a very pretty flight … the apparatus had the appearance of a huge flying fish.' He also gathered from the grapevine that '… Mr Bass will later this week take the flying boat to Messrs. White and Thompson's shed at Bognor.' During this period Porte flew the Curtiss himself on a number of occasions.

During his sojourn at Brighton, the American must have been impressed both by Porte's skilled handling of the flying boat and his knowledgeable interest in its construction. The result was an invitation to Porte to Hammondsport to participate in his next venture. Meanwhile, Bass's negotiations had borne fruit and, early in 1914, White and Thompson signed a 12-year contract for the exclusive agency and manufacturing rights for the Curtiss flying boats 'in the UK and its Dominions'. Unfortunately, a few months later, Ernie Bass crashed his 'F' boat on the Cote d'Azur and it had to be returned to Middleton for repair – and eventual transformation!

Over in the USA, Curtiss had been approached by an American store owner, Rodman Wannamaker, who aspired to sponsoring a flying boat capable of crossing the Atlantic 'to celebrate a hundred years of peace between Britain and America'. Perhaps he also had an eye on the *Daily Mail*'s £10,000 prize for the first transatlantic aeroplane flight. Fittingly, Wannamaker suggested its two pilots should be drawn one from each nation. The American was a Lt. J.H. Towers of the US Navy, while Lt. Porte represented Britain.

In April 1914 Porte joined Curtiss at Hammondsport, where he played a significant and innovative part in the design of the new machine. The result was a 72 ft. wing-span, twin-engined flying boat powered by two tractor Curtiss 90 hp OX5 engines and known as the *America*. It was ready in June. Such, though, was the 'suck it and see' philosophy of aircraft design in those days, that only during tests did it become clear the plane was incapable of leaving the water with the fuel load necessary to cross the Atlantic.

1914 was also the year that the patriotic proprietor of the *Daily Mail* sponsored the 'Round Britain Seaplane Race'. Boldly, White and Thompson entered two machines. The first – 'Flying boat No. 1', as it was known in the works – was substantially Thompson's design although heavily influenced by the Curtiss *America*. Power was derived from two 100 hp Curtiss-Austin engines mounted in pusher form. Yet, apart from the fact that Captain Loftus Bryan first flew it, little about the aircraft's performance is known. Perhaps this was because 'Flying boat No. 2' proved markedly the superior machine. In fact, this was none other than Ernie Bass's American 'F' boat, repaired after its crash, its Anzani engine replaced with an Austro-Daimler, re-hulled by Saunders' of Cowes and re-winged with Royal Aircraft Factory No. 9 Section wings by White and Thompson. At any rate, it was deemed 'British' enough to enter the race.

Then Britain declared war on Germany. This, of course, put paid to the *Daily Mail* Circuit Race and brought John Porte hurrying back to England to rejoin the Navy, his health apparently restored. Within a few days, the Admiralty visited Middleton and commandeered both the 'Circuit' flying boats. However, this cloud proved to have a silver lining. For No. 2 attracted the attention of the RNAS, who purchased the prototype and followed it up with an order for another eight slightly modified machines. In its production form it was designated the White and Thompson No.3; their first viable type brought some much needed money into the Middleton till!

In British Naval circles it had long been of concern that, in the event of war, our shipping would be at the mercy of the German submarines. Yet, in 1914, the country possessed no specialised aircraft capable of mounting long-distance anti-submarine patrols. Aware of this, Porte approached Captain Murray Suter – his old boss in subs, now in charge of the Navy Air Department – and prevailed upon him to purchase two 'Americas' for the RNAS. Although incapable of flying the Atlantic and poor on the sea, they had the making of a tolerable anti-submarine patrol flying boats, with a few modifications, Porte judged.

From this point forward, John Porte's work,* crucial as it proved to be in the prosecution of the war against the German U-boats, becomes rather remote from Middleton. So let it suffice to say that in 1915 he was placed in charge of the RNAS's Experimental Seaplane Station at Felixstowe, a large flying-boat base with facilities for manufacturing aircraft.

After flying the two Curtisses under North Sea conditions, John Porte embarked on a painstaking programme of experimental work on the hulls of a number of American flying boats, resulting in the greatly improved 'Porte hulls' Nos. 1 and 2 that were to become the common element of the extended family of Felixstowe flying boats – mostly designed by himself – many hundreds of which paid a great part in ridding the seas around Britain and the Mediterranean of the German U-boat menace.

Wing Commander John Porte CMG died in 1919, the victim of his old malady and overwork; he was only 36. In his official history of *The War in the Air (1914-18)*, Sir Walter Raleigh pens this appreciation of John Porte: 'The shortest possible list of those who saved their country in its hour of need would have to include his name.' There could have been no better tribute to the young naval Lieutenant who, six years earlier, had pranged White and Thompson's second protoype on Middleton beach.

Late in 1914 White and Thompson decided to invest in the services of a chief designer. Thus there arrived on the Middleton scene Percy Beadle, an original and imaginative aircraft designer who had been responsible for the Twickenham-built pre-war Perry-Beadle sponson-winged flying boat. In the meantime Neptune appears to have restored the storm-ravaged beach. And none too soon, for Beadle's first project was for another land plane, a side-by-side two-seater of dubious purpose with a 70 hp Renault engine. In fact, its chief claim to fame – apart from having 'looped-the-loop' in the hands of Clifford Prodgers, an Admiralty test pilot who had yet to make his name with Handley Page – lay in its Williams-built monocoque fuselage clad in Saunder's 'Consuta' cedar panels which, when varnished, gave it a scaly appearance and led to the RNAS christening it the 'Bognor Bloater'. Yet, the Navy must have considered it filled some kind of niche – training, perhaps. At all events, they ordered 14 of them.

The year 1915 saw the parting of the ways of Dr White and Norman Thompson, the former having decided to resume his medical career. And with that the firm's name was changed to the Norman Thompson Flight Co. Ltd. Henceforth, most new aircraft types were prefixed NT. Thompson

---

* A much fuller account of Porte's fascinating service career is to be found in Michael Goodall's book, *The White and Thompson File*, published by Air Britain.

109 The 'Bognor Bloater'. Fourteen were built, one of which looped the loop.

and Beadle now settled down to two years of productive energy with designs for various niches of flying-boat use. In late 1915 they embarked on what was to be Thompson's most important project to date; a twin-engined flying boat – designated the NT4 – based on what had been learned from the Circuit Race Flying Boat No. 1 and incorporating a number of details from the Curtiss 'America' patents.

Aesthetically, the four-bay biplane NT4s were graceful-looking machines; although distinctly 'Curtiss' in appearance, they were no mere clones of the American design. Much about them was pure Thompson Flight Company: they were 'pushers' rather than tractors; the wing-span was greater (78 ft. 7 in. against 72 ft.), and they had finer lines. Their military equipment consisted of a Lewis gun and bomb racks. An innovation was the equipping of one of them with a Davis recoilless gun mounted above the cockpit. The enclosed, glazed cabins on the production models must have come as a blessing to their crews.

Initially the NT4s were powered by 150 hp Hispano-Suiza engines but later, when they were fitted with the geared 200 hp version, they became known as NT4As, and had a top speed of 95 m.p.h. at 2,000 ft. Altogether some fifty of these flying boats were constructed at their factory at Middleton, the hulls being made in the yard of William's, their subsidiary, at Littlehampton. In January 1917 a new prototype was unwrapped, the NT2B; in fact, it was a scaled-up version of the successful little White and Thompson No. 3, which had in turn evolved from Ernie Bass' pre-war Circuit flying boat No. 2. With a wing-span of 48 ft. 5 in., it was powered in the first place by a 160 hp pusher Beardmore engine, but ended up being fitted with a variety of power plants according to their erratic availability, including the 200 hp Hispano-Suizas which had to be slew-mounted to counteract torque.

At all events, it appears to have been what the Admiralty were looking for as a two-seater, side-by-side, dual-control trainer. Initially an order for

110 A graceful NT4A poses outside one of the erecting sheds at Middleton.

one was received, then for ten, then for more – and still more. In fact, such was the demand it became necessary to farm out some of the NT2Bs to other constructors, both Supermarine and Saunders being glad to build sizeable batches of what eventually became the RNAS's standard trainer. By the end of the war, some 156 of the 195 ordered had been produced, making it the most successful of Norman Thompson Flight Company's designs.

Another product from Percy Beadle's drawing board at about this time was the Norman Thompson N1B. With a hint of the Walrus yet to come, was a two-seater, high-speed, flying-boat fighter powered by a 200 hp Hispano-Suiza engine. At Middleton expectations were high: a top speed of 108 m.p.h., a climb to 20,000 feet in 18½ minutes – an unheard-of performance for a flying boat at the time. But when it was tested with a full military load at the RNAS station on the Isle of Grain it failed to live up to any of its promises and any thoughts of its production were abandoned.

In 1917 Thompson fell foul of the Admiralty. Since early 1915 the Curtiss Company had ignored his firm's 'exclusive rights' to benefit from the import of flying boats into the UK. Thompson had not received a single penny of commission from any of the Admiralty orders. But when he applied to the courts for permission to sue Curtiss for breach of contract, his application was refused; twice – once by the Ministry of Munitions, doubtless with the connivance of their head, Winston Churchhill. Those in the know believed that too many high-ranking feathers would be ruffled if Thompson resorted to this sort of thing! Instead, there followed what he claimed to be a spiteful and underhand campaign by the Admiralty and its acolyte departments to disadvantage him, even to the extent of putting him out of business.

Whether it was the company's money problems, or whether it had anything to do with the N1B débâcle, is conjectural, but in the autumn of that same year Percy Beadle decided to leave Norman Thompson. And with

111 The NT2B trainer, Thompson's most prolific design, of which some 150 were built. He was also able to cite promised orders for aircraft which were unaccountably cancelled and the Admiralty insisting that he constantly enlarge his manufacturing space – for orders that never materialised, including twenty NT4As. He claimed he was kept short of engines. His accounts remained unpaid and letters pleading settlement went unanswered; by late 1917 his factory was working at one third of its earlier capacity. Already he was in severe financial trouble.

his departure 'came to an end eight years of creative endeavour at Middleton with little of note emerging thereafter'. Even the NT2C of 1918 was merely the wings of an NT4a attached to a Porte hull, although, but for the Armistice, it might have become an effective replacement for the NT4s. As it was, only two were built.

The peace bells that gave tongue across the Sussex countryside on 11 November 1918 must have sounded more like a death-knell to Thompson, all but bankrupt since April, ruined by the Admiralty's vendetta against him, they being his sole customer. Neither was there any sign that he had up his sleeve the design for a civil aeroplane to meet the needs of a post-war market. After the war, justifiably awash with bitterness at the way his country had treated him, Norman Thompson removed himself and his family to France where he spent the rest of his life. He died in the mid-1950s.

Early to pounce upon the Flight Company's liquidated remains was fast-moving Handley Page, scavenging for machine tools and material stocks to carry off to their Cricklewood eyrie. But for two of the erecting sheds there awaited an unexpected after-life, which can be explained by a glance at the Bognor Council minutes dated 2 April 1921: '... the Council proceeded to Middleton Aerodrome and inspected the building offered for sale for £1,000 by the Webley Construction Company'. Yet, by the time what was to become Bognor's Pavilion had been dismantled, transported to its new site behind the Merchant Taylors' Ladies Home in West Street, re-erected, and given a couple of pebbledash turrets at its south end, the cost – to a back-

112 The aftermath. Thompson's old works became the New City Holiday Club, seen here in the early 'thirties.

ground of unedifying Council rancour – had risen to over £17,000. On 22 September 1922 'the Bognor UDC Winter Gardens Pavilion' was opened with the staging of an Ideal Homes Exhibition.

The other shed was purchased by Norman Wilmott for incorporation in his West End Garage in Aldwick Road. What was left of the Middleton works became a holiday camp called the New City Holiday Club. And it was to those smoke-blackened walls, the last witnesses of Thompson's Icarian dreams, that my father took me on the Christmas Day of 1929.

Only a few years had elapsed since Claude Grahame-White and the Pashleys had brought the aeroplane age to Bognor with their prehistoric flying machines. Yet, by 1918, the Sussex skies had lost all trace of innocence. Passing aircraft – many from the recently opened aerodromes at Tangmere and Ford – were no longer a sight to marvel at; crawling laboriously at their top 95 m.p.h. past the end of the Pier, Thompson's flying boats had ceased to rate the pointing finger as, indeed, had the RNAS 'blimps' patrolling the Channel from their arboreal lairs at Polegate and in Slindon Woods. The sound of aero engines in the Bognor sky had become as commonplace as the roar of the breaking waves. So I can remember few summer days in the 'thirties when the sky was free from the sound of aircraft. On Bognor beach we played under the leisurely moving shadows of Avro 504s pulling their wavering banners, exhorting the holiday crowds to dose themselves with Bile Beans or to nourish their minds with the *News of the World*. From Tangmere, the Hawker Furys of Nos 1 and 43 Squadrons of the RAF flew their immaculate formations along the coast.

With club flying flourishing from aerodromes at Shoreham, Yapton, Portsmouth and Redhill, we were treated to a never-ending cavalcade of De Havilland Tiger, Leopard and Puss Moths, Comper Swifts, BA Swallows and Percival Gulls, their pilots unable to resist the temptation to fly low over the sunburnt shrimpers and bathers pottering among the Bognor Rocks. Now and again we caught glimpses of those old Croydon residents, the Behemoth biplanes of Imperial Airways, the Handley Page 42s bearing those sonorous names, *Heracles*, *Hannibal* and *Hengist*, etc. But West Sussex wasn't their natural habitat until, in 1939, the war drove them, camouflaged, on fitful visits to Tangmere in the course of their new RAF transport duties.

It only remains for me to blow the dust from that memory of another sticks-and-string aeroplane of those early days. On a winter's afternoon in 1934, as the lamps were coming on around the Pier, I remember seeing a Vickers Virginia bomber, sombre in its dark green war paint, clawing its crabwise path through a howling nor'easter, as it took all of ten minutes to fly from somewhere over Chichester before disappearing into scudding clouds in the direction of Littlehampton.

Sir Alan Cobham

The Bognor sky was always a livelier place when that intrepid aviator, Sir Alan Cobham, was in the district. Already renowned for his epic flights to Australia and Africa, one of his earliest visits to the town was in 1929, in the course of his Municipal Airports Campaign. Backed by the Air Ministry, who paid him £48 for each town visited, and sustained by the generosity of Sir Charles Wakefield, who underwrote the cost of giving 'flips' to 10,000 schoolchildren, Sir Alan's mission was to persuade quite small towns like Bognor to have their own aerodromes. Yet the Council was dubious; there were murmurs of 'propaganda'. So it may have been the offer of free flights in his DH61, *Youth of Britain*, for the Councillors, local nabobs and 'school children who had attained some scholarly distinction' which caused them suddenly to take a more charitable view.

At any rate, to mark the great aviator's visit, invitations were extended to Bognor's well-born for speeches and a decorous lunch – paid Dutch – held at the Pavilion. For the rest of the day, from a field near the *Robin Hood* pub at Woodgate, the time was spent flying the lucky ones over the town so they could spot their houses from the air. But although Sir Alan failed to tempt the Council to become air-minded on this occasion, the idea of a Bognor airport* refused to go away.

In the 'thirties the indefatigable Sir Alan was back again, this time with his Air Display – or, more properly, National Aviation Day – (no one ever used the term 'Flying Circus' within his hearing!) From 1932 to 1935[†] it was

---

* The Government's Maybury Report of 1939 considered it almost impossible for a small municipal airport to be an economical proposition.

† After the 1935 tour, Sir Alan sold his air display to C.W.A. Scott who, with Tom Campbell Black, had won the Macpherson Robertson air race to Melbourne in 1934. In their hands it became known as the Empire Air Display. But in the popular mind all air shows tended to enjoy the appellation 'Alan Cobham's'.

113 Sir Alan Cobham.

a regular event at Bognor. The arrival was heralded by a formation flight along the seafront; once it included an autogyro. 'Fly with Alan Cobham' cried the banner trailing behind the old Avro 504. It was echoed on the poster pinned to the bus shelter under the elm in Aldwick Road. Arrows pointing 'To the Air Display' spattered the countryside … 'Mother, do you think we could we have some money, please, for Alan Cobham?'

At Chalcraft Farm, my brother and I abandoned our bikes in a ditch and made towards the tannoy's metallic voice with its backdrop of ice-cream tricycles, newspaper placards, St John's Ambulance and advertisments for Exide, Lucas and Castrol. Of course, the Law had to be there, too: 'Specials' in their peaked caps and well-creased trousers. Soon we were absorbed in a motley of sunburnt holiday makers, sandalled children and farm workers dressed in their Sunday best. And, every now and then, that heady cocktail of crushed grass and spent aviation fuel was sniffed.

It was an afternoon to savour the tactile pleasure of running one's fingers over fabric-covered wings, to touch the varnished propeller of the DH61 or inhale the smell of burnt Castrol from the Mongoose-engined Avro 504N. Soon we were being treated to a noisy fly-past of all the aircraft – the giant Handley Page Airliner, Tiger Moths, an Avro Tutor and a Cadet, as well as the autogyro and the old Avro 504 – flat out at 100 m.p.h. Then came that kaleidoscopic memory of bombing an 'eloping' couple in a jalopy with bags of flour, inverted and 'crazy' flying, besides a programme of pylon racing and death-defying loops and spins, each surely terminal – but never quite – and, of course, Geoffrey Tyson in the Fox Moth picking up a flag on the tip of his wing.

All too quickly it was time for the Grand Finale. Slowly the Handley Page flew over the field, a small figure standing on its wing; suddenly a 'chute billowed in the slipstream and down drifted the afternoon's heroine – on this occasion it was Sir Alan's fearless *parachutiste*, Miss Naomi Heron-Maxwell – who landed in the middle of the field amidst a wave of relieved and admiring applause. We couldn't raise the wind for a trip in the 504 or the Giant Airliner that afternoon because our 'flip' allowance had been mortgaged a few weeks earlier at Heston aerodrome with a five-minute flip round the Southall gasometer in a Leopard Moth, whose pilot entertained us with the non-stop humming of 'Shoeshine Boy'. As our late afternoon shadows pedalled home along Chalcraft Lane, I daresay we were quite oblivious of how deeply etched in our minds had been the impressions of that cracking afternoon, thanks to Sir Alan Cobham – and our mother's ready purse.

Sir Alan applied his mind to many aspects of aviation. One of these was the ineluctable fact that more power was needed to get an aircraft off the

114 The Handley Page W10 tanker tops up Sir Alan's Airspeed Courier somewhere off the Bognor coast.

ground than required to sustain it in flight afterwards. Clearly, if a plane could be 'topped up' in the air by a 'tanker', its range – and payload – would be greatly increased. It was to explore and exploit this imaginative concept, that Cobham founded Flight Refuelling Ltd at Ford aerodrome in 1934. Soon the sight of an old Handley Page W10 or Harrow bomber, connected by its umbilical re-fuelling hose to Sir Alan's Airspeed Courier, or perhaps an HP Heyford, became an everyday phenomenon as they droned along the Bognor coastline.

Pushed out of Ford by the Navy in 1940, and with flight-refuelling operations at low ebb, Sir Alan eventually found his way to the Morgan Motor Company's works at Great Malvern in Worcestershire. There he began to attract service work peripheral to military flying. Soon he was involved in experiments with self-sealing petrol tanks, wing de-icing equipment and a method for the aerial towing of Hawker Hurricanes to Malta! After the war, his firm became established players in high-tech aerospace research while remaining front-runners in the provision of sophisticated re-fuelling equipment and techniques which are used by virtually all the airforces of the western world. In 1969 Sir Alan retired and was succeeded as Chairman and Managing Director by his son, Michael.

In 1994, 65 years after its fumbling beginnings at Ford aerodrome, Flight Refuelling Ltd became part of Cobham plc, currently (2000) capitalised at £550 million with a healthy quotation on the London Stock Exchange. Before the war Sir Alan and his wife, Gladys, with their two sons, Geoffrey and Michael, made their home at Old Point at Middleton, only a stone's throw from Norman Thompson's disused slipway, parts of which were still visible in the 1960s.

A Zeppelin passes by

As the silvery-grey German airship D-LZ127 – the giant *Graf Zeppelin* – slid along the English south coast on a July evening in 1938 on her Round Britain cruise, the twenty-five or so passengers must have been mildly interested to find themselves peering down at one of Britain's premier naval bases. But to the posse of mufti-clad Kriegsmarine intelligence officers, snapping away through their powerful telephoto lenses, the sight of Ports-mouth dockyard laid out below must have seemed like a gift on a plate. At any rate, the vehemence with which the Germans denied that they were engaged in espionage,* only went to convince Winston Churchill that that was exactly what they were up to!

115 The *Graf Zeppelin* turns north over the Arcade on her Round-Britain cruise in July 1938.

Minutes later the huge airship would have been over the Selsey Lifeboat Station with a fine view of Pagham Harbour and our patchwork of fields stretching to the Downs on their port side. Did the sight of Bognor Pier ahead cause even a ripple of interest? As they drew nearer to it, the more hawk-eyed on board might have observed a man and two boys gazing up at their eastwardly progress. 'Quickly, boys – come out and look at this,' my father had shouted from the garden just as we had started on our late Heinz beans on toast.

With the last of the sun glinting on her side, the *Graf Zeppelin* presented a picture of buoyant majesty as she slowly purred past us and began to turn inland after passing the Pier. But above the Dark Lane elms the rooks were up-in-wings about it, *caw-cawing* loudly at the intrusion into their airspace of this alien shape. Or was it the purpose of the airship's mission that caused them such disquiet? Rooks, after all, are very wise! Anyway, it was a long time before they regained their composure on that warm July evening in 1938.

* * *

An Airport for Rose Green?

Although outwardly resistant to Sir Alan Cobham's entreaties to bring Bognor into the air age, the Council never quite shook off the notion of a municipal aerodrome. Like the proverbial bad penny, it kept on turning up. As early as 1928 and again in 1934 the Council toyed with the idea of building an airfield on a site south of Chalcraft Lane where Westmeads now sprawls. Then, a year later, representatives of Bognor, Littlehampton and

---

* Mr Churchill was not amused. In the House of Commons he questioned these Zeppelin flights over our coastline. Would, he asked, the German authorities allow our aeroplanes to fly over the Kiel Canal or the Rhine Valley without questioning our motives? (*Hansard*, 10 July 1938)

Arundel Councils had a look at a site at Shripney, although this time it was the Air Ministry who wouldn't play. In 1937, however, there was a flurry of excitement when rumours began to circulate about 'an aerodrome to be built near Bognor' which was likely to have the Ministry's blessing.

Now, of course, my brother and I regarded any new aerodrome nearly on our doorstep as being in the same 'Good Thing' category as Odeons and bathing pools! The difficulty was, though, finding out exactly where it was to be built. Fearful of land speculators, the Council for a long time kept its location a closely guarded secret. But the less guileful West Sussex County Council eventually let the cat out of the bag when they issued a Public Zoning Notice. It was to be at Rose Green, north of Rose Green Road, west of the Lower Bognor Road and extending to Copyhold and Lagness Farms; 230 acres – larger than Tangmere – at the cost of £20,000.

Although the Council explained *ad nauseam* that the land was only to be *reserved* for an aerodrome and did not commit them to actually building one, this cut no ice with the local residents, who were quite sure they knew the thin end of a wedge when they saw it! At a packed public meeting held in the Village Hall on 14 October 1937 the West Ward representatives voiced their implacable opposition: 'this ghastly plot' … 'the Council had no mandate' … 'this reckless expenditure must stop' … 'it will constitute a menace to the town', etc., etc. Noise, crashing aircraft, the adverse effect on the new Rose Green School and the fear that it would provoke the Germans into dropping bombs on Bognor, all were wheeled out in defence of Aldwick and Rose Green in the face of this 'preposterous proposal'.

In fact – apart from my brother and myself – the new aerodrome seems to have had only two other friends: the editor of *Air Review*, Leonard Taylor, who considered Bognor was worth an airport, and Mr H.W.E. Thomas, Chairman of the Council, who firmly believed the town's very future depended on it. 'What', he asked, rhetorically, 'will the children of your children say when, one day, they find Bognor has no aerodrome?' A few heads may have hung in shame, but that sort of clairvoyance was beyond most of the audience. What mattered at the end of that stormy meeting was the uncompromising tone of the West Ward electors' resolution: 'that we emphatically object to the Council proceeding any further in the matter of acquiring a site for a civil airport near Rose Green'.

At the Town Hall on 29 December Captain Corbishley held up the bathing pool débâcle of the previous year as a terrible warning to the Special Purposes Committee. He didn't want that all over again. 'We are living beyond our means: we have enough land.' Councillor T.W. Marshall, for his part, thought 'the money was better spent on ARP'. Suddenly, political prudence prevailed. Forthwith the Town Clerk was instructed to discontinue his negotiations for the land. And thus, unloved, another Town Hall brainwave came to naught. So, making Bognor air-minded remained an uphill task, until the town became surrounded by airfields in 1943. But that was wartime and the purpose sterner.

It might be supposed that by now Bognor's pre-war graveyard of Lost Causes must be full. But, no, there is room for one more – and a rather grand one at that!

Pagham International!

By 1939 a boy was expected to know his Lysander from his Blenheim, his Whitley from his Hampden. But, for those ungifted in aircraft recognition, there was always one plane that defied anonymity, the four-engined Short Empire flying boat. In their silver-and-blue Imperial Airways livery and bearing classical names such as *Canopus*, *Cassiopea* and *Circe*, the sturdily handsome C-Class flying boats epitomised an innovative, pioneering and self-confident Great Britain, as they criss-crossed the equator daily, carrying passengers and the Royal Mail between Southampton Water and those romantic-sounding outposts of the British Empire, Durban, Karachi, Sydney, Singapore *et al.*

But when the news reached my ears that Imperial Airways proposed to quit Southampton Water and set up their Empire flying boat base at Pagham Harbour, I couldn't greet the news with the same enthusiasm as I might have a few years earlier. For, as the reader will recall, I had fallen under the spell of the lonely fascination of the Harbour and its birds. And for neither was this good news.

It began in January 1939 when Mr W.A. Thornton, the owner of 'this muddy wilderness', made an application to the Air Ministry 'to develop the derelict Pagham Harbour ... into an Empire Flying Boat base'. One has to feel some sympathy for William Thornton, a considerable landowner in the Pagham area. He was getting on in years and the never-ending battle to stabilise the harbour's mouth in its 1910 position was a constant drain on his resources. Nor did the ducks and waders pay any rent. But quite suddenly a sparkling star began to rise above the Church Norton horizon.

With the ever-growing volume of shipping in Southampton Water posing both a danger to their flying boats and disruption to their timetables, Imperial Airways were looking for a less congested base. So, when the Navy turned down their application to use Langstone Harbour, this lord of the manor of Selsey and his eminent London aerodrome designer, Mr Baillie Stewart, must have felt that Pagham Harbour was in with a chance.

Baillie Stewart's scheme was Olympian. He intended 'dredging between three and four feet of mud out of the harbour', hardening the shores and providing a sluice at the Chuch Norton mouth. The main terminal buildings – with a rail link to Chichester using the route of the old Selsey Tramway – he had located at the Sidlesham end of Pagham Wall. On an enlarged shingle bank south-east of the harbour mouth he proposed there should arise a luxury hotel.

And there was more to come. For after the 'Pagham and Bremere Rifes had been filled-in and diverted', it was Baillie Stewart's plan to form a large circular-shaped land aerodrome on what are now Honer and Bowley farms extending to Pagham Road. So, at the cost of £750,000, the harbour stood shortly to become Imperial Airways' main British base for their Empire flying boats: Pagham International! The only snag was the plans had yet to pass muster with the Air Ministry.

Amongst the less ornithologically interested Bognor traders, hoteliers and local press, the scheme was greeted with rapture! 'The prosperity of Bognor will be assured for ever,' claimed the *Observer.* Might not this be the

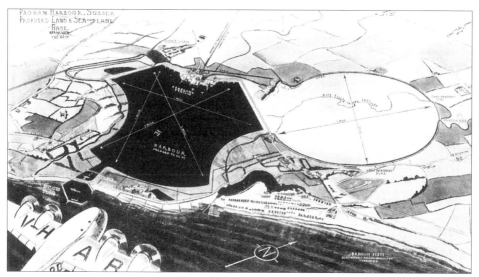

116 An artist's impression of Pagham Harbour re-modelled to become Imperial Airways' main Empire flying base in the UK. Certain features stand out: the Lagoon just above the North sign, the main terminal buildings east of Sidlesham, the proposed circular aerodrome on Honer and Bowley farms, and an hotel built on the widened shingle bank seen in front of the aircraft's nose.

town's long-sought crock of gold? Just think, thousands of well-heeled air travellers on stop-overs with wads of $ bills burning holes in their pockets; picture those long queues, on cold January afternoons, struggling to get into Butlin's Zoo, or hundreds of gum-chewing Californians shivering in their snow-dusted overcoats as they listened to the Bognor Regis Municipal Orchestra playing selections from *Chu Chin Chow* in the roofless Western Bandstand Enclosure. What a prospect!

Even C.G. Grey, the wordly editor of the *Aeroplane*, reckoned 'the Pagham scheme should be given earnest consideration'. So did Nigel Tangye, the aeronautical journalist, as well as many others eminent in the world of commercial flying. At the Chamber of Commerce it was all champagne and Bognor prawn canapés! Yet, there is one curious feature of those heady days – which of course happened long before those hallowed words 'conservation' and 'environment' came to mean just about anything the speaker wanted them to mean: it was the marked absence in the local papers of any letters of protest from furious naturalists and apoplectic ornithologists, wringing their hands on account of the disastrous effect a busy flying boat base would have on the Harbour's birds, flora and fauna.

In fact, only the Rev. A.A. Evans, writing in the *Sussex County Magazine*, seems to have shown anything but indifference to the fate of Pagham's birds. Even Sir Arthur Smith Woodward, a council member of the Sussex Archaeological Society, speaking at Aldwick, could think of nothing more breast-beating to say than 'he hoped that we would be able to enjoy the waterfowl for a little longer'. But he then added – with rare insight – that as Pagham Harbour had been the scene of so many failed enterprises in the past why should this one fare any better? Could he still remember an earlier scheme dreamed up for Pagham Harbour in 1924 by the National Seaplane

Club, an organisation formed 'to practise the new and virile sport of seaplaning'? There was to have been a large club building, an hotel, a ballroom, restaurant and 'amusements' – not to mention bungalows and 'beach-huts to let' – all within sight of Pagham church. And dozens of 'virile' seaplanes, too! In 1926 it was only merciful insolvency which prevented a Mr Smallman-Smith from starting a seaplane club on Pagham Lagoon.

At the Air Ministry in London's Kingsway, hard-nosed civil servants set about giving the Pagham Harbour application a good going-over. Rather too good, in fact. For by the time they had finished, they had propounded a view not half as rosy as those of Mr Thornton and the Bognor Chamber of Commerce. One can only admire the Ministry's prescience. They concluded that in the medium term they might be dealing with 'giant flying boats requiring take-off and landing zones of up to four miles'. With commendable foresight they even envisaged the eventual eclipse of the flying boat by 'large, multi-engined aircraft operating from aerodromes close to the major centres of population'. In any case, they didn't think Southampton Water was anything like so bad as Imperial Airways made out. It was, they concluded, a non-starter. And with that, the unfortunate Mr Thornton's plan for Pagham International was consigned to Bognor's scrapheap of lost causes; but at least Pagham's wintering dunlin and a young birdwatcher could breathe again!

In 1943 the executors of the late W.A. Thornton had one last shot at getting rid of their wretched harbour. It was offered to the Air Ministry. But a more vulnerable location for a flying boat base at that time would have been difficult to find. Their offer was declined. And if the reader wonders what happened after that, may I point them to *A Postscript from Iraq*, to be found on page 287 of this book.

20

Growing Up

A note on newts. And a time of change.

Once upon a time, the filigree of medieval ditches which drained our Aldwick Hundred was inhabited by a multitude of crested newts living out their slithery lives, blowing tiny bubbles and showing off their frilly parts. But that was before the Great March to the Water's Edge of the never-had-it-so-good 'wrinklies'. Within a few years the ditches had disappeared under miles of concrete roads lined with endless rows of new bungalows, houses and Marley patios. Sniffily – and who shall blame them? – the newts moved out. Yet, even today, here and there, in remote pools and ditches among the discarded remains of children's first-generation computers and the jagged wrecks of supermarket trollies, occasionally, *Triturus cristatus* may still be found.

But here is a tip. Avoid like the plague the young, inexperienced ones, the ones which have had their crests cut off to remind their parents of their rebelliousness. Seek, instead, an Elder; an experienced Elder with a sense of genealogy is always best. For almost certainly you will find him mighty in the telling of the great *Triturus* sagas of the past, of how one of his revered ancestors was hailed as being the last of the *Trituruses* ever to be caught by that young, fair-haired newt-hunter chap, you know the one – had his base-camp in South Avenue. Must've been back in '36. No, he tells a lie, it was '35. Or was it '37? Anyway, don't forget to note everything he says. But leave the jar – newts are now protected by the Law!

Well, it stands to reason, doesn't it? I mean, there must have been a final, ultimate, very last time those frayed cuffs were plunged deep into muddy ditch-water in pursuit of one of old *T. cristatus*'s forebears. I daresay it was about the same time that I made that quantum leap into long trousers which, I remember, coincided with Mrs Simpson going off with our King. My mother thought it shameful. Mr Baldwin and the Archbishop of Canterbury seemed to think it a bit rich, too. 'Queen Simpson'; it didn't sound right.

The snag was I was growing up. I had kicked the *Hotspur* and given up walking through bovine leavings; even the Pier's slot-machines had lost their allure. Brother Rog had inherited my roller-skates and little Julian my Dinky Toys. Secretly, I had even taken now and then to combing my hair without my mother's badgering. It was all reflected in a weekly stipend which had been upwardly adjusted across the board to a gradely 1s. 6d. On top of that I had shaken hands with a real Duke, an event on which the less socially secure may secretly crave expansion!

Well, this was how. One Saturday morning, when my father was motoring me down to Bognor, there arose some imperative of business which caused him to call upon His Grace at Harrowlands, the Newcastles' pile at the end of a rhododendron-lined drive near Dorking. The butler and a bouncy, Debrett-looking, golden retriever answered the door-bell. For a while I was parked in the spacious, entrance hall – which my father had recently designed – where I filled in time making friends with old Bouncy and indolently turning a few pages of *The Tatler* and *Farmer and Stockbreeder*.

Eventually the butler returned and shepherded me into a large room with an oak-beamed ceiling filled with elegant furniture, green-and-white striped cushions, gold-framed ancestral portraits and an array of vases with that British Museum look. My father introduced me to the Duke. From the leather-bound sleeve of a sports jacket I was offered a well-manicured ducal hand. I shook it nervously and mumbled 'Sir' instead of 'Your Grace'. With that he gave the bell-pull a sharp tug. Not, though, you will be relieved to hear, for my removal to the Tower, but for his housekeeper to bring me a glass of orange squash, it being a very hot day.

After all these years I have to admit the precise cut and thrust of our conversation rather escapes me. But I do remember him asking me whether I played cricket for my school: 'Yes, Your Grace, for the Second XI.' (Mercifully he didn't ask my highest score: 7). 'Was I going to watch the South Africans play at Lords?' Yes, I was going with a friend. 'Might I be coming over to watch the old timber mill chimney toppled over next week?' Yes, I was; my brother too; both of us looked forward to seeing it come crashing down. I thought I might steal the initiative by mentioning that I had seen a fox in the estate gravel pit. 'Foxes? – the damned place is stiff with 'em,' he replied vehemently. He asked me whether I proposed to become an architect like my father when I grew up. Well, I hoped so – if I was clever enough. Then my heart warmed to him when he let slip that at school he had hated Latin.

Next, he told us about his own son, Pilot Officer Sir Archibald Clinton-Pelham-Hope,* doing night-flying exercises over London in Hawker Demons.

---

* As the Duke of Newcastle's heir apparent, Sir Archibald Clinton-Pelham-Hope's official title was Lord Lincoln, Deputy Lord of the Manor of Worksop. This entitled him to play a significant role in the Coronation ceremony in May 1937. His duties included, at one stage of the proceedings, holding the satin cushion on which rested the Sovereign's glove, and at others relieving His Majesty of the orb and 'the sceptre with the cross' and being at his side 'to support the King's right elbow'. On 7 May 1937 Lord Lincoln attended a dress rehearsal at Westminster Abbey.

When he returned to Harrowlands the next day it was to find my father, Frank Alford, having tea with the Duke. Consequently, my father became privy to the Lincoln story. Afterwards, he made some notes in his nearly illegible hand on the back of a drawing, which my mother later deciphered for posterity:

'Frank very entertained today at the Duke of Newcastle's. Lord Lincoln to tea full of his experiences of the previous day's rehearsal for the Coronation. He says the King is a very nice fellow, jolly and not as nervous as he expected. The rehearsal was a very important one including crowning with the real crown. There were only a few present: the King and Queen, the Archbishop of Canterbury, and the Dukes, namely Norfolk, Somerset, Lincoln himself and Sutherland.

'The King then astonished the Archbishop by taking off his coat to try on the robes! When the white glove was brought to him on the satin cushion, he (the King) said, 'Oh, don't spoil it. Let's use that one' – pointing at Lincoln's leather glove resting on a chair. So this was the one used for the rehearsal.

'The Queen was more nervous – and critical – than he was and watched every move closely. Once, she told him to sit more upright! An amusing incident occurred when it was found that the King was about to be burdened with the Bible and sceptre both at the same time; 'You take this (the

And how the herons had taken all the fish from his terrace pond. I said what a nice dog he had. No, it wasn't his; 'the clumsy damned brute' belonged to his daughter, Lady Doria. Then we went to a small room where he showed us some Roman pots and other artefacts that had been dug up on the estate. Another glass of orange squash and that, as I recall it, brought our *tête à tête* to a close. Once more I was offered the ducal hand. Then the butler and the retriever – still bouncing – came in to show us to the front door.

So, after newts, what? Gone with them my very young childhood; gone, too, those vestigial dreams of being a Schneider Trophy Pilot, capturing the World Speed Record from Sir Malcolm Campbell on Daytona Beach, or being a top-link driver on the Cheltenham Flyer. Now it was that putative 'best-time-of-your-life' stuff spread between London and Bognor, the hum-drum of homework, Latin, awful French irregulars, sines, cosines, quadratics and two-pad cricket in the Second XI.

My education received an upwards nudge when I was given a junior ticket for Bognor's homely little Public Library which had just been trans-ferred from the Water Tower Building to 'Hansfords Hall' – the old Congregational Sunday school building in Sudley Road – approached in those days by a long passage next door to Hansford's shop in London Road. From its shelves I learned the less reputable secrets of the Hollywood Stars, how to construct a vivarium and the story of Howard Carter's discovery of the treasure-filled tomb of the little princeling, Tutankhamun. Gradually I worked my way through Richard and Cherry Kearton's natural history books, became hooked on Biggles and tripped over Jeeves.

For a long time the 'news' in my father's *Morning Post* meant Don Bradman's latest century and Harold Larwood's bodyline bowling, which made D.R. Jardine's team so unpopular with the Australians in 1933. Naturally, the Sussex County Cricket team could count me a loyal sup-porter, with John Langridge my hero, so how he had fared against Somerset or Notts was something on which I should keep my eye; likewise the bowling figures of the great Maurice Tate turning the new ball against Kent. Gradually, though, my eyes began to tarry among the pages of proper news; the carryings-on of the controversial vicar of Stiffkey,[†] destined to meet his Maker in a lion's cage at a zoo in Skegness; the sad Jarrow Marches; the death of Lawrence of Arabia, and the destruction of the Crystal Palace by fire in December 1936. My father had taken us up to Richmond Hill to watch it.

But, for those with eyes to see with, it was the reports of rearmament, the bellicose rantings of Hitler, Mussolini's Million Gleaming Bayonets and

---

sceptre), Lincoln,' he said – and turned, nearly poking Lincoln's eye out with it! The whole rehearsal seems to have been carried out in a more or less light-hearted way. Lord Lincoln said that although people are inclined to deprecate all this pomp and ceremony, he nevertheless felt tremendously thrilled to find himself standing by the King's shoulder and to realise he was participating so closely in the crowning of the world's most important monarch and ruler of the greatest Empire that had ever existed.'

The Duke told Frank that Lord Lincoln's American wife was getting a 'tremendous kick out of the whole thing!'

† The Rev. H. Davidson, who conducted a highly publicised protest against the Church's decision to deprive him of his living after the courts had found him guilty of immoral conduct.

117 Looking west along the High Street in about 1932. Already the motor car is beginning to dominate the scene.

the pictures of a defenceless Guernica destroyed by Franco's bombs which reduced the future to uneasy guesswork. To my generation this was our backcloth to growing up: Mussolini's invasion of Abyssinia in 1935 followed less than a year later by Hitler's annexation of the Rhineland; still in my mind is that picture of Nazi stormtroopers goose-stepping across an iron bridge. Then, in October 1936, came the Berlin-Rome Axis Agreement and the orchestrated spleen of the Nazi's Nuremburg rallies.

So it was all the more curious how a lot of folk remained sanguine of these sinister omens. One such was a Felpham resident who had been holidaying near Nauheim in August 1936. One day he was flattered to receive 'a finely lettered invitation' to a nearby 'Hitler Youth Encampment'. On his return, he couldn't wait to share his enthralling experience with the readers of the *Bognor Regis Post*:

> … we were taken in the charge of two Camp Commandants who welcomed us in English and French. Then, about 300 boys aged from fourteen to eighteen marched forward and went through various evolutions and exercises … later we all sat down in rows on both sides of long tables like a collection of schoolchildren. And I never remember such an atmosphere of simple, natural jollity.

While we were enjoying cakes and coffee the boys sang Nazi songs and went through more evolutions ... as we drove away they saluted us with up-lifted arms.

It is real national socialism translated into practice and is an example to the world ... the boys wear a brown shirt, brown shorts and a black scarf loosely tied ... the greatest defence of Fascism is the Hitler Youth Movement which gives opportunities of a natural, healthy, social holiday to scores of thousands of young lads who, if they were in England, France or America, wouldn't have a chance. None of the Democratic nations who profess to study the people have helped the underdog as he is being helped in Germany by Hitler and the 'Strength Through Joy' movements. As we drove back, the country people saluted us ... and every village was decorated with the Swastika flag in honour of the Olympic Games ...
F.E.C. August 1936

Then there was a Mr Williams who was one of the Bognor and Brighton Legionaires who went to Germany in 1935 on a goodwill visit. Evidently he made a friend there; in June 1936 the *Bognor Regis Post* published a letter he had received from 'Herr H.M'.

Dear Mr Williams,

It is a long time since I last heard from you. In the meantime the situation in Europe is a little altered by the courageous delivery act by Adolf Hitler on March 7th. We are now a Sovereign people ... the proposals of Adolf Hitler for 25 years of peace are so important, they could be the beginning of a new era in Europe. While you were in Germany you saw the people in their love for Adolf Hitler. He is sincere. No, he is not a Dictator because he is supported by the whole people because he is our Saviour ...

Your very sincere German friend, H.M.

At Bognor, the same sort of gullibility must have seized the Vice Chairman of the Urban District Council when he gave a welcoming Nazi salute to a 'goodwill mission' consisting of a bunch of stormtroopers whose number included Hauptsturmfuhrer Schroder, the leader of Hitler's personal bodyguard.

Another source of disquiet during the 'thirties was Sir Oswald Mosley's pro-German – and virulently anti-Jewish – British Union of Fascists, the 'Blackshirts'. Some readers may still remember the disturbances they caused in the East End of London. Their posters proclaiming 'Mosley for Peace' and 'Mind Britain's Business' were spattered everywhere. The Bognor area seems to have been particularly attractive to them. They had offices in the Arcade and a holiday camp at Selsey. I can still recall watching one of their rallies being held in a field somewhere near Church Farm at Pagham. On 3 March 1935, at a meeting held in the Pier Hall, the audience had been harangued by a certain William Joyce, black-shirted against an effusion of Union Jacks and Fascist flags. Four years later this one-time resident of the Bay Estate was to become better known as the sneering Lord Haw-Haw of Reichsender Bremen, infamous for his constant, demoralising questioning of 'Where is the *Ark Royal*?' In February 1938 Mosley himself addressed what the

Bognor Oberver described enthusiastically as 'a very fine crowd' at the Theatre Royal.

But the mouthings of those Churchill was to call 'these dilettante, purblind worldlings' were forgotten in the spring of 1937. For, thanks to Mrs Wallis Simpson, we now had a proper Sovereign with a charming wife and two pretty daughters. The Coronation of King George VI was booked for 12 May. Majestically, the great tapestry of state began to unfurl. With municipal bonhomie, Bognor Council allocated £700 for general fun and games which they hoped donations from 'various organisations' would raise to £1,000. It included £61 5s. for 'coloured woollen bunting', £45 for two thousand engraved teaspoons to be distributed to schoolchildren and £75 for fireworks in the West Car Park. More dubious was the item of £8 5s. for the hire of an 'ape's dress' from Barnum's.

Soon, a fluttering red, white and blue canopy dappled the town; 'Long Live Their Majesties' hung on every lamp-post and banners draped the fronts of all the best buildings. In Chapel Street the decorations were said to be without peer. And of course the Bognor traders joined in, too: Messrs Olby offered a patriotic line in flag-poles and, for those short of a flag to break upon it, Lemmon's in London Road could supply a large Union Jack for 3s. 6d.; the International Stores promised 'a colourful portrait of Their Majesties' to any of their customers purchasing 2s. 9d. worth or more of 'Empire grown products'; for their part, Osborne's the bakers were taking orders for Coronation cakes iced in red, white and blue. On the Newtown Estate – not to be outdone – Neal's, the developers, had opened a Coronation Show House in Coronation Drive. Expansively, the Council agreed to let their employees have the day off on full pay.

Alas, 12 May dawned a day of leaden clouds and heavy rain. Undaunted, though, sharp on 10.30 a.m., a signal of 'twenty one rocket guns' signalled the move-off of the procession. Soon the marchers and floats – headed by a contingent of Police and the British Legion Band – were threading their splashy route through the umbrella-lined streets followed by many of Bognor's well-known institutions, St John's Ambulance, the Red Cross, Boy Scouts, Girl Guides and the Fire Brigade. There was ironic applause for the Council's float – a send-up depicting the bathing pool débâcle of a few months earlier. Marching, too, that morning were the Royal and Ancient Order of Buffaloes, the British Union of Fascists and the Legion of Frontiersmen headed by Captain Harding of the Marine Riding School, on whose saddles we had only recently learned to ride. For the less inhibited, there was dancing between puddles in the High Street.

In the afternoon, at the Hampshire Avenue Recreation ground, to a background of thunder and lightning, Mr R. Bottrill conducted a choir of 3,000 schoolchildren as they squelched their way through 'Rule Britannia' and 'Land of Hope and Glory', with ice-creams afterwards as a reward. And, for those with the stamina, there was the chance to top off that joyful, soggy day with more dancing until the early hours of the morning, to the music of Billy White and his Orchestra at the Pavilion.

But all that is hearsay! For, to tell the truth, I spent that ermine day with my mother's umbrella, a packet of sandwiches and a bottle of lemonade, perched on a kerbstone in the Mall, surrounded by cheering schoolchildren as the King and Queen's coach drove past. It was the recognised path to a coronation mug. So we had to wait for Saturday to join in Bognor's celebrations. That night the Marine Park Gardens were floodlit as a torchlight procession wended its way towards the lighting of an Imperial bonfire in the West Car Park for 'the greatest firework display in Bognor's history'.

With the crack of 'twenty one red maroons' the show was opened. Soon the smell of spent gunpowder spread over the waves of 'ooohs' and 'aaaahs' which greeted the massed roman candles, the cascades of golden rain and the giant catherine wheel which – like all catherine wheels – needed a shove to get it going. Overhead, fusillades of bursting rockets rent starlit holes in the velvet night. All too soon, though, it was time for the grand finale, the torching of a spectacular 'fire-portrait' of His Majesty and the words 'Long May He Reign'.

As the murmurs of appreciation and the last strains of the National Anthem died away, a ripple of applause brought the great show to an end. All that remained was for the Council to take down the town's decorations and find a good home for '180 unclaimed commemorative teaspoons'. It seemed a pity that coronations didn't happen more often.

* * *

By 1938 my brother and I had spent nearly half our lives at Bognor since the family first came to South Avenue nine years earlier. We had grown to know the district like the backs of our hands and had made many friends there. Certainly our roots were more deeply entrenched at Aldwick than in our West London suburb.

Like most children, we also had an eagle eye for change. And in those few years before the war, Bognor was firmly in its throes – I mean, quite apart from getting a new King and Queen! Although, come to think of it, it must have been to celebrate the latest chapter in the House of Windsor that the Highways and Foreshore Committee decided the time had come to extinguish the puddles of Aldwick Gardens under six inches of concrete and to light it with electric lamps. Strange that something which, a few years earlier, would have caused me much anguish, suddenly sounded not a bad idea at all. I suppose that was what growing up meant. Anyway, my late grandmother, I know, would have been overjoyed.

Within our short perspective, it seemed not all that long since we had said farewell to Mr George Tate's unsprung Red Rover buses and seen the last of the Southdown's open-top double-deckers, as well as watch the rather super bus station being built. It was in the field of transport, too, there now awaited another change. For 1938 was the year the Southern Railway line from Bognor to London was due to be electrified. But when we saw those headless, dark green caterpillars creeping and sparking over the level-crossing, they had little of the appeal of the steam trains pulled by the old B4s and H2 Atlantics that they'd replaced; *Hengistbury Head* on a London Bridge excursion I can recall.

118 The last scheduled steam-hauled train from Victoria arrives at Bognor on 2 July 1938.

119 A four-unit electric train, having passed the Bersted crossing, makes its way towards Barnham.

And, with electrification, Bognor found itself with a new landmark, a chic signal-box, centrally heated, flat-roofed and with fashionably curved ends. The *Observer* thought putting it by the level-crossing a missed opportunity; far better that it should have been placed on the Esplanade where it would have looked so much nicer than the new shelters!

So, in spite of our tender years, my brother and I were able to look back at a whole litany of changes. Of course, many of them were trivial. Dark Lane was one: nearly car-less when we first knew it in 1929, it was now so blocked with motors at weekends that the police had taken to booking the drivers who asserted their birthright to ignore the 'Waiting Prohibited' signs; 'A Police State, that's what it's becoming,' growled my father. And, no doubt, it was the 50,000 visitors and their cars which poured into the town on August Bank Holiday in 1937 that prompted Morton Swinburne to warn his readers that traffic-lights must soon come to Bognor – 'they were quite easy to understand and people would get used to them in time'; well, hadn't we already Belisha crossings in Aldwick Road and elsewhere? Meanwhile, the queues of traffic at the level-crossing on Saturday mornings and at Fontwell on Sunday nights became the stuff of legend. A twenty-minute crawl before the constable on point duty let us on to the A29 was often the price of a weekend at Aldwick.

Even the days of our cesspit – with those red-letter visits from the Rural District Council's 'gulper' – were numbered. For in 1937 the Council had let it be known that the whole area was to be sanitised with the introduction of mains drainage. Soon, Aldwick village was cut off from the rest of the world by a deep, barely-moving trench. The work took months. And to all these changes could be added the ever-increasing numbers of new houses and bungalows we encountered as we cycled round the district. In Crescenta Walk houses now covered fields in which we had once caught butterflies with our shrimping nets. Such was the attraction of the Bay Estate the polar-bear-rug-owning classes had filled many of the plots with a variety of architectural fantasies. In Apple Grove, Allaway and Partners were asking £1,295 for 'bijou' houses enjoying the facilities of 'all-weather tennis courts', a bowling green and their own drinking hole, the *Tithe Barn Club* run by the playboy and speedboat racer, Sir Ronald Gunter.

Not far away, Willowhale Farm had long ago swopped its barley crop for a harvest of modern residences. Everywhere, it seemed, builders were at work; on the Summerley Estate at Felpham and in Nyewood Lane, where the new Kyoto Court* boasted a Japanese garden. At King's Beach, Pagham bungalows were on offer at £650 a time, while just off the Chichester Road the Durlston Estate was growing furiously.

If demolition equated to 'change' then, in those years before the war, there was a lot of that about, too. A quota of my time was given over to watching the dismemberment of the Water Tower in London Road and, in 1938, I felt bound to lend half-an-eye to the demolition of Derby House in

---

* The original Kyoto Court (1937) was built by Mr A.H. Winham, who later burnt his fingers in a failed attempt to develop the site of Bognor Lodge, although that did not prevent the house from being pulled down. In 1973 Kyoto Court was demolished and re-hashed on more modern lines by the London architects Austin Vernon and Partners.

the High Street (fortunately not a patch, architecturally, on its neighbour Valhalla), to allow for the widening of Lyon Street. Somehow the demolition of Bognor Lodge seems to have escaped my notice but, from an historical standpoint, it was a tragedy.

Then, early in that same year, while out on my bicycle, I came upon a pile of rubble which was all that was left of Sir Arthur du Cros' Craigweil House. While it had lain empty, our friends and us had often played in its overgrown garden. There were a few who thought it should have become a national shrine to mark the recovery of King George V, but that proved a non-starter compared with the more seductive notion of filling the site with houses. At least the £20,000 Welte-Mignon organ found a good home at the little 12th-century church at Patcham, near Brighton, to which it was donated by Sir Arthur. With the great house gone, its garden quickly became 'Craigweil-on-Sea; the Heart of the Sunny English Riviera', as it began inexorably to fill with a rich assortment of corbelled gables, Georgian carriage lamps and gravelled drives.

Another change we couldn't have failed to observe was in London Road where the Bognor Constabulary had abandoned their little blue-lamp police cottage opposite the *Alexandra Inn*, and had moved further east into a smart, and much larger, neo-Georgian Police Station, the brainchild of Mr Stillman FRIBA, the County Architect. Not even the Bognor Fire Brigade was immune from change. Since 1934, the old 'No. 1' Leyland had been joined by a Leyland Cub Escape, which had coincided with replacement of the Volunteers' brass helmets* by black ones made of leather. Then, in 1937, a third appliance had arrived. But to two connoisseurs of fire engines, the new Dennis Emergency Tender looked rather bland with its crew seated comfortably inside instead of having to hang on for dear life outside!

One change, insignificant in itself, but charged with political overtones, might have been observed on the seafront where, since 1935, the Parade Inspectors had taken to wearing on their uniforms the badge of Bognor's new municipal crest. A closer look showed it to bear the motto 'Action'. To most people this seemed nothing worse than a rather inept word inspiring the citizens of a quiet, slightly backward south coast resort. But to those with the right political antenna, Bognor's motto wasn't just inept; it was outrageous! For *Action* was the name of the official newspaper of the British Union of Fascists. Nor was this mere coincidence. In fact the device had been dreamed up by Councillor Hudson, who represented Felpham and was a close friend and admirer of Sir Oswald Mosley, as well as being an active leader in the Bognor branch of that dubious organisation. The motto seems to have had few friends and, after consultations with the College of Arms, the Council quietly dropped the offending word while its perpetrator and his wife were otherwise engaged on the Isle of Man.

Down on the sands, another sign of the times was the gradual dis-appearance of the little beach shows, ousted by the indoor comfort of the more sophisticated 'revues' which were becoming the rage, such as *The Revuettes* at the Roof Garden Theatre and *Dazzle* at Pierrotland. The

---

* Leather helmets were introduced because of the brass ones proving lethal when they came into contact with electric wires. And, of course, they were lighter.

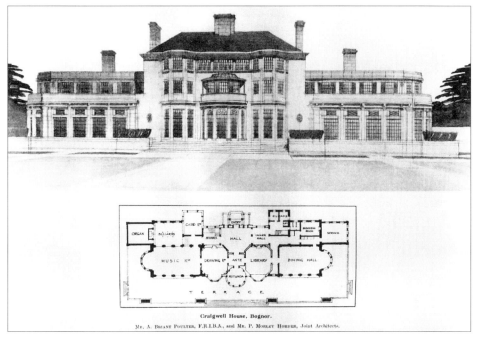

Craigwell House, Bognor.

Mr. A. Briant Poulter, F.R.I.B.A., and Mr. P. Morley Horder, Joint Architects.

120 The architect's drawings for the refurbishment of Craigweil House for Sir Arthur du Cros in about 1926. Three years later he was able to offer it to King George V for the royal convalescence. Mr Morley Horder went on to do the landscaping at the new Aldwick Place for Rowland Rank.

demolition of the old Western Bandstand and its replacement with the new Band Enclosure was another alteration to a familiar setting. An advertisement for lectures at the Picturedrome entitled 'Gases; persistent and non-persistent' suggested change of a more ominous kind. Just in time, Roger and I had learned to ride on the sands. For, in 1937, in an apparent attempt to court maximum unpopularity, the Council decided to introduce two highly controversial measures which certainly amounted to change – and of the severest order.

First, the Council's eyes had fallen upon riders with horses 'of over 12 hands using the beach'. In response to the unsubstantiated complaints from a vociferous few – Councillor Eastland was one who considered riding on the beach a 'dangerous and objectionable habit' – it was decided, in spite of this harmless pastime having enjoyed an entirely accident-free history, to restrict riding to certain unpopular hours during the summer season; instead, it was proposed to shunt equestrians on to a sort of 'Rotten Row' to be constructed in the West Car Park.

Of course, there was uproar! Riders and non-riders alike thought the Council must have taken leave of its senses! Naturally much of the opposition came from the equestrian lobby. Mr Therwell of the Milton Riding stables said he would leave Bognor if it came about – and he did! At the Marine Riding Stables in Aldwick Road, Captain Harding – one of those dismissive of the 'Rotten Row' idea owing to the danger from motor cars – predicted his trade would soon face bankruptcy. 'When did you last see a

Councillor on a horse?' he asked, pertinently. Britain's champion jockey, Steve Donohue, claimed that many Grand National horses had benefitted from walks on the beach and, if the ban were instituted, threatened never to come to Bognor again and get all his horsey pals to follow him. The Marchioness of Cambridge, on behalf of her daughter, the Lady Mary,

121 A riding school out for a trot on Bognor sands. In 1937 the Council banned 'this popular pastime' from the beach.

complained bitterly in a letter to the *Post* that riding on the sands was one of the reasons why they had come to Bognor at all. Over the Mounted Gymkhana and Donkey Derby, held in the field opposite the Duck Pond, hung a cloud of equestrian gloom.

As the row proceeded there was a call to turn out of office every Councillor who had 'voted for this lunacy'. Firmly on the side of the horses, the *Post* opined 'that some of the best people ride'. It was all too exasperating for one of the *Post*'s correspondents. 'Wouldn't it be simpler for the Council to put the beach out-of-bounds to everything and everybody?' he asked.

Yet, regardless of any evidence to the contrary, the Council managed to convince itself of a chapter of horrendous accidents waiting to happen. On 19 August 1938 the Home Office confirmed the riding ban. Soon, up went the warning notices: 'No riding permitted between Gloucester Road and Fish Lane 10 am – 7 pm on Good Friday and the four following days and between these hours on any day between the Saturday before Whitsun and September 30th'. Clearly, any horserider reading the new notice would do well to be accompanied by a solicitor!

The other piece of Council-inspired change – and many thought it mean and spiteful – was to rescind 'Sandscratcher' Samuel Mather's licence on the specious grounds that his artistry denied holiday-makers use of the beach and the crowds he attracted constituted 'an obstruction on the Promenade'. Yet, weren't his unique sand-drawings the sort of thing which encouraged parents to bring their children to Bognor? And didn't the Daily Mirror Eight take up just as much beach and attract even larger crowds? But, apart from one Councillor who felt it a shameful way to treat this elderly ex-service-man, Mather's history of sand-scratching on Bognor beach since 1907 failed to melt Town Hall hearts.

122 'Sandscratcher' Mather at work, delighting the crowds with his art, opposite the Steyne.

Other changes we couldn't have failed to notice – quite apart from the recently arrived Odeon cinema in London Road – were the sudden appearance of a GPO telephone box at the end of Aldwick Gardens and a new roundabout at the crossroads. Already I had christened the newly opened Felpham by-pass (June 1938), pedalling my way to Ford aerodrome. And now – much to the consternation of the local shopkeepers – there were rumours that it was planned to make London and Sudley Roads into a one-way traffic system. Change and more change seemed the order of the day. Might it go on for ever?

* * *

By 1937 – Morris Eights and Hoovers apart – it was the cocktail cabinet and the radiogram that had come to reflect the *dolce vita* of South Avenue, the tokens by which its residents might stake out their social aspirations and point the way ahead in matters of taste and fashion. Although my parents eschewed the former, there came the day, just before Christmas, when the Southern Railway delivered to Idlewylde a large cardboard box containing a radiogram. Curved of the edge-parts and lustrous in veneer, it answered to the golden-Gothic name of BARKER'S.* Beneath its pneumatically hinged lid lurked every mechanical and radiophonic felicity, an automatic record-changer of human ingenuity and a turntable beholden to neither 'wow' nor 'woof'. It boasted 'superhet' tuning across an array of exotic-sounding stations, from Bordeaux La Fayette to Athens, from Rome to Fecamp, via Kalundborg and Riga, each with its own distinctive screech, whistle, snatch of morse code or hullabaloo of Bolivian street riot.

* In 1937 a well-known department store in Kensington High Street, west London.

From its moving-coil loudspeaker the brochure assured its owner of reproduction much superior to the real thing. What it didn't mention, though, was the gramophone's huge appetite for expensive fibre-tipped needles. But at least it was goodbye to acid batteries (which, in Southdown buses, were 'not to be placed upon the seats'). BARKER'S long list of virtues quickly revealed the woeful inadequacies of our current stock of tormented Parlophone, HMV and Brunswick records, as every scratch, serration and footmark became magnified a hundredfold. So pennies were added to Christmas Postal Orders and parental subsidies begged. Our next stop was Eroica's Music Salon in the High Street, opposite the Post Office. Soon the ten-inch labels of Columbia, Eclipse and Zonophone brought to our home the music of the great dance bands of the 'thirties.

To Harry Roy at the Mayfair Hotel and Lew Stone from the Café de Paris, we added Ambrose's Embassy Club Orchestra playing 'A Nightingale sang in Berkeley Square' and Roy Fox's easily remembered 'June in January'. Daily, our ears were soothed by Jack Hylton's version of 'Dark Town Strutter's Ball' and Billy Cotton bashing out 'Flat Foot Floogie with The Floy Floy'. At high tea, 'Just the Time for Dancing' was a prelude to Henry Hall and his BBC Dance Orchestra rendering 'Red Sails in the Sunset', or we polished off the lemon-curd tarts to the strains of 'Deep Purple' played by the inimitable Victor Silvester and his Ballroom Orchestra.

Then, one evening, semi-comatose and faced with the gall and wormwood of the Second Punic War, I was arrested in mid-pencil-chew by an ear-catching euphony floating from BARKER'S loudspeakers. With no musical vocabulary at my command, I was reduced merely to judging it to be, well, 'beautiful'. The piece turned out to be the 'Four Ways Suite' by a certain Eric Coates. But for me its attraction lay not only in its lilting melodies ('light in substance but impeccable in workmanship' says *Collins Music Encyclopedia* of Coate's compositions), for suddenly I became aware of the new-found pleasure of listening to all the instrumental strands of a full-blooded orchestra.

A few days later, my fist full of mortgaged coin, I paid another visit to Mr Bedford – Eroica's proprietor – before bicycling home clasping my first, shiny, 12-inch 78: the music of Eric Coates, including his 'Four Ways Suite'. And only the dilatoriness of history prevented this gifted composer of 'In Town Tonight', 'The Dam Busters March' and 'Sleepy Lagoon' – said, so we are told, to have been inspired by the distant view of Bognor from Selsey in fading evening light – settling at The Holdynge in Aldwick Avenue early enough to have had the pleasure of sharing with me the occasional complimentary performance of 'At the Dance' played *fortissimo-fortissimo* if he ever chose to stroll past our open French windows.

So with 'Summer Days' came the end of dance music. Soon Coates was joined by Tchaikovsky's 'Pathetique', then Schubert's 'Trout', until, in due course, BARKER'S moving coils were employed on overtime pounding out Brahms 'Piano Concerto No. 2' – subject only to my father's peremptory requests to 'turn that damned thing down'. Oh yes, and Arthur Askey's 'Bee Song'.

But BARKER'S light-hearted days were hardly begun before they were over. For on the Ides of March 1938 we listened on the BBC's National

123 Not exactly a great conflagration; more a fire in an umbrella stand at 16 Wychwood Close, Craigweil in about 1938. But the fire brigade rules required the presence of two appliances, in this case the Leyland Cub Escape (right) and the recently acquired Dennis 'limousine' tender.

Programme to the news that the German Army had crossed the border into Austria. At the Picturedrome I watched the Pathé Gazette newsreel showing Hitler haranguing a wall-to-wall carpet of 'sieg heil-ing' stormtroopers with the Luftwaffe roaring overhead. 'Ein Reich, Ein Volk, Ein Fuhrer', it all looked a bit unsettling.

Regardless, though, of these dark omens, one weekend in May my father took the family to have a look at four acres of Wealden hillside encircled by oak trees at Slinfold, near Horsham. He was minded to buy and build on it our country house. Meanwhile, as Aldwick's fields surrendered to Bognor's expanding town and as we contemplated what Aldwick Gardens might look like under six inches of concrete, as we deplored the disappearance from the beach of 'Scratcher' Mather and the riding-school horses and feigned not to hear the distant chants of war, it was time to admit that our 'pioneering' days in this little corner of Aldwick had run their course; like it or not, we had become part of Bognor's suburbia. So, what might the future bring?

Well, one thing it brought happened on 20 August 1938, when Len Hutton scored a record-breaking 364 of England's total of 904 for 7 declared against the Australians at the Oval. Yet the great hero's astronomical score came as no surprise to those locals who had witnessed him and Hedley

Verity practising on Aldwick beach, while they were staying at the *Victoria Hotel* in West Bognor, a few days before the match.

Yes, everything was changing all right. And now there was to be a change to the pattern of our holidays. For hitherto our lives had been spent almost entirely between the creosoted fences and pebble dash chimneys of our Middlesex suburb and the Owers' flashing beacon off Bognor's sandy rim. The time had come, my parents concluded, for their sons to see a bit more of the Great-Out-There. So, sometime in August, we swopped the still-dusty potholes of South Avenue for a fortnight of clotted-cream teas, saffron cake and the implacable drizzle of Tavistock and Dartmoor. After fighting our wind-buffeted way to the top of every Tor in sight, and spending hours contemplating the rain sheeting down on the bleak, ducklessness of Burrator Reservoir, our West Country holiday came to its soggy end. Wistfully, we looked forward to feeling once more Bognor's pulse and, perchance, a glimpse of her famous sun.

Late that Saturday afternoon the family's return to its native heath became a tour of inspection as we drove through the town reviewing the changes that seemed constantly awaiting our appraisal. One recent new-comer we couldn't have missed was Burton's. In 1937 they had built their new stores – 'this cathedral of commerce', as they so lyrically put it – upon two of the last residential sites in London Road, The Lawns and Mr Palmer's Ivy Lodge. So, with Marks and Spencer's next door and Wool-worth's and Timothy White's only a few steps away, there were now four major stores on its west side. And already there were rumours that W.H. Smith's were shortly to join them. On the opposite side of the road, well-established and thriving, stood Hansford's the outfitters, Sainsbury's, Dutton and Thorogood and Dewhurst's the butchers, not to mention Shirley Brother's walk-round stores that now occupied part of the old waterworks site, to all of which Sir Arthur Blomfield's St John's Church, with its towering steeple, added a note of architectural and spiritual distinction.

So, with the recently opened biscuit-coloured Southdown Bus Station in the High Street (can the reader remember the polished brass bell, from an eponymous Great War sloop, that hung in the foyer?), our new Odeon cinema in London Road and the ever-decorous Arcade, the centre part of the town presented an air of prosperous well-being. My mother, I know, pre-ferred shopping in Bognor to our west London suburb.

But perhaps that was the town seen through rose-tinted spectacles after our visit to the West Country. Here is a less flattering view which appeared in the *Post* that same August:

> Your streets are drab and dirty, your tumble-down shacks, your decay-ing hoardings, your ugly tin-roofed shanties, your hideous coloured gasometer which extends its hand of greeting as you enter the town, all resemble Ypres at its war-time worst – and your cesspits stink!

In the same spirit of municipal castigation, Mrs Rudolph Stawell, the author of *Motoring in Kent and Sussex*, had her reservations about the place, too. She wrote, 'Only, I think, the devoted lovers of Marine Parades will wish to tarry in Bognor.'

The last stage of our journey was marked by shouts and screams from the Dodgems and the funfair's raucous clamour in the lee of the Zoological Alps, as we drove past 'Butlin's – the Rendezvous of Bognor', where the Esplanade's *éminence grise* continued to apply himself to catering for the swarms of 'the wrong sort of visitor'. But at least Butlin had brought some kind of life to the old Cabbage Patch site. And no doubt the Treasurer was glad of the rates – which were more than he could have reckoned on had it been laid out as a Municipal Gardens, the idea mooted by the Council in 1923, when it let slip the chance of buying one of Bognor's most valuable sites.

A few minutes later, with the curving lines of the new Western Band Enclosure behind us, we were driving into the evening sun past Silverston Avenue – where Bert Seymour was putting up the last of his houses – and along Aldwick Road, now widened, pavemented and lit as far as Hammond's Corner. Growing taller by the year, the new windbreak conifers planted by Rowland Rank had begun to stamp one kind of mark upon the landscape, while the new mock-medieval houses opposite and the still-treeless gardens of Crescenta Walk and Westingway impressed another. Bearing its 'Tamplin's Brighton Ales and Stouts' frieze, the No. 50 double-decker bus coming towards us from Pagham looked as modern as anything we'd seen in London.

At last we came to Mrs Duffin's Slated Barn Stores – re-opened after being badly damaged by a petrol-pump fire the previous summer – and turned into Aldwick Gardens. Minutes later my father had unlocked the back door of the bungalow and gone to the loggia to bring in the two boxes of groceries left by Mr Gates from the village stores. Already my mother had put the kettle on. In the living room my brother and I had begun sorting out our fishing tackle for the next day on the Pier, while Julian had picked up where he had left off a fortnight earlier on his Meccano crane. In the ditch at the bottom of the garden Judy was more convinced than ever that she could smell rabbits. Thus, life started up again at Idlewylde.

Only a few days later we heard the imperative rasp of Hitler's voice as he lay claim to Czechoslovakia's Sudetenland. Throughout September 1938 international tension mounted. From the new ARP Headquarters at Cole-brook House, gasmasks were handed out in thousands; on the Hampshire Avenue recreation ground, and elsewhere, trench digging proceeded urgently, and unsuspecting families were ordered by billeting officers to be ready to share their homes with the expected flood of evacuees from London. Home Office pamphlets on 'The Protection of Your Home Against Bombs' were stuffed through every apprehensive householder's letterplate.

Then, on 30 September, Chamberlain arrived back at Heston aerodrome waving his 'Peace for our time' message; there was to be no war! Pending full comprehension of its shameful contents, a wave of relief swept the country. We weren't going to be gassed or bombed; we could forget that baleful acronym, ARP! And with that, the Council cancelled any further issuing of gasmasks and halted its trench digging. The folk threatened with half-a-dozen noisy little evacuees from London could breath again – or at least, that's what they thought!

During that same month, a letter from the Duke of Newcastle's agent arrived at 19 Hanover Square. It contained instructions for my father to proceed with the preparations of plans for 250 houses on a site near Betchworth in Surrey. Already pinned on his drawing-board were the preliminary drawings of Hundred Oaks, the name for our proposed country house at Slinfold. Down at Aldwick we were only just getting used to the sight of the family's new six-cylinder Packard gleaming in the driveway at weekends.

At last, my parents' years of sacrifice and relentless hard work had begun to show a small reward. Little, though, could we have guessed how short-lived were to be those halcyon days.

124 Town crest, 1935

21

War Again

In the event of war. Accommodation required for Lady. Bognor district.
Particulars and terms to Box No … a leaf in the wind.

Bognor Regis Post, June 1939.

The whole might and fury of the enemy must be very soon turned on
us.

Winston Churchill, 18 June 1940.

On Christmas Day 1938, my mother presented me with a Lett's Diary.
From then on, every day, I made a schoolboy entry – remarkable mainly for
their excruciating vapidity. Certainly it and the others diaries I kept for the
next five years were never intended for public consumption. Yet, to reread
the inelegant prose written between 1939 and 1940 – which provides a
thread of continuity to this chapter – is to relive a period unique in Britain's
history. The reader will be relieved to learn, though, that I propose to draw
only upon those of my scribblings which will help convey a picture of the
exceptional times in which we lived.

We can, for instance, ignore with advantage the words 'homework' and
'revision' which appear on nearly every page; likewise 'cleaned out rabbits',
which occurs sporadically; so also 'bought new saddle-bag and mud-guards'
on 20 January 1939. Visits to the cinema figure prominently; at least once
a week, sometimes more. At Bognor's Odeon Theatre on Saturday 4 February I saw *Pygmalion* and fell under the spell of Wendy Hiller and had to
stay on to see it round again. And so the cryptic word 'puncture' on 22 February brings me to the 23rd, when 'searchlights and flares over London'
proved to be a harbinger of things to come. Then, on the 27th, the entry:
'Told that in the event of war, the school will be evacuated to Wiltshire'
shows only too clearly we were no longer living in normal times.

My father was sure that war was now inevitable. And, in that event, he
had it in mind that we would move down to Aldwick so as to escape the
rain of bombs everyone supposed would fall upon London immediately
hostilities were declared. His idea was to build an air-raid shelter under the
bungalow with an escape to the garden. But addressing the Middleton
Society in March, Mr Ward-Price, the well-known journalist – with that
insight journalists enjoy – was of the opinion that all this panic was
unnecessary: '… I am quite sure Hitler will not go to war in 1939.' Another
journalist, Mr Morton Swinburne of the *Bognor Regis Post*, was equally
unperturbed: 'All this talk of evacuation is the usual cock-and-bull rumours
spread by irresponsible females with too little to occupy their minds.' Then,

with measured gravity, he turned to the Arundel Flower Show: 'People who can grow a 29lb marrow need fear nothing,' he declared.

Rather less droll, though, was the burden of the Home Office letter which arrived at Bognor's Town Hall on 8 April 1939. This was a copy of ARP Circular No. 86/1939 *Acceleration of Civil Defence Measures* which, in effect, ordered Local Authorities to drop everything else and concentrate their minds on perfecting their Air Raid Precaution arrangements.

At Bognor's ARP HQ at Colebrook House, lessons had been learned since the Chief Constable of West Sussex had been severely critical of the Council's unreadiness at the time of the Czech crisis in 1938. So, on 31 May, Captain H.W.E. Thomas, Chairman of the ARP Committee, was able to report that 'remarkable progress' had been made putting things right. The petty bickering that had plagued his department had given way to some semblance of 'unity of purpose and common desire'. They now had more equipment. The importance of 'brief and concise messages' had not gone unheeded and well-meaning over-zealousness – the cause of many mishaps and misunderstandings during exercises – was being dealt with as the need arose. To save money, for example, the Bognor Council had insisted on the various shifts of the AFS volunteers sharing working uniforms. This was not popular and each shift demanded its own. The Council dug its heels in; so did the volunteers – by going on strike! The Home Office was asked to mediate: to the Council's chagrin, they came down firmly on the volunteers' side. The cost of the additional uniforms was £125.

And there was more yet. A comprehensive ARP training programme had been instituted and air-raid shelters planned at the Pavilion, the Isolation Hospital and at Snook's Corner. Shortly, a street-wardening scheme would be introduced. The only black spot was the chronic shortage of nurses, special constables and 96 firemen. That same April the Home Office ordered a national ARP test under blackout conditions. 'Realism' was to be its theme. Captain Thomas hoped 'the public would take it seriously and refrain from practical joking'. Nor should they crowd round the 'incidents'.

Entering into the spirit of the thing, Bognor's AFS detachment decided that instead of going first to Felpham church for a pre-test briefing, they would leave the station only when they heard the siren at 10 p.m. – 'in the name of realism'. So it wasn't until the crew got to the church that they discovered they had gone past the fire they were meant to extinguish. Hurriedly, they turned round and eventually found it in the East Car Park. Urgently, hoses were run out to the nearest hydrant. And that was when it was realised their only hydrant key had fallen off the appliance during the journey. Luckily, nearby was a telephone box; a call to the duty officer in Clarence Road and a new key would be quickly sent out. But they hadn't reckoned on the local air-raid warden being an expert at inventing imaginary situations of wild improbability. This particular phone box, he insisted sternly, 'was unavailable having been wrecked by enemy action!' After a few curt words the firemen hurried back to the telephone near the church – only to learn to their dismay that, 'in the name of realism', all the hydrant supplies in that part of Felpham had been cut off. In the meantime the fire had burnt itself out.

Links Avenue in Felpham was the scene of our intrepid crew's next 'incident'. Alas, the nearest hydrant was again labelled 'dry'. The only alternative was the Aldingbourne Rife, where a perverse tide had caused the water level to be unusually low. With selfless courage, one of the firemen grabbed the hose and struggled down the steep bank in the dark. Suddenly there was a cry and a loud splash as our hero lost his footing on the damp grass and, 'in the name of realism', fell into the water. Only because the fire was kept going by volunteers were the drier members of the crew eventually able to extinguish it.

Bognor's AFS had known better nights – especially when they discovered they had overlooked three 'casualties' who had stayed most of the dark hours in the car park waiting to be 'rescued'. Nor was Warden No. 275 best pleased having to submit a claim for the loss of her dentures in another 'incident'. Clearly, realism had its price! It was only when the real bombs began to fall and the Auxiliary Fire Service and other Civil Defence units were asked to draw upon their reserves of skill and courage in deadly earnest, that they were able to look back at the wealth of learning contained in those petty irritations they had encountered during their days and nights of training.

As July became that scorching August of 1939, two well-remembered events figure in my diary. One was the opportunity which arose for my brother to go to France with our cousin Joan to stay with her friends near Dieppe. Although the international situation remained disquieting, my parents must have considered peace still had a little way to run. So on 9 August my father drove Joan and Roger down to catch the Channel Packet from Newhaven. The other event was the arrival of my cousin Arthur – plus bicycle – who came down from Glasgow to stay with us for a fortnight. Over a glass of Tizer I learned he had plans to train as a wireless operator in the Merchant Navy. It sounded a nice, cushy job. And think of all that travel – free!

So, for most of that fortnight, detached from the ominous comings and goings of Messrs Chamberlain, Daladier, von Ribbentrop and the voice of the carpet-chewing Fuhrer, we idled away our time pedalling the narrow, scarce-trafficked lanes that wandered through a West Sussex countryside dressed in her harvest finery. Earnley and South Mundham; Sidlesham and Aldingbourne; Binsted, Oving and West Stoke, hamlets left stranded in an ochre sea of reaped fields rippled with lines of wigwam stooks. At Henty and Constable's newly opened *King's Beach Hotel* at Pagham, my sophisticated cousin bought himself half-a-pint of bitter while I stuck to Pink's ginger beer.

At last the weather broke and gave us the opportunity to seek asylum at our luxurious Odeon cinema. From the ninepennies, sustained by a bag of sticky popcorn, we gave our minds to every intellectual twist and turn of Jack Buchanan and Googie Withers in *The Gang's All Here* and watched the London balloon barrage go up on the Movietone News. Afterwards, on the rain-soaked pavement, we totted up our financial resources: fourpence each – just enough for fish and chips from Day's Fish Restaurant in the High Street. To make it an 'occasion' we took our *News of the World*-wrapped feast and finished it off under the shelter of the Pier.

Those early days of August also bought to our territory a rash of posters heralding the imminent arrival of a circus, Bertram Mills' in the Bottom Field. On our doorstep – how absolutely wizard! When the multi-coloured wagon train crawled into the field, Arthur and I followed in its wake for, to tell the truth, we still found circuses full of wonder. Tall poles had been stayed into the clay. On the ground lay an amorphous mound of canvas. Upon the Major Domo's sharp commands, purpose and order sprang to attention. Expert hands gripped the ropes; so did ours. The Major Domo shouted 'One, two, three – and heave!' We heaved, too. Slowly, foot by foot, the shapeless canvas was reared up until, almost imperceptibly, it was transformed into the Big Top, voluptuously trembling in the summer breeze. Soon it was filled with seats. Then in went the circus ring; sawdust was poured on the ground. Next, the Great Frederico's trapeze was hung from above. The air smelt of bruised grass and Grindl's gambolling elephants. A big cat roared, the bunting fluttered and the Booking Office opened. 'Roll-up, Roll-up!' Naturally, we weren't going to miss any of this!

Quickly the days fled by until the morning arrived when my father took us all to Bognor station to see Arthur off to Glasgow. It wasn't until 1946 that I saw my cousin again, and learned how he had been three times bombed, twice torpedoed and seen a dozen ships sunk before his eyes on those ghastly Murmansk convoys. And all that travel – free!

On 23 August my parent's calculation that there was enough peacetime left to accommodate Roger's holiday suffered a rude rebuff when Germany signed a non-aggression pact with Russia and Mr Chamberlain warned the Fuhrer that Britain would fulfill her guarantees to Poland. Never had the abyss of war looked closer.

> **Diary, 22 August**: 'Hitler sounds as if he really does mean business. Situation pretty bad. Went with mother by bus to Ferring for tea with Aunts Marjory and Vera. Played tennis in evening. Dad tried phoning Rog but no luck.'
>
> **Dairy, 23 August**: 'Bought Aircraft Recognition book. Hitler still talking. Russo-German pact signed. Nothing from Rog. Mower bust so couldn't do lawn.'
>
> **Diary, 24 August**: 'Things still look pretty grim. Tried to phone Dad but lines full. Still no news of R. Saw Vickers Wellesley. Took Judy for walk in Yeoman's Acre.'

On the Promenade it could have been any hot August day; the familiar patchwork of shuffling holiday makers, licking cornets, snapping Brownies, chastising offspring and stopping now and then to watch Bognor's Clown, Punch and Judy or the Daily Mail Sandcastle Competition below the Western Bandstand Enclosure. Pasted on the Culver Cottage notice-board, a poster reminded stage lovers that John Gielgud was directing Zena Dare in *Spring Meeting* at the Theatre Royal. In a cloud of spray, Albe Ide's *Miss Magic* roared past the end of the Pier. Only the words scribbled on the newsvendor's placard cast a jarring note: 'Emergency Latest; Hitler in Session with War Chiefs'.

Diary, 26 August: 'Dad down from London. Still no word of Rog. Had two bathes. Trenches being dug at Pavilion. Cycled to Tangmere. Hurricanes now joined by a squadron of Gladiators. Saw Fairey Battle take off. Did drawing of Aldwick Barn. Not bad.'

Well, it *was* a bit worrying. Every attempt to get in touch with their cherished boy in France had failed. The French telephone system, dodgy at the best of times, was now in a state of paralysis as their army was mobilised and people began to move out of the more bombable towns. But, at last, to everyone's relief, we were advised through a roundabout route that young Roger had been put on a boat in the care of a kind and reliable stranger. On the Monday afternoon, happily oblivious of all the fuss that he'd caused, my brother arrived back in his Motherland for a dockside reunion of hugs and kisses from his thankful parents.

Diary, 29 August: 'Had bathe. Went fishing on Pier. Rog caught a red mullet. News still bad.'

On our way back from the Pier we came across sunburnt holiday makers and toddlers in bathing-drawers enthusiastically helping Council workmen and the police with filling sandbags. Happy sand-baggery was also in full swing on the Bay Estate dunes. In his study my father applied himself to designing our new air-raid shelter; fingers crossed it would ward off bombs. But at least the Alfords were to be spared the misery of the bottom-of-the-garden 'Anderson' shelter.

125 Below the Promenade visitors and children help Council workmen fill sandbags, August 1939.

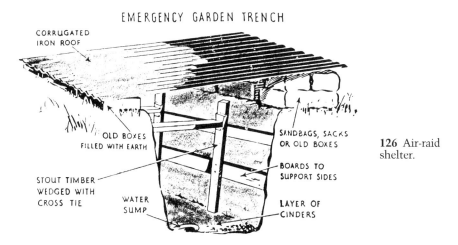

126 Air-raid shelter.

Meanwhile, on 26 August, the Chairman of the Bognor Council's ARP Committee was able to announce that a Control Centre had been established at the Police Station in London Road and the promised shelters built. In addition, trenches for 780 persons had been dug and Wardens named for every road; South Avenue could feel secure in the hands of our neighbours, Messrs Prior and Gentle. On behalf of the Fire Brigade, Acting Chief Officer Leslie Walwin confidently claimed that 'Bognor was the best protected town on the south coast' … with 250 men, four fire engines and twelve trailer pumps stationed in the High Street, Clarence Road, Aldwick and at Felpham. Less sanguine, though, were Reynolds' the undertakers, where Mr Frank had stocked up with an extra supply of coffin-elm imported from Holland.

> **Diary, 1 September**: '**GERMANY INVADES POLAND**! Cycled over to Tangmere. Ansons gone. Hurricanes dispersed and the Squadron of Gladiators now near perimeter fence. No flying. Listened to wireless in evening.'

That morning the familiar national and regional radio programmes disappeared from the airwaves and were replaced by a newcomer called the BBC Home Service. On the 1 o'clock News for the first time we heard the word 'Blitzkrieg' as the German Panzers thrust their way towards Warsaw. Insistently, it was drummed into listeners' heads that the 'blackout' – the restriction which was to most transform the nation's life – was to become effective from that night.

> **Diary, 2 September**: 'Bognor practically empty. 3,000 evacuees expected. Had bathe. Bought water colours from Goughs.'

Preferring to ignore the great international drama unfolding in front of it, the *Bognor Regis Post* devoted its front page to the Golden Weddings of two well-known local couples. The 'Sunshine Page' they called it, unheedful of the shadow cast by the adjoining announcement: 'NOTICE. The sirens of the ARP organisation will in future be used only for the purpose of TRUE AIR RAID WARNINGS'.

All day lorries carted their loads of sandbags required to protect buildings suddenly precious and vital: the Town Hall, the new Police Station and the ARP HQ at Colebrook House. Gradually the newly opened Fire Station in Clarence Road, the Post Office and the Memorial Hospital began to disappear behind a rising tide of sandbags. So, too, did dozens of AFS and Warden's Posts. The public shelter in the Odeon's basement and the Southern Railway's signal box by the level-crossing each claimed their share of sandbags.

Not unreasonably, the local traders sought business and profit from the Emergency. Lewis and Co. advertised 'a recent delivery of stout black-out paper'. For the same purpose, Staley's were offering black twill at 1s. 11½d. per yard. For anti-shatter adhesive tape and sandbags the public needed look no further than Olby's in Hawthorn Road. G.A. Culverwell Ltd, the builders, let it be known they were 'specialists in blast walls' and R.H. Hill looked forward to receiving orders for 'reinforced concrete air-raid shelters'. If Reynolds Ltd were a little reticent about the emergency it was because their minds were more on celebrating the opening of their rebuilt High Street stores, poshly clad in Portland stone.

From Elmer to Pagham, holiday homes were locked up, beach huts secured, removal vans loaded, farewells exchanged and outstanding accounts settled – or not – as financial circumstances permitted. Under the blacked-out roof of a railway station spattered with notices sternly asking 'Is your journey really necessary?', visitors heading for home and an uncertain future became entangled with the train-loads of labelled and pale-faced evacuees coming in the opposite direction as the WVS and Red Cross shepherded them to Southdown buses waiting to take them to Reception Centres for corned-beef sandwiches, bottles of milk and tearful billets. Across the nation hung an air of unreality overlaid with apprehension.

Diary, 3 September: 'WAR DECLARED ON GERMANY at 11.15 am! Dug bait. Went to church with mother in evening. Got in two bathes.'

'If you're going down to the beach', said my father, 'you ought to be back here by eleven to hear Chamberlain; this is history in the making, old chap.'

127 Staley's advertisement.

New Delivery of **COMPLETE BLACKOUT** Fabric

FINE BLACK TWILL ITALIAN CLOTH, 40 INCHES WIDE
1/11¼ per yard
(3 PIECES ONLY)

SUPERIOR QUALITY BLACK DOWNPROOF SATTEEN
48 INCHES WIDE
3/6 per yard
(1 PIECE ONLY)

Both of these Fabrics are absolutely effective.

STALEYS **BOGNOR REGIS**

Phone 224

Like millions of other families that Sunday morning, we gathered round the wireless; Downing Street and eleven strokes of Big Ben. Then the Prime Minister's crumpled voice; the melancholy reasons for the failure of the British Government's negotiations; the ultimatum sent to Hitler. At last came the kernel of his announcement, '... I have to tell you now that no such undertaking has been received and that, consequently, this country is at war with Germany.'

'Drawing pins!' cried my mother, responsible for our blackout. 'We've not a single one left and there were none in the shops yesterday.' 'Well, I've seen it coming for years,' growled my father. Later that day he returned to London to see how this momentous news was going to affect our daily bread. In the event of an air raid, he reckoned he'd be safe under the stairs of our house at Isleworth.

In the evening, carrying our respirators, my mother and I made our way to St Richard's church to pray that the Allies would win and no one we knew would get hurt. With my call-up date less than two years away, perhaps she said a special prayer for me. A few hours later the Germans sunk the SS *Athenia* with heavy loss of life including many children. But at Aldwick, twenty-four hours without bombs seemed to have induced a mood of unbridled recklessness:

> **Diary, 4 September**: 'To Pier. Caught a quite nice shoal-bass. Patched Li-Lo. Cycled to Pagham Harbour and Sidlesham. Very hot. Tried out new [bicycle] lamp-shield in black-out. Useless.'

With the longer nights, the blacked-out street lamps and the darkened shop windows turned the town into a camp of Stygian darkness inhabited by shadowy figures tripping over street kerbs and colliding with sandbags. Quickly the shops emptied of torches, batteries, blackout material and drawing pins.

One of the first victims of the Defence Regulations were the cinemas, which immediately closed. For most people – after the blackout – it was their first sacrifice for King and Country. It was also a measure felt deeply by myself, the more so as there was still no sign of any enemy air activity. However, on 12 September the Home Office relented.

> **Diary, 14 September**: 'Went fishing. No luck. In evening to cinema; *Lambeth Walk* with Lupino Lane. Jolly good. Warsaw still holding out. Petrol rationing soon.'

With the visitors gone, Bognor's residents could take stock of the war so far. Still filled with unsold goods – except the foodshops, due to 'hoarding' – display windows were rapidly disappearing behind a patterning of anti-shatter lattices and diamonds. In the streets notices began to appear pointing to Air Raid Shelters, Civil Defence, AFS and First Aid Posts. The tops of pillar boxes were painted with a pigment that turned them into gas indicators. At the Town Hall the ceiling of the Rates Department was strengthened with steel beams to act as an air-raid shelter. From Colebrook House, backsliders were still being issued with gasmasks. Forthwith, the buses travelling within sight of Tangmere aerodrome had their windows obscured and an armed soldier posted on the platform to discourage spies from taking photographs. At the Pavilion the new 'British Restaurant' was offering the cheapest lunches in town, 6d. for adults, 3d. children. In the surrounding countryside tractors and ploughs were gradually turning the grassland into arable as the farmers bowed to the Min of Ag's exhortation to 'Plough Now!'

Outside the Arcade the *Daily Mail* placard, 'War Latest; Poles Counter-attack', was a poignant reminder of a brave people being put to sword. But the housewives of Bognor could do nothing other than carry on with their shopping. Meanwhile, the County's Chief ARP Officer felt it necessary to issue a stern warning that respirator boxes were meant for gasmasks – not 'for storing blackberries and other fruits of the earth'.

But, gradually, life after dark became a little easier as the street-lamps were allowed a glimmer of light and the road signs were lowered to catch the reluctant glow from shrouded car lights. In the High Street the blued-out bus station took on the gloomy visage of a district morgue. On the unlit roads accidents mounted alarmingly. But if the roads suffered a surfeit of blackness, that wasn't the RAF's opinion of Bognor seen at night from the air. 'One of the worst blacked-out towns on the south coast', expostulated these connoisseurs of utter darkness.

And with that the air-raid wardens found a sense of purpose. To improve the town's standard of 'obscuration', they set about a campaign of knocking at doors and reprimanding householders for the smallest chinks of escaping light – although seemingly quite unconcerned for the all-illuminating flashes from the new electric trains. The trouble was we'd had no bombs!

It wasn't long before the Regional Commissioner, the Air Raid Controller and the ordinary wardens came to be regarded as Enemies of the People and 'Little Hitlers'. 'What did they do except listen to gas lectures and play darts during the day and emerge from their sandbag burrows at night to harass the innocent public?' wrote a wrathful correspondent to the *Post*. It was only after a minor bomb-fall in London Road nearly a year later that the air-raid wardens came to be seen in a more favourable light.

With the commencement of petrol rationing in October (120 miles a month), the number of cars in the town fell abruptly, bringing an unfamiliar quietness to the roads. Suddenly people's voices and footsteps sounded curiously louder, as struggling through the blackout proved a catalyst for shedding lifetimes of reserve. At the bus-stops complete strangers smiled at each other and embarked upon family histories while they waited for the arrival of the gloomily-lit 51 Circular Service. But the hotels and boarding-house proprietors were in sore straits. At a standing-room-only meeting at the Picturedrome, the Bognor Regis Hotels and Apartments Association complained that their businesses were being ruined by the Defence Regulations; 'from being a "boom" town it has become a "bust" one'. They demanded a hefty reduction in their rates.

> **Diary, 26 September**: 'Cycled over to Tangmere; usual Gladiators and Hurricanes. Also an Ensign. Went to flicks and saw *Ask a Policeman*. Very funny. In evening read *But Soft; We Are Observed* and listened to w'less.'

With no sign of action, the 'Bore War' continued to drag on through October into November. British nerve was tested by the *Tatler's* lament that 'hostilities are upon us just as cubbing begins' and by the notice in the *Observer* stating that 'in future the Cowdray Hounds will meet on Midhurst Common at ten o'clock instead of eleven to defeat the blackout'. Dances continued to be held at the Pavilion and at the *Elmer Hotel*. The Chesney Allens, Phyllis Robins and Vera Lynn were expected to share a table for Christmas dinner at Middleton's New Country Club while, at the Sports Club, 11-year-old Alan Loveday gave a violin recital accompanied by Mrs Millar on the piano. All the cinemas were open; so was Butlin's. And there was little – apart from No. 8 batteries and drawing pins – that couldn't be bought in the shops.

With all worthwhile 'war news' suppressed by D-notices, it was only a matter of time before the *Post* was 'reduced to twelve pages to conserve newsprint'. Bognorians became the anonymous 'inhabitants of a South Coast town'. With the cancellation of the Duke of Newcastle's scheme to build 250 houses near Betchworth in Surrey, my father's architectural practice suffered a body blow. Soon other jobs dissolved as his clients went off to war or to their air-raid shelters in the country. The office at Hanover Square had to be closed. No longer could we afford to run two houses and the one at Isleworth was let on a regulated rent to two sisters on 'work of national importance'. Petrol rationing meant the thirsty Packard spent most of its time in the drive. So my father bought a bike and changed from Abdulla cigarettes to Players Weights. Gradually our stringent economies began to bite.

The declaration of war also marked a change in my educational circumstances. Threatened with evacuation to far-off Wiltshire, I had left my West London school and the question was – what next? For the time being I signed on at the Chichester Art School, in those days above the Butter Market in North Street. Here it was hoped that, freed from the burden of Latin ablatives and the Dissolution of the Monasteries, those little signs of imagination and creativity I had occasionally displayed might be given room to grow. Under the critical eye of our 'instructor', Mr R.F. Champ ARCA, life drawing took the place of chemistry and history took on a new meaning with the study of the ancient constructions of Egypt, Greece and Rome. My father bought me a velvet-lined box of compasses, a drawing-board, and a mahogany tee-square embellished with my initials. Had the boy the talent to become an architect?

On most days, to save money, I cycled to and from Chichester. Thus, Morell's Farm, the *Royal Oak* at Lagness, Runcton's *Walnut Tree Inn*, the watercress beds at Vinnetrow Farm and Bartholomew's Mill at Bognor Bridge became the day-marks by which I measured time and distance. Glorious autumn mornings shared with untidy flocks of peewit contrasted with journeys home through impenetrable darkness in the course of which instinct rather than my defence-regulated cycle-lamp kept me out of the ditches. Sometimes my way was lit by the candle-power of the slender-fingered searchlights probing the sky over Hayling Island. But under the keen light of a full moon there was poetry in those leagues, dressed in their silver lace.

> **Diary, 23 November**: 'Dad down with billiard table. Forgot balls. Mended fence. In evening they went to the cinema. Stayed at home and worked on Riding Stables drawings. Listened to *Band Wagon*.'

Gradually our evenings became geared to listening to *Garrison Theatre, Hi-Gang* and Tommy Handley's imperishable *ITMA*, with its cast of highly imitable voices: Funf, Mrs Mopp and the Colonel ('I don't mind if I do'). Wednesday nights were the preserve of Sir Adrian Boult conducting the BBC Symphony Orchestra from Bedford. Together with J.B. Priestley's *Postscripts* and the *Midweek Matinee* voices of Carleton Hobbs, Norman Shelley and Patricia Burke, the BBC did its best to take our minds off the voice of the sneering Lord Haw Haw and the wicked magnetic mines.

On the sideboard, the Phoney War was reflected in our abandoned gasmasks languishing among the precious No. 8 batteries, the ear-plugs and the Ministry of Food's recipes for nettle purée and how to make a single egg do an omelette for six. Then, with the approach of that first wartime Christmas, the temperature began to drop. Soon Britain and the rest of Europe lay paralysed in the grip of the worst freeze-up since 1894. Our water main froze and had to be nursed back to health with the alchemy of blow-lamp and intemperate language.

In Bognor the wrapped-up crowds, obedient to the traders' entreaties to 'shop early and beat the blackout', bent to their Christmas victualling in the teeth of a bitter wind that swept down London Road and turned the Arcade into a wind tunnel. At Toyland, Goodacre's and Burgess' Bazaar parents spent far more on toys than they had ever intended – well, next year might there be any? And everywhere the 'Merry Christmas' message had to run the gauntlet of stern exhortations to 'Dig for Victory', 'Invest in War Savings', 'Walls have Ears' and 'Be like Dad – Keep Mum'. 'Courage, Resolution and Cheerfulness' was expected by the Home Office of every Bognorian.

Yet, there was still no shortage of a wide range of seasonal goods. Only the search for bananas, citrus fruits, marzipan and the crunchy kind of chocolate liqueurs turned a shopping trip into a treasure hunt. So it was to general rejoicing that my mother returned from a shopping trip bearing a wickered jar of preserved ginger! Thus, heroic deprivation was hardly the theme of our first wartime Christmas. As usual the decorations were pinned up; as usual the fairy lights failed to work because of the wrong plug. For the umpteenth time, Bennett's in Linden Road supplied our Christmas tree, specially trained to spread its needles all over the bungalow before Twelfth Night.

In the kitchen my mother busied herself with the Christmas pudding and mince pies made from carefully hoarded pre-war ingredients. From Targett's in West Bognor, a turkey, too late for seasonal resentment, awaited the oven and its call to higher duty. Then, the next thing we knew, it was that frost-brittle morning filled with 'Happy Christmas, dears', the rustle of presents being unwrapped and the crackle of a log fire burning in the grate. With touching gratitude, my father thanked me for my gift-wrapped pair of No. 8 batteries. From BARKER'S loudspeaker The Enigma Variations – a present from my mother – Elgared *fortissimo* the length and breadth of the bungalow. 'Would it not be a good idea if you all cleared off for a good long walk while I got on with the cooking?' suggested my mother.

Two hours later, famished and just in time for the 1 o'clock News, my father, his three sons and Judy – that bane of the burrowing classes – could have been found stumbling across the frozen corrugations of the Bottom Field, as they made their way back to the icy pavements and hoar-frosted roofs of Aldwick Gardens. Soon we were hanging up overcoats and kicking off wellies in a bungalow filled with the thyme-and-parsley smell of Christmas cooking.

'For what we are about to receive' … first helpings and seconds ('eat up the sprouts, there's a good boy'); crackers with mottoes of familiar banality, whistles, snow-storms and paper hats; then the Christmas pudding in flames. 'Might I play the 'Nimrod' bit once more?' – well, at least it was a change from Jack Payne banging out 'The Flat Foot Floogie with the Floy Floy'! My father leaned over and gave my mother a 'thankyou' kiss for the delicious spread. Then, with becoming ostentation, he lit up his last peace-time Cuban Corona, made perfect by being rolled on a dusky maiden's thigh – well, that's what he said, honestly!

Nineteen more renditions of 'Hark The Herald Angels', 33 of 'Run Rabbit Run' and heaven knows how many sessions of Sandy MacPherson on the BBC Theatre Organ and, lo, it was New Years Eve. We heard it in on BARKER'S: Will Fyffe in the studio and the Lord Archbishop of Canterbury at Lambeth Palace, twelve strokes of Big Ben, *Auld Lang Syne* and a Watchnight Service. My father took a tin tray and banged it merrily outside in the snow-mantled garden. And so the family found itself in 1940 with history still playing its cards pretty close to its chest.

Cycling to and from Chichester during that bitterly cold winter was a trial of endurance in the face of blinding snow, ice and slush. On the worst days I was allowed the luxury of the centrally-heated 59 Midhurst bus as it prowled the frost-trampled stops, scooping up the little knots of Chichester High School pupils filled with early morning chatter and their 'war work' elders wrapped in after-breakfast silence.

But retracing that serpentine, ice-covered road, in a bus with shrouded lights, made heroes of our drivers. After Runcton I was often the only passenger left. Then the conductor would divest himself of his ticket-machine, put his feet up on a seat, light a fag and invite me to philosophic discussion. At Hewarts Lane a glimpse of the 'Royal Key to Health' sign was followed by the manurey smell of Aldwick Farm. 'Slated Barn coming up,' said my friend as he rang the bell. The bus slowed to a halt under the elm. 'Goodnight, Guv.' 'Goodnight.' Ding-ding.

From my drawing-board above the cheesy aroma of John Nash's Butter Market, there flowed – trickled is, perhaps, a better word – those encouraging signs of hesitant creativity. I tried my hand at drawing from the 'antique' and did my term of 'life' *viz* the female nude. Oh! but how to square the blushing instinct to avert my eyes from a lady in so vulnerable a state of déshabillé with the academic necessity of having to examine closely each pendulous breast, bulging thigh and roll of fat about her ribs?

I designed a riding stables and a house in a forest; another exercise was to measure and draw one of the Wren House fireplaces, with my instructor approving of the result. At night, making careful notes, I plodded through Ruskin's *Stones of Venice* and Banister Fletcher's *History of Architecture on the Comparative Method*. And, in between, I became seduced by the designs of Frank Lloyd Wright, Corbusier and Mies van der Rohe from the pages of the *Architectural Review*.

In summer, for lunch, I bought pork pies from Kimbell's in East Street and ate them under the Cathedral's buttresses; in winter I bought pork pies from Kimbell's and heated them up on the model's four-bar fire – until Mr Champ complained that my share of their electricity bill far exceeded my whack in fees. But by that time the school was beginning to empty of pupils. Sometimes I seemed the only person left in the building.

Said Mr Churchill: 'More than a million German soldiers ... are drawn up, ready to attack at a few hours notice all along the frontiers of Luxembourg, Belgium and Holland. At any moment these neutral countries may be subjected to an avalanche of steel and fire' (in a world broadcast, 30 March 1940).

At last the departing redwing and the unfolding buds of March shouldered that bruising winter of 1940 into folklore and set a path for spring. Soon my journeys to Chichester were rewarded with the warm scent of mayflower and the songs of chiff-chaff and whitethroat debating, or the sweetness of the skylark's voice bubbling above the fields of grazing cows from Aldwick Farm. Each day I pedalled past the smelly wash from Crimsham Farm, past the half-way *Walnut Tree* and on to Heaver's Pit* where the clattering machinery spawned their gravel tumuli, ivory against a spring-blue sky. But now we had the thunder of the Hawker Hurricanes, as their pilots practised killing games above the Sussex Plain. For that fateful day in May was drawing nigh.

> **Diary, 10 May 1940**: 'Things are beginning to happen! The German Army has attacked Belgium and Holland! Churchill now Prime Minister. Played tennis; muscles still stiff. Discussed lettuces with Firemen.'

For the rest of the day the family became glued to BARKER'S as we devoured the flood of communiques, bulletins and newsflashes pouring from its speakers. The BBC newsreaders, as a measure of security, suddenly dropped their traditional anonymity and divulged their names. Soon we could differentiate between the voices of Alvar Lidell and Frank Phillips, or Stuart Hibberd and Bruce Belfrage.

Hastily my father consulted our *Daily Express* war map; for heaven's sake where were Moerdjik, Maastricht and the River Meuse? Should we stick our coloured pins into Gronigen, Tongres and Dinant? Then came the news that Rotterdam had been bombed and captured by sky-borne troops. So this was the war for which we had waited! Somehow, it seemed difficult to believe it was really happening. But we needn't have bothered about coloured

---

* Now the Southern Leisure Centre.

pins. For only a few days later the newsreaders were intoning locations more familiar; the Maginot Line ignominiously by-passed and left in the German Army's wake as the Panzers streamed through Sedan and the dark forests of the Ardennes. On the 18th St Quentin fell; then Arras and Cambrai.

> **Diary, 19 May**: 'Planted lettuces. Things not going too well in France. Amiens and Abbeville have fallen. Took Judy down to beach for walk. Got on with perspective. Mrs Gentle's chimney caught fire. Listened to Churchill.

> **Diary, 24 May**: 'Dad down from London. In evening took Judy for walk on beach. Heard rumble of gunfire from east and saw smoke on horizon. Very bad news from France. Started *How Green is my Valley* by A.J. Cronin. Aunt Marjory to tea.'

Of course, no one doubted the Allies were going to win. Yet the position still sounded a bit disturbing. Confidently, though, we awaited the great counter-attack which would restore our national pride and military fortunes. Instead the picture grew only more grave as the sweeping black arrows on the *Daily Telegraph* war map began swinging northward when Von Kliest's panzers headed for Boulogne and Calais. Then it began to sink in: the BEF was all but trapped!

By command of the King, Sunday 26 May was designated a National Day of Prayer. Less than forty-eight hours later came the shattering news of the Belgian capitulation. Now it became clear that the British Army was in full retreat, their goal a beach-head on the Channel coast. For a few days the news was opaque. Suddenly the eyes of the world became focused on the little French port of Dunkirk. On that same 26 May the BBC broadcast an enigmatic message instructing small boat owners 'to proceed to the usual assembly points'. Security inhibited more. Within hours, from Margate to Cowes, skippers of the 'little boats' were weighing anchor for their journey to the Dover ports, unguessed at dangers and the greatest seaborne rescue in history: Operation Dynamo.

At Bognor, Bob Ragless, skipper of the seventy-seater pleasure boat *Bluebird*, also heard the call. So did Billy Welfare Senior, in charge of *Silver Spray*. Soon the two boats were ploughing their way towards Rye Harbour. Shaping a course in that direction, too, was the RNLI's Eastbourne boat, the old *Jane Holland* I had last seen at Selsey in 1927. From William Osborne's yard at Littlehampton, the cabin cruisers *Gwen Eagle* and *Bengeo* slid down the Arun and swung on to an easterly bearing. 'The situation of the British and French armies now engaged in a most severe battle and beset on three sides and from the air is evidently extremely grave … meanwhile the House should prepare itself for hard and heavy hearings', warned a sonorous Winston Churchill in the House of Commons (28 May 1940).

Less sonorous my diary for the same day:

> **Diary, 28 May**: 'With John (Allen) to Butlin's. Had long ride on Dodgems for only a tanner. Listened to wireless in evening. British Army withdrawing to coast. All terribly serious. Mowed lawn. Saw heron over Dark Lane.'

Meanwhile, in the air, the Tangmere squadrons were among the Sector A fighters ordered, day after day, to patrol the pitiless Dunkirk beaches and the French hinterland. Between 20 and 27 May, in air battles over Arras, Bethune, St Pol and Dunkirk, 145 Squadron accounted for 11 of the enemy at the cost of six of their own with three pilots saved. On 1 June, at odds of seven to one, No. 43 Squadron, lately returned from Scotland, shot down nine Huns and damaged six others at the cost of one pilot lost and one wounded. But on the 7th, over Amiens, the tables were turned when Messerschmitts made spiteful play with 43's Hurricanes; eight were lost although six pilots made it back to Tangmere.

And all the while, thousands of feet below the weaving RAF fighters, the 'little boats', the paddle-steamers, destroyers, dredgers and trawlers laboured with tireless valour for eight long days and nights to perform the 'Miracle of Dunkirk'. By 3 June more than 224,000 men of the BEF had been returned to their native shore, surprised to find themselves regarded as unwashed and unshaven heroes. 'Bognor men safely back' read the *Observer's* headline triumphantly on 18 June.

After it had made a number of trips to the Dunkirk beaches in the hands of a Royal Navy crew, the Admiralty requisitioned the 1929-built *Bluebird*, decked-out and fitted her with bunks at Osborne's Littlehampton yard, and sent her as deck-cargo to the Mediterranean. There, the little Bognor boat served as a hospital tender during the Siege of Tobruk. In 1945 she was returned to England and, after being remodified, found her way to St Mawes in Cornwall where Vanessa Mills tells me she saw her earning a living as a ferry in 1991.

Now the word 'invasion' hung on every lip. With the Army in a calamitous state, only the Royal Navy and Fighter Command of the RAF stood between our island and Hitler's voracious military machine drawn up twenty miles from Dover and only eighty from Aldwick's sands. In the newspapers appeared the silhouettes of German troop-carrier planes we could shortly expect to see. Within a few days an array of wooden scaffold poles, discarded agricultural machinery and broken-down cars began spreading over the local fields to prevent the enemy's gliders and planes from landing. Even the trunks of the Bay Estate palm trees, killed off by the bitter winter, found a last and valiant role.

Name-boards which might have helped disoriented invaders establish their whereabouts were hastily removed. The large BOGNOR REGIS sign on the signal box by the level-crossing was among the first to go; quickly, the town's name was painted-out on the station seats. No sign was too small to qualify. They disappeared from the estate agents' flag-boards, from the sides of lorries, delivery vans and shop blinds. Soon the directional road signs vanished, too, until there were only a couple left which might have helped the enemy: one was outside Bognor's Town Hall and the other, incised in stone, gazed down from over the new Fire Station in Clarence Road. Of course, the immediate effect of all this anonymity was to spread untold confusion among the innocent visitors, assuming they could even find the town in the first place!

But whither Bognor's military defences in that early summer of 1940? To begin with, the town found itself in the defence area allocated to 3 Division under the command of the then little-known General B.G. Montgomery. But, by the beginning of July, their place had been taken by the 10th Infantry Brigade of 4 Division, lately returned from France. Quickly, the townsfolk became familiar with one of their units, the 2nd Battalion of the Beds and Herts, charged with guarding Bognor's coast. These excerpts from their Regimental War Diary shows a nation awaiting a cataclysmic event:

2 July. 'Information rec'vd that paratroops expected imminently. Work continues on Battalion defences.' [Anti-invasion measures]

6 July. 'One Tommy-gun received for instruction.'

11 July. '10.38 am, message rec'vd that enemy craft approaching Portsmouth. Work continues on Battalion defences.'

12 July. 'REs started work building concrete blocks; 4ft. cubes weighing 8 tons. [Generally, they were 6ft. cubes and weighed nearer 14 tons.]

20 July. 'Curfew established on front. Civilians must be away by 21.30 hrs. Cycle patrols over defence area. Observation points instituted at [*inter alia*] Pagham Point, Lidsey Lodge, the Salt House, Morells Farm and Gasworks. Liason exercise with LDVs. Level crossing and Felpham bridge [*inter alia*]; holes dug for mining.'

4 Aug. 'Heavy sea-mist. Special attention required. 28 civilian m/cycles received for patrolling. Battalion defence work continues.'

13 Aug. 'Heavy explosions and smoke from W. Wittering direction.'

16 Aug. '13.00 hrs. 42 Ju.88s attacked Tangmere 7 down.' [Wrong in almost every detail!]

Around the south-east coast the Army, aided by 150,000 civilians, set about the Herculean task of surrounding the beaches, dunes and promenades with mines, barbed wire and concrete blocks. At Bognor, Royal Engineer Field Companies began erecting anti-invasion barriers constructed from miles of tubular scaffolding. Armed strong points disguised as ice-cream kiosks appeared in the East and West Car Parks. A concrete pill-box was constructed at the bottom of Nyewood Lane. Another arose near the *Nelson Arms* on the A259. In due course the Marine Café – once our ice-cream mecca – became the cookhouse for the Royal Fusiliers. At the other end of the Esplanade the Eastern Bandstand was demolished to prevent it fouling the field of fire from the Army's nearly non-existent guns. In Aldwick Avenue, mere camouflage netting failed to disguise the arrival in the garden of Mrs Shippam's house, Sea Marge, of a 5.5 inch ex-naval gun manned by the Royal Artillery.

To deny the invaders a toe-hold on Bognor's promenade three bays of the Pier were blown up – breaking nearby windows in the process. Garnished with rolls of barbed wire and sandbags, with a pom-pom and an Oerlikon machine-gun mounted at its sea-end, it became a Royal Naval Observation Post with the name of HMS *St Barbara*, the theatre destined to become a gunnery lecture hall.

Sir Anthony Eden's earlier call on 14 May for Local Defence Volunteers had fallen on ready ears. Spontaneously, leaders stepped forward. At the

128 At Tangmere the Hurricanes wait ... and wait.

Pavilion on the 19th of that month Colonel Jackman addressed 500 men, many of them Great War veterans. That night, for the first time since the Bognor Fencibles had stood-by to repel Napoleon's army in 1800, patrols were sent out to protect Britain's shores from the threat of invasion by an enemy far more formidable.

Bognor's LDV platoon was led by Colonel Jackman and by Colonel Byrne, a legend with the bat at Bognor's Cricket Club. At Aldwick, Colonel Gamble and Captain Freddie Watson, both of Aldwick Hundred, paraded their men outside their HQ in Wychwood Close. Other platoons were raised at North Bersted and Pagham. On 9 June Mr Jack Langmead's 200-strong platoon was inspected by General Ashmore at the Middleton Sports Club. My father joined up and received his LDV armband, and Roger remembers being taken by him to a demonstration of molotov cocktails at the cricket ground in Hawthorn Road.

> **Diary, 13 June**: 'Made two blocks for Chichester Art Society mono-gram. Air-raid siren at 1.30 pm. Nothing happened. Did sketch of Yeoman's Acre stile.'

That air-raid alert was to be the first of many. To mark for posterity every siren wail we heard during that momentous summer, we drove a one-inch nail into a piece of wooden board. Soon we had to call at George White's for more nails!

> **Diary, 18 June**: 'Helped Dad put up wire-mesh fence for chickens. Bought Blue Eagle tennis racquet; lovely job 30s. Played Ken and beat him 6-3, 1-6, 6-2. Two bathes. The French all but finished by the sound of it. Listened to Mr Churchill in evening.'

Our ally's difficulties and Winston Churchill's 'finest hour' speech apart, it is the 'chickens' in that entry which introduced a new dimension to our wartime lives – and larder. They had their roots in a sudden faltering in the supply of real eggs which our dietically-correct mother regarded as funda-mental to her family's health at a time when the choice of food was becoming more restricted. The taste of reconstituted-egg omelettes proved a salutary experience and galvanised her into action in a quite unexpected direction.

129 Bognor, defended by a pea-shooter and a posse of Top Brass, awaits the enemy onslaught. A posed photograph taken by Frank L'Alouette on behalf of the Ministry of Information, June 1940.

'If we have plenty of eggs, my dears,' she declared, 'then at least we shan't starve.' And with that my good mother was off to W.H. Smith's for a book on chicken culture. Within a few days the garden shed was requisitioned to become the hen house and half the hallowed lawn was coralled-off with wire netting. With curiosity, we awaited the arrival of a dozen 'point of lay' Light Sussex pullets from Eastergate. Soon the smell of boiling chicken mash and balancer meal began to permeate every room in the bungalow.

Success was not immediate. My mother was forbearing; perhaps they were only 'point-of-thinking-about-laying' birds. Then, one morning, there was a triumphal whoop from the direction of the chicken house and into the kitchen she swept, proudly holding a rather small, grubby egg. It was the first of thousands our hens were to lay for us during the war. I still treasure my mother's 'chicken book' although not so much for the astronomical numbers of eggs produced by her 'gals' during those years of rationing and shortages, as for her scribbled notes in the margins.*

* For example: '**June 6 1944**. Light Sussex in broody pen. "Speckles" definitely egg eater! Wakeful night. 8 o'clock news of invasion of Europe via mouth of Seine and Cherbourg! Planes with green lights that we saw last night were parachute carriers. Terrific air activity all day. ... **August 27 1944**. Flying bomb in Bognor; terrific damage. Roger to the rescue! Not many eggs today. [My brother was in a Rescue Party stationed at Aldwick. The scene of the incident was Shelley Road.] ... **February 23 1945**. Cooke's chickens very fit, laying like mad. Allies in Cologne. Pullet broody. ... **May 8 1945**. Unconditional surrender! Bonfire! ... **July 23 1945**. Put 4 doz eggs in waterglass. 1st street lamp lighted in Aldwick Gardens; great excitement. Crowds stood round to admire!'

Diary, 25 June: 'Air-raid alert 12.10-2.15 am. Nothing happened. Bought tennis balls. Played Ken on Swansea courts. France has capitulated. Miss Spiridion to tea in garden. Alert 1.30-3.35 pm.'

Diary, 3 July: 'Air-raid shelter started. Alert at 12.20 am. Bombs dropped in sea off Craigweil. Rumour that Prom is to be subjected to a curfew. Said I would help Mr Field with his shelter. 2 alarms later in morning.'

Diary, 5 July: 'School. Started Trajan lettering exercise. Went to lecture on Renaissance Art VG. Beach closed as we are now in a Defence Area. 10 pm Curfew in Bognor. Chatted to Firemen in evening. V. nice chaps.'

The Chief Constable's fiat that forthwith the beach was to be closed and a 10 p.m. curfew imposed on the Promenade brought the war home to us with a jolt as we bade au revoir to Aldwick sands for the next four years.

From 10 July, the Germans began trailing their coat over the North Sea and Channel convoys in an attempt to lure the RAF into combat – and speedy attrition. It is from this date the Battle of Britain is deemed to have begun.

Diary, 11 July: 'Air-raid alert 6-7.05 pm. Heavy artillery and machine-gun fire from west of Pagham Harbour. AA puffs over Portsmouth. Saw 4 He.111s accompanied by Me.109s. 4 down. Helped Dad with air-raid shelter. 12 air-raid warnings so far.'

130 An ex-naval gun being manhandled into the garden of Sea Merge in Aldwick Avenue.

131 Hawker Hurricanes of 601 Squadron being re-fuelled at Tangmere during the Battle of Britain. The rightmost figure in a peaked cap is Squadron Leader Max Aitken, their Commander.

The Luftwaffe mounted a heavy raid on Portsmouth at about 6 p.m. What we heard was the destruction of an He.111 which was shot down on East Beach, Selsey at 6.15 p.m. by 145 Squadron from Tangmere. The '4 down' figure, like most estimates of enemy planes destroyed during the Battle of Britain, was highly suspect.

At about 5.15 p.m. on 19 July, six 43 Squadron Hurricanes were 'bounced' by Me.109s. Sgt. Buck was drowned at sea. Another plane belonged to Fl. Lt. J.W.C. Simpson who, after shooting down an Me.109, was himself shot down off Felpham. He baled out and landed safely in a cucumber frame at Worthing.

> **Diary, 26 July**: 'Dad down for weekend. Cycled to Midhurst. New aerodrome near Goodwood. We are now out of Curfew Area so beach may be re-opened. Alerts at 9.47-10.25 am and 12 noon-12.55 pm. 25 nails in board.

This was Westhampnett aerodrome, a satellite of Tangmere. The morning alert was due to an enemy attack on a convoy off the Isle of Wight.

Inspired by the great air battles taking place over south-east England, 'Spitfire Funds' to raise the £5,000 cost of a fighter were inaugurated all over the country. At Bognor it was launched by the *Bognor Regis Post*. With patriotic generosity, the Aldwick Home Guard Platoon donated their July government allowance to the fund which, on the 10 August, stood at £873. By 2 November it had risen to £1,491; the Odeon cinema added £43 3s. 4d. Although the full sum was never reached, on 16 May 1942 a cheque for £2,660 18s. 3d. was handed over to the Ministry of Aircraft Production. In the same selfless spirit, Bognor's housewives responded to the Ministry of

Supply's appeal for aluminium pots and pans for making into aircraft. Soon the WVS were standing over an ever-growing mountain of saucepans at the Gas Company's premises at No. 7 London Road.

Another Ministry campaign was for scrap metal for turning into munitions. A ready source were the wrought- and cast-iron gates and railings surrounding public gardens, country estates and great houses. At Aldwick Place Mrs Margaret Rank felt it a privilege to hand over Baron Grant's gates for smashing up and loading onto lorries. The railings to Aldwick Grange and Waterloo Square swiftly followed them. Much of this scrap was never used and the nation was needlessly deprived of many irreplaceable works of the blacksmith's and founder's art – but that is being wise after the event.

> **Diary, 12 August**: 'Air-raid warnings at 9.37-9.50 am and 11.55-1.05 pm. Terrific gunfire and heavy bombing over Pompey. Air fight off Bognor. Another alert at 10-2.15 pm. To Odeon and saw *Let George Do It*. Quite funny. Goldfinches in garden. Fed horse in Bottom Field.'

The 'air fight' involved a flight of Hurricanes from 213 Squadron stationed at Exeter which tangled with German fighters off Bognor, resulting in the loss of two of their aircraft with their pilots.

> **Diary, 15 August**: 'Air-raid alarms 7.40-8.20 am and 5.25-7.50 pm. Much AA fire and machine-gunning. Saw Ju.88 being chased by Hurricanes. Helped with threshing at Hammonds Barn. Told Ju.88 down near Earnley. On news 182 Huns down – greatest number so far! Yippee! Another air-raid alert 11.47-11.57 pm.'

The widespread raids of the 15th proved to be the Luftwaffe's maximum effort during the Battle. Again, though, the number of enemy aircraft destroyed – often compiled in the heat of battle – proved greatly exaggerated and was later adjusted to 75. But history confirms it was still a glorious victory which finally marked the failure of the Luftwaffe's attempt to defeat the RAF.

By the middle of August 1940, though, air-raid warnings had become endemic. We became used to a background of mysterious thuds and bangs, the abstract patterns of vapour trails and the roar of Rolls-Royce Merlins overhead. So, on the 16th, having had three false alarms already between midnight and midday, we didn't take too much notice when, just before lunch, the Steam Laundry siren in Hawthorn Road wailed yet again. A squadron of Hurricanes climbed over Pagham heading in the general direction of Selsey. Not long afterwards came the muffled rumblings of a fierce action out of sight.

But hardly had I put on a gramophone record to take us up to the 1 o'clock News than we heard the sound of more aircraft overhead, but these had an engine note strange to our ears. Rushing out into the garden, followed by Judy – who loved any kind of 'rushing' – my brother and I peered up into the sky. Our sharp eyes quickly picked up 13 aircraft flying at a great height in close formation, their silhouettes and duck-egg blue undersides unmistakable; Ju.87b's – Stukas … and flying north. Gosh! Tangmere! My mother's plea for us to come in and finish our lunch went unheeded.

132 The skeins of battle.

To get a better view we stood on the arch of the garden fountain. Half a minute later we could still see the formation faintly as they reached their target. Suddenly the Stukas began to up-end as they commenced their pitiless dives, almost leisurely at first, but swiftly gathering speed as they howled down on their target. All at once great fountains of brown smoke and debris erupted against the outline of the Downs. Seconds later our ears were assailed by the mighty 'woomphs' of exploding bombs and the angry response from the airfield's defences.

On the aerodrome: devastation. The cathedral-like hangars lay collapsed in a tangle of twisted roof trusses and fallen masonry; personnel lay mortally wounded, torn apart by flying steel; precious aircraft and many motor vehicles blazed fiercely among the dust-laden chaos and unexploded bombs. Gradually a great mushroom of smoke spread over the station. And, with it, a short-lived hush fell upon the countryside.

Through the open French windows, opposing the evil that lurked in the afternoon sky, flowed the rousing march 'Northwards' from Eric Coates' 'Four Ways Suite', our preferred background music for watching air battles. But all too quickly this was drowned by the whine of overstretched Jumo engines as the attackers surged into view over Miss Bradshaw's house opposite, fleeing at tree-top level towards the Channel and the safety of their Brittany lairs.

But for many it was too late. For it was just then that the Ju.87b's of Stukageschwader II's 3rd Staffel ran into the arms of 43 Squadron returning from breaking up the Luftwaffe formations over Bembridge. It was supported now by 601 County of London Squadron led by none other than Squadron Leader Sir Archibald Clinton-Pelham-Hope – son and heir of the Duke of Newcastle – and was quickly joined by 602 Squadron's Spitfires up from Westhampnett (whose CO, on seeing Tangmere attacked, had taken off without the Group Controller's permission). The three squadrons now set about exacting retribution from the marauders.

Before our astonished eyes, across the skies over Aldwick, Rose Green and Nyetimber, a roof-top air battle developed, savage and patternless; a melée of aircraft flying in all directions to the chattering accompaniment of machine-guns and the sound of tortured engines. The combined firepower of a Hurricane and a Spitfire knocked bits off one of the Stukas; another raider was being chased back towards Tangmere before suddenly turning south again, dropping earthwards. Attempting to avoid its assailant's guns, yet another, its swastikas clearly visible, jinked and twisted desparately over our heads before it was lost to view beyond the Dark Lane elms. At Runcton spent bullets broke greenhouse panes and links of ammo-belt tinkled down in Rose Green Road.

133 At 1 p.m. on 16 August 1940 Mr Frank L'Alouette, Bognor's official war photographer, happened to be near Colworth railway bridge just as the German Stukas began their attack on Tangmere aerodrome.

Meanwhile, on the loggia, Judy lay panting, curious in her spaniel mind as to what kind of noisy game this was meant to be! Within minutes it was all over. As the sound of aircraft died away, a deep silence descended upon Aldwick Gardens. Soon, the loudest sounds were the voices of neighbours as they emerged from their houses, many of them suggesting hopefully that all the German planes had been shot down.

Over at Tangmere, the RAF contemplated its shattered aerodrome,* while continuing to refuel and re-arm the Hurricanes whose pilots were to labour long into the dusk of that sultry summer's day. But at least 601 Squadron had the additional satisfaction, a couple of hours later, of seeing their CO bring down an Me.110 in the grounds of Shopwyke House.

Not wishing to provoke unduly the attention of the Luftwaffe, my mother had moved the wobbly tea table from the garden to the shelter of the loggia. And it was while we were seated there, about to start on the marrow-jam sandwiches, that the bush-telegraph brought to our ears the news that one of the Stukas had come down by the Pagham Rife – 'over Sefter School way'. Hastily excusing ourselves, my brother and I grabbed our bikes. Soon we were making our way across the little packhorse bridge that led to Bowley Farm.

And there it was, a Ju.87b, dark, sinister – and much the worse for wear: peppered with bullet holes, its wing-tips reduced to tatters and the propeller smashed to firewood from having flown through a belt of trees. The

* The Station Records show that three civilians and ten RAF personnel were killed and another 20 injured. In addition three radar-equipped Blenheims of the Fighter Interceptor Unit were written off and four damaged. Seven Hurricanes and a Miles Magister were also damaged. Much motor transport, too, was destroyed.

134 Wrecked from flying through a belt of trees, this Ju.87b, its gunner dead and pilot mortally wounded, crash-landed on Bowley Farm near Sefter School after attacking Tangmere aerodrome, 16 August 1940.

mortally injured pilot, his gunner dead, had managed to land the plane more or less in one piece. Black, sour-smelling oil dripped from its still-warm engine; blood spattered the cockpit canopy through which the rear gun still pointed menacingly. On the ground lay pieces of torn metal and a map-case. To record the event for posterity, Frank L'Alouette, Bognor's official war photographer, was there to take the picture which appears above. Later we learned that the mortally wounded pilot had been removed to hospital and his gunner to the mortuary.* But this maimed and humiliated Stuka served to convince us that the war was as good as won!

Two days later there was more excitement. From early morning on 18 August it had been nothing but air-raid warnings right up to lunch-time at 4.23 a.m., 11 o'clock and again just after 1 p.m., with the all-clear sounding some fifty minutes later. So far, though, there was nothing to show for them around Bognor. Anyway, it seemed a good opportunity to take Judy for 'walkies' in Yeoman's Acre. And it was while she was snuffling around in her favourite ditch that the air-raid siren wailed again. Almost immediately the western sky seemed full of Hurricanes. From the Selsey direction came the sound of guns and the crash of bombs as the Luftwaffe put its mind to the elimination of Thorney Island aerodrome. Another group of dive bombers, meanwhile, was on its way to deliver the *coup de grâce* to Gosport aerodrome. But faulty intelligence had led the enemy to make their main target of that afternoon the harmless Fleet Air

---

* Initially the bodies of both crew, Oberfeldwebel Willi Witt, the pilot, and his gunner, Feldwebel Heinz Rockstascel, were buried at the Portsdown Military Cemetery, but in the 1960s they were re-interred at the German Military Cemetery at Cannock Chase, Staffordshire.

135 Ford aerodrome blazes after being attacked by German dive bombers on 18 August 1940.

Arm training establishment at Ford in the mistaken belief that it was an RAF fighter station.

A little after 2.30 p.m., residents on the front at Felpham and Middleton had a ringside view as a line of thirty Ju.87b's of StG77, protected by nearly as many Messerschmitt 109s, flew past them on their way to bringing to an end the useful lives of HMS *Peregrine* and the frail-looking radar masts at Poling. A minute or two later came the air-compressing crash of a sustained tattoo of exploding bombs as the attack began; then the far-off sound of machine-gun fire and glimpses of dot-sized aircraft wheeling in the hazy sky as 602's Spitfires mixed it with the German bandits. Distant fire-engine bells signalled the AFS units hurrying to the scene – including the pump from the Aldwick Gardens station. At Littlehampton people saw a blazing Ju.87 go into the sea. On Elmer beach young Sgt Basil Whall had to be helped ashore from his ditched Spitfire, having earlier shot down two Junkers, one of which came down nearly intact on Ham Manor golf course, and thereby contributed to his eventual award of the DFM. Pilot Officer H.W. Moody, his Spitfire badly savaged, had no option but to land his plane through the smoke on Ford itself. The raid cost the enemy four Stukas shot down, but a Hurricane and its pilot were lost at sea. Meanwhile, on fire-swept HMS *Peregrine*, 28 naval personnel lay dead, another 70 injured. Ruptured fuel tanks and workshops blazed; a dozen Blackburn Sharks, Albacores and Fairey Swordfishes had been destroyed and an equal number damaged. In one of the hangars Sir Alan Cobham's Flight Refuelling AW23 and two of his Handley Page tankers had come temporarily to the end of their flying days. And so, too, for the time being, had Ford aerodrome. A few weeks later the station was paid-off pending repair and refurbishment, before being taken over by the RAF in November.

This seemed quite enough 'walkies' for one afternoon! So, putting Judy on the lead, I set off home. But barely had I reached our garden than I heard bursts of machine-gun fire from over Pagham way. In the sky was the silhouette of a flaming Hurricane spiralling earthwards; of a parachute, no sign. Seconds later a column of black smoke rising from near Summer Lane at Nyetimber marked the death of Sgt. Redvers Hawkings of 601 Squadron from Tangmere, another name on the long Roll of Honour. That evening the firemen at the Slated Barn AFS post showed us a brass hose-nozzle full of shrapnel dents they had retrieved from the Ford station fire engine which had received a near-miss. It is now on display at the West Sussex Fire Brigade Headquarters at Chichester.

> **Diary, 26 August**: 'Alerts 12.50-1.15 pm, 1.50-1.55 pm, 4.15-5.45 pm. Big air battle over Selsey, 2 Huns shot down. One of ours lost but pilot baled out and landed in sea off Pier. Rescued by fishermen unharmed. Saw him brought ashore. Went to flicks and saw *Charlie's Big Hearted Aunt*. Not v. good. Alarm 10.55-11.25 pm. Searchlights but nothing happened.'

At about 4.30 that afternoon, I happened to be cleaning my bike when the far-off sound of aircraft engines and the crackle of machine-gun fire made me look up. High in the sky over Selsey a little white blob hung like a sixpence – a parachute. Slowly it descended, drifting eastwards along the coast, its pendent flier anonymous. One of ours or one of theirs? And it took a long time to come down; three or four minutes. At last the dangling figure disappeared behind the Aldwick Place elms. By then Ernie Ragless' boat was on its way to rescue the pilot – although not before he had enlisted the help of two soldiers from the Beds and Herts, armed with rifles. Well, you could never be too sure! He turned out to be Sgt Cyril Babbage, whose Westhampnett-based Spitfire had been shot down by an Me.109 during an abortive raid on Portsmouth.

Babbage seems to have enjoyed a charmed life. On 14 September he made a forced landing at Shoreham after a fight over Beachy Head, the 27th saw his plane damaged by a Ju.88 over Dungeness, and on 12 October, he put his plane on its back during an emergency landing in a field at Iford, near Lewes. Ernie Ragless,who kept in touch with him, told me that he died in his bed at Gloucester in 1989.

That August, of 1940, the Channel was stained red with blood. Only a few days after he had rescued Babbage, Ernie found the bullet-ridden body of an RAF Flight Lieutenent floating in the sea, still attached to his parachute. He tied it to a buoy and called the Air-Sea Rescue people. In the House of Commons Winston Churchill spoke of Fighter Command's travail: 'Never before in the field of human conflict was so much owed by so many to so few.'

> **Diary, 29 August**: 'Went into town. Bought *Trent's Last Case* (Bentley). In evening over to Rife. Came back with dive-brake from Ju.87b.'

The forlorn Stuka still stood near the Pagham Rife where it had come down 11 days earlier. The gawpers having gawped their fill, I decided to have a last

136 Spitfire pilot Sgt. Cyril Babbage is brought ashore, none the worse for his ducking. The group in the picture are, left to right, Albe Ide, Ernie Ragless, two soldiers, Babbage, Nelson Ide and another soldier.

look myself – and perhaps pick up some trivial memento, a rivet or a piece of bent metal. With studied indifference I strolled round the machine, watched with matching indifference by two privates of the Beds and Herts Regiment sitting on the tail-board of their Morris van. Somehow we fell to chatting. Clearly, guarding two tons of junk aluminium had lost its appeal. So when I mentioned trivial mementos, they seemed suddenly to scent escape to a life more purposeful. And that was when three pairs of eyes fell shamelessly upon the Stuka's loose port dive-brake. Even with the contents of their vehicle's tool-box it took quite a lot of getting off. But at last it lay in the grass at my feet. So, after thanking my browned-off collaborators for their assistance, I set off on my bike carrying the dive-brake over my shoulder.

All went well until I arrived at Aldwick crossroads – for coming towards me was a policeman on a bike! Suddenly my air-brake felt about fifty feet long! But the mind of the Law must have been more on the prospect of its Woolton Pie supper than on the entrails of a defunct German bomber; at any rate, he cycled past unseeing either of me or of my ill-gotten trophy. A few minutes later I was safely home. But the glory days of showing-off my loot to friends and impressionable relations were fairly short-lived. Quite soon my mother claimed it enjoyed neither beauty nor purpose, and the air-brake was consigned to the loft. And there it mouldered for the best part of half a century until, in 1986, it began a new lease of life at Tangmere's Military Aviation Museum where it has been reunited with all the other miscellanea from the Bowley Farm Stuka. (Roger also did some collecting from this Stuka and still has one of its panels, showing production number

5618, with a bullet hole through it. This panel retained that sour oily smell for years.)

> **Diary, 9 September**: 'To Slinfold with Dad. Ju.88 down off Craigweil. One of crew found dead in Willowhale Ave. Listened to wireless and read in evening. No. 17 Avenue Road [near our Isleworth house] has received a direct hit.'

> **Diary, 14 September**: '2.30 pm. Bombs dropped in London Road. Knight's shop wrecked also house in Den Ave. Bought *The Hound of the Baskervilles* by Conan Doyle. Helped Mr. Hammond with the roof of his air-raid shelter. Dad back from London. Reports huge damage. May move to Slinfold.'

With the onset of September, the night skies became the barely disputed dominion of the Heinkels and Dorniers as their engines throbbed their de-synchronised trails across the Sussex coast on their way to London and other targets. On the other side of the Channel, with Teutonic urgency, Hitler's armies were preparing *Operation Sea Lion*, the invasion of Great Britain. On their maps was Bognor's name. 'We must expect many lodg-ments or attempted lodgments to be made on our island simultaneously', said Winston Churchill to the House of Commons sitting in secret session on 17 September 1940.

But to the Bognor Civil Defence officers and the West Sussex Police, the notion of a 'lodgment' in their area had long been foreseen. For, ever since they had received a Civil Defence memo from Tunbridge Wells, dated 19 August 1940, dealing with just such a possibility, they had been studying and formulating their plans. Amongst their more radical provisions was a scheme for the evacuation of a large part of the civilian population of Bognor and its surrounding area. They were 'to be shepherded along roads and paths other than those used for military movement', to get them the fifteen miles to Amberley Station for onward transmission to 'Purley, East Croydon and London'. It was evidently assumed that Barnham and Ford Junctions had been bombed. The Fire Brigade units were classified as non-combatants and were to try and save their equipment, failing which it was to be destroyed.

Those residents left behind were issued with 'A Notice to Householders; Instructions in case of a State of Emergency caused by a threatened landing of the enemy'. Notice of an impending attack was to be given 'by the firing of maroons'. But its severest warning read, 'In no case must there be any attempt at resistance by civilians either with firearms or otherwise. Any such attempts might bring the most terrible consequences upon the whole district.' The lessons learned so bitterly by our late allies were not to go unheeded at Bognor.

The possibility that the enemy might make a 'lodgment' somewhere on our flat and virtually undefended coast had also long concerned my father. If this should happen and our quiet roads and fields become torn by machine-gun and mortar fire, what would – or could – we do? At the best we should become *bouches inutiles*, at the worst we might all be killed! The Home Office pamphlet 'If the Invader Comes' was adamant that the civil population should 'stay put' so as not to clutter the roads with disorganised refugees pushing hand-carts as had happened in France. If we were to move we had to make up our minds rather quickly.

Of course, with the superior wisdom that hindsight lends, it now sounds bizarre. But, in early September 1940, history remained equivocal, unscripted. My parents were invited to toss a coin on their children's behalf, Julian only six. It was a cruel dilemma. But what if …? And it was that same worrying question which was just then exercising the consciences of millions of other parents faced with the terrible responsibility of protecting themselves and their young from the frightfulness of total war, those newsreel images from France still fresh in every mind. Might it be them next?

The majority of folk, of course, had to rely on the officially inspired evacuation schemes. But a small number chose to act independently by sending their offspring out of the country altogether; and at that time nowhere sounded safer than the New World. However, for one Bognor family bound for Canada, it proved to be a case of out of the frying pan into the fire – or rather into the Atlantic Ocean! For on 22 September 1940 the BBC announced that the *City of Benares*, carrying a large number of children, had been torpedoed in the Atlantic at night. We now know that of her precious cargo of a hundred evacuees only 13 were rescued. Mercifully, among this pitiful fraction were the Bech family from West Drive on the Bay Estate, Barbara (14), Sonia (11), Derek (9) and their mother, Marguerite.

After hearing the 'abandon ship' order on the tannoy, they arrived on deck to a scene of chaos; upturned lifeboats, people without lifebelts and figures struggling in the sea. Someone pointed to a davit rope connected to Lifeboat No. 4, just launched. Could anyone climb down it? Trained at school to climb a rope, Barbara – believing the family were close behind her – grasped it and slid safely down into the heaving boat. But when brother Derek, assisted by a seaman, tried to follow her down a rope ladder, it was only to find that Lifeboat No. 4, and his sister, had been swept away. Hastily he had to be hauled back by unseen hands onto to a deck which was sloping more acutely by the minute as the stricken liner began to sink. Still agonisingly uncertain of the fate of the rest her family, Barbara witnessed not long afterwards the awesome sight of the great liner, her lights still blazing, slipping stern-first below the waves.

In fact – soaked, cold and terrified – the rest of the Bechs plus the 3rd Engineer and an elderly woman passenger, were aboard a small oil-drum raft faced with the prospect of trying to survive the roaring white-necked waves of a wild Atlantic night. And already the raft showed signs of disintegrating. More than once Marguerite, her fingers badly bleeding from being crushed by the moving drums, thought the most merciful end might be for them to hold hands and slip into the sea; twice young Sonia was washed overboard and, with difficulty, retrieved. Yet, somehow they hung on a little longer … and a little longer … until, in the grey half-dawn, they were spotted by a lifeboat from the SS *Marina*, one of the U-boat's earlier victims. And only just in time, for the raft couldn't have lasted much longer. Neither could its six occupants, upon whom the effect of 14 hours of exposure was beginning to tell.

Meanwhile, the Royal Navy destroyer, HMS *Hurricane*, was thrashing her way at top speed towards the scene of the disaster. But by the time she had arrived in the debris-covered area and commenced her search the motley collection of lifeboats and rafts was tossing about over many square miles of ocean, and it wasn't until later in the afternoon that willing naval hands helped the survivors from the *Marina's* open boat onto the deck of the British warship.

Barbara's fate was now the family's main concern. Was she safe? Was her boat still afloat, even? One can only guess at the seething doubts that must have passed through Marguerite's mind as she went around seeking crumbs of information about the fate of Lifeboat No. 4 from the officers and rescued

137 The Bech family safe in Glasgow. From left to right: Barbara, Derek, their mother and, far right, Sonia. The boy in the middle is Colin Ryder Richardson, who received the King's Commendation for Bravery in the Merchant Navy, the youngest recipient ever.

passengers. Ironically, the lack of news of Barbara's boat was due to its being in good condition and in the hands of a competent crew. It was for that reason the destroyer's Captain left its rescue until nearly last. So it was only some hours later, when *Hurricane* edged alongside Lifeboat No. 4 to take on board its cold but otherwise unscathed occupants, that Marguerite Bech knew for certain that her whole family had survived. Mere words are not designed to measure her relief.

At all events, a few days later they were disembarked, safe and sound, 'at a Scottish port'. And as soon as she could, Mrs Bech made her way into Glasgow where she bought all her family new gabardine overcoats; hats, too, which in the accompanying photograph obscures the fact that only a few days earlier they had been snatched from the roaring Atlantic. But the fate that overtook those other 87 innocent young children is something they can still never forget. And that is how, by the Grace of God, our family are able to count Barbara, Sonia and Derek amongst our dearest friends.

But for us in Aldwick, as the Hurricanes and Spitfires roar overhead, all is rendered transient, censored – or rationed – as our lives are re-written in a script that only the future will decipher. Hourly we await the landing barges, the gliders and parachute troops dropping from the sky; the Local Defence Volunteers are on the lookout for nuns with hairy legs, while, from under Dark Lane's arching elms, the rookly clamour has fled before the tramp of army boots and strident-voiced commands.

If we could have thought about a book such as this when Roger and I were still exploring our territory around Aldwick, these closing chapters would have aimed no higher than to portray the last, precious years of our childhood, invoking memories of Aldwick Beach set against a tasteful composition of seaweedy breakwaters and a crimson sun sinking behind Selsey Bill. But, alas, all of this was to be set at naught by the momentous events sweeping France, by the concertinas of barbed wire between us and Aldwick Beach and by the anti-glider poles sprouting from the fields. Instead, these lines have to reflect the avalanche of history that piled up around us and brought such a dramatic end to our childhood. At this, her Finest Hour, Britain was standing unbent, defiant … and alone!

So, heart-searching done with, the painful decision was made. The family would move to Slinfold. The idea of a country mansion might have to go unrealised, but our recently acquired neighbours were willing to rent us part of The Chalet, a jerry-built bungalow adjoining our land. And at least we could 'Dig for Victory' on an heroic scale and, with our Light Sussex and Buff Orpington's eggs, be all but self-supporting. My father bought a Min of Ag and Fish book on market gardening. To my parents' three sons, the idea of being the Swiss Family Alford in the heart of the Sussex Weald was not without its attractions. It was only spoilt by the wrench of leaving Bognor. Yet, what if …?

On 17 September 1940, having made sure we'd left nothing in the air-raid shelter – whose main purpose so far had been to keep the milk cool – the bungalow was locked up. The chickens had been sent on in advance. On the strength of our last few petrol coupons, my parents, little Julian, a sack of oatmeal from Isted's and Judy, drooling in anticipation of meeting a better class of rabbit, set off in the car to the safety of the north Sussex country-side. Detailed to carry a couple of cardboard attaché cases, a meat mincer and the dinner plates, Roger and I followed by train.

Of course, had we consulted Nostradamus, we'd have discovered rather earlier that the 17th was a day on which travel was ill-advised. For, on Barnham station, my plates slipped their packaging, fell to the platform and proceeded to cut noisy figures-of-eight around the empty Nestlés Chocolate machine, under the station trolley and behind a crate of disbelieving Khaki Campbells, before describing a gracious *pas de deux* at the feet of an astonished ticket collector. Phew – not one broken! But that only presaged a disagreeable journey of stops and starts caused by the exigencies of war. At Christ's Hospital we arrived just in time to see the 'Slinfold Flyer' disappearing out of the station, leaving us two hours to wait until the next.

Then it started to rain; nor had we brought our macs; and we'd finished the Spam sandwiches.

To burden the reader with yet another vicissitude that befell these two bedraggled refugees upon arrival at their rural asylum would be an uncalled-for imposition. So let it suffice if I say that it hinged on the discovery of a circular 12-inch hole in the ground a few yards from The Chalet's wall. The village bobby stood up, brushed the grass from his trousers, replaced his tin hat and turned to my father: 'An unexploded bomb, sir!' And on that ominous note this story must draw to a close. If you harbour some faint vision of Roger and me on Barnham station, in pursuit of our dinner plates as they danced to the siren's wail, then you see us as we bade farewell to the childhood we were leaving behind amongst the fields of Aldwick, the streets of Bognor and the Paradise Rocks.

A Postscript from Iraq

1943; a map reference in a featureless desert.
And I learn that Pagham Harbour lies in peril!

HQ Troop was restless; for weeks we'd seen no mail. 'Sandstorms', insisted the Tech. Adj.; 'Patience', counselled the Padre; 'More likely bloody sunk', growled the SSM, darkly, from under his bug-net. Then, in the afternoon, a billowing dust cloud on the far side of the wadi heralded the arrival of the brigade 15 cwt; on board were two sacks of the stuff. APO had sent it by mistake to Basra docks where we had unloaded the tanks a few days earlier.

In my bundle was the familiar, chewed-up copy of the *Bognor Regis Post* sent me by my father. Around an item he thought I might find of interest he had drawn a red line. 'Bognor of the Future!' cried the headline. Closer examination showed the writer – the town's Surveyor and Engineer – had been on a creative binge, re-planning the seafront. Certain passages stood out: 'the raw material which the enterprising engineer dreams of' … 'an area which calls for development and imagination' … 'the Brooks with its fifteen acres of fields' … 'and perhaps later, Pagham Harbour with all its possibilities.' He looked forward to a brightly illuminated seafront 'eight miles long'. The more I read the more depressed I became!

Survival apart, my war aims were pretty innocuous. But they all had a thread in common: it was one day to return and walk again those lonely, windswept shores of Pagham Harbour, to watch the black-and-white dunlin clouds, and to remind my ears of the calls of redshank, curlew and golden plover. It was a reassuring sheet-anchor in a life which threatened to be a bit more hazardous than I'd bargained for. For, ever since that summer afternoon in 1934 when I had leaned my bike against a dilapidated old shack – that it was called the Salt House I was unaware – and for the first time wandered across the Dyke and heard those strange wader calls echoing over the gull-pocked mud, the Harbour had cast its gentle spell upon me. Only the hand of man was capable of destroying this peaceful wilderness of marsh and mud-flat. It was impossible to envisage it being part of a brightly lit 'seafront eight miles long'.

Now, it is a well-known fact that when engineers and surveyors start talking about 'possibilities', 'development' and Pagham Harbour, all in the same breath, it is time to torch the beacons and make for the barricades! Over my dead body would my greenshank, grey plover and restless turnstone be seen against a background of multi-storey hotels and strings of sodium street lights. Twenty-seven hundred miles away, Pagham Harbour lay in peril! So I reached for my quill. Between swatting flies in the shadow of our tank, I composed an inflammatory draft, another more temperate and eventually settled for a sweetly reasoned letter to the editor of the *Bognor Regis Post*.

Its gist was simple. I suggested that in any post-war redevelopment plan, besides curbing the westerly sprawl of Pagham's shacky bungalows – and anything worse which might follow – consideration should also be given to insuring the protection of the Harbour's ever more vulnerable natural life by designating the whole area a 'Bird Reserve'. Just what it might entail, I had no real idea; planning legislation in those days was a closed book to me. In any case, this same thought must have occurred to lots of other folk much better informed about this sort of thing than I. Wasn't it merely stating the obvious? Was it worth writing the letter, even? Nevertheless, I pressed on, signed the thing and shoved the envelope into the Squadron Office post-box. Soon I forgot all about it, as mail to the UK was still tortuously slow.

With a change in the war situation, the day came when the basalt boulder-fields and the flat-topped village mounds, shimmering their mirage-dance in the blaze of the Badiet esh Sham, slid from our driving mirrors for the last time; the serpentine climb through the snow-capped Lebanons into the clean, cool air of Zahle shortened the lives of the tank transporters by months and left our ears to pop on the escarpment descent into the perfumed suffocation of the Levant. Our new camp near Beirut stood among giant cedars; through the open hut windows drifted the scent of bougain-villea and acacia. On to my bed Tubby, the post-corporal, had chucked a bundle of mail which had been chasing me for days. Unmistakable was the frayed-edged copy of the *Bognor Post*.

Just then the fate of Pagham Harbour must have slipped my mind. So all the greater my surprise when I opened the paper. For there, marked with that familiar red line, and dated 3 July 1943, was my letter – in Morton Swinburne's column. Of course, the rest of the crew wanted to see it, if only to confirm their long-held belief of my incipient dottiness. A few weeks later another *Post* arrived. This time my letter had become the subject of Edmond M. Venables' 'Natural Science Scrapbook'. Such an idea, he wrote, 'was deserving of sympathetic consideration'. Also enclosed was a cutting from the *West Sussex Gazette*: 'one cannot help but feel touched by this appeal from a soldier far away in a foreign land … who was still thinking of Pagham and feeling anxious about its birds. It is much to be hoped that something on the lines he suggests will be done.'

Then, a few days later, I received a letter from this very Mr Venables himself, congratulating me on 'this overdue initiative'. More correspondence followed. A letter from Sir Richard Gregory FRS of Middleton Manor said he thought the idea would have popular backing 'and was proposing to talk about it to some of his friends'. The contents of another, signed by a Mr S.J. Teideman of North Bersted, suggested my notion had rung a bell with a knowledgeable ornithologist. Anyway, they all welcomed the Bird Reserve idea and sounded enthusiastic about pursuing it. They wished me well and hoped I would get in touch with them when I returned home. But that had to wait, as we had yet to endure the wickedness of the Appennine Marchiagno and the trek to Venice.

So Pagham Harbour remained on the back-burner until about the time HQ Troop floated its hush-hush Shermans on the quiet reflections of the black volcanic hills surrounding Lago di Bracciano, north of Rome. For it was there I received another *Bognor Post*. It was dated 10 February 1945. This time the letter from 'the soldier in the Middle East' had grabbed the front page with a banner headline! 'The Future of Pagham Harbour; proposal to establish a Nature Reserve.' It went on to refer to an influential committee consisting of Sir Richard Gregory FRS, Dr H.L. Lucking and Mr E.M. Venables which had been formed to enlist the sympathy of the West Sussex County Council Planning Department. Meanwhile, Mr Teideman was busy raising the matter with the Committee for Nature Reserves in Post-War Britain. Pagham Harbour's future sounded as if it was in the best of hands. And none too soon; already the RAF were using it as a rocket range.

To our travels there seemed no end. After Venice came Greece – with time enough to dawdle on Athens' deserted Acropolis, to drink of the Theseion caressed by a pendent moon, and, with the aid of a ladder surplus to the Wehrmacht's needs, to make a measured drawing of the little Temple of Nikè Apteros above the Odeion of Herodes Atticus. Six more months; blissful ones.

Then, one day, I learned that my number had come up for demob. A fortnight later I was lugging my kit-bag up the gangway of a cross-Channel paddle-steamer at Calais. On a pouring wet afternoon, late in August 1946, I found myself at the Army's Demobilisation Depot at York. After being 'tried on' for my new suit by an Issuing Clerk trained to kit out gorillas above the waist and Armenian midgets below, I was handed a Ration Book, a wodge of clothing coupons, a palmful of coin in lieu of the unexpired portion of the day's ration, and a single Rail Warrant to Bognor Regis via Barnham Junction. Over yon, jerked the Quartermaster's head, I would find the door to Civvy Street.

Self-consciously attired in an ill-fitting navy-blue pinstripe and green pork-pie hat and carrying a parcel of War Department underwear on the end of a piece of string, I made my way to the railway station. And that was the end to all that.

> **Diary, 14 September 1946**: 'Cycled to Pagham early a.m. Hard to believe that last time here was Sept/1940. Not much change except for a few old bomb craters, rolls of barbed wire, concrete blocks and knocked-out target tanks on the shingle bank. Many curlew … a few widgeon … dunlin clouds over Church Norton … etc., etc.'

I forget where we first met. At a house in Victoria Drive, I think; a gathering of the Pagham Harbour Preservation Committee. At any rate, it was where I was first introduced to the person of Martin Venables. He greeted me warmly. But as we chatted a curious feeling stole over me that I had seen this chap somewhere before. But where? After all, I had been away from Bognor for more than four years. So it was only when he began to talk learnedly of the London clay, Cretaceous and Eocene strata, of iron pyrites, shark's teeth and his pre-war discovery of fossil insects from the Aldwick Beds that suddenly the penny dropped. That was where I had seen him; on our beach, just before the war! Surely this was the fellow in rolled-up trousers, a knapsack on his back and carrying a sieve, I could still remember paddling and exploring among the rockpools. So that was what he'd been looking for – fossils! And thus it transpired I had known Martin Venables for far longer than I could have imagined. From that meeting stemmed a friendship I was to treasure for the next forty-five years.

The Pagham Harbour Preservation Committee was begat of the Bognor Regis Natural History Society, founded in 1938 by Martin Venables with the help of Morton Swinburne FZS and Capt. D.S. Hancock, FRMetS, the Headmaster of Greenways School in Hawthorn Road. In 1946 the P.H.P. Committee was a well deep in talent and wisdom. Its Chairman was Sir Richard Gregory Bt., FRS, for 21 years Professor of Astronomy at Queen's College, Harley Street in London, but best known as the reforming editor of *Nature*, from which he had retired in 1938, although he and his wife had come to live in Bognor seven years earlier. One of his closest friends had been the author H.G. Wells. Now immersed in local affairs, he was President of both the South Eastern Union of Scientific Societies and the Bognor Regis and District Horticultural Society, besides being a founder member of the Bognor Regis Natural History Society. Another appointment he enjoyed was that of Honorary Life President of the United Nations Society.

I have been unable to trace any committee minutes from this period – 1945-50 – but I do remember the Committee's Hon. Sec. was Stanley Tiedeman who, in spite of his confinement to a wheelchair, was an active ornithologist of the old school; a counter of primaries and an expert on 'little brown jobs' seen at prodigious distances. His notebooks are an immaculate record of every bird he saw. In Dr Lucking, a retired chemist – and ex-Hon. Treasurer of the Ice Cream Association of Great Britain – we had a man of public stamp: a member of Bognor Regis Council, a Rural District Councillor and Chairman of the Middleton Parish Council who, at critical junctures, could be relied upon to have the ear of the County's Planning Department.

The Committee was also fortunate to have enlisted the help of the legendary Dorothy French whose knowledge of the Harbour's flora was profound, authoritative – and often in Latin. Even plodding around the Lagoon with her in soaking rain in search of the Lesser Swine-Cress or Crested Dog's Tail, was a memorable – if somewhat soggy – experience. In 1962 the Bognor Regis Natural Science Society published her seminal work, *The Flora of Pagham Harbour.*

Purposely, though, I have left to last the Committee's king-pin, its roving commissioner and inspirational dynamo: Martin Venables, naturalist and self-taught geologist, whose work on Bognor's London clay deposits was to bring him the Geologists' Association's Foulerton Award in 1949, and whose impish mind shone a light on every corner of natural history. Although a fruit and apple grower by profession, he was, by inclination, also an ornithologist, artist and teacher. As an accomplished journalist he is best known for his articles on natural history which appeared weekly as the 'Selborne Notes' in the *West Sussex Gazette* and under the title of 'Natural Science Scrapbook' in the *Bognor Regis Post.* Taxidermy was another of his skills, again self-taught. And, to round off, he was also a non-practising Buddhist, a lover of heavy horses and, as a one-time Group Leader in Bognor's Civil Defence, no stranger to the thick end of many wartime

138 This RAF reconnaissance photo of Pagham Harbour was taken on 31 August 1941. Mr Thornton's new harbour mouth at the Church Norton end still appears to be holding up. At the upper right can be seen the semi-circle of St Thomas' Drive and a string of three bomb craters about a quarter of a mile to its west. There is another large crater some half a mile north west of Church Norton. The Lagoon (mid right) following the earlier, sinuous course of the Rife is clearly visible. Keen eyes will pick out Little Welbourne, Pagham Wall and the church.

139 E.M. Venables FGS, FRHS.

bombing incidents; in fact, only a *bon viveur* was he not!

Of course, it was rather gratifying to see how my 'Nature Reserve' idea had caught on. The snag was, though, that having to devote all my concentration and every waking minute to my architectural studies, I was able to attend only a few of their meetings. And when I did it was to prove a somewhat humbling experience. For all the members – except me – appeared to be learned authorities on one or another niche of the natural life of Pagham Harbour.

By this time the Committee had settled down to its role as the Nature Reserve pressure group and moral custodian of the Harbour. It applied itself to a wide spectrum of business. For instance, in July 1946 there was a request by the local branch of the Workers Association for Martin Venables and Miss French to give them a conducted tour of the Harbour. Sometime afterwards we discussed a communication from Mr T. Hayward, Clerk of the WSCC – himself an ardent ornithologist – 'inviting the views of the Committee upon the desirability of creating Pagham Harbour a nature conservancy in order to preserve the flora and fauna of that area for the future'. Another subject requiring discussion was the fear of 'pedalos' on the Lagoon. Meanwhile, to keep up our spirits in the winter of 1946, Mr Teideman conducted a survey of tits breaking into milk bottle tops.

But in February 1947 a serious threat presented itself when it was learned that the Air Ministry had it in mind to use Pagham Harbour as a bombing range. Predictably, opposition was strident; although, against a government department enjoying such Draconian powers, the outcome was uncertain. So it seemed prudent for the Committee to prepare for the worst. The question was, how would the birds and the plants take to being daily stonked by bombs?

And it was that pregnant question that brought me my one, brief moment of glory on the Committee. High explosives, my Pagham Harbour niche! For this was a subject on which I could address the members with authority. Thus, I was able to relate how, in Italy, I had observed that during the breeding season many birds seemed almost oblivious of even the most intense artillery barrages: swallows and hoopoes near Ancona; breeding moorhens and coots raising their young amongst the bomb craters in the Spandau-raked reed-beds south of the Po River. What did this tell us? Might not Pagham's birds be less disturbed by a few practice bombs than by hundreds of holiday makers? For his part, Stanley Teideman believed the birds – apart from the few singled out by Fate to receive direct hits – would survive the ordeal as they had being regularly rocketed by RAF fighters only a few years earlier. Dorothy French felt a bombing range was the ultimate means of protecting Pagham's plant-life – always on the understanding she could have access to the range when the red flags were down. But it was never a popular idea and I suspect many of the public marked us down as Quislings of the Nature Reserve!

As it turned out, our fears proved groundless. In the face of vehement opposition from the WSCC, the local Parish Councils, the Press and almost everyone else – including our own Committee* – the Air Ministry withdrew their threat. Yet, I have often wondered whether the use of the Harbour as a bombing range might not have been in the Little Tern's best interests!

By 1950 it was clear that the bureaucratic process for turning the Harbour into a *de facto* Nature Reserve was going to be grindingly slow, its feasibility often in doubt. But at least the existing Wild Bird Protection Act could be implemented. And in a very curious way. For Phillip Hawes, Secretary of the Pagham Wildfowlers and Conservation Association, contrived to have two – and later a further twenty – of its members enrolled as Special Constables. This meant they could keep an eye on those pedestrians who strayed into nesting areas, egg-thieves and the indiscriminate shooters. For their part, the planning authorities curbed the westward sprawl of the bungalows. And a variety of circumstances put paid to the plans of a local businessman who considered buying Pagham Harbour as a site on which to float caravans disguised as 'houseboats'.

In fact, nothing much else happened until 1962. In that year, A.E.E. Marr of the Sussex Naturalist Trust (in conjunction with the Sussex Ornithological Society, and using much material provided by Major W.W.A. Phillips of the Bognor Regis Natural History Society) produced for submission to the West Sussex County Council a comprehensive and authoritative paper titled 'A Report on the Scientific Interest of Pagham Harbour with Proposals for the Establishment of a Nature Reserve'. This, with the backing of the Pagham and West Sussex Wildfowling and Conservation Association, seems to have done the trick. At last, in June 1964, the West Sussex County Council – clearly influenced by the Trust's report – announced that, under the National Parks and Access to the Countryside Act, the Secretary of State had confirmed that from July of that year Pagham Harbour would become operative as a Nature Reserve, administered by the County Council's Countryside Committee. It was just twenty-one years of Bureaucracy since I had written my letter from Iraq!

Eventually I had to move to London, with time spent watching birds at Pagham Harbour an unaffordable luxury. Nevertheless, whenever I was in Bognor I used to make a point of calling on Martin Venables, first at the Lyon Street Museum where, in 1949, he had been appointed Curator of the hitherto little-known Guermonprez Natural History Collection, and then, after 1969, at the Manor House in Chichester Road to where it had been shifted. And it was at the Manor House that I spent many happy hours drinking cups of tea, asking questions and watching Martin and his assistant, Joy White, performing their Pharaonic rites on some cormorant, curlew or tufted duck as they went about the task of supplementing the

---

* In May 1953 the Pagham Harbour Preservation Committee became a sub-committee of the Bognor Regis Natural History Society.

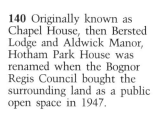

140 Originally known as Chapel House, then Bersted Lodge and Aldwick Manor, Hotham Park House was renamed when the Bognor Regis Council bought the surrounding land as a public open space in 1947.

Guermonprez standing-and-perching birds with specimens in the flying mode. Hanging from the ceiling, with wings outstretched, their verisimilitude beggared belief.

The career of Henry Leopold Guermonprez (1858-1924) appears to have been underwritten by that inestimable boon, a private income; 'modest but adequate', as he describes it. Indeed, although he qualified as an Associate of the Royal Institute of British Architects, there is no evidence that he ever needed to practise his profession to keep a roof over his head. Instead he was able to devote himself to his passion for the study of the natural history of West Sussex, although it was in and around the Bognor area that his keen eyes and enquiring mind reaped their richest harvest. From London's Chelsea, Guermonprez and his ailing parents first came to live at 6 Albert Road in Bognor in about 1892. But within a year his father died and shortly afterwards the family moved to Dalkeith, another house in the same road. In 1897 Henry married a Miss Clara Phelps about whom little is known except that 'she was small, pretty and a good singer'.

Although the study of natural history had long been his primary interest, it was only in the thirty years following his arrival in Bognor that he set about seriously collecting, classifying and documenting a vast hoard of specimens: plants, mammals, birds, insects, reptiles and marine life. He was also a skilled taxidermist, although his birds seemed to have survived better than the mammals and fishes. Guermonprez' accomplishment as a botanist is mentioned by Wooly-Dod in his *Flora of Sussex*. Nor were his activities restricted to natural history. He described the discovery of the remains of a 13th-century chapel at Manor Farm, Nyetimber (now Barton Manor), part of which Lindsay Fleming believed to be Saxon. In 1906 he was appointed to edit the 'Selborne Notes' in the *West Sussex Gazette* which he ran successfully for some years, although J.J. Thompson, the paper's editor, complained occasionally of the excessive amount of material Guermonprez submitted!

Towards the end of his life, he was involved with the Marshall Avenue find of 90 Bronze-Age axes, or palstaves, on which he wrote a paper that appeared posthumously in the *Sussex Archaeological Collections*. The axe-heads eventually found a home at Dalkeith which, at the time of his death in 1924, had every semblance of a major museum collection. Yet, neither this remarkable, self-taught naturalist – Gerard Young calls him the Gilbert White of Bognor – nor his collection have ever been as well-known as they deserve. To some extent this was due to the very private nature of the man, a characteristic borne out in his obituary published in the *West Sussex Gazette* on 21 December 1924, which refers to his having 'lived a retiring life'. He appears, for instance, to have had little to do with the many local natural history societies which flourished at this time and, considering the scope of his work, he published relatively few papers. Indeed, if he set out to hide his light under a bushel, he seems to have been almost too successful!

Still in the ownership of the Guermonprez family, Dalkeith remained the home of the collection until 5 February 1943, the day Bognor suffered a severe air raid. A bomb fell in Albert Road close to the house causing much structural damage and endangering its irreplaceable contents. By a stroke of luck, Group Leader E.M. Venables of the Civil Defence Service happened to be on duty in the area. He knew the collection well and was able to arrange for its immediate salvage and temporary protection. This wartime incident marked a watershed in the collection's history. For, in 1944, the West Sussex County Council accepted the Guermonprez family's offer of it as a gift, conditional upon it being used to form the nucleus of a Bognor Regis Museum 'under the observation and supervision' of that gallant ex-Chief Air Raid Warden, geologist, naturalist and soon-to-be-appointed Curator of the new Lyon Street Museum, Martin Venables.

But the Manor had a major drawback: it was extremely damp and the very last place to store a valuable collection. Yet, not far away, stood a great house which – if it could be saved from demolition – would have made a far better home. For, long before Martin retired in 1974, the Battle for Hotham Park House, headed by that champion of the town's historic past, Gerard Young, was still in full swing. When Bognor's founder, Sir Richard Hotham Kt., built himself a stylish Regency house on a fine wooded site bounded by what is now the Upper Bognor Road and the High Street he lit the fuse of a controversy which was to explode among the citizens of his town a hundred and eighty years later. Those readers who cannot remember the great Hotham Park House saga of the 1970s may benefit from this brief synopsis. After Sir Richard died, in 1799, Chapel House – an allusion to the private chapel he added to it – passed through various ownerships until, in 1857 (by which time it had become known as Bersted Lodge), it fell into the hands of the Fletcher family. The last of their line to live there was William Holland Ballett Fletcher, who changed its name yet again to Aldwick Manor. He died in 1941.

In 1947 Bognor Council bought the site on behalf of the town for £40,000 and, after naming it Hotham Park, designated it a public open space to be augmented with some simple amusements for children. Meanwhile, Sir Richard's old pile – now re-christened Hotham Park House – was found to be in a parlous structural condition due to years of neglect and a period of damaging wartime occupation by the Army. Utterly regardless of this, though, the Council then almost immediately let the house on a 21-year *non-repairing* lease to the Ministry of Pensions and Social Insurance. So, by the time it reverted to the Council in 1968, the Knight's old house was in an advanced and accelerating state of decay. At the Town Hall influential voices recommended its demolition.

The future of Hotham Park House became a Bognor *cause célèbre*, giving rise to a long-running battle between what – for the purposes of this chapter – we will call the Philistines and the Angels; those who sought its demolition and replacement with some kind of a modern entertainment facility (the perennial Winter Gardens was a strong contender; a beer garden less so) versus that body of local opinion which believed Sir Richard's historic house should be saved and restored to become the home of a Bognor Regis Museum with its core exhibit the Guermonprez Collection of Sussex flora and fauna. This was Martin Venables' most cherished wish. The moment of truth came in 1969 when a structural survey revealed that to restore the house and raise it to the standard of 'a public building', suitable for a museum, would cost £110,000. Whether or not they could afford expenditure of this magnitude was to occupy a great deal of the Council's attention over the next three years.

Meanwhile, in February 1970, the *Bognor Regis Post* conducted a poll which showed that the Angels had it over the Philistines by 608 votes to 253. Persuaded of the way the wind of public opinion was blowing, the Council grudgingly agreed to fund half the cost of restoration on the condition that the public and various charitable bodies raised the other £55,000.

141 The Friends gather to admire the model of Hotham Park House. Left to right: the author, Margaret Powell and Mrs Jean Rose.

Some time before these events, Councillor Margaret (Maggie) Culver – a diehard Angel and seasoned campaigner for the building's restitution – had formed the Friends of Hotham Park House, a pressure group for the purpose of preventing demolition by the Council. Accorded the status of a registered charity, the Friends turned their attention to raising this great sum of money. Enthusiastically they set about organising dinners, wine-and-cheese parties, coffee mornings and evening 'do's at Shripney Manor. But, by 1971, in spite of donations and promises from the Pilgrim's Trust, the Georgian Group, an interest-free loan from the County Council and a promise of 'the last £5,000' from Mrs Margaret Rank and her son John, the Friends' contribution was a mere £1,500. The gap looked unbridgeable.

Of course, the Friends' discomfiture was eagerly seized upon by the Philistine section of the Council; they were able to point out that, although they had kept their part of the bargain by giving the Friends more than a year to find a sizeable part of the other £55,000, clearly the task had been beyond them. At a meeting held on 20 July the Council decided Sir Richard

Hotham's house would have to be demolished. To no one was this a more bitter blow than Martin Venables, who saw his last hope of the Museum Collection ever being properly housed in Bognor disappearing.

Between 1972 and 1973 the Collection was dispersed, a sizeable part being taken by the Portsmouth City Museum, who marked the occasion the following year with an exhibition of the Guermonprez section, towards the cost of which the Friends made 'a generous contribution'. The birds in flying mode went to a museum at Harlow in Essex.

In the meantime, the siege of Hotham Park House continued for the simple reason that, before they could demolish the house, the Council had to apply to the Department of the Environment to have its Listed Building status removed. Their application, however, elicited a fairly cool reply from the Minister, who 'regretted this highly-graded building should be allowed to decay', and suggested they spend some money on essential and emergency repairs, pending any decision to which the Department might come. The Council's response was to allocate £500 a year for the purpose, a mere flea-bite in the context of the remedial work needed.

However, on April Fool's Day 1974 Bognor Regis Council ceased to exist when the town was joined with Arundel and Littlehampton in a shotgun marriage which spawned the new Arun District Council. Like the Ancient Mariner's albatross, Hotham Park House now hung round the new Council's neck. Unable to demolish it, unwilling – as had been Bognor – to spend enough on the fabric to properly preserve it, Sir Richard's house continued its genteel, downhill slide to ultimate dereliction. But, for those who clutched at straws, at least it was still there, albeit ridden with dry-rot and deathwatch beetle. And there was no doubt that the majority of the more thoughtful townsfolk, including many of the Bognor members on the new Council, still hoped 'something might turn up' to stave off execution. But as 1974 turned to 1975 and no magic wand was forthcoming, it looked increasingly clear that the end of Hotham Park House must be in sight.

By that date, the Friends – on whose committee I now found myself – had gloomily to admit that the £16,000 accumulated in total was still far distant from the £60,000 (the figure had increased at the rate the building was deteriorating and inflation was accelerating) needed to save this historic house. With touching faith, we continued with yet more dinner parties and coffee mornings to raise pitifully small sums of money. From outside the town, the Friends enlisted the help of well-known personalities sympathetic to our cause: the poet Robert Graves, the authoress Margaret Powell, of *Upstairs, Downstairs* fame, and Lord Bessborough, an influential Sussex preservationist. All did their bit. A model of Hotham Park House in a perspex case was commissioned and placed on display in local schools to attract interest and donations from pupils, parents and staff.

In the meantime, a piquant telephone conversation had taken place between Jean Rose, the Friends' Chairman, and her old political acquaintance, Peter Walker MP, Minister of State for the Environment. The result was Hotham Park House was hastily raised from a Grade II to a Grade II* Listed Building. Still the controversy raged. Councillor Shearing, an influential Philistine, announced he looked forward to entering the house seated on a bulldozer, to which Jean Rose spiritedly retorted, 'that she would be there waiting for him'!

In 1976 an exasperated Arun District Council applied to the Department for permission to demolish Hotham Park House, Grade II* or not; the Department ordered an Inquiry to take place the following year. Jean Rose's despairing view was that 'unless a kindly person with cash to spare' could be found, the end of the house must be in sight. It was what we all thought. And it was just as we were asked to swallow this bitter pill that, suddenly, the future of Hotham Park House was transformed in a way no one could have foreseen. For out of nowhere, in February 1977, there arrived in Bognor the person for whom the Friends had prayed in the shape of Mr Abraham Singer, a Buckinghamshire businessman with a penchant for restoring old buildings. He thought he could make a go of Hotham Park House by converting it into flats, including one for his own family. Of course the Friends would have preferred the infeasible museum, but we were beggars, not choosers. Clearly flats were the only lifeline left to throw to the Knight's historic home. But our relief at having outwitted Mr Shearing and his bulldozer was palpable!

Soon the house was girdled in scaffolding as the skips began to fill with all that was beyond repair. Over the ensuing months Mr Singer and his builder strove to overcome a multitude of structural problems, many unforeseen, as local craftsmen applied their skills to the restoration, repair and replacement of the original plaster, timber and cast-iron details; careful research ensured that, where possible, the new paintwork matched the colours of the 1790s. At last, in the summer of 1978, the great act of resuscitation was complete – or almost so, for cost had prevented restoration of the canopy on the front elevation. But that is to cavil. The fact was, Sir Richard Hotham's house stood, if anything, in a sounder structural condition than when it was first built. And for that the town owed Mr Singer a mighty 'thankyou'. If some claimed they could hear old Bognor's heart beating again, who could have doubted them?

Before the Friends of Hotham Park House went their different ways, I was asked to design and arrange the fixing of a slate plaque with gold lettering to one of the gate-posts, commemorating the victorious outcome of their six-year struggle to save the one-time home of Bognor's founder, Sir Richard Hotham, Kt.

* * *

With semi-retirement, I felt I must visit Pagham Harbour again to see how it had fared since becoming a Nature Reserve. I drove in at Ferry Field on a spring afternoon. There for the first time I saw the tastefully designed information hut, the inviting car parks, neat paths and the notices reminding the visitors to keep to them. A small van had 'Pagham Harbour Nature Reserve' written on its side. One notice pointed to a Nature Trail and another 'to the hide'. On sale in the hut, its walls decorated with educational diagrams, were books on birds, key-rings, mugs and badges. It even boasted loos.

142 View of Pagham Harbour from Church Norton.

143 Visitors' Centre, Pagham Harbour Nature Reserve.

144 Ferrypool – a part of Pagham Harbour Nature Reserve

Outside in the car park, Ford Transits disgorged their project-bent children to jar the horizon with multi-coloured anoraks and trousers. Around the shore roamed young men carrying powerful-looking telescopes on tripods. Past me rushed a breathless twelve-binoc party from Penge: '... seen yesterday near the sluice', said a voice. Little did the poor whatever-it-was know what was coming to it! In reply to my question, a young man wearing a symbol of authority divulged that last year the Harbour had attracted over 100,000 visitors!

Suddenly I felt a stranger, an oddity in this great space of marsh and sky. Was this really where I had once sat, alone, hearing for the first time the wild calls of marsh-birds? Or, *sans* binoculars, strained my eyes to make sketches of the birds so that I could find their names in Lansborough Thompson's handsome tome? Even after the war – when we still had ration-cards – a deserted Pagham Harbour seemed to belong to just God and myself on the afternoon that I tried out a pair of ex-Luftwaffe binoculars on some bar-tailed godwits, their balletic grace reflected in a pool. And now this great wild and natural thing had become a Committee in County Hall.

And then it dawned on me. Hijacked, that was what it had been! The days of my solitary hobby of watching birds on this once-remote, unpeopled marsh, all those years ago, had been usurped of adventure and mystery and re-born as the Birding Industry. Ornithology had become Birdwatching, 'Twitching' its cousin; and my old Harbour was reduced to an Educational Experience. So this was the Nature Reserve my letter from Iraq had spawned!

In truth, how could it have been otherwise? After all, 1934 is almost prehistoric to a lot of folk; Britain has become a very different place. How

145 Harbour centre.

could the Harbour of my youth have remained unaffected by the tide of sociological change that has marked the last thirty years, thirty years of 'more', more wealth, more cars, more leisure and more education? And endless TV programmes plugging wildlife and encouraging millions to visit places such as nature reserves and nature trails to see these wonders for themselves. I shall withdraw those carping paragraphs and, instead, ungrudgingly, offer my congratulations to the West Sussex County Council and the staff of the Nature Reserve – who have had to deal with the real world as they find it at the end of the 20th century – on the way they have exercised their custodianship of Pagham Harbour. And not only for their duty of care for the well-being of its birds and plants, but also in the way they have coped with the thousands of twitchers, birders (perish the word!), ornithologists, botanists, day-outers – and their motor cars – and provided all those fluorescently-garbed kids with such an enticing educational entrée into the Harbour's wildlife. And no less worthy of tribute is the imaginative manner in which the Pagham and West Sussex Wildfowling and Conservation Association have renovated and converted the Salt House – that 'dilapidated old shack' of my childhood – into an Information Centre for those entering the Reserve from the Pagham end.

Yet, as I made my way back to my car, I couldn't help but feel how privileged I had been, as a young lad, to have stumbled across – and then come to love – those primordial acres before they became so jolly well managed!

When Martin Venables retired to Eastgate House in Chichester I continued to call on him from time to time, always staying twice as long as I had intended, so much was there to talk about, including the idea for this book. Just before Christmas 1990 I spoke on the phone to this tireless scribe, thanking him for sending me a newspaper cutting that had been read to him by his mother, when he was about six years old, describing the destruction by fire of Paradise at Aldwick. At the same time I arranged to visit him a day or two after the New Year. He was to make us a cup of tea and afterwards I would take him for a drive around his – and my – old haunts, Pagham Harbour, the Lagoon, St Mary's church at South Bersted and Marine Drive for a look at his beloved Bognor Rocks – with fingers crossed that the tide would be out!

I arrived at Eastgate House to find Martin's Christmas mail still outside his front door. There was no reply to my knock. I sensed something ominous and made further inquiries. Only then did I learn that my old friend had passed away in St Richard's Hospital a few days earlier, on 29 December. Downcast, I drove away, but, as I turned towards the Hornet, I couldn't help my mind wandering back to the desert of Iraq in 1943 and that letter I had written in the shadow of my tank.

Tern Island

After Martin Venables' death, his many friends expressed a wish to commemorate his life in a way which would have been close to his heart. Thanks to the imagination and energy of Phillip Hawes, Secretary of the Pagham and West Sussex Wildfowling and Conservation Association, this took the form of an exercise in practical conservation on behalf of the indigenous colony of Little Terns. It involved the moving of 2,500 tonnes of shingle to create an artificial island, off the Church Norton spit on the south side of the Harbour, on which it is hoped they may nest more safely than in the past.

146 The Estuary in the Reserve.

The Story of a Seedling Apple

Seedling apples are not really my *forte*; aspidistras and *ficus benjamina*, that thing which starts dropping its leaves the moment the over-pampering garden centre is out of sight, perhaps, but not fruit trees. Yet, it would be remiss of me not to record the chronicle of one special seedling which, besides providing the family with a slow-motion close-up of Creation doing her stuff, can also be counted as a stitch in the rich tapestry of Aldwick's history.

The saga opened on a spring day in 1955 when my mother drew my attention to a plant which had misguidedly rooted itself in the middle of her garden path. That she insisted on calling it a sapling seemed rather over-egging what I took to be a weed. But, apparently, in that little stalk she perceived some secret cypher; a secret so deep as to be, to me, entirely absent. As bidden, though, I dug it up and she replanted it in a nearby bed. 'Probably only a crab apple – but you can never be quite sure', she murmured. From then on, whenever I visited Aldwick my mother insisted I come with her to inspect what by now, I had to agree, had rather more the appearance of a tree than at our first encounter. Asked what I thought of it, I conceded it looked a nice little specimen – and no show-off, either. She was still pretty sure it was a crab.

Many years passed. (Incidentally, that phrase reflects an observable trait in fruit trees; arboreal urgency is quite unknown. So this is the speeded-up version of what really took a dreadfully long time.) Then, one day in the spring of 1961, while I was in London, I received an excited telephone call from Aldwick. The tree had flowered; covered with blooms; spectacular! I must come down and pay it homage. Finding that Bognor could offer other business as well, the next weekend I set off. Hardly had I got out of the car than my mother grabbed my arm and marched me down the garden to introduce me to its scattering of pinkish-white flowers. 'Very pretty – in fact, almost like a Dutch oil painting,' I said, feeling that a little intellectual padding was called for. Then, a few days later, a small green apple appeared and immediately fell off.

The following year it was a repeat performance, but this time the tree bore a dozen small red apples. Glory be! Still my mother thought it merely a crab – until they began to grow larger than any wild apple she'd ever seen. It was then she made a telephone call to our mutual friend, that eminent apple grower and horticulturalist, Martin Venables. In due course a cycle-clipped Martin turned up on his bike and was shown the tree. After close inspection and deliberation he announced great tidings! For, he exclaimed, what he beheld was no ordinary ugly-duckling crab, but a seedling apple! Something unusual among that genus of forbidden fruit, it would soon become a handsome swan! Then he pointed at a nearby crab apple tree, the

147 Doris Alford with *Aldwick Beauty* – 'chance grown'.

one chosen by my mother and planted on Mr Rank's land thirty years earlier, 'And that is probably where it began.' It only remained for the new tree to teach my mother how easy it had been to raise her three sons compared with raising this fruit of her garden path.

From that moment the new seedling assumed the status of a *prima donna*. Upon Martin's recommendation it had to be be moved to a position where it would have more space and a better view of the sun. Round it was placed a wire cage with a stern notice saying 'DO NOT TOUCH'. Daily the tree was inspected by my mother; devotedly she mulched, watered and sprayed it. The next year it bloomed so profusely that a pair of bullfinches turned up to have a look. Panic! For suddenly it dawned on her that her precious tree was surrounded by enemies! For what about the blackbirds and squirrels, let alone all the creepy-crawly tormentors with long Latin names? From Isted's in London Road yards of green netting were ordered and a sticky band placed round its pampered midriff. Soon it was burdened down with apples. And they swelled and swelled and became redder and redder.

In July – which was distinctly early – the six largest were placed in a silver-plated fruit dish from where their sweet scent filled the living room. Martin confirmed them to be a 'discovery' and promised that next year its fruit would be even larger. Meanwhile the family was invited to bend the knee to *Aldwick Beauty*, the name by which – subject to HM's Government's permission – my mother had already decided it should be known. With that dedication found among few but apple growers, Martin visited both tree and proprietress at regular intervals. Sage were his nods and stern his rebukes; he commiserated with my mother's depression brought on by the sight of a single crinkled leaf.

Sure enough, the following year the tree was still heavier of apple, a lot of them large. 'Good taste, good texture, nice appearance; skin rich-red merging to yellow and flesh tending to pink, small stalk, early cropping and about five to the pound.' But that, said Martin, was the good news. The bad was that my mother would now have to take seriously the admin. side: the tree would need to undergo National Fruit Trials; a patent had to be applied for. The next day she went off and bought a manila file on which she wrote in large capitals 'ALDWICK BEAUTY'. In the spring of 1968, Brinkman's Ltd of Bosham, the well-known nurserymen and fruit-growers – and eventually my mother's agents – arrived with a sharp knife to take some cuttings. Soon forty trees were growing there on a variety of stocks.

Eventually, in 1970, fifteen years after we'd rescued the tree from our garden path, two grafts were planted on probation at the Ministry's National Fruit Trials establishment at Brogdale in Kent and a further two at the RHS's garden at Wisley. Then came the task of dealing with the Plant Variety Rights Office in Cambridge to obtain the *Aldwick Beauty* patent; forms and more forms. Was her apple 'distinct, uniform and stable'? It sure was. By now her file was bulging. But, at last, in 1976, amongst great rejoicing at Idlewylde, the patent was granted and thereafter nothing could sunder *Aldwick Beauty* from the name of Doris Alford.

Meanwhile, my mother awaited anxiously the Ministry's verdict. Had she nurtured a little genius or a mindless dolt …? And 'wait' was the operative word, as her trees idled away another eight years swanning it up in the best parts of Kent and Surrey. This slow procession of time might have dented the enthusiasm of many a soul. Not Doris Alford, though. Buoyed up by her apple winning a couple of Firsts at the Bognor Horticultural Society Show, by encouraging sales at Brinkman's and the attention of the apple-growing cognoscenti at the RHS Exhibition at Vincent Square, she pressed on lovingly mulching, pruning and spraying. And not only the *Aldwick Beauty* mother-tree, but now its three daughters. Suppose they turned out to be a second Cox's? What if royalties from millions of trees planted all over the world proved a passport to serious riches? Swiss bank accounts! A Chateau Beauté d'Aldwick at St Tropez! Ferraris all round! But by 1978 the moment of truth was nigh.

Now, as the Ministry pointed out in a letter designed to sweeten Brogdale's bitter pill, there is a world of difference between a 'good' apple and a 'commercial' one. Size, and only moderate keeping qualities, in spite of its rich taste, precluded lorry-loads of *Aldwick Beauty* ever reaching Sainsbury's and Tesco's shelves. Apparently, it was a verdict pronounced upon many garden-seedlings. On the other hand (the letter continued), with all its other qualities – appearance, texture and taste – there was no reason why such a nice dessert apple tree shouldn't 'prove a popular addition to the amateur grower's orchard'. But behind that word 'amateur' wasn't there a barely concealed sneer? At least we hadn't exchanged contracts on that villa at St Tropez!

In fact, many of my mother's trees still flourish in and around Bognor as well as further afield and are highly regarded by their owners. At Sennicotts, near Chichester, Mr John Rank's gardener, Don Tester, has them magnificently espaliered on a south-facing wall. Others grow successfully in Suffolk and in Worcestershire, where a number of *Aldwick Beauty* trees flourish in an orchard which once echoed to the shouts of Major General Massey's Scots' Horse during the Civil War.

Like my mother, Martin Venables' sister, Mary, was a prolific poet. The *Aldwick Beauty* saga inspired her to write these charming verses:

WASSAIL

Twin apple trees in Eden
Long ago, time out of mind,
Grew close together, each in its kind
Sprang from God-thought
Miraculous, Divine.
In one did life abound
Knowledge the other found
Where the spying serpent twined.

From this ancient ancestry
Of primal parentage we see
This wondrous archaean mystery
Whence sprang the Alford apple-tree;
Wind-blown, chance-thrown, chance-grown

A miracle-to-be.
God Bless this tree!

F.M. Venables

Appendix

William Tate

Born in 1850, William Tate's early life, the family's emigration to Australia and his return, with wife, to his native Sussex a few years later to resume his work as cabinet-maker and furnisher, are more than adequately recorded in Gerard Young's *A History of Bognor Regis* and in Tate's obituary published in the *Bognor Regis Post* on 19 December 1931. The turning point in his career, though, came some time in the mid-1880s, when he decided to drop cabinet-making and become instead an entrepreneurial builder – working on his own developments as well as acting as a general building contractor – a step which was to result in his becoming the pre-eminent constructor of 20th-century bricks-and-mortar Bognor.

Amongst his first jobs was the construction of Park Terrace in West Bognor, one of the surviving elements of Arthur Smith's imaginative, but mainly unrealised, Victoria Park scheme of the 1870s. He built houses in many parts of the town; Campbell Road he developed in its entirety. Other areas he helped to shape were Gordon Avenue, Canada Grove and Ockley Road. Over at Felpham he refurbished the late William Haley's Turret House in Limmer Lane, which became his home. Then, in 1891, he was elected a member of the Local Government Board and almost immediately resigned his office, putting his firm to work building the sea-wall and promenade between York Road and Gloucester Road at a price hitherto regarded as being quite beyond the Board's financial reach.

During 1900, in his capacity as a general builder, he completed what must have been two 'plum' jobs, the Princess Mary Memorial Home and the Victorian Convalescent Home for Surrey Women on the Esplanade. To make his day, he had

148 William Tate.

the honour of shaking hands with the Duke and Duchess of York, who opened them on 9 July. 'What Bognor needs', said William Tate, a year or two after his royal handshake, 'is less trees and more buildings.' And with that, in the wooded grounds of York House in the High Street, he opened his first Bognor landmark, the Edwardian Arcade of 1902 – a prosperous shopping centre to this day. He built a private electricity generating plant on the site of the old Southdown bus garage in Lyon Street* to light his own buildings.

---

* The Lyon Street site of the generating station is mentioned in a hand-written note in a pamphlet on the Bognor Gas and Electricity Company by Wallace Hammond, in the Gerard Young collection.

The year 1909 marked the commencement of the great Kursaal entertainment complex extending from the Esplanade to Belmont Street. White-stuccoed, copper-domed and soaring, it included a theatre equipped for showing films, a roller-skating rink and a general purpose Hall, destined to become Pierrotland. The inauguration, in 1911, of this much-acclaimed building coincided with Tate's election as Chairman of the Urban District Council. If anyone had the right to feel that 'he'd made it', it must have been William Tate! The following year, perhaps feeling that he'd done his stint for the town, he retired to Southsea at the age 62 where he lived until his death at the age of 81 in December 1931.

Oswald Bridges

Another shaper of early 20th-century Bognor, Bridges was appointed in 1896. Until he retired, in 1923, he played a major creative role overseeing Bognor's rapid transformation from a still recognisable seaside 'village' into a modern town run by an Urban District Council.

149 Oswald Bridges.

One of Bridges' earlier jobs (1904) was the design of the little Western Bandstand on the old 'boat pound' site opposite the *Royal Norfolk Hotel*, where my mother must have been amongst its first patrons during her visit to Bognor in that year. Built by Mr J.H. Redman of North Bersted, it cost £60. In 1914 his most important project was the strengthening of the sea-wall east of the Pier.*

Other buildings bearing his signature were the High Street Fire Station, housing schemes in Gravits Lane and Mons Avenue, as well as the embayment and beach-ramps at the end of York Road and West Street. With the burgeoning motor traffic, his remit came to include highway improvements and the provision of road signs.

During the early 'twenties 'Ossy' Bridges was instrumental – along with Tom Tregear – in providing Bognor Bowling Club with a permanent headquarters and greens in Waterloo Square. But, gradually, more and more of his time was taken up vetting applications for the flood of new houses being built in the area. With retirement, he entered local politics, serving as a Councillor from 1929 to 1935. Two years were spent as Chairman of the UDC. He also qualified as an architect, counting among his many clients Billy Butlin and the Bognor Pier Company, for whom he designed the new landing stage opened in 1935. He died in October 1946 aged seventy-seven.

---

* It is said that the bull-nosed section of the the top of the sea-wall, which successfully broke the power of the waves, was his own invention.

Index

compiled by Jill Ford

150 Scott Ragless (centre), winner of the 1900 Bognor Regatta.

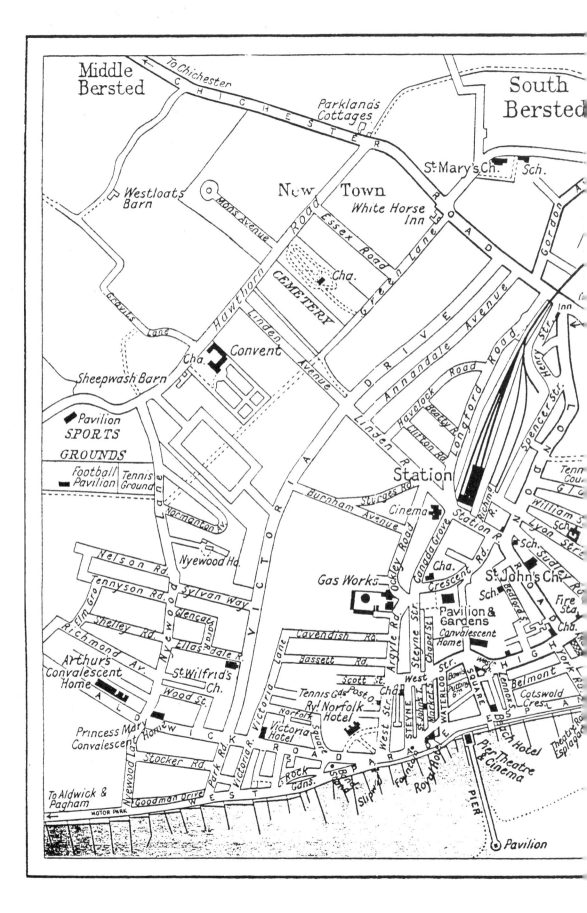